BOUNDARIES

A Customized Reader

General Editors

Bradley R.E. Wright
University of Connecticut

Ralph B. McNeal, Jr.
University of Connecticut

Compiled by

Derek Evans
Social Deviance 1650

Pearson Custom Publishing

New York   Boston   San Francisco
London   Toronto   Sydney   Tokyo   Singapore   Madrid
Mexico City   Munich   Paris   Cape Town   Hong Kong   Montreal

Senior Vice President, Editorial and Marketing: Patrick F. Boles
Senior Sponsoring Editor: Robin J. Lazrus
Development Editor: Abbey Lee Briggs
Associate Editor: Ana Díaz-Caneja
Marketing Manager: Jack Cooney
Operations Manager: Eric M. Kenney
Database Product Manager: Jennifer Berry
Rights Manager: Katie Huha
Art Director: Renée Sartell
Cover Designers: Renée Sartell and Kristen Kiley

Cover Art: "Chain with Broken Link," courtesy of Emanuele Taroni/PhotoDisc; "Fence," courtesy of PhotoDisc; Ernesto Rios Lanz/Sexto Sol (photographers), "Shadow Hands image," courtesy of Ernesto Rios Lanz and Sexto Sol/Getty Images; JoSon (Photographer), "Shatter Glass image," courtesy of SuperStock, Inc.

**Pearson
Custom Publishing**
is a division of

ISBN 10: 055826865X
ISBN 13: 9780558268657

Package ISBN 10: N/A
www.pearsonhighered.com   Package ISBN 13: N/A

ACKNOWLEDGEMENTS

The success of *Boundaries* could not have occurred without the attention of our reviewers. Those who have reviewed the content are experts in the field of sociology and criminal justice, and have influenced our decisions about the direction that a revision should take. With sincere thanks, we acknowledge:

Ann M. Borden, Peter M. Carlson, *Christopher Newport University; University of Central*; Mirelle Cohen, *University of Puget Sound*; Norman Conti, *Duquesne University*; Christopher T. Godialis, J.D., *Iona College and Sacred Heart University*; Andy Hochstetler, *Iowa State University*; Alan Horowitz, *University of Delaware*; Jo Ellyn Johnson, *Richard J. Daley College*; Joyce D. Meyer, *Parkland College*; P.J. McGann, *University of Michigan*; Marilyn D. McShane, *University of Houston-Downtown*; Stacey Nofziger, *University of Akron*; Timothy O'Boyle, *Kutztown University*; Peter Parilla, *University of St. Thomas*; Curt Sobolewski, *Indiana University South Bend*; Paul Stretesky, *Colorado State University*. Yvonne Villanueva-Russell, *Texas A&M University, Commerce*; Kimberly A. Vogt, *University of Wisconsin, La Crosse*; Patrick D. Walsh, *Loyola University New Orleans*

FOREWORD
By William J. Chambliss

One of the most effective classroom pedagogies available is to have students read original research in the form of published articles. This provides the students not only with the data and theories that drive the discipline but it also enables them to get a sense of the craft. In the past, books have traditionally served the purpose of bringing together the literature on a particular subject. Often these books fail to provide an instructor with the most important articles to the course and often contain many articles the instructor does not want to assign.

Now there is an alternative to the traditional "reader" that enables instructors to pick and choose precisely those articles that are most important to their method of teaching the course. *Boundaries: Readings in Deviance, Crime, and Criminal Justice* creatively edited by Bradley R. E. Wright and Ralph McNeal, both of the University of Connecticut, provides a collection of more than 400 of the most influential articles in the field of sociology and criminal justice. It is an unbiased, eclectic collection of academic journal articles and book chapters which survey the past 70 years in both fields. Classic and contemporary selections can be found within the collection, and they range from the harshest criticism to the most defensive posture in the literature. To add additional perspective, every article is introduced with an editor-written headnote, and concludes with several thought-provoking discussion questions. More importantly, the collection represents what the editors claim: there is a wide range of articles covering deviance, crime, and criminal justice.

Instructors will find this collection timely and unlimited in its flexibility. Each reader can be easily updated and modified at the beginning of each semester. The end result is an attractive paperback reader with the articles arranged in accordance with the professor's own choice. I have been using *Boundaries* for several years and am very happy with the results.

∮ Contents ∰

Contents

Contents

A Typology Based on Middle-Class Norms

CHARLES R. TITTLE AND RAYMOND PATERNOSTER

What makes a particular behavior deviant? Many sociologists subscribe to the normative explanation for deviant behavior—behavior that violates the norms of a society is considered deviant. But it is not always easy to determine exactly what the norms are, especially since norms vary by race, gender, age, social class, culture, and time. In this selection, Charles Tittle and Raymond Paternoster present a typology of deviance based on middle class norms. While the authors admit the typology is far from perfect, it is a starting point for further discussion about which norms are most important and how to classify deviant behavior based on the violation of these norms.

The scheme to be presented takes middle-class American (U.S.) norms as its reference base. It demonstrates the variety of deviant behaviors that can be recognized from just one normative perspective. After studying this typology you should be able to appreciate the volume and diversity of deviance that is possible when numerous normative contexts, over time and both within and across modern societies, are taken into account. In addition, this classification scheme illustrates why indigenously created categories, such as crime, cannot be incorporated into deviance typologies as separate and distinct categories, or types, of deviance. In considering the classification, you should be particularly alert to inclusiveness (does every deviant act from the middle-class point of view fit somewhere in the scheme?) as well as mutual exclusivity (does a given deviant act fit in one and only one category?). Moreover, you should critically assess how well the norms described in the typology actually reflect middle-class expectations. Although this scheme is more adequate than most, it too is defective in some important respects. Finding

"A Typology Based on Middle-Class Norms," by Charles R. Tittle and Raymond Paternoster, reprinted from *Social Deviance and Crime: An Organizational and Theoretical Approach,* 2000, Roxbury Publishing Company.

these defects will sharpen your understanding of the relativity and complexity of deviance.

The classification scheme is summarized in Table 1. Ten middle-class norms are identified and listed in Column 1. Associated with each norm is a category of deviant behavior listed in Column 2. Column 3 lists specific examples of the various deviant acts within each category. The scheme ranks norms from most to least important for middle-class people.

Although any such ranking is necessarily arbitrary, this one is based on three specific criteria. One is dominance. Where there are conflicts between the demands of two or more norms, the dominant norm takes precedence. For instance, the norm of *privacy* may sometimes conflict with the norm of *loyalty*. In most contests between the two, the norm of loyalty has prevailed; hence, it is probably perceived by most middle-class Americans to be more important. A second criterion has to do with the emotional investment most people have in the norm. The affect associated with the norm of *participation* usually turns out to be much less than that associated with the norm of *prudence;* therefore, it seems clear that prudence is regarded as more important than participation. Finally, the probability, severity, and institutionalization of sanctions for acts of deviance, as well as the chances of long-lasting stigma for violators, are taken to indicate the importance of the norm to middle-class people. For example, *intrusion* normally results in official, fairly severe sanction for offenders, and it usually carries a stigma lasting long after the official sanction ends. In contrast, *uncouth* conduct is rarely sanctioned officially, and any stigma that grows out of informal sanction is short-lived. Therefore, we conclude that the norm of *privacy* (violated by intrusion) is more important to middle-class citizens than the norm of *courtesy* (violated by *uncouthness*).

With this criteria in mind, let us turn the typology itself and examine the various norms and associated deviance.

*£*oyalty/*A*postasy

A primary, and possibly the most important, norm among middle-class Americans concerns the ultimate right of the group or collectivity to sustain itself through subordinating individual interests to group survival. Recognition of this right is expressed in the norm of loyalty. By middle-class standards, all people must commit themselves to the group or society as a whole and maintain that commitment against all challenges. Any behavior that seems to express disloyalty, weak commitment, or disrespect for the group is, therefore, unacceptable. Such behavior can be referred to as *apostasy*. Behaviors within the category of apostasy include revolutionary actions, betrayal of government secrets, cooperation with an enemy nation (treason), draft dodging, defiling the flag, surrendering one's citizenship, and advocating contrary government philosophies.

TABLE 1 *A Classification of U.S. Middle-Class Deviance*

Norm	Deviance	Examples
Group Loyalty	Apostasy	Revolution, Betraying national secrets, Treason, Draft dodging, Flag defilement, Giving up citizenship, Advocating contrary government philosophy
Privacy	Intrusion	Theft, Burglary, Rape, Homicide, Voyeurism, Forgery, Record spying
Prudence	Indiscretion	Prostitution, Homosexual behavior, Incest, Bestiality, Adultery, Swinging, Gambling, Substance abuse
Conventionality	Bizarreness	"Mentally ill behavior" (handling excrement, nonsense talk, eating human flesh, fetishes), Separatist life styles
Responsibility	Irresponsibility	Familiy desertion, Reneging on debts, Unprofessional conduct, Improper role performance, Violations of trust, Pollution, Fraudulent business
Participation	Alienation	Non-participatory life styles (hermitry, street living), Perpetual unemployment, Receiving public assistance, Suicide
Moderation	Hedonism-Asceticism	Chiseling–Rate busting, Atheism–Fanaticism, Teetotaling–Alcoholism, Total honesty–Total deceit, Hoarding–Wasting, Ignoring children–Smothering them
Honesty	Deceitfulness	Selfish lying, Price-fixing, Exploitation of the weak and helpless, Bigamy, Welfare cheating
Peacefulness	Disruption	Noisy disorganizing behavior, Boisterous reveling, Quarreling, Fighting, Contentiousness
Courtesy	Uncouthness	Private behavior in public place (picking nose, burping), Rudeness (smoking in prohibited places, breaking in a line), Uncleanliness

Revolutionary actions such as participation in a conspiracy to overthrow the government obviously display disloyalty, as do selling of military secrets to an enemy and gunrunning during war or helping an invader to establish control over an area. In a less obvious way, attempts to avoid the draft are taken to the indicative of disloyalty to the group, another way of saying that the person lacks the commitment to sacrifice for the interests of the group. And defiling the flag or advocating another governmental or economic philosophy (such as communism) is assumed to prove that the person holds the group in such low regard that he would be disloyal in a critical situation.

Deviance in Everyday Life

The United States Supreme Court in 1989 declared that the burning of the American flag was protected expression under the First Amendment. In this case, *Texas v. Johnson* 491 U.S. 397 (1989), the defendant, Gregory Lee Johnson, burned an American flag on the steps of Dallas City Hall to protest the policies of President Ronald Reagan. He was tried, convicted, and sentenced to one year in jail and fined $2,000 under a Texas statute that outlaws desecrating the flag. The Supreme Court argued that the fact that an audience may find a particular expression of speech offensive or disloyal does not justify it being prohibited.

Clearly, most middle-class Americans endorse the norm of loyalty and consider it exceptionally important. No personal or other group obligation can excuse apostate behavior, and middle-class people usually display disgust and loathing for those who are guilty. Moreover, violations of the norm of loyalty almost always result in sanctions—often quite severe—and they usually evoke lifetime stigmatization whether or not there is official sanction.

᛭

*P*rivacy/*I*ntrusion

A second major middle-class American norm revolves around the concept of privacy. It holds that every person has the right to exclusive control over some things, especially private places and personal items. Sometimes there are disputes about the limits of exclusive control; for example, do parents or pet owners have a right to abuse their charges? Moreover, exclusive control over property is limited in view of potential consequences for others (you cannot burn your own house if it poses a fire hazard for other homes), and exclusivity is never absolute. In addition, the fact of ownership may be disputed. But, when exclusive control is recognized, the principle of privacy prevails; that is, only the owner may invade that domain. Hence the associated deviance is called *intrusion,* and it consists of acts that deny the controller or owner of some domain the exclusivity implied by ownership. Examples of intrusion include theft, burglary, rape, homicide, voyeurism, forgery, and record spying (unauthorized examination of bank accounts, hospital records, or other confidential information).

Deviance in Everyday Life

Video surveillance is rapidly becoming a tool of corporate management. Also, many city and town squares and streets are being monitored by video cameras, as are shopping centers and their parking lots, and convenience stores. Video cameras are being installed in many workplaces, enabling management to keep an eye on workers.

Theft constitutes intrusion because it deprives the owners of exclusive control over their property. Burglary, of course, involves invasion of a private space, which usually provokes in the victim a sense of having been "violated." Rape is a deviant action in violation of the norm of privacy because most middle-class people believe that a person's body is a private domain to be entered only by request or permission. Forgery denies exclusive use of a signature and often implies usurpation of private funds, opinions, or duties.

The strength of emotion surrounding the norm of privacy is perhaps best grasped by considering the intrusion called voyeurism. Most people who discover that they have been under surveillance, without permission, while bathing, performing personal functions, engaging in sexual activities, or even working, feel an overwhelming sense of distress that they have been violated. This is particularly interesting since such individuals have not actually been injured or harmed in a tangible sense. Yet they feel abused because their expectation of privacy was overriden, thus denying them the exclusive control that all expect.

Of course, most acts of intrusion are subject to sanction and, indeed, typically are sanctioned. In fact, most acts of intrusion are among the most feared of crimes, the so-called "index crimes" for which the FBI collects and publishes statistics. Yet the stigma and sanction are not as severe or long lasting as in the case of apostate behavior. It appears that recognition of the ultimate superiority of the group, reflected in the norm of loyalty, supersedes the rights of the individual, as it must for society to continue. In the final analysis, the only persons who may intrude into private domains with impunity are official representatives of the collectivity who act on authority of the group as a whole. Thus the government may confiscate property (with fair compensation, at least from the government's point of view) when it exercises the right of eminent domain, or where tax assessments are not paid and the property is offered for public sale. Government agents may enter private residences uninvited if authorized by court orders, and the state may even claim a citizen's life in the interest of group survival as when the individual is sent to die in combat or when the courts decide that the person must be executed. Similarly, the police and court officials may look at private records under authorized conditions, and the state is sometimes even authorized to forcefully invade a person's body to perform court-ordered sterilization, test for a driver's possible intoxication, or to search for evidence of illegal activity.

Deviance in Everyday Life

In a *New York Times* public opinion poll, 43 percent of respondents favored a Constitutional Amendment that would allow a woman to have an abortion only in order to save her life. A comparable poll in Ohio found that 47 percent of those asked would allow an abortion only when it was necessary to save the life of the mother

Hence almost every domain of privacy may be set aside by the superior right of the group as a whole. This even extends to the question of rape. When law enforcement personnel search the inner cavities of human persons in search of illegally smuggled drugs, they are actually committing acts that would constitute criminal assault or rape were they not authorized by the state as an enforcement procedure. How far this would extend is unknown, of course, but it is conceivable that the government might even forcefully intrude into a woman's body for sexual or reproductive purposes should voluntary reproduction decline to the point where population maintenance were threatened. At present in the United States, many people would favor laws that force women to bear children once they are impregnated, even if that conception were the result of rape or incest, and even if the bearing of the child would cost the mother's life. Many believe it only a small step to requiring women to become pregnant.

𝒫rudence/𝒥ndiscretion

The third most important normative area among middle-class American appears to be that concerning *prudence*. All people are expected to exercise selectivity in the practice of activities that are pleasurable. They are to use pleasure as a means to an end, not as an end in itself, and the expression of pleasure must be within specified limits or boundaries. The prescribed end is expected to be some contribution to the economic or social maintenance of society. A person is supposed to avoid activities that are frivolous or primarily oriented around self-gratification as well as activities that may involve nonproductive emotional involvements or that may disrupt productive emotional ties. Violation of the norm of prudence can be characterized as *indiscretion*. Indiscrete behavior would include prostitution, homosexual behavior, bestiality, adultery, incest, swinging, gambling, and abuse of drugs.

Prostitution (sexual activities as a commercial exchange), swinging (consensual exchange of sexual partners among married people), and bestiality (sexual activities with animals) all involve sexual interaction without emotion, thus challenging the usual linkage between emotional involvement and sexual expression that motivates the establishment and maintenance of stable, productive, and socially useful unions. Homosexual behavior (sexual relations with someone of one's own gender, incest (sexual relations with a relative), and adultery (sexual relations of a married person with someone other than his or her spouse) may involve emotional attachments that cannot be productive and that may provoke disruptive conflicts. Gambling and abusive recreational drug use convey images of obsession with self-gratification and frivolity. All of these indiscrete behaviors are sanctionable, but most of them usually do not receive official sanctions. They all do, however, ordinarily provoke substantial stigma from others, which expresses fairly long-lasting group disapproval.

𝒞onventionality/𝘉izarreness

A fourth norm of middle-class America mandates that all must practice personal habits and lead lives that are similar to the conventions followed by most middle-class people. Violations of the norm of conventionality are called *bizarre* behavior; that is, relative to most middle-class people, the behavior in question is unusual or statistically atypical to such an extent that the sanity or "normality" of the individual is questioned. But not all statistically unusual behavior is deviant by middle-class standards. To qualify as bizarre, the behavior must be incomprehensible to the typical person. The average middle-class individual must be unable to imagine herself or anyone like her committing such an act; that is, the behavior must not have a good reason behind it. Some atypical behaviors are readily understandable to "normals." Clearly, religious celibacy is acceptable since it reflects devotion to an established faith and is believed to be good and useful. Likewise, skydiving, while unusual, is nevertheless comprehensible as a recreational search for adventure—fulfillment of the individualistic ideal of bravery—and is therefore not deviant. On the other hand, total sexual abstinence for no apparent good reason (such as among wedded people who fail to consummate the marriage) would be bizarre. And handling rattlesnakes as a part of religious ritual (La Barre, 1969) would seem to most middle-class people to be senseless and unacceptable, particularly if it were seen as an obligation that might endanger the young.

Other examples of unusual behavior that most middle-class people cannot imagine for sane people include consuming or playing with excrement, talking in nonsensical ways to others or to oneself—perhaps through unique sounds and words—or conversing with unseen creatures. Similarly, hiding from or attempting to counteract perceived threats or dangerous moves by individuals who "normals" do not believe are making such threats or dangerous moves, as well as eating the flesh of a human corpse, are acts so unthinkable that most middle-class people consider them indicative of "mental illness." Other bizarre acts may be considered deviant by middle-class standards but are not taken as evidence of total sickness. Strange sexual preferences like rubber fetishes (inability to experience orgasm unless wearing rubber garments), masochism (depriving sexual pleasure from personal physical pain), or desires to be diapered and powdered by a sexual partner are instances of unacceptable or bizarre behaviors qualifying as "perversions."

Another kind of conventional behavior that is deviant by middle-class standards is that manifest in separatist life styles. One of the most dramatic and well-known groups that practice unusual living styles are the Amish, a sectarian religious group that resides in Pennsylvania, Ohio, Indiana, and other parts of the Midwest (Ammon, 1989; Hostetler, 1980, 1989). The Amish shun modern society and its conveniences, choosing instead to live in primitive farming communities. They plow their fields with horse-drawn implements, transport themselves in buggies, and refuse to use electricity or appliances in their homes. They dress in plain black "pilgrim" styles, eschewing any adornments such as jewelry or personal comforts like gloves. The Amish resist modern education and refuse on religious grounds to serve in the armed forces.

8

Other groups, like the Hare Krishna, separate themselves less completely but nevertheless are thought of as a bizarre because of their unusual styles of dress (long flowing colorful robes, shaven heads except for a long pigtail at the back of the head, and sandals), and their evangelistic behavior on city streets and in airports, where they accost and attempt to convert passersby. And still other groups earn the deviant designation by periodically removing all clothes while performing ordinary tasks. Nudists who occasionally spend a weekend or a vacation at a "camp" are deviant enough, but those who live at nudist camps year round are considered to be especially perverted.

Deviance in Everyday Life

One example of behavior that is bizarre by middle-class standards was exhibited by a group of religious cult members referred to under the name of Heaven's Gate. The group was founded by Marshall Herff Applewhite and Bonnie Lu Nettles, who shared an interest in philosophy and metaphysics. The two founders of the group went by various aliases such as Bo and Peep, Guinea and Pig, and "The Two." Their religion consisted of a combination of Christian theology, folk wisdom, and a firm belief in UFOs. Bo and Peep believed that they were extraterrestrials who would lead their followers to a higher level of existence. They believed that their escape would come via a spaceship that hid in the tail of the comet Hale-Bopp. In order to reach the spaceship, however, followers had to shed their human skin. On March 28, 1997, authorities in San Diego, California, discovered the bodies of 39 members of this cult who had committed suicide.

Finally, a life style organized around night activity arouses suspicion, and if a person is unable to provide a reasonable excuse (such as nighttime job), he or she is defined as probably doing bizarre behavior, although less reprehensible than the behaviors already mentioned. Since most middle-class folks work in the daytime and sleep at night (at least the late night), going out only in the early evening, they regard those who are up and about, especially if out on the streets, during the wee hours as somewhat bizarre and possibly up to no good. Few allowances are made for those who simply like to sleep during the day and visit, paint, or jog late in the night.

Some of the activities described here as bizarre behavior are subject to some form of official sanction; usually, however, sanctions are informal—ridicule, harassment, and rejection. Many of the more bizarre acts are

9

formally sanctioned by incarceration in mental institutions, where therapists are employed to help their practitioners "recover," which means to begin to act in conventional ways. In all instances, however, there is a strong tendency toward stigmatization, which can be erased only with great difficulty. Probably the best example of stigmatization for "mental illness" is the case of Thomas Eagleton, a United States senator from Missouri who was the Democratic nominee for vice-president of the United States in 1972. When it became known that he had at one time been treated by a psychiatrist for emotional problems and had been given electroshock treatments, he was forced off the ticket, despite the fact that the treatment had taken place sometime in the past and had apparently been successful since the candidate was not then suffering from those emotional problems and gave no evidence of being prone to psychiatric difficulties. Stigmatization of those whose bizarre behaviors are not usually thought of as evidence of mental illness is common as well. It is unlikely that an Amish person could easily overcome the stigma of "ignorant" and "backward" should he or she choose to assimilate, or that even a "night person" could ever fully escape suspicion if his or her life were scrutinized in a police investigation.

𝒭esponsibility/𝒥rresponsibility

Another norm of middle-class Americans prescribes responsible conduct. People, especially those on whom others depend, must be reliable. Violations of this norm constitute instances of *irresponsible* behavior. Examples include family desertion, refusal or failure to meet financial obligations, negligence in maintaining property or performing occupational roles, failure to fulfill professional standards, violations of trust, pollution of the environment, and selling defective, harmful, or useless products or services.

For instance, parents are expected to provide financial and emotional support for children, and spouses are required to fulfill marital obligations toward each other. Children and spouses, as well as members of the larger society, have a stake in faithful parental and marital role performance. When husbands or wives desert families, for whatever reason, they leave their dependants open to potential harm, and they may be helping to create burdens for the community should the children or deserted spouse need public assistance. This is thought by middle-class people to be irresponsible. Similarly, all individuals who participate in the world of commerce must be able to rely upon each other for basic financial dependability that justifies the trust on which contracts are based. Individuals, therefore, commit deviance when they renege on debts, delay payments, or evade contractual obligations.

Owners or managers of property are similarly expected to behave responsibly so that other property owners, innocent bystanders, or consumers of goods and services will not be harmed. Property owners must keep their buildings in good repair and cut the lawn so that property values in the area will not deteriorate. Moreover, owners are supposed to make sure their property does not pose a danger to others. For instance, a homeowner who leaves a swimming pool open and unattended entices neighborhood children to the dangerous possibility of drowning and is therefore guilty of irresponsibility.

Professionals such as physicians, lawyers, accountants, and police bear a special middle-class responsibility. Norms prescribe that they perform competent services for those who entrust themselves as clients, including in the case of the police, the entire community, and that the interests of the clients must take precedence of the self-interests of the practitioners. A physician who performs unnecessary surgery simply for the purpose of earning the fee for service is engaging in irresponsible behavior, as is one who prescribes medicine to be bought in a pharmacy the physician owns, or who reports to unrelated third parties about the illnesses of another. Similarly, a male physician who takes advantage of female patients who trust him to examine their unclothed bodies behaves irresponsibly and deviantly in violation of the role obligations of a physician. And it is deviant for a physician to keep people sick to guarantee income rather than to help them recover.

Other examples of professional irresponsibility include graft, theft, or burglary by police officers. Middle-class people regard as irresponsible, as well as intrusive, stealing by a police officer who is called to investigate a crime but ends up taking things. Similarly, police who fail to make an arrest in exchange for a payoff or sexual favors behave irresponsibly. And, of course, brutality or the use of force simply to graftiy personal whims or to satisfy aggressive tendencies is unacceptable. Finally, police who use their positions, uniforms, or coercive power to enjoy privileges or to escape the law themselves garner the enmity of the middle class. This occurs at the level of police bribery or graft, and may be felt at a more minor level when citizens see police officers accepting "free" meals or drinks.

Deviant conduct of an irresponsible type also includes embezzlement or other forms of diverting organizational funds or equipment to private use. Within this category are fraudulent pyramid schemes, where entrepreneurs induce investors to put up money with the promise of a high rate of return but actually use the money put up by new investors as the "profit" for old investors (after taking their cut). These schemes are fraudulent because no actual produce or service is produced. When new investors can no longer be found, the entire pyramid collapses.

Deviance in Everyday Life

Medical frauds, including anti-aging potions, arthritis remedies, diet gimmicks, and ineffective cancer treatments, cost Americans billions of dollars a year. Not only do medical frauds cost us money, they may also be costing us our health by luring us away from effective medical treatment. Why are we so enthralled by medical quackery? Because we want to believe in medical miracles and are convinced by the promises of easy treatments and cures made by unscrupulous medical quacks. Want to lose weight? Here are your options: (1) eat better, eat less, and stick to a regular exercise routine, or (2) sit on the couch with an electronic "muscle stimulator" attached to your flabby areas that effortlessly removes the unwanted pounds. Now, which option sounds more appeal?

Over the past several decades, the interdependency of human social life has become more fully recognized by middle-class people; as a result, the number and types of possibly irresponsible behaviors as expanded. Some of the newest, and to some extent still controversial, forms of deviance concern behavior that jeopardizes others through damage to the environment—even small incremental damages. Just as individuals may endanger public health and safety by spitting on the sidewalk, dumping garbage on the street, or putting carbon residues into the air through their automobile exhausts, now corporations are being held responsible for polluting the environment through discharge of toxic chemicals into rivers or the air, or by destruction of natural protective systems such as forests or sand dunes. Similarly, although swindlers have always been considered to be doing deviance by selling defective home siding (so-called "Tin Men") or roof painting jobs, now "respectable" businesses are being castigated for marketing defective or dangerous products, such as automobiles with improperly designed gasoline tanks that explode on rear-end impacts or children's pajamas that are excessively flammable (see Simon and Eitzen, 1993). The major forms of deviance involving useless products or services are medical frauds. Charlatans often sell ineffective or dangerous machines or drugs to desperate people who suffer continuous pain or incurable diseases.

The reason some of these newer forms of irresponsible behavior are controversial is the inherent conflict between the norm of responsibility and the norm of privacy. Although most middle-class people probably believe it is deviant behavior to sell a toy that has a high probability of injuring a child, some people would maintain that it is the responsibility of a parent to refuse to purchase such a toy or to teach the child how to use it safely. These people also probably believe that prohibiting a company from selling such an item is an invasion of the privacy of the owners and managers of the company. In like manner some would maintain that it is the individuals' responsibility to make wise choices and to protect themselves from market shenanigans; therefore, to them selling a useless or even harmful medical nostrum is not a deviant act.

Clearly, many potentially deviant acts are moving toward deviant status, and some that are now thought of as irresponsible could in the future sink back into acceptability with a slight turn of opinion. Nevertheless, it is likely that all those mentioned here as violating the norm of responsibility are deviant. Yet the ambivalence of these norms is reflected in the relative leniency of official sanctions. Even though the listed behaviors may be disapproved, usually they go unpunished or, if violations are punished, they are given only a "slap on the wrist." More often, these transgressions provoke private civil suits and some stigma, although usually not great or long lasting.

Participation/Alienation

Another middle-class norm specifies that everybody will take an active part in the social and economic life of the community or society and in the institutions it spawns. Those who fail to participate are guilty of *alienation*, unless they can provide an acceptable excuse. Deliberate defiance of the participation norm is illustrated by hermits, tramps, and bums, as well as by suicides. The perpetually unemployed, those receiving public assistance, the aged, and the handicapped all exhibit forms of involuntary alienation, but they are nevertheless held in contempt unless their inactivity is justified. It may be excused by visible physical defects but only if the symptoms are sufficiently debilitating to make participation impossible, or by an individual's reputation for perseverance that allows the middle-class audience to conclude that the nonparticipator has done all he or she could to fulfill expectations.

Almost every generation has its prominent examples of bohemians—those who reject middle-class standards of morality, work, or politics and withdrawn into a world of their own. In the 1950s it was "beatniks"; the 1960s and 1970s had "hippies"; and the 1980s were the time of "punks." The hippies of the 1960s are probably best known because they were so numerous and had such an important impact on society. They became famous for "dropping out" of the middle-class system and "turning on." Many young people of that era came to regard traditional work ethics as dehumanizing; conventional nuclear families too confining; middle-class sexual mores as being "up-tight"; and prohibitions on mind-altering drugs as fearful avoidance of self-actualization. They traded the "status seeking" of the establishment for subsistence living, communal sharing, sexual freedom, and drug-induced visions of what might be. Their very existence insulted middle-class standards, and so hippies came to symbolize deviant behavior in the minds of the middle class. Contempt is heaped upon any individual or group that denies the validity of the middle-class system by self-conscious refusal to play the game.

Denial of that validity is also evident among those who will not try, those who fail, those who live as parasites on the system, or those who escape completely, and they all earn a disreputable status. Hermits refuse to try, chronically unemployed street people fail, and loafers exploit public services—all forms of the deviance termed alienation. But alienation is more dramatically displayed by suicide. With the exception of altruistic acts of self-destruction, where somebody sacrifices his or her life to save others, suicide makes the ultimate statement of nonparticipation and so it is proportionally stigmatized—although the stigma ironically applies to the relatives of the deceased.

The importance of the norm of participation is shown by the suspiciousness with which the middle class regards any deviation. People receiving public assistance are assumed to be chiselers or "welfare cheats" unless they can individually redeem themselves, and middle-class people are ever alert to detect any evidence of immorality, deceit, or laziness by welfare mothers, the infirm, or the aged that would confirm their suspicions. If a person is inactive because of age, he or she must not be seen walking without a crutch or a cane. An unemployed man must not laugh, drink beer, or be seen in recreation, no matter how long he has been unemployed or how hard he has searched for a job; nor must he refuse any kind of employment, no matter how degrading or dangerous it might be. And nonparticipating handicapped individuals must show their handicap so observers will know they have a right to be excused from the alienated status. Otherwise, such persons will be regarded as fakes and cheats, false claimants to special dispensation.

14

Although alienation is rarely dealt official punishment, it is the object of constant informal sanctions, and its practice carries a stigma that may endure into future generations, as when the police suspiciously keep a close watch on children from welfare families. Some bohemian behavior is illegal, and it is sometimes managed by arrest and prosecution or sometimes simply by police harassment, but usually bohemians suffer ostracism, criticism, and name calling. Likewise, the behavior of tramps, bums, street people, and welfare recipients is also sometimes a matter of official review but more often an object of informal scorn. The nonparticipation of the aged, handicapped, infirm, and suicides is almost completely a matter of informal criticism.

*M*oderation/*H*edonism and *A*seticism

Middle-class Americans subscribe to Emerson's golden mean. All things should be in moderation, and extremes of any kind—even for desirable activities—are unacceptable. This concern with moderation produces judgment of act as deviant that fall on one end or another of a continuum from hedonism (too much of something) to asceticism (not enough of something). These rules of moderation apply to all realms of activity from work to play. Thus it is good to nurture a child but it is bad to practice "smother love" (hedonism) or to reject a child; one is expected to perform an honest day's work, but it is wrong to be a "workaholic" or "rate-buster" (Roethlisberger and Dickson, 1964 [1939]); it is good to drink socially but unacceptable to abuse alcohol or to teetotal.

The American middle-class ethic of moderation is really one of "sensible" compromise, well-roundedness, and adaptability. This can be seen most clearly in the apparent ambivalence that surrounds important issues like religion. While the middle class respects religion, regards itself as fundamentally religious, and promotes a religious outlook on life style and politics, it is clear that both atheists and fanatics are viewed with some measure of disgust. Although many religions teach that a believer should give up worldly goods to promote righteousness, and although members of the middle class believe in philanthropy, they would think actually giving away all one's property to charity a very foolish thing, just as they would regard hoarding one's possessions like a miser as inappropriate. Many religions also teach loving forgiveness of abuse (turn the other cheek), and the middle class does embrace patience and love, but it also regards too much pacifism as unacceptably "wimpish." In like manner, most religions endorse the virtue of modesty,

15

which is embraced by the middle class, but the middle class rejects failure to "toot your own horn" as much as they do bravado.

The golden mean rules the middle-class psyche especially in matters of politics. Extreme conservatives as well as extreme liberals are anathema. The ideal politician is middle of the road, moderate, balanced. And while middle-class Americans ostensibly love freedom and hate totalitarianism, they tolerate "extremes in the defense of freedom" no better than extremes in the service of dictatorship. The history of American government has shown a repeated cyclical pattern as the pendulum swings from the "liberalism" of one generation of governmental policy to the "conservatism" of the next, each in its turn laying claim to having brought policy back to the middle ground.

Here, as with most deviance, violations are sometimes managed by formal sanctions but more often by informal reactions. While an administrator who cuts too many corners may be arrested, most simply find themselves on more and more precarious ground with their peers and coworkers. And administrators who slavishly adhere to the rules may find themselves formally dismissed because of an inability to get the job done, but more likely they will simply go nowhere in the organization, a type of informal reaction. Moreover, in most areas there are no formal sanctions to deal with hedonism or asceticism. Those who extravagantly waste their money are ridiculed and pitied as are those who penuriousness deprives them of important comforts. But neither is formally dealt with unless the behavior is also so bizarre as to invoke the intervention of mental health personnel. And the "greasy grind," curve busting student along with the "space cadet" are subject to no more punishment than occasional scorn, ridicule, or social isolation.

Honesty/Deceitfulness

The middle-class normative system requires a certain degree of honesty, at least in important things. Everybody is expected to avoid lying, fraud, or misrepresentation, but this prohibition is subject to the restraint of the golden mean mentioned before. Persons who exceed the limit of tolerance for mendacity are exhibiting the deviance of *deceitfulness*. Examples include selfish lying, price-fixing by business people, fraudulent business activities, exploitation of the weak and helpless, bigamy, and welfare cheating.

Unfortunately, the limits within which honesty is to be practiced are not consistent across social contexts; the norm is situationally variable. For example, if you visit a sick male friend and are struck by his poor appearance, it is not good manners for you to tell him how bad he looks. Even if the man proclaims it himself, you are supposed to assure him that he will soon be well. Or if you are a male and your girlfriend buys a new dress and seeks your opinion, you mustn't tell her that you think it's ugly; middle-class norms call for diplomatic concealment in cases like this where the truth serves only to hurt someone. But when the sick person gets well and asks if you covered for him at work during the illness, you can't, according to the norm of honesty, say you did if, in fact, you didn't. Or if the girlfriend with the new dress asks her boyfriend what he did that day she was shopping, the fellow must not deny that he was with friends she does not like. There seems to be an understanding that selfish lying, which promotes one's personal interest, is unacceptable but that unselfish lying, which serves an altruistic purpose, is all right. Yet even this guideline is not infallible. An individual who lies in a court of law to protect a friend is no less guilty of perjury than one who lies to save his own skin; both will be condemned as disreputable, although the latter perhaps more thoroughly than the former.

Similar ambivalence prevails on the organizational level. Large businesses may peg their own prices at the level set by the dominant firm in an industry, all the time pretending that their pricing is a response to supply and demand market forces, without earning a characterization as deceitful. But companies actually meeting to discuss pricing is a form of conspiracy in violation of the law of middle-class ethics. Another example is the case of a defense industry that persuades the Navy to buy its airplanes by general arguments suggesting the plane will be better and cheaper than those produced by its competitors. Such rhetoric is regarded as good business even if the company knows it has underestimated the cost and may not actually be able to fulfill the plane's performance requirements. But the same company will be deceitful if it actually falsifies test data, as the Goodrich corporation did in some of its brake operation tests for the A7D Light Attack Aircraft (Vandiver, 1996). Of course, knowing ahead of time just where the dishonesty of salesmanship stops and the deceitfulness of fraud begins is not easy.

Deceitfulness is also expressed when someone takes advantage of people unable to defend themselves, but here again a fuzzy line separates deviance and conformity. A storekeeper who charges exorbitant prices to migrant laborers who must trade in his store because they have no transportation to shop elsewhere is regarded as somewhat unsavory but still within the bounds of acceptable capitalism. But a storekeeper who shortchanges migrant laborers because they are unfamiliar with American money is deceitful.

Finally, those who receive services from governmental or private organizations through misrepresentation are regarded as disreputable if their deceit is blatant and technically in violation of the spirit of written laws or regulations. The welfare mother who claims her children have no father to support them when she, in fact, has an employed husband is condemned, whereas a person might be applauded for simply neglecting to reveal a disqualifying injury in order to obtain employment. A male senator who operates a farm at a loss in order to offset tax liabilities in other areas is regarded as a clever operator, but he is labeled disreputable when he conceals from tax officials the actual income he earns from speeches or other services rendered.

Peacefulness/Disruption

Quiet, tranquility, and order are the hallmarks of American middle-class communities and social life. Middle-class people dislike contentiousness and conflict; they seek agreement, cooperation, and harmony. Violations of these norms are called disruption. Examples include noisy or disruptive protests; boisterous revelry; quarrels, fights, or brawls, particularly in open or public places; and disagreeableness or contentiousness.

Contentiousness is disruptive because it disturbs the air of tolerance that middle-class people like to display. In conversation, one is supposed to avoid conflict-generating topics, and if they are broached, every point of view is to be granted respect if not equal validity. And if someone believes something passionately, he or she is to show restraint in its presentation and defense. In all things a person is expected to be reasonable. Those who have a "negative" attitude, who like to argue, who are loud and boisterous, or who don't want to go along with the group are regarded as disruptive and may be excluded from further group interaction, gossiped about, or ridiculed (although probably not face to face). The ultimate expression of this norm is evident in hospitals when people are dying. No matter how much pain the person is suffering or how dreadful the prospect of death, a dying individual is cajoled to restrain any groans, screams, or yells on the grounds that the noise disturbs others and is in bad taste as well (Sudnow, 1967). Hence one must even bear the agony of death in conformity with the peacefulness norm of the middle class, whose influence permeates hospitals and other social institutions dealing with sickness and death.

According to middle-class rules, one must express political anger, frustration, or chagrin through quiet, dignified methods, not loud, garish, or unrestrained protests. A quiet vigil in an unobtrusive place may be all right, although letters to political figures would be preferable. Marching in the streets, blocking access to buildings, and drowning out speakers with chants and catcalls are prohibited because they are clearly in violation of the norm of peacefulness. Thus, any form of political expression that inconveniences others or disturbs the peace and tranquility is deviant.

While the middle class tolerates ritualized occasions for bending the rules of peacefulness, they nevertheless require that parties and celebrations be restrained and restricted to particular places, times, and occasions, and within the bounds of proper decorum. The music should be confined to the host's home, the guests should not become intoxicated, and the entertainment should consist of quiet conversation on trivial subjects. Never should activities become raunchy or disorderly, wake up the neighbors, or involve indiscretion. Middle-class fun is peaceful and calm (and, remember, moderate).

Finally, when conflicts do occur, they are to be handled in a "mature," private manner. A husband and wife are not to yell at each other in public or in the presence of others; they are to maintain a façade of peaceful happiness or tolerance, at least until they are in a private place. Parents are prohibited from yelling at or disciplining children in company; family members must excuse themselves to private quarters. Adults who end up in angry conflict are never to employ fisticuffs or other forms of physical aggression or even to raise their voices to levels that might inconvenience others.

In short, any behavior that interferes with the orderly peaceful flow of life must be avoided. Consideration for others is paramount, so disruption is regarded as unacceptable, to be managed mainly by avoidance or informal means, although sometimes by official sanctions, as when the police break up noisy parties, arrest participants in a fight, or disperse demonstrators who block traffic.

Courtesy/Uncouthness

Finally, there are a large number of middle-class rules concerning interpersonal interaction. The point of these middle-class norms is to ensure that an individual's behavior does not make the ordinary business of social intercourse too unpleasant and that necessary accommodation to other people be elevated to a civilized plane. Therefore, in almost every realm of activity there are middle-class norms requiring that the presence of others be taken into account so that they are not offended. Violations of those norms constitute a form of deviance called *uncouthness*.

Uncouth behavior includes any private behavior that is done in public—passing gas, scratching one's genitals, picking one's teeth or nose, spitting, performing bodily functions, vomiting, sleeping, burping, or having sex.

Such behavior tends to offend others by introducing unpleasant smells, sounds, and sights. In the middle-class mind, it is enough that one endure these things when they are personally generated without having to share other's experience of them as well. Other rude acts are smoking in an elevator or a nonsmoking section of a restaurant, rushing ahead of someone to go through a door; interrupting a person who is speaking, breaking into a ticket line, or coughing and sneezing without covering one's mouth. Failing to keep one's body clean or to use deodorant is a form of uncouthness that offends others, as are crude table manners like making slurping noises while eating soup or drinking coffee.

The usual method of dealing with these transgressions is informal—a reaction of disgust or sometimes deliberate silence, followed by ostracism of the guilty party. Very rarely are there official sanctions for uncouthness, although sometimes arrests are made for sleeping or performing bodily functions in public places.

An instance in which formerly acceptable behavior is now becoming uncouth and for which formal sanctions are coming to replace informal sanctions is smoking behavior. Up until recently, smokers were relatively free to practice their habit just about anywhere. Although it was considered good manners to ask permission from those nearby, most smokers rarely bothered to ask and were seldom regarded as deviant. Within the past decade or so, however, smoking behavior has become much less tolerated. As medical evidence has accumulated showing that smoking damages not only the health of the smoker but also that of innocent bystanders, expectations have developed that smokers will confine their activities to designated areas and will honor the wishes of those who want to be protected. And in many places laws now require such segregation on airplanes, in restaurants, theaters, public buildings, and some places of employment. The full transition has not yet occurred, however. Although the airlines are held responsible for enforcing the smoking segregation under threat of the Civil Aeronautics Board, most other enforcement remains informal.

Summary

This typology of middle-class norms and deviance shows that there are enormous numbers and kinds of deviance—far more than usually come to mind when the subject of deviance is discussed. It is easy to imagine the large number and variety of deviant acts that would be evident if we built typologies based on the norms of all social classes, regions, ethnic groups, or sub-cultures. Yet if we were to construct such typologies, we would find substantial overlap with this one. That is because the middle class dominates U.S. society, both by imposing its standards through the schools, the mass media, and the law and by enjoying a degree of natural hegemony in behavior styles and thinking that flows from the admiration and emulation of those with higher status. For example, lower-class norms differ a little bit in a few of the categories, but, by and large, the lower class shares most norms with the middle class. And so it is for almost any normative reference we might choose. The fact is, there is considerable evidence of an overarching American culture exhibiting remarkable degrees of normative agreement. Nevertheless, we must be attuned to the many variations that do exist.

References

La Barre, Weston. 1969. They Shall Take Up Serpents: Psychology of the Southern Snake-Handling Cult. New York: Schocken.

Roethlisberger, Fritz, and William J. Dickson. 1964 [1939]. Management and the Worker. New York: John Wiley and Sons.

Simon, David R., and D. Stanley Eitzen. 1993. Elite Deviance, 4th Ed. Boston: Allyn and Bacon.

Sudnow, David. 1967. Passing On: The Social Organization of Dying. Englewood Cliffs, NJ: Prentice-Hall.

Vandiver, Kermit. 1996. "Why should my conscience bother me? Hiding aircraft brake hazards." Pp. 118–138 in Corporate and Governmental Deviance, edited by M. D. Ermann and R. J. Lundman. New York: Oxford.

❧ ❧ ❧

Questions

1. How well do the norms listed reflect middle-class expectations? Explain.

2. How inclusive is the typology (i.e. does the typology capture all forms of deviant behavior)?

3. What other norms would you include in this typology? Why?

4. Can specific behavior be classified in only one given category (i.e. how well does the typology reflect *exclusivity*)?

5. The typology clearly addresses middle-class norms and expectations. How might the typology be different if it were based on lower-class and/ or upper-class norms and expectations?

The Normal and the Pathological

EMILE DURKHEIM

What is normal for a society? What is pathological? Though many people consider crime "non-normative" and therefore believe it should be eliminated from society, Emile Durkheim disagrees. In this classic essay, Durkheim addresses the conditions under which pathological behavior emerges. He then uses crime to illustrate the functional necessity of such behavior for society.

. . .

*I*f there is a fact whose pathological nature appears indisputable, it is crime. All criminologists agree on this score. Although they explain this pathology differently, they none the less unanimously acknowledge it. However, the problem needs to be treated less summarily.

. . . Crime is not only observed in most societies of a particular species, but in all societies of all types. There is not one in which criminality does not exist, although it changes in form and the actions which are termed criminal are not everywhere the same. Yet everywhere and always there have been men who have conducted themselves in such a way as to bring down punishment upon their heads. If at least, as societies pass from lower to higher types, the crime rate (the relationship between the annual crime figures and population figures) tended to fall, we might believe that, although still remaining a normal phenomenon, crime tended to lose that character of normality. Yet there is no single ground for believing such a regression to be real. Many facts would rather seem to point to the existence of a movement in the opposite direction. From the beginning of the century statistics provide us with a means of following the progression of criminality. It has everywhere increased, and in France the increase is of the order of 300 per cent. Thus there is no phenomenon which represents more incontrovertibly all the symptoms of normality, since it appears to be closely bound up with the conditions of all collective life. To make crime a social illness would be to concede that sickness is not something accidental, but on the contrary derives in certain cases from the fundamental constitution of the living creature. This would be to erase any distinction between the physiological and the pathological. It can certainly happen that crime itself has normal forms; this is what happens, for instance, when it reaches an excessively high level. There is no doubt that this excessiveness is pathological in nature. What is normal is simply that criminality exists, provided that for each social type it does not reach or go beyond a certain level which it is perhaps not impossible to fix in conformity with the previous rules.[1]

We are faced with conclusion which is apparently somewhat paradoxical. Let us make no mistake: to classify crime among the phenomena of normal sociology is not merely to declare that it is an inevitable though regrettable phenomenon arising from the incorrigible wickedness of men; it is to assert that it is a factor in public health, an integrative element in any healthy society. At first sight this result is so surprising that it disconcerted even ourselves for a long time. However, once that first impression of surprise has been overcome it is not difficult to discover reasons to explain this normality and at the same time to confirm it.

In the first place, crime is normal because it is completely impossible for any society entirely free of it to exist.

Crime, as we have shown elsewhere, consists of an action which offends certain collective feelings which are especially strong and clear-cut. In any society, for actions regarded as criminal to cease, the feelings that they offend would need to be found in each individual consciousness without exception and in the degree of strength requisite to counteract the opposing feelings. Even supposing that this condition could effectively be fulfilled, crime would not thereby disappear; it would merely change in form, for the very cause which made the well-springs of criminality to dry up would immediately open up new ones.

Indeed, for the collective feelings, which the penal law of a people at a particular moment in its history protects, to penetrate individual consciousnesses that had hitherto remained closed to them, or to assume greater authority—whereas previously they had not possessed enough—they would have to acquire an intensity greater than they had had up to then. The community as a whole must feel them more keenly, for they cannot draw from any other source the additional force which enables them to bear down upon individuals who formerly were the most refractory. For murderers to disappear, the horror of bloodshed must increase in those strata of society from which murderers are recruited; but for this to happen the abhorrence must increase throughout society. Moreover, the very absence of crime would contribute directly to bringing about that result, for a sentiment appears much more respectable when it is always and uniformly respected. But we overlook the fact that these strong states of the common consciousness cannot be reinforced in this way without the weaker states, the violation of which previously gave rise to mere breaches of convention, being reinforced at the same time, for the weaker states are no more than the extension and attenuated form of the stronger ones. Thus, for example, theft and mere misappropriation of property offend the same altruistic sentiment, the respect for other people's possessions. However, this sentiment is offended less strongly by the latter action than the former. Moreover, since the average consciousness does not have sufficient intensity of feeling to feel strongly about the lesser of these two offences, the latter is the object of greater tolerance. This is why the misappropriator is merely censured, while the thief is punished. But if this sentiment grows stronger, to such a degree that it extinguishes in the consciousness the tendency to theft that men possess, they will become more sensitive to these minor offences, which up to then had had only a marginal effect upon them. They will react with greater intensity against these lesser faults, which will become the object of severer condemnation, so that, from the mere moral errors that they were, some will pass into the category of crimes. For example, dishonest contracts or those fulfilled dishonestly, which only incur public censure or civil redress, will become crimes. Imagine a community of saints in an exemplary and perfect monastery. In it crime as such will be unknown, but faults that appear venial to the ordinary person will arouse the same scandal as does normal crime in ordinary consciences. If therefore that community has the power to judge and punish, it will term such acts criminal and deal with them as such. It is for the same reason that the completely honourable man judges his slightest moral failings with a severity that the mass of people reserves for acts that are truly criminal. In former times acts of violence against the person were more frequent than they are today because respect for individual dignity was weaker. As it has increased, such crimes have become less frequent, but many acts which offended against that sentiment have been incorporated into the penal code, which did not previously include them.[2]

In order to exhaust all the logically possible hypotheses, it will perhaps be asked why this unanimity should not cover all collective sentiments without exception, and why even the weakest sentiments should not evoke sufficient power to forestall any dissentient voice. The moral conscience of society would be found in its entirety in every individual, endowed with sufficient force to prevent the commission of any act offending against it, whether purely conventional failings or crimes. But such universal and absolute uniformity is utterly impossible, for the immediate physical environment in which each one of us is placed, our hereditary antecedents, the social influences upon which we depend, vary from one individual to another and consequently cause a diversity of consciences. It is impossible for everyone to be alike in this matter, by virtue of the fact that we each have our own organic constitution and occupy different areas in space. This is why, even among lower peoples where individual originality is very little developed, such originality does however exist. Thus, since there cannot be a society in which individuals do not diverge to some extent from the collective type, it is also inevitable that among these deviations some assume a criminal character. What confers upon them this character is not the intrinsic importance of the acts but the importance which the common consciousness ascribes to them. Thus if the latter is stronger and possesses sufficient authority to make these divergences very weak in absolute terms, it will also be more sensitive and exacting. By reacting against the slightest deviations with an energy which it elsewhere employs against those what are more weighty, it endues them with the same gravity and will brand them as criminal.

Thus crime is necessary. It is linked to the basic conditions of social life, but on this very account is useful, for the conditions to which it is bound are themselves indispensable to the normal evolution of morality and law.

Indeed today we can no longer dispute the fact that not only do law and morality vary from one social type to another, but they even change within the same type if the conditions of collective existence are modified. Yet for these transformations to be made possible, the collective sentiments at the basis of morality should not prove unyielding to change, and consequently should be only moderately intense. If they were too strong, they would no longer be malleable. Any arrangement is indeed an obstacle to a new arrangement; this is even more the case the more deep-seated the original arrangement. The more strongly a structure is articulated, the more it resists modification; this is as true for functional as for anatomical patterns. If there were no crimes, this condition would not be fulfilled, for such a hypothesis presumes that collective sentiments would have attained the degree of intensity unparalleled in history. Nothing is good indefinitely and without limits. The authority which the moral consciousness enjoys must not be excessive, for otherwise no one would dare to attack it and it would petrify too easily into an immutable form. For it to evolve, individual originality must be allowed to manifest itself. But so that the originality of the idealist who dreams of transcending his era may display itself, that of the criminal, which falls short of the age, must also be possible. One does not go without the other.

Nor is this all. Beyond this indirect utility, crime itself may play a useful part in this evolution. Not only does it imply that the way to necessary changes remains open, but in certain cases it also directly prepares for these changes. Where crime exists, collective sentiments are not only in the state of plasticity necessary to assume a new form, but sometimes it even contributes to determining beforehand the shape they will take on. Indeed, how often is it only an anticipation of the morality to come, a progression towards what will be! According to Athenian law, Socrates was a criminal and his condemnation was entirely just. However, his crime—his independence of thought—was useful not only for humanity but for his country. It served to prepare a way for a new morality and a new faith, which the Athenians then needed because the traditions by which they had hitherto lived no longer corresponded to the conditions of their existence. Socrates's case is not an isolated one, for it recurs periodically in history. The freedom of thought that we at present enjoy could never have been asserted if the rules that forbade it had not been violated before they were solemnly abrogated. However, at the time the violation was a crime, since it was an offence against sentiments still keenly felt in the average consciousness. Yet this crime was useful since it was the prelude to changes which were daily becoming more necessary. Liberal philosophy has had as its precursors heretics of all kinds whom the secular arm rightly punished through the Middle Ages and has continued to do so almost up to the present day.

From this viewpoint the fundamental facts of criminology appear to us in an entirely new light. Contrary to current ideas, the criminal no longer appears as an utterly unsociable creature, a sort of parasitic element, a foreign, unassimilable body introduced into the bosom of society.[3] He plays a normal role in social life. For its part, crime must no longer be conceived of as an evil which cannot be circumscribed closely enough. Far from there being cause for congratulation when it drops too noticeably below the normal level, this apparent progress assuredly coincides with and is linked to some social disturbance. Thus the number of crimes of assault never falls so low as it does in times of scarcity.[4] Consequently, at the same time, and as a reaction, the theory of punishment is revised, or rather should be revised. If in fact crime is a sickness, punishment is the cure for it and cannot be conceived of otherwise; thus all the discussion aroused revolves round knowing what punishment should be to fulfil its role as a remedy. But if crime is in no way pathological, the object of punishment cannot be to cure it and its true function must be sought elsewhere.

Endnotes

[1] From the fact that crime is a phenomenon of normal sociology it does not follow that the criminal is a person normally constituted from the biological and psychological viewpoints. The two questions are independent of each other. This independence will be better understood when we have shown later the difference which exists between psychical and sociological facts.

[2] Calumny, insults, slander, deception, etc.

[3] We have ourselves committed the error of speaking of the criminal in this way through not having applied our rule (cf. *Division du travail social,* pp. 395, 396).

[4] But, although crime is a fact of normal sociology, it does not follow that we should not abhor it. Pain has likewise nothing desirable about it: the individual detests it just as society detests crime, and yet it is a normal physiological function. Not only does it necessarily derive from the very constitution of every living creature, but it plays a useful and irreplaceable role in life. Thus it would be a peculiar distortion to represent our thinking as an apologia for crime. We would not even have envisaged protesting against such an interpretation were we not aware of the strange accusations and misunderstandings to which one is exposed in undertaking to study moral facts objectively and to speak of them in language that is not commonly used.

❃ ❃ ❃

Questions

1. Why does Durkheim contend that crime is not only normal but necessary in society?

2. How does crime contribute to the development of, or a change in, society?

3. If Durkheim's view of crime is accurate, how effective can we expect social sanctions to be in deterring crime? How effective might various reform efforts be?

4. Think of specific crimes that occur on your campus. How would Durkheim explain the existence or prevalence of these crimes?

Moral Entrepreneurs: The Creation and Enforcement of Deviant Categories

HOWARD BECKER

Behavioral norms, or unspoken rules, exist at all levels of society. Some of these tell us how we should behave, while others tell us how we should not behave. How do specific rules come into existence? In this selection, Howard Becker addresses this question by examining the impact of "rule creators." He also explores the ways in which norms are enforced ("rule enforcers") and the relationship between rule creators and rule enforcers.

Rules are the products of someone's initiative and we can think of the people who exhibit such enterprise as *moral entrepreneurs*. Two related species—rule creators and rule enforcers—will occupy our attention.

☺ Rule Creators

The prototype of the rule creator, but not the only variety as we shall see, is the crusading reformer. He is interested in the content of rules. The existing rules do not satisfy him because there is some evil which profoundly disturbs him. He feels that nothing can be right in the world until rules are made to correct it. He operates with an absolute ethic; what he sees is truly and totally evil with no qualification. Any means is justified to do away with it. The crusader is fervent and righteous, often self-righteous.

It is appropriate to think of reformers as crusaders because they typically believe that their mission is a holy one. The prohibitionist serves as an

"Moral Entrepreneurs: The Creation and Enforcement of Deviant Categories," by Howard Becker, reprinted from *Outsiders: Studies in the Sociology of Deviance*, 1963, pp. 147–163. Copyright © 1963 by the Free Press.

excellent example, as does the person who wants to suppress vice and sexual delinquency or the person who wants to do away with gambling.

These examples suggest that the moral crusader is a meddling busy-body, interested in forcing his own morals on others. But this is a one-sided view. Many moral crusades have strong humanitarian overtones. The crusader is not only interested in seeing to it that other people do what he thinks right. He believes that if they do what is right it will be good for them. Or he may feel that his reform will prevent certain kinds of exploitation of one person by another. Prohibitionists felt that they were not simply forcing their morals on others, but attempting to provide the conditions for a better way of life for people prevented by drink from realizing a truly good life. Abolitionists were not simply trying to prevent slave owners from doing the wrong thing; they were trying to help slaves to achieve a better life. Because of the importance of the humanitarian motive, moral crusaders (despite their relatively single-minded devotion to their particular cause) often lend their support to other humanitarian crusades. Joseph Gusfield has pointed out that:

> The American temperance movement during the 19th century was a part of a general effort toward the improvement of the worth of the human being through improved morality as well as economic conditions. The mixture of the religious, the equalitarian, and the humanitarian was an outstanding facet of the moral reformism of many movements. Temperance supporters formed a large segment of movements such as sabbatarianism, abolition, woman's rights, agrarianism, and humanitarian attempts to improve the lot of the poor. . . .

> In its auxiliary interests the WCTU revealed a great concern for the improvement of the welfare of the lower classes. It was active in campaigns to secure penal reform, to shorten working hours and raise wages for workers, and to abolish child labor and in a number of other humanitarian and equalitarian activities. In the 1880's the WCTU worked to bring about legislation for the protection of working girls against the exploitation by men.[1]

As Gusfield says,[2] "Moral reformism of this type suggests the approach of a dominant class toward those less favorably situated in the economic and social structure." Moral crusaders typically want to help those beneath them to achieve a better status. That those beneath them do not always like the means proposed for their salvation is another matter. But this fact—that moral crusades are typically dominated by those in the upper levels of the social structure—means that they add to the power they derive from the legitimacy of their moral position, the power they derive from their superior position in society.

Naturally, many moral crusades draw support from people whose motives are less pure than those of the crusader. Thus, some industrialists supported Prohibition because they felt it would provide them with a more manageable labor force.[3] Similarly, it is sometimes rumored that Nevada gambling interests support the opposition to attempts to legalize gambling in California because it would cut so heavily into their business, which depends in substantial measure on the population of Southern California.[4]

The moral crusader, however, is more concerned with ends than with means. When it comes to drawing up specific rules (typically in the form of legislation to be proposed to a state legislature or the Federal Congress), he frequently relies on the advice of experts. Lawyers, expert in the drawing of acceptable legislation, often play this role. Government bureaus in whose jurisdiction the problem falls may also have the necessary expertise, as did the Federal Bureau of Narcotics in the case of the marijuana problem.

As psychiatric ideology, however, becomes increasingly acceptable, a new expert has appeared—the psychiatrist. Sutherland, in his discussion of the natural history of sexual psychopath laws, pointed to the psychiatrist's influence.[5] He suggests the following as the conditions under which the sexual psychopath law, which provides that a person "who is diagnosed as a sexual psychopath may be confined for an indefinite period in a state hospital for the insane,"[6] will be passed.

> First, these laws are customarily enacted after a state of fear has been aroused in a community by a few serious sex crimes committed in quick succession. This is illustrated in Indiana, where a law was passed following three or four sexual attacks in Indianapolis, with murder in two. Heads of families bought guns and watch dogs, and the supply of locks and chains in the hardware stores of the city was completely exhausted. . . .
>
> A second element in the process of developing sexual psychopath laws is the agitated activity of the community in connection with the fear. The attention of the community is focused on sex crimes, and people in the most varied situations envisage dangers and see the need of and possibility for their control. . . .
>
> The third phase in the development of these sexual psychopath laws has been the appointment of a committee. The committee gathers the many conflicting recommendations of persons and groups of persons, attempts

to determine "facts," studies procedures in other states, and makes recommendations, which generally include bills for the legislature. Although the general fear usually subsides within a few days, a committee has the formal duty of following through until positive action is taken. Terror which does not result in a committee is much less likely to result in a law.[7]

In the case of sexual psychopath laws, there usually is no government agency charged with dealing in a specialized way with sexual deviations. Therefore, when the need for expert advice in drawing up legislation arises, people frequently turn to the professional group most closely associated with such problems:

> In some states, at the committee stage of the development of a sexual psychopath law, psychiatrists have played an important part. The psychiatrists, more than any others, have been the interest group back of the laws. A committee of psychiatrists and neurologists in Chicago wrote the bill which became the sexual psychopath law of Illinois; the bill was sponsored by the Chicago Bar Association and by the state's attorney of Cook County and was enacted with little opposition in the next session of the State Legislature. In Minnesota all the members of the governor's committee except one were psychiatrists. In Wisconsin the Milwaukee Neuropsychiatric Society shared in pressing the Milwaukee Crime Commission for the enactment of a law. In Indiana the attorney-general's committee received from the American Psychiatric Association copies of all of the sexual psychopath laws which had been enacted in other states.[8]

The influence of psychiatrists in other realms of the criminal law has increased in recent years.

In any case, what is important about this example is not that psychiatrists are becoming increasingly influential, but that the moral crusader, at some point in the development of his crusade, often requires the services of a professional who can draw up the appropriate rules in an appropriate form. The crusader himself is often not concerned with such details. Enough for him that the main point has been won; he leaves its implementation to others.

By leaving the drafting of the specific rule in the hands of others, the crusader opens the door for many unforeseen influences. For those who draft legislation for crusaders have their own interests, which may affect the legislation they prepare. It is likely that the sexual psychopath laws drawn by psychiatrists contain many features never intended by the citizens who spearheaded the drives to "do something about sex crimes," features which do however reflect the professional interests of organized psychiatry.

◉ The Fate of Moral Crusades

A crusade may achieve striking success, as did the Prohibition movement with the passage of the Eighteenth Amendment. It may fail completely, as has the drive to do away with the use of tobacco or the anti-vivisection movement. It may achieve great success, only to find its gains whittled away by shifts in public morality and increasing restrictions imposed on it by judicial interpretations; such has been the case with the crusade against obscene literature.

One major consequence of a successful crusade, of course, is the establishment of a new rule or set of rules, usually with the appropriate enforcement machinery being provided at the same time. I want to consider this consequence at some length later. There is another consequence, however, of the success of a crusade which deserves mention.

When a man has been successful in the enterprise of getting a new rule established—when he has found, so to speak, the Grail—he is out of a job. The crusade which has occupied so much of his time, energy, and passion is over. Such a man is likely, when he first began his crusade, to have been an amateur, a man who engaged in a crusade because of his interest in the issue, in the content of the rule he wanted established. Kenneth Burke once noted that a man's occupation may become his preoccupation. The equation is also good the other way around. A man's preoccupation may become his occupation. What started as an amateur interest in a moral issue may become an almost full-time job; indeed, for many reformers it becomes just this. The success of the crusade, therefore, leaves the crusader without a vocation. Such a man, at loose ends, may generalize his interest and discover something new to view with alarm, a new evil about which something ought to be done. He becomes a professional discoverer of wrongs to be righted, of situations requiring new rules.

When the crusade has produced a large organization devoted to its cause, officials of the organization are even more likely than the individual crusader to look for new causes to espouse. This process occurred dramatically in the field of health problems when the National Foundation for Infantile Paralysis put itself out of business by discovering a vaccine that eliminated epidemic poliomyelitis. Taking the less constraining name of The

National Foundation, officials quickly discovered other health problems to which the organization could devote its energies and resources.

The unsuccessful crusade, either the one that finds its mission no longer attracts adherents or the one that achieves its goal only to lose it again, may follow one of two courses. On the one hand, it may simply give up its original mission and concentrate on preserving what remains of the organization that has been built up. Such, according to one study, was the fate of the Townsend Movement.[9] Or the failing movement may adhere rigidly to an increasingly less popular mission, as did the Prohibition Movement. Gusfield has described present-day members of the WCTU as "moralizers-in-retreat."[10] As prevailing opinion in the United States becomes increasingly anti-temperance, these women have not softened their attitude toward drinking. On the contrary, they have become bitter at the formerly "respectable" people who no longer will support a temperance movement. The social class level from which WCTU members are drawn has moved down from the upper-middle class to the lower-middle class. The WCTU now turns to attack the middle class it once drew its support from, seeing this group as the locus of acceptance of moderate drinking. The following quotations from Gusfield's interviews with WCTU leaders give some of the flavor of the "moralizer-in-retreat":

> When this union was first organized, we had many of the most influential ladies of the city. But now they have got the idea that we ladies who are against taking a cocktail are a little queer. We have an undertaker's wife and a minister's wife, but the lawyer's and the doctor's wives shun us. They don't want to be thought queer.

> We fear moderation more than anything. Drinking has become so much a part of everything—even in our church life and our colleges.

> It creeps into the official church boards. They keep it in their iceboxes. . . . The minister here thinks that the church has gone far, that they are doing too much to help the temperance cause. He's afraid that he'll stub some influential toes.[11]

Only some crusaders, then, are successful in their mission and create, by creating a new rule, a new group of outsiders. Of the successful, some find they have a taste for crusades and seek new problems to attack. Other crusaders fail in their attempt and either support the organization they have created by dropping their distinctive mission and focusing on the problem of organizational maintenance itself or become outsiders themselves, continuing to espouse and preach a doctrine which sounds increasingly queer as time goes on.

❧ Rule Enforcers

The most obvious consequence of a successful crusade is the creation of a new set of rules. With the creation of a new set of rules we often find that a new set of enforcement agencies and officials is established. Sometimes, of course, existing agencies take over the administration of the new rule, but more frequently a new set of rule enforcers is created. The passage of the Harrison Act presaged the creation of the Federal Narcotics Bureau, just as the passage of the Eighteenth Amendment led to the creation of police agencies charged with enforcing the Prohibition Laws.

With the establishment of organizations of rule enforcers, the crusade becomes institutionalized. What started out as a drive to convince the world of the moral necessity of a new rule finally becomes an organization devoted to the enforcement of the rule. Just as radical political movements turn into organized political parties and lusty evangelical sects become staid religious denominations, the final outcome of the moral crusade is a police force. To understand, therefore, how the rules creating a new class of outsiders are applied to particular people we must understand the motives and interests of police, the rule enforcers.

Although some policemen undoubtedly have a kind of crusading interest in stamping out evil, it is probably much more typical for the policeman to have a certain detached and objective view of his job. He is not so much concerned with the content of any particular rule as he is with the fact that it is his job to enforce the rule. When the rules are changed, he punishes what was once acceptable behavior just as he ceases to punish behavior that has been made legitimate by a change in the rules. The enforcer, then, may not be interested in the content of the rule as such, but only in the fact that the existence of the rule provides him with a job, a profession, and a *raison d'être*.

Since the enforcement of certain rules provides justification for his way of life, the enforcer has two interests which condition his enforcement activity: first, he must justify the existence of his position and, second, he must win the respect of those he deals with.

These interests are not peculiar to rule enforcers. Members of all occupations feel the need to justify their work and win the respect of others.

Musicians, as we have seen, would like to do this but have difficulty finding ways of successfully impressing their worth on customers. Janitors fail to win their tenants' respect, but develop an ideology which stresses the quasi-professional responsibility they have to keep confidential the intimate knowledge of tenants they acquire in the course of their work.[12] Physicians, lawyers, and other professionals, more successful in winning the respect of clients, develop elaborate mechanisms for maintaining a properly respectful relationship.

In justifying the existence of his position, the rule enforcer faces a double problem. On the one hand, he must demonstrate to others that the problem still exists: the rules he is supposed to enforce have some point, because infractions occur. On the other hand, he must show that his attempts at enforcement are effective and worthwhile, that the evil he is supposed to deal with is in fact being dealt with adequately. Therefore, enforcement organizations, particularly when they are seeking funds, typically oscillate between two kinds of claims. First, they say that by reason of their efforts the problem they deal with is approaching solution. But, in the same breath, they say the problem is perhaps worse than ever (though through no fault of their own) and requires renewed and increased effort to keep it under control. Enforcement officials can be more vehement than anyone else in their insistence that the problem they are supposed to deal with is still with us, in fact is more with us than ever before. In making these claims, enforcement officials provide good reason for continuing the existence of the position they occupy.

We may also note that enforcement officials and agencies are inclined to take a pessimistic view of human nature. If they do not actually believe in original sin, they at least like to dwell on the difficulties in getting people to abide by rules, on the characteristics of human nature that lead people toward evil. They are skeptical of attempts to reform rule-breakers.

The skeptical and pessimistic outlook of the rule enforcer, of course, is reinforced by his daily experience. He sees, as he goes about his work, the evidence that the problem is still with us. He sees the people who continually repeat offenses, thus definitely branding themselves in his eyes as outsiders. Yet it is not too great a stretch of the imagination to suppose that one of the underlying reasons for the enforcer's pessimism about human nature and the possibilities of reform is that fact that if human nature were perfectible and people could be permanently reformed, his job would come to an end.

In the same way, a rule enforcer is likely to believe that it is necessary for the people he deals with to respect him. If they do not, it will be very difficult to do his job; his feeling of security in his work will be lost. Therefore, a good deal of enforcement activity is devoted not to the actual enforcement of rules, but to coercing respect from the people the enforcer deals with. This means that one may be labeled as deviant not because he has actually broken a rule, but because he has shown disrespect to the enforcer of the rule.

Westley's study of policemen in a small industrial city furnishes a good example of this phenomenon. In his interview, he asked policemen, "When do you think a policeman is justified in roughing a man up?" He found that "at least 37% of the men believed that it was legitimate to use violence to coerce respect."[13] He gives some illuminating quotations from his interviews:

> Well, there are cases. For example, when you stop a fellow for a routine questioning, say a wise guy, and he starts talking back to you and telling you you are no good and that sort of thing. You know you can take a man in on a disorderly conduct charge, but you can practically never make it stick. So what you do in a case like that is to egg the guy on until he makes a remark where you can justifiably slap him and, then, if he fights back, you can call it resisting arrest.

> Well, a prisoner deserves to be hit when he goes to the point where he tries to put you below him.

> You've gotta get rough when a man's language becomes very bad, when he is trying to make a fool of you in front of everybody else. I think most policemen try to treat people in a nice way, but usually you have to talk pretty, rough. That's the only way to set a man down, to make him show a little respect.[14]

What Westley describes is the use of an illegal means of coercing respect from others. Clearly, when a rule enforcer has the option of enforcing a rule or not, the difference in what he does may be caused by the attitude of the offender toward him. If the offender is properly respectful, the enforcer may smooth the situation over. If the offender is disrespectful, then sanctions may be visited on him. Westley has shown that this differential tends to operate in the case of traffic offenses, where the policeman's discretion is perhaps at a maximum.[15] But it probably operates in other areas as well.

Ordinarily, the rule enforcer has a great deal of discretion in many areas, if only because his resources are not sufficient to cope with the volume of rule-breaking he is supposed to deal with. This means that he cannot tackle everything at once and to this extent must temporize with evil. He cannot do the whole job and knows it. He takes his time, on the assumption that the problems he deals with will be around for a long while. He establishes priorities, dealing with things in their turn, handling the most pressing problems immediately and leaving others for later. His attitude toward his work, in short, is professional. He lacks the naive moral fervor characteristic of the rule creator.

If the enforcer is not going to tackle every case he knows of at once, he must have a basis for deciding when to enforce the rule, which persons committing which acts to label as deviant. One criterion for selecting people is the "fix." Some people have sufficient political influence or know-how to be able to ward off attempts at enforcement, if not at the time of apprehension then at a later stage in the process. Very often, this function is professionalized; someone performs the job on a full-time basis, available to anyone who wants to hire him. A professional thief described fixers this way:

> There is in every large city a regular fixer for professional thieves. He has no agents and does not solicit and seldom takes any case except that of a professional thief, just as they seldom go to anyone except him. This centralized and monopolistic system of fixing for professional thieves is found in practically all of the large cities and many of the small ones.[16]

Since it is mainly professional thieves who know about the fixer and his operations, the consequence of this criterion for selecting people to apply the rules to is that amateurs tend to be caught, convicted, and labeled deviant much more frequently than professionals. As the professional thief notes:

> You can tell by the way the case is handled in court when the fix is in. When the copper is not very certain he has the right man, or the testimony of the copper and the complainant does not agree, or the prosecutor goes easy on the defendant, or the judge is arrogant in his decisions, you can always be sure that someone has got the work in. This does not happen in many cases of theft, for there is one case of a professional to twenty-five or thirty amateurs who know nothing about the fix. These amateurs get the hard end of the deal every time. The coppers bawl out about the thieves, no one holds up his testimony, the judge delivers an oration, and all of them get credit for stopping a crime wave. When the professional hears the case immediately preceding his own, he will think, "He should have got ninety years. It's the damn amateurs who cause all the heat in the stores."

Or else he thinks, "Isn't it a damn shame for that copper to send that kid away for a pair of hose, and in a few minutes he will agree to a small fine for me for stealing a fur coat?" But if the coppers did not send the amateurs away to strengthen their records of convictions, they could not sandwich in the professionals whom they turn loose.[17]

Enforcers of rules, since they have no stake in the content, of particular rules themselves, often develop their own private evaluation of the importance of various, kinds of rules, and infractions of them. This set of priorities may differ considerably from those held by the general public. For instance, drug users typically believe (and a few policemen have personally confirmed it to me) that police do not consider the use of marijuana to be as important a problem or as dangerous a practice as the use of opiate drugs. Police base this conclusion on the fact that, in their experience, opiate users commit other crimes (such as theft or prostitution) in order to get drugs, while marijuana users do not.

Enforcers, then, responding to the pressures of their own work situation, enforce rules and create outsiders in a selective way. Whether a person who commits a deviant act is in fact labeled a deviant depends on many things extraneous to his actual behavior: whether the enforcement official feels that at this time he must make some show of doing his job in order to justify his position, whether the misbehaver shows proper deference to the enforcer, whether the "fix" has been put in, and where the kind of act he has committed stands on the enforcer's list of priorities.

The professional enforcer's lack of fervor and routine approach to dealing with evil may get him into trouble with the rule creator. The rule creator, as we have said, is concerned with the content of the rules that interest him. He sees them as the means by which evil can be stamped out. He does not understand the enforcer's long-range approach to the same problems and cannot see why all the evil that is apparent cannot be stamped out at once.

When the person interested in the content of a rule realizes or has called to his attention the fact that enforcers are dealing selectively with the evil that concerns him, his righteous wrath may be aroused. The professional is denounced for viewing the evil too lightly, for failing to do his duty. The moral entrepreneur, at whose instance the rule was made, arises again to say that the outcome of the last crusade has not been satisfactory or that the gains once made have been whittled away and lost.

◎ Deviance and Enterprise: A Summary

Deviance—in the sense I have been using it, of publicly labeled wrongdoing—is always the result of enterprise. Before any act can be viewed as deviant, and before any class of people can be labeled and treated as outsiders for committing the act, someone must have made the rule which defines the act as deviant. Rules are not made automatically. Even though a practice may be harmful in an objective sense to the group in which it occurs, the harm needs to be discovered and pointed out. People must be made to feel that something ought to be done about it. Someone must call the public's attention to these matters, supply the push necessary to get things done, and direct such energies as are aroused in the proper direction to get a rule created. Deviance is the product of enterprise in the largest sense; without the enterprise required to get rules made, the deviance which consists of breaking the rule could not exist.

Deviance is the product of enterprise in the smaller and more particular sense as well. Once a rule has come into existence, it must be applied to particular people before the abstract class of outsiders created by the rule can be peopled. Offenders must be discovered, identified, apprehended and convicted (or noted as "different" and stigmatized for their nonconformity, as in the case of legal deviant groups such as dance musicians). This job ordinarily falls to the lot of professional enforcers who, by enforcing already existing rules, create the particular deviants society views as outsiders.

It is an interesting fact that most scientific research and speculation on deviance concerns itself with the people who break rules rather than with those who make and enforce them. If we are to achieve a full understanding of deviant behavior, we must get these two possible foci of inquiry into balance. We must see deviance, and the outsiders who personify the abstract conception, as a consequence of a process of interaction between people, some of whom in the service of their own interests make and enforce rules which catch others who, in the service of their own interests, have committed acts which are labeled deviant.

Endnotes

[1]Joseph R. Gusfield, "Social Structure and Moral Reform: A Study of the Woman's Christian Temperance Union," *American Journal of Sociology,* LXI (November, 1955), 223.

[2]*Ibid.*

[3]See Raymond G. McCarthy, editor, *Drinking and Intoxication* (New Haven and New York: Yale Center of Alcohol Studies and The Free Press of Glencoe, 1959), pp. 395–396.

[4]This is suggested in Oscar Lewis, *Sagebrush Casinos: The Story of Legal Gambling in Nevada* (New York: Doubleday and Co., 1953), pp. 233–234.

[5]S. Edwin H. Sutherland, "The Diffusion of Sexual Psychopath Laws," *American Journal of Sociology,* LVI (September, 1950), 142–148.

[6]*Ibid.,* p. 142.

[7]*Ibid.,* pp. 143–145.

[8]*Ibid.,* pp.145–146.

[9]Sheldon Messinger, "Organizational Transformation: A Case Study of a Declining Social Movement," *American Sociological Review,* XX, (February, 1955), 3–10.

[10]Gusfield, *op, cit.,* pp. 227–228.

[11]*Ibid.,* pp. 227, 229–230.

[12]See Ray Gold, "Janitors Versus Tenants: A Status-Income Dilemma," *American Journal of Sociology,* LVII (March, 1952), 486–493.

[13]William A. Westley, "Violence and the Police," *American Journal of Sociology,* LIX (July, 1953), 39.

[14]*Ibid.*

[15]See William A. Westley, "The Police: A Sociological Study of Law, Custom, and Morality" (unpublished PhD. dissertation, University of Chicago, Department of Sociology, 1951).

[16]Edwin H. Sutherland (editor), *The Professional Thief* (Chicago: University of Chicago Press, 1937), pp. 87–88.

[17]*Ibid.,* pp. 91–92.

Questions

1. What role do "moral crusaders" play in the development of rules and laws? Cite some contemporary examples of successful and unsuccessful moral crusades.

2. Becker discusses the role of professionals, in particular psychologists, in creating some rules. Do you think the role of professionals has become more or less prominent in recent times? Provide examples to support your claim.

3. What is the relationship between rule enforcers and rules? How might rule enforcers' differential enforcement of rules lead to problems when people are dealing with deviance and crime?

4. Becker contends that rule creators are concerned with rule content but not enforceability, and that rule enforcers are concerned with enforceability but not content. What kinds of problems may arise from these two groups' having competing interests?

5. What does Becker mean when he claims that rule enforcers must deal with a "double problem"? How might this "double problem" be resolved?

Social Structure and Anomie

ROBERT K. MERTON
Harvard University

This classic article by Robert Merton explains the role of social structure in generating anomie, or a sense of lawlessness and alienation, within individuals. Merton also discusses the intersection between one's adoption (or not) of culturally prescribed goals and one's adoption (or not) of accepted means of achieving those goals. Merton's resulting framework identifies particular responses to stress and anomie, including conformity, innovation, ritualism, retreatism, and rebellion.

There persists a notable tendency in sociology theory to attribute the malfunctioning of social structure primarily to those of man's imperious biological drives which are not adequately restrained by social control. In this view, the social order is solely a device for "impulse management" and the "social processing" of tensions. These impulses which break through social control, be it noted, are held to be biologically derived. Nonconformity is assumed to be rooted in original nature.[1] Conformity is by implication the result of an utilitarian calculus or unreasoned conditioning. This point of view, whatever its other deficiencies, clearly begs one question. It provides no basis for determining the nonbiological conditions which induce deviations from prescribed patterns of conduct. In this paper, it will be suggested that certain phases of social structure generate the circumstances in which infringement of social codes constitutes a "normal" response.[2]

The conceptual scheme to be outlined is designed to provide a coherent, systematic approach to the study of socio-cultural sources of deviate behavior. Our primary aim lies in discovering how some social structures *exert a definite pressure* upon certain persons in the society to engage in nonconformist rather than conformist conduct. The many ramifications of

"Social Structure and Anomie," by Robert Merton, reprinted from *American Sociological Review*, vol. 3, 1938, pp. 672–682.

the scheme cannot all be discussed; the problems mentioned outnumber those explicitly treated.

Among the elements of social and cultural structure, two are important for our purposes. These are analytically separable although they merge imperceptibly in concrete situations. The first consists of culturally defined goals, purposes, and interests. It comprises a frame of aspirational reference. These goals are more or less integrated and involve varying degrees of prestige and sentiment. They constitute a basic, but not the exclusive, component of what Linton aptly has called "designs for group living." Some of these cultural aspirations are related to the original drives of man, but they are not determined by them. The second phase of the social structure defines, regulates, and controls the acceptable modes of achieving these goals. Every social group invariably couples its scale of desired ends with moral or institutional regulation of permissible and required procedures for attaining these ends. These regulatory norms and moral imperatives do not necessarily coincide with technical or efficiency norms. Many procedures which from the standpoint of *particular individuals* would be most efficient in securing desired values, e.g., illicit oil-stock schemes, theft, fraud, are ruled out of the institutional area of permitted conduct. The choice of expedients is limited by the institutional norms.

To say that these elements, culture goals and institutional norms, operate jointly is not to say that the ranges of alternative behaviors and aims bear some constant relation to one another. The emphasis upon certain goals may vary independently of the degree of emphasis upon institutional means. There may develop a disproportionate, at times, a virtually exclusive, stress upon the value of specific goals, involving relatively slight concern with the institutionally appropriate modes of attaining these goals. The limiting case in this direction is reached when the range of alternative procedures is limited only by technical rather than institutional considerations. Any and all devices which promise attainment of the all important goal would be permitted in this hypothetical polar case.[3] This constitutes one types of cultural malintegration. A second polar type is found in groups where activities originally conceived as instrumental are transmuted into ends in themselves. The original purposes are forgotten and ritualistic adherence to institutionally prescribed conduct becomes virtually obsessive.[4] Stability is largely ensured while change is flouted. The range of alternative behaviors is severely limited. There develops a tradition-bound, sacred society characterized by neophobia. The occupational psychosis of the bureaucrat may be cited as a case in point. Finally, there are the intermediate types of groups where a balance between culture goals and institutional means is maintained. These are the significantly integrated and relatively stable, though changing, groups.

An effective equilibrium between the two phases of the social structure is maintained as long as satisfactions accrue to individuals who conform to both constraints, viz., satisfactions from the achievement of the goals and satisfactions emerging directly from the institutionally canalized modes of striving to attain these ends. Success, in such equilibrated cases, is twofold. Success is reckoned in terms of the product and in terms of the process, in terms of the outcome and in terms of activities. Continuing satisfactions must derive from sheer *participation* in a competitive order as well as from eclipsing one's competitors if the order itself is to be sustained. The occasional sacrifices involved in institutionalized conduct must be compensated by socialized rewards. The distribution of statuses and roles through competition must be so organized that positive incentives for conformity to roles and adherence to status obligations are provided *for every position* within the distributive order. Aberrant conduct, therefore, may be viewed as a symptom of dissociation between culturally defined aspirations and socially structured means.

Of the types of groups which result from the independent variation of the two phases of the social structure, we shall be primarily concerned with the first, namely, that involving a disproportionate accent on goals. This statement must be recast in a proper perspective. In no group is there an absence of regulatory codes governing conduct, yet groups do vary in the degree to which these folkways, mores, and institutional controls are effectively integrated with the more diffuse goals which are part of the culture matrix. Emotional convictions may cluster about the complex of socially acclaimed ends, meanwhile shifting their support from the culturally defined implementation of these ends. As we shall see, certain aspects of the social structure may generate countermores and antisocial behavior precisely because of different emphases on goals and regulations. In the extreme case, the latter may be so vitiated by the goal emphasis that the range of behavior is limited only by considerations of technical expediency. The sole significant question then becomes, which available means is most efficient in netting the socially approved value.[5] The technically most feasible procedure, whether legitimate or not, is preferred to the institutionally prescribed

47

conduct. As this process continues, the integration of the society becomes tenuous and anomie ensues.

Thus, in competitive athletics, when the aim of victory is shorn of its institutional trappings and success in contests becomes construed as "winning the game" rather than "winning through circumscribed modes of activity," a premium is implicitly set upon the use of illegitimate but technically efficient means. The star of the opposing football team is surreptitiously slugged; the wrestler furtively incapacitates his opponent through ingenious but illicit techniques; university alumni covertly subsidize "students" whose talents are largely confined to the athletic field. The emphasis on the goal has so attenuated the satisfactions deriving from sheer participation in the competitive activity that these satisfactions are virtually confined to a successful outcome. Through the same process, tension generated by the desire to win in a poker game is relieved by successfully dealing oneself four aces, or, when the cult of success has become completely dominant, by sagaciously shuffling the cards in a game of solitaire. The faint twinge of uneasiness in the last instance and the surreptious nature of public delicts indicate clearly that the institutional rules of the game *are known* to those who evade them, but that the emotional supports of these rules are largely vitiated by cultural exaggeration of the success goal.[6] They are microcosmic images of the social macrocosm.

Of course, this process is not restricted to the realm of sport. The process whereby exaltation of the end generates a *literal demoralization*, i.e., a deinstitutionalization, of the means is one which characterizes many[7] groups in which the two phases of the social structure are not highly integrated. The extreme emphasis upon the accumulation of wealth as a symbol of success[8] in our own society militates against the completely effective control of institutionally regulated modes of acquiring a fortune.[9] Fraud, corruption, vice, crime, in short, the entire catalogue of proscribed behavior, becomes increasingly common when the emphasis on the *culturally induced* success goal becomes divorced from a coordinated institutional emphasis. This observation of crucial theoretical importance in examining the doctrine that antisocial behavior most frequently derives from biological drives breaking through the restraints imposed by society. The difference is one between a strictly utilitarian interpretation which conceives man's ends as random and an analysis which finds these ends deriving from the basic values of the culture.[10]

Our analysis can scarcely stop at this juncture. We must turn to other aspects of the social structure if we are to deal with the social genesis of the varying rates and types of deviate behavior characteristic of different societies. Thus far, we have sketched three ideal types of social orders constituted by distinctive patterns of relations between cultural ends and means. Turning from these types of *culture patterning,* we find five logically possible, alternative modes of adjustment or adaptation *by individuals* within the culture-bearing society or groups.[11] These are schematically presented in the following table, where (+) signifies "acceptance," (-) signifies "elimination" and (±) signifies "rejection and substitution of new goals and standards."

		Culture and Goals	Institutionalized Means
I.	Conformity	+	+
II.	Innovation	+	-
III.	Ritualism	-	+
IV.	Retreatism	-	-
V.	Rebellion[12]	±	±

Our discussion of the relation between these alternative responses and other phases of the social structure must be prefaced by the observation that persons may shift from one alternative to another as they engage in different social activities. These categories refer to role adjustments in specific situations, not to personality *in toto.* To treat the development of this process in various spheres of conduct would introduce a complexity unmanageable within the confines of this paper. For this reason, we shall be concerned primarily with economic activity in the broad sense, "the production, exchange, distribution and consumption of goods and services" in our competitive society, wherein wealth has taken on a highly symbolic cast. Our task is to search out some of the factors which exert pressure upon individuals to engage in certain of these logically possible alternative responses. This choice, as we shall see, is far from random.

In every society, Adaptation I (conformity to both culture goals and means) is the most common and widely diffused. Were this not so, the stability and continuity of society could not be maintained. The mesh of expectancies which constitutes every social order is sustained by the modal behavior of its members falling within the first category. Conventional role behavior oriented toward the basic values of the group is the rule rather than the exception. It is this fact alone which permits us to speak of a human aggregate as comprising a group or society.

Conversely, Adaptation IV (rejection of goals and means) is the least common. Persons who "adjust" (or maladjust) in this fashion are, strictly speaking, *in* the society if not *of* it. Sociologically, these constitute the true "aliens." Not sharing the common frame of orientation, they can be included within the societal population merely in a fictional sense. In this category are *some* of the activities of psychotics, psychoneurotics, chronic autists, pariahs, outcasts, vagrants, vagabonds, tramps, chronic drunkards and drug addicts.[13] These have relinquished, in certain spheres of activity, the culturally defined goals, involving complete aim-inhibition in the polar case, and their adjustments are not in accord with institutional norms. This is not to say that in some cases the source of their behavioral adjustments is not in part the very social structure which they have in effect repudiated nor that their very existence within a social area does not constitute a problem for the socialized population.

This mode of "adjustment" occurs, as far as structural sources are concerned, when both the culture goals and institutionalized procedures have been assimilated thoroughly by the individual and imbued with affect and high positive value, but where those institutionalized procedures which promise a measure of successful attainment of the goals are not available to the individual. In such instances, there results a twofold mental conflict insofar as the moral obligation for adopting institutional means conflicts with the pressure to resort to illegitimate means (which may attain the goal) and inasmuch as the individual is shut off from means which are both legitimate *and* effective. The competitive order is maintained, but the frustrated and handicapped individual who cannot cope with this order drops out. Defeatism, quietism and resignation are manifested in escape mechanisms which ultimately lead the individual to "escape" from the requirements of the society. It is an expedient which arises from continued failure to attain the goal by legitimate measures and from an inability to adopt the illegitimate route because of internalized prohibitions and institutionalized compulsives, *during which process the supreme value of the success-goal has as yet not been renounced.* The conflict is resolved by eliminating *both* precipitating elements, the goals and means. The escape is complete, the conflict is eliminated and the individual is a-socialized.

Be it noted that where frustration derives from the inaccessibility of effective institutional means for attaining economic or any other type of highly valued "success," that Adaptations II, III, and V (innovation, ritualism and rebellion) are also possible. The result will be determined by the particular personality, and thus, the *particular* cultural background, involved. Inadequate socialization will result in the innovation response whereby the conflict and frustration are eliminated by relinquishing the institutional means and retaining the success-aspiration; an extreme assimilation of institutional demands will lead to ritualism wherein the goal is dropped as beyond one's reach but conformity to the mores persists; and rebellion occurs when emancipation from the reigning standards, due to frustration or to marginalist perspectives, leads to the attempt to introduce a "new social order."

Our major concern is with the illegitimacy adjustment. This involves the use of conventionally proscribed but frequently effective means of attaining at least the simulacrum of culturally defined success—wealth, power, and the like. As we have seen, this adjustment occurs when the individual has assimilated the cultural emphasis on success without equally internalizing the morally prescribed norms governing means for its attainment. The question arises, While phases of our social structure predispose toward this mode of adjustment? We may examine a concrete instance, effectively analyzed by Lohman,[14] which provides a clue to the answer. Lohman has shown that specialized areas of vice in the near north side of Chicago constitute a "normal" response to a situation where the cultural emphasis upon pecuniary success has been absorbed, but where there is little access to conventional and legitimate means for attaining such success. The conventional occupational opportunities of persons in this area are almost completely limited to manual labor. Given our cultural stigmatization of manual labor, and its correlate, the prestige of white collar work, it is clear that the result is a strain toward innovational practices. The limitation of opportunity to unskilled labor and the resultant low income can not compete *in terms of conventional standards of achievement* with the high income from organized vice.

For our purposes, this situation involves two important features. First, such antisocial behavior is in a sense "called forth" by certain conventional values of the culture *and* by the class structure involving differential access to the approved opportunities for legitimate, prestige-bearing pursuit of the culture goals. The lack of high integration between the means-and-end elements of the cultural pattern and the particular class structure combine to favor a heightened frequency of antisocial conduct in such groups. The second consideration is of equal significance. Recourse to the first of the alternative responses, legitimate effort, is limited by the fact that actual advance toward desired success-symbols through conventional channels is, despite our persisting open-class ideology,[15] relatively rare and difficult for those handicapped by little formal education and few economic resources. The dominant pressure of group standards of success is, therefore, on the gradual attenuation of legitimate, but by and large ineffective, strivings and the increasing use of illegitimate, but more or less effective, expedients of vice and crime. The culture demands made on persons in this situation are incompatible. On the one hand, they are asked to orient their conduct toward the prospect of accumulating wealth and on the other, they are largely denied effective opportunities to do so institutionally. The consequences of such structural inconsistency are psychopathological personality, and/or antisocial conduct, and/or revolutionary activities. The equilibrium between culturally designated means and ends becomes highly unstable with the progressive emphasis on attaining the prestige-laden ends by any means whatsoever. Within this context, Capone represents the triumph of amoral intelligence over morally prescribed "failure," when the channels of vertical mobility are closed or narrowed[16] *in a society which places a high premium on economic affluence and social ascent for all its members.*[17]

This last qualification is of primary importance. It suggests that other phases of the social structure besides the extreme emphasis on pecuniary success, must be considered if we are to understand the social sources of antisocial behavior. A high frequency of deviate behavior is not generated simply by "lack of opportunity" or by this exaggerated pecuniary emphasis. A comparatively rigidified class structure, a feudalistic or caste order, may limit such opportunities far beyond the point which obtains in our society today. It is only when a system of cultural values extols, virtually above all else, certain *common* symbols of success *for the population at large* while its social structure rigorously restricts or completely eliminates access to approved modes of acquiring these symbols *for a considerable part of the same population,* that antisocial behavior ensues on a considerable scale. In other words, our egalitarian ideology denies by implication the existence of noncompeting groups and individuals in the pursuit of pecuniary success. The same body of success-symbols is held to be desirable for all. These goals are held to *transcend class lines,* not to be bounded by them, yet the actual social organization is such that there exist class differentials in the accessibility of these *common* success-symbols. Frustration and thwarted aspiration lead to the search for avenues of escape from a culturally induced intolerable situation; or unrelieved ambition may eventuate in illicit attempts to acquire the dominant values.[18] The American stress on pecuniary success and ambitiousness for all thus invites exaggerated anxieties, hostilities, neuroses and antisocial behavior.

This theoretical analysis may go far toward explaining the varying correlations between crime and poverty.[19] Poverty is not an isolated variable. It is one in a complex of interdependent social and cultural variables. When viewed in such a context, it represents quite different states of affairs. Poverty as such, and consequent limitations of opportunity, are not sufficient to induce a conspicuously high rate of criminal behavior. Even the often mentioned "poverty in the midst of plenty" will not necessarily lead to this result. Only insofar as poverty and associated disadvantages in competition for the culture values approved for *all* members of the society is linked with the assimilation of a cultural emphasis on monetary accumulation as a symbol of success is antisocial conduct a "normal" outcome. Thus, poverty is less highly correlated with crime in southeastern Europe than in the United States. The possibilities of vertical mobility in these European areas would seem to be fewer than in this country, so that neither poverty *per se* nor its association with limited opportunity is sufficient to account for the varying correlations. It is only when the full configuration is considered, poverty, limited opportunity and a commonly shared system of success symbols, that we can explain the higher association between poverty and crime in our society than in others where rigidified class structure is coupled with *differential class symbols of achievement.*

In societies such as our own, then, the pressure of prestige-bearing success tends to eliminate the effective social constraint over means employed to this end. "The-end-justifies-the-means" doctrine becomes a guiding tenet for action when the cultural structure unduly exalts the end and the social organization unduly limits possible recourse to approved means. Otherwise put, this notion and associated behavior reflect a lack of cultural coordination. In international relations, the effects of this lack of integration are notoriously apparent. An emphasis upon national power is not readily coordinated with an inept organization of legitimate, i.e., internationally defined and accepted, means for attaining this goal. The result is a tendency toward the abrogation of international law, treaties become scraps of paper, "undeclared warfare" serves as a technical evasion, the bombing of civilian populations is rationalized,[20] just as the same societal situation induces the same sway of illegitimacy among individuals.

The social order we have described necessarily produces this "strain toward dissolution." The pressure of such an order is upon outdoing one's competitors. The choice of means within the ambit of institutional control will persist as long as the sentiments supporting a competitive system, i.e., deriving from the possibility of outranking competitors and hence enjoying the favorable response of others, are distributed throughout the entire system of activities and are not confined merely to the final result. A stable social structure demands a balanced distribution of affect among its various segments. When there occurs a shift of emphasis from the satisfactions deriving from competition itself to almost exclusive concern with successful competition, the resultant stress leads to the breakdown of the regulatory structure.[21] With the resulting attenuation of the institutional imperatives, there occurs an approximation of the situation erroneously held by utilitarians to be typical of society generally wherein calculations of advantage and fear of punishment are the sole regulating agencies. In such situations, as Hobbes observed, force and fraud come to constitute the sole virtues in view of their relative efficiency in attaining goals,—which were for him, of course, not culturally derived.

It should be apparent that the foregoing discussion is not pitched on a moralistic plane. Whatever the sentiments of the writer or reader concerning the ethical desirability of coordinating the means and goals phases of the social structure, one must agree that lack of such coordination leads to anomie. Insofar as one of the most general functions of social organization is to provide a basis for calculability and regularity of behavior, it is increasingly limited in effectiveness as these elements of the structure become dissociated. At the extreme, predictability virtually disappears and what may be properly termed cultural chaos or anomie intervenes.

The statement, being brief, is also incomplete. It has not included an exhaustive treatment of the various structural elements which predispose toward one rather than another of the alternative responses open to individuals; it has neglected, but not denied the relevance of, the factors determining the specific incidence of these responses; it has not enumerated the various concrete responses which are constituted by combinations of specific values of the analytical variables; it has omitted, or included only by implication, any consideration of the social functions performed by illicit responses; it has not tested the full explanatory power of the analytical scheme by examining a large number of group variations in the frequency of deviate and conformist behavior; it has not adequately dealt with rebellious conduct which seeks to refashion the social framework radically; it has not examined the relevance of cultural conflict for an analysis of culture-goal and institutional-means malintegration. It is suggested that these and related problems may be profitably analyzed by this scheme.

Endnotes

[1] E.g., Ernest Jones, *Social Aspects of Psychoanalysis*, 28, London, 1924. If the Freudian notion is a variety of the "original sin" dogma, then the interpretation advanced in this paper may be called the doctrine of "socially derived sin."

[2] "Normal" in the sense of a culturally oriented, if not approved, response. This statement does not deny the relevance of biological and personality differences which may be significantly involved in the *incidence* of deviate conduct. Our focus of interest is the social and cultural matrix; hence we abstract from other factors. It is in this sense, I take it, that James S. Plant speaks of the "normal reaction of normal people to abnormal conditions." See his *Personality and the Cultural Pattern*, 248, New York, 1937.

[3] Contemporary American culture has been said to tend in this direction. See André Siegfried, *America Comes of Age,* 26–37, New York, 1927. The alleged extreme(?) emphasis on the goals of monetary success and material prosperity leads to dominant concern with technological and social instruments designed to produce the desired result, inasmuch as institutional controls become of secondary importance. In such a situation, innovation flourishes as the *range of means* employed is broadened. In a sense, then, there occurs the paradoxical emergence of "materialists" from an "idealistic" orientation. Cf. Durkheim's analysis of the cultural conditions which predispose toward crime and innovation, both of which are aimed toward efficiency, not moral norms. Durkheim was one of the first to see that "contrairement aux idées courantes le criminel n'apparait plus comme un être radicalement insociable, comme une sorte d'elément parasitaire, de corps étranger et inassimilable, introduit au sein de la société; c'est un agent régulier de la vie sociale." See *Les Régles de la Méthode Sociologique,* 86–89, Paris, 1927.

[4] Such ritualism may be associated with a mythology which rationalizes these actions so that they appear to retain their status as means, but the dominant pressure is in the direction of strict ritualistic conformity, irrespective of such rationalizations. In this sense, ritual has proceeded farthest when such rationalizations are not even called forth.

[5]In this connection, one may see the relevance of Elton Mayo's paraphrase of the title of Tawney's well known book. "Actually the problem is *not that of the sickness of an acquisitive society; it is that of the acquisitiveness of a sick society.*" *Human Problems of an Industrial Civilization,* 153, New York, 1933. Mayo deals with the process through which wealth comes to be a symbol of social achievement. He sees this as arising from a state of anomie. We are considering the unintegrated monetary-success goal as an element in producing anomie. A complete analysis would involve both phases of this system of interdependent variables.

[6]It is unlikely that interiorized norms are completely eliminated. Whatever residuum persists will induce personality tensions and conflict. The process involves a certain degree of ambivalence. A manifest rejection of the institutional norms is coupled with some latent retention of their emotional correlates. "Guilt feelings," "sense of sin," "pangs of conscience" are obvious manifestations of this unrelieved tension; symbolic adherence to the nominally repudiated values or rationalizations constitute a more subtle variety of tensional release.

[7]"Many," and not all, unintegrated groups, for the reason already mentioned. In groups where the primary emphasis shifts to institutional means, i.e., when the range of alternatives is very limited, the outcome is a type of ritualism rather than anomie.

[8]Money has several peculiarities which render it particularly apt to become a symbol of prestige divorced from institutional controls. As Simmel emphasized, money is highly abstract and impersonal. However acquired, through fraud or institutionally, it can be used to purchase the same goods and services. The anonymity of metropolitan culture, in conjunction with this peculiarity of money, permits wealth, the sources of which may be unknown to the community in which the plutocrat lives, to serve as a symbol of status.

[9]The emphasis upon wealth as a success symbol is possibly reflected in the use of the term "fortune" to refer to a stock of accumulated wealth. This meaning becomes common in the late sixteenth century (Spenser and Shakespeare). A similar usage of the Latin *fortuna* comes into prominence during the first century B.C. Both these periods were marked by the rise to prestige and power of the "bourgeosie."

[10]See Kingsley Davis, "Mental Hygiene and the Class Structure," *Psychiatry,* 1928, 1, esp. 62–63; Talcott Parsons, *The Structure of Social Action,* 59–60, New York, 1937.

[11]This is a level intermediate between the two planes distinguished by Edward Sapir, namely, culture patterns and personal habit systems. See his "Contribution of Psychiatry to an Understanding of Behavior in Society," *Amer. J. Sociol.,* 1937 42:862–70.

[12]This fifth alternative is on a plane clearly different from that of the others. It represents a *transitional* response which seeks to *institutionalize* new procedures oriented toward revamped cultural goals shared by the members of the society. It thus involves efforts to *change* the existing structure rather than to perform accomodative actions *within* this structure, and introduces additional problems with which we are not at the moment concerned.

[13]Obviously, this is an elliptical statement. These individuals may maintain some orientation to the values of their particular differentiated groupings within the larger society or, in part, of the conventional society itself. Insofar as they do so, their conduct cannot be classified in the "passive rejection" category (IV). Nels Anderson's description of the behavior and attitudes of the bum, for example, can readily be recast in terms of our analytical scheme. See *The Hobo*, 93–98, *et passim*, Chicago, 1923.

[14]Joseph D. Lohman, "The Participant Observer in Community Studies," *Amer. Sociol. Rev.*, 1937, 2:890–98.

[15]The shifting historical role of this ideology is a profitable subject for exploration. The "office-boy-to-president" stereotype was once in approximate accord with the facts. Such vertical mobility was probably more common then than now, when the class structure is more rigid. (See the following note.) The ideology largely persists, however, possibly because it still performs a useful function for maintaining the *status quo*. For insofar as it is accepted by the "masses," it constitutes a useful sop for those who might rebel against the entire structure, were this consoling hope removed. This ideology now serves to lessen the probability of Adaptation V. In short, the role of this notion has changed from that of an approximately valid empirical theorem to that of an ideology, in Mannheim's sense.

[16]There is a growing body of evidence, though none of it is clearly conclusive, to the effect that our class structure is becoming rigidified and that vertical mobility is declining. Taussig and Joslyn found that American business leaders are being *increasingly* recruited from the upper ranks of our society. The Lynds have also found a "diminished chance to get ahead" for the working classes in Middletown. Manifestly, these objective changes are not alone significant; the individual's subjective evaluation of the situation is a major determinant of the response. The extent to which this change in opportunity for social mobility has been recognized by the least advantaged classes is still conjectural, although the Lynds present some suggestive materials. The writer suggests that a case in point is the increasing frequency of cartoons which observe in a tragi-comic vein that "my old man says everybody can't be President. He says if ya can get three days a week steady on W.P.A. work ya ain't doin' so bad either." See F.

W. Taussig and C. S. Joslyn, *American Business Leaders,* New York, 1932; R. S. and H. M. Lynd, *Middletown in Transition,* 67 ff., chap. 12, New York 1937.

[17]The role of the Negro in this respect is of considerable theoretical interest. Certain elements of the Negro population have assimilated the dominant caste's values of pecuniary success and social advancement, but they also recognize that social ascent is at present restricted to their own caste almost exclusively. The pressures upon the Negro which would otherwise derive from the structural inconsistencies we have noticed are hence not identical with those upon lower-class whites. See Kingsley Davis, *op cit.,* 63; John Dollard, *Caste and Class in a Southern Town,* 66 ff., New Haven, 1936; Donald Young, *American Minority People,* 581, New York, 1932.

[18]The psychical coordinates of these processes have been partly established by the experimental evidence concerning *Aspruchsniveaus* and levels of performance. See Kurt Lewin, Vorsatz, Wille and Bedurfnis, Berlin, 1926; N. F. Hoppe, "Erfolg und Misserfolg," *Psychol. Forschung,* 1930, 14:1–63; Jerome D. Frank, "Individual Differences in Certain Aspects of the Level of Aspiration," *Amer. J. Psychol,* 1935, 47:119–28.

[19]Standard criminology texts summarize the data in this field. Our scheme of analysis may serve to resolve some of the theoretical contradictions which P. A. Sorokin indicates. For example, "not everywhere nor always do the poor show a greater proportion of crime . . . many poorer countries have had less crime than the richer countries. . . . The [economic] improvement in the second half of the nineteenth century, and the beginning of the twentieth, has not been followed by a decrease of crime." See his *Contemporary Sociological Theories* 560–61, New York, 1928. The crucial point is, however, that poverty has varying social significance in different social structures, as we shall see. Hence, one would not expect a linear correlation between crime and poverty.

[20]See M. W. Royce, *Aerial Bombardment and the International Regulation of War,* New York, 1928.

[21]Since our primary concern is with the socio-cultural aspects of this problem, the psychological correlates have been only implicitly considered. See Karen Horney, *The Neurotic Personality of Our Time,* New York, 1937, for a psychological discussion of this process.

Questions

1. How is the intersection between goals and means relevant for generating deviant behavior?

2. How might you extend Merton's athletics analogy (that is, winning is the goal and "by all means necessary" is the strategy) to explain deviant behavior? Cite examples from the world of sport that fit each of Merton's five categories.

3. According to Merton, which of the following would have the greatest effect on the generation of deviant behavior: highly placed goals that may be unreasonable or unattainable *or* structurally blocked access to legitimate means of achieving the goals? Explain your reasoning.

4. Which type of deviant behavior does Merton's theoretical framework best describe? Does his theory work better for some subgroups than others? If so, which group's deviant behavior does the theory best explain?

5. To what degree does Merton's framework reflect society's motto of "by whatever means necessary" to achieve specific goals? With what type of behavior or action might you typically associate this statement?

A Theory of Differential Association

EDWIN H. SUTHERLAND AND DONALD R. CRESSEY

Theories abound regarding what causes people to commit crime. In this selection, Edwin Sutherland and Donald Cressey present a theory that they call differential association. According to this theory, people learn to commit crime from others through personal interaction. They commit actual crimes when conditions (which the authors call definitions) favorable to crime outweigh those unfavorable to crime.

The following statements refer to the process by which a particular person comes to engage in criminal behavior.

1. *Criminal behavior is learned.* Negatively, this means that criminal behavior is not inherited, as such; also, the person who is not already trained in crime does not invent criminal behavior, just as a person does not make mechanical inventions unless he has had training in mechanics.

2. *Criminal behavior is learned in interaction with other persons in a process of communication.* This communication is verbal in many respects but includes also "the communication of gestures."

3. *The principal part of the learning of criminal behavior occurs within intimate personal groups.* Negatively, this means that the impersonal agencies of communication, such as movies and newspapers, play a relatively unimportant part in the genesis of criminal behavior.

4. *When criminal behavior is learned, the learning includes (a) techniques of committing the crime, which are sometimes very complicated, sometimes very*

simple; (b) the specific direction of motives, drives, rationalizations, and attitudes.

5. *The specific direction of motives and drives is learned from definitions of the legal codes as favorable or unfavorable.* In some societies an individual is surrounded by persons who invariably define the legal codes as rules to be observed, while in others he is surrounded by persons whose definitions are favorable to the violation of the legal codes. In our American society these definitions are almost always mixed, with the consequence that we have culture conflict in relation to the legal codes.

6. *A person becomes delinquent because of an excess of definitions favorable to violation of law over definitions unfavorable to violation of law.* This is the principle of differential association. It refers to both criminal and anti-criminal associations and has to do with counteracting forces. When persons become criminal, they do so because of contacts with criminal patterns and also because of isolation from anticriminal patterns. Any person inevitably assimilates the surrounding culture unless other patterns are in conflict; a southerner does not pronounce *r* because other southerners do not pronounce *r*. Negatively, this proposition of differential association means that associations which are neutral so far as crime is concerned have little or no effect on the genesis of criminal behavior. Much of the experience of a person is neutral in this sense, e.g., learning to brush one's teeth. This behavior has no negative or positive effect on criminal behavior except as it may be related to associations which are concerned with the legal codes. This neutral behavior is important especially as an occupier of the time of a child so that he is not in contact with criminal behavior during the time he is so engaged in the neutral behavior.

7. *Differential associations may vary in frequency, duration, priority, and intensity.* This means that associations with criminal behavior and also associations with anticriminal behavior vary in those respects. "Frequency" and "duration" as modalities of associations are obvious and need no explanation. "Priority" is assumed to be important in the sense that lawful behavior developed in early childhood may persist throughout life, and also that delinquent behavior developed in early

childhood may persist throughout life. This tendency, however, has not been adequately demonstrated, and priority seems to be important principally through its selective influence. "Intensity" is not precisely defined, but it has to do with such things as the prestige of the source of a criminal or anticriminal pattern and with emotional reactions related to the associations. In a precise description of the criminal behavior of a person, these modalities would be rated in quantitative form and a mathematical ratio be reached. A formula in this sense has not been developed, and the development of such a formula would be extremely difficult.

8. *The process of learning criminal behavior by association with criminal and anticriminal patterns involves all of the mechanisms that are involved in any other learning.* Negatively, this means that the learning of criminal behavior is not restricted to the process of imitation. A person who is seduced, for instance, learns criminal behavior by association, but this process would not ordinarily be described as imitation.

9. *While criminal behavior is an expression of general needs and values, it is not explained by those general needs and values, since noncriminal behavior is an expression of the same needs and values.* Thieves generally steal in order to secure money, but likewise honest laborers work in order to secure money. The attempts by many scholars to explain criminal behavior by general drives and values, such as the happiness principle, striving for social status, the money motive, or frustration, have been, and must continue to be, futile, since they explain lawful behavior as completely as they explain criminal behavior. They are similar to respiration, which is necessary for any behavior, but which does not differentiate criminal from noncriminal behavior.

It is not necessary, at this level of explanation, to explain why a person has the associations he has; this certainly involves a complex of many things. In an area where the delinquency rate is high, a boy who is sociable, gregarious, active, and athletic is very likely to come in contact with the other boys in the neighborhood, learn delinquent behavior patterns from them, and become a criminal; in the same neighborhood the psychopathic boy who is isolated, introverted, and inert may remain at home, not become acquainted with the other boys in the neighborhood, and not become delinquent. In another situation, the sociable, athletic, aggressive boy may become a member of a scout troop and not become involved in delinquent behavior. The person's associations are determined in a general context of social organization. A child is ordinarily reared in a family; the place of residence of the family is determined largely by family income; and the delinquency rate is in many respects related to the rental value of the houses. Many other aspects of social organization affect the kinds of associations a person has.

The preceding explanation of criminal behavior purports to explain the criminal and noncriminal behavior of individual persons. As indicated earlier, it is possible to state sociological theories of criminal behavior which explain the criminality of a community, nation, or other group. The problem, when thus stated, is to account for variations in crime rates and involves a comparison of the crime rates of various groups or the crime rates of a particular group at different times. The explanation of a crime rate must be consistent with the explanation of the criminal behavior of the person, since the crime rate is a summary statement of the number of persons in the group who commit crimes and the frequency with which they commit crimes. One of the best explanations of crime rates from this point of view is that a high crime rate is due to social disorganization. The term *social disorganization* is not entirely satisfactory, and it seems preferable to substitute for it the term *differential social organization*. The postulate on which this theory is based, regardless of the name, is that crime is rooted in the social organization and is an expression of that social organization. A group may be organized for criminal behavior or organized against criminal behavior. Most communities are organized for both criminal and anticriminal behavior, and, in that sense the crime rate is an expression of the differential group organization. Differential group organization as an explanation of variations in crime rates is consistent with the differential association theory of the processes by which persons become criminals.

❧ ❧ ❧

Questions

1. How would you summarize Sutherland and Cressey's theory in just one sentence?

2. What is "differential association"?

3. Which one of the nine theoretical statements listed in this reading is most central to differential association theory, and why?

4. Are there certain types of crimes for which this theory would not work well? If so, what are they, and why would the theory not apply in these cases?

5. How might public policy makers use differential association theory to reduce or prevent crime?

A Control Theory of Delinquency

TRAVIS HIRSCHI

In this chapter from his well-known book, Travis Hirschi presents his theory of social control. He starts with the assumption that all people have reasons for wanting to commit crimes. Thus we must ask: Why do some people not commit crimes? Hirschi answers that social bonds—particularly attachment, commitment, involvement, and belief—can restrain people from acting on their desire to act illegally.

"The more weakened the groups to which [the individual] belongs, the less he depends on them, the more he consequently depends only on himself and recognizes no other rules of conduct than what are founded on his private interests."[1]

*C*ontrol theories assume that delinquent acts result when an individual's bond to society is weak or broken. Since these theories embrace two highly complex concepts, the bond of the individual to society, it is not surprising that they have at one time or another formed the basis of explanations of most forms of aberrant or unusual behavior. It is also not surprising that control theories have described the elements of the bond to society in many ways, and that they have focused on a variety of units as the point of control.

I begin with a classification and description of the elements of the bond to conventional society. I try to show how each of these elements is related to delinquent behavior and how they are related to each other. I then turn to the question of specifying the unit to which the person is presumably more or less tied, and to the question of the adequacy of the motivational force built into the explanation of delinquent behavior.

Elements of the Bond

Attachment

In explaining conforming behavior, sociologists justly emphasize sensitivity to the opinion of others.[2] Unfortunately, . . . they tend to suggest that man is sensitive to the opinion of others and thus exclude sensitivity from their explanations of deviant behavior. In explaining deviant behavior, psychologists, in contrast, emphasize insensitivity to the opinion of others.[3] Unfortunately, they too tend to ignore variation, and, in addition, they tend to tie sensitivity inextricably to other variables, to make it part of a syndrome or "type," and thus seriously to reduce its value as an explanatory concept. The psychopath is characterized only in part by "deficient attachment to or affection for others, a failure to respond to the ordinary motivations founded in respect or regard for one's fellows";[4] he is also characterized by such things as "excessive aggressiveness," "lack of superego control," and "an infantile level of response."[5] Unfortunately, too, the behavior that psychopathy is used to explain often becomes part of the *definition* of psychopathy. As a result, in Barbara Wootton's words: "[The psychopath] is . . . *par excellence*, and without shame or qualification, the model of the circular process by which mental abnormality is inferred from anti-social behavior while anti-social behavior is explained by mental abnormality."[6]

The problems of diagnosis, tautology, and name-calling are avoided if the dimensions of psychopathy are treated as causally and therefore problematically interrelated, rather than as logically and therefore necessarily bound to each other. In fact, it can be argued that all of the characteristics attributed to the psychopath follow from, are effects of, his lack of attachment to others. To say that to lack attachment to others is to be free from moral restraints is to use lack of attachment to explain the guiltlessness of the psychopath, the fact that he apparently has no conscience or superego. In this view, lack of attachment to others is not merely a symptom of psychopathy, it *is* psychopathy; lack of conscience is just another way of saying the same thing; and the violation of norms is (or may be) a consequence.

For that matter, given that man is an animal, "impulsivity" and "aggressiveness" can also be seen as natural consequences of freedom from moral restraints. However, since the view of man as endowed with natural propensities and capacities like other animal is peculiarly unpalatable to sociologists, we need not fall back on such a view to explain the amoral man's aggressiveness.[7] The process of becoming alienated from others often involves or is based on active interpersonal conflict. Such conflict could easily supply a reservoir of *socially derived* hostility sufficient to account for the aggressiveness of those whose attachments to others have been weakened.

Durkheim said it many years ago: "We are moral beings to the extent that we are social beings."[8] This may be interpreted to mean that we are moral beings to the extent that we have "internalized the norms" of society. But what does it mean to say that a person has internalized the norms of society? The norms of society are by definition shared by the members of society. To violate a norm is, therefore, to act contrary to the wishes and expectations of other people. If a person does not care about the wishes and expectations of other people—that is, if he is insensitive to the opinion of others—then he is to that extent not bound by the norms. He is free to deviate.

The essence of internalization of norms, conscience, or superego thus lies in the attachment to others.[9] This view has several advantages over the concept of internalization. For one, explanations of deviant behavior based on attachment do not beg the question, since the extent to which a person is attached to others can be measured independently of his deviant behavior. Furthermore, change or variation in behavior is explainable in a way that it is not when notions of internalization or superego are used. For example, the divorced man is more likely after divorce to commit a number of deviant acts, such as suicide or forgery. If we explain these acts by reference to the superego (or internal control), we are forced to say that the man "lost his conscience" when he got a divorce; and, of course, if he remarries, we have to conclude that he gets his conscience back.

This dimension of the bond to conventional society is encountered in most social control-oriented research and theory. F. Ivan Nye's "internal control" and "indirect control" refer to the same element, although we avoid the problem of explaining changes over time by locating the "conscience" in the bond to others rather than making it part of the personality.[10] Attachment to others is just one aspect of Albert J. Reiss's "personal controls"; we avoid his problems of tautological empirical observations by making the relationship between attachment and delinquency problematic rather than definitional.[11] Finally, Scott Briar and Irving Piliavin's "commitment" or "stake in conformity" subsumes attachment, as their discussion illustrates, although the terms they use are more closely associated with the next element to be discussed.[12]

*C*ommitment

"Of all passions, that which inclineth men least to break the laws, is fear. Nay, excepting some generous natures, it is the only thing, when there is the appearance of profit or pleasure by breaking the laws, that makes men keep them."[13] Few would deny that men on occasion obey the rules simply from fear of the consequences. This rational component in conformity we label commitment. What does it mean to say that a person is committed to conformity? In Howard S. Becker's formulation it means the following:

> First, the individual is in a position in which his decision with regard to some particular line of action has consequences for other interests and activities not necessarily (directly) related to it. Second, he has placed himself in that position by his own prior actions. A third element is present though so obvious as not to be apparent: the committed person must be aware [of these other interests] and must recognize that his decision in this case will have ramifications beyond it.[14]

The idea, then, is that the person invests time, energy, himself, in a certain line of activity—say, getting an education, building up a business, acquiring a reputation for virtue. When or whenever he considers deviant behavior, he must consider the costs of this deviant behavior, the risk he runs of losing the investment he has made in conventional behavior.

If attachment to others is the sociological counterpart of the superego or conscience, commitment is the counterpart of the ego or common sense. To the person committed to conventional lines of action, risking one to ten years in prison for a ten-dollar holdup is stupidity, because to the committed person the costs and risks obviously exceed ten dollars in value. (To the psychoanalyst, such an act exhibits failure to be governed by the "reality-principle.") In the sociological control theory, it can be and is generally assumed that the decision to commit a criminal act may well be rationally determined—that the actor's decision was not irrational given the risks and costs he faces. Of course, as Becker points out, if the actor is capable of in some sense calculating the costs of a line of action, he is also capable of calculational errors: ignorance and error return, in the control theory, as possible explanations of deviant behavior.

The concept of commitment assumes that the organization of society is such that the interests of most persons would be endangered if they were to engage in criminal acts. Most people, simply by the process of living in an organized society, acquire goods, reputations, prospects that they do not want to risk losing. These accumulations are society's insurance that they will abide by the rules. Many hypotheses about the antecedents of delinquent behavior are based on this premise. For example, Arthur L. Stinchcombe's hypothesis that "high school rebellion . . . occurs when future status is not clearly related to present performance"[15] suggests that one is committed to conformity not only by what one has but also by what one hopes to obtain. Thus "ambition" and/or "aspiration" play an important role in producing conformity. The person becomes committed to a conventional line of action, and he is therefore committed to conformity.

Most lines of action in a society are of course conventional. The clearest examples are educational and occupational careers. Actions thought to jeopardize one's chances in these areas are presumably avoided. Interestingly enough, even nonconventional commitments may operate to produce conventional conformity. We are told, at least, that boys aspiring to careers in the rackets or professional thievery are judged by their "honesty" and "reliability"—traits traditionally in demand among seekers of office boys.[16]

Involvement

Many persons undoubtedly owe a life of virtue to a lack of opportunity to do otherwise. Time and energy are inherently limited: "Not that I would not, if I could, be both handsome and fat and well dressed, and a great athlete, and make a million a year, be a wit, a bon vivant, and a lady killer, as well as a philosopher, a philanthropist, a statesman, warrior, and African explorer, as well as a 'tone-poet' and saint. But the thing is simply impossible."[17] The things that William James here says he would like to be or do are all, I suppose, within the realm of conventionality, but if he were to include illicit actions he would still have to eliminate some of them as simply impossible.

Involvement or engrossment in conventional activities is thus often part of a control theory. The assumption, widely shared, is that a person may be simply too busy doing conventional things to find time to engage in deviant behavior. The person involved in conventional activities is tied to appointments, deadlines, working hours, plans, and the like, so the opportunity to commit deviant acts rarely arises. To the extent that he is engrossed in conventional activities, he cannot even think about deviant acts, let alone act out his inclinations.[18]

This line of reasoning is responsible for the stress placed on recreational facilities in many programs to reduce delinquency, for much of the concern with the high school dropout, and for the idea that boys should be drafted into the Army to keep them out of trouble. So obvious and persuasive is the idea that involvement in conventional activities is a major deterrent to delinquency that it was accepted even by Sutherland: "In the general area of juvenile delinquency it is probable that the most significant difference between juveniles who engage in delinquency and those who do not is that the latter are provided abundant opportunities of a conventional type for satisfying their recreational interests, while the former lack those opportunities or facilities."[19]

The view that "idle hands are the devil's workshop" has received more sophisticated treatment in recent sociological writings on delinquency. David Matza and Gresham M. Sykes, for example, suggest that delinquents have the values of a leisure class, the same values ascribed by Veblen to *the* leisure class: a search for kicks, disdain of work, a desire for the big score, and acceptance of aggressive toughness as proof of masculinity.[20] Matza and Sykes explain delinquency by reference to this system of values, but they note that adolescents at all class levels are "to some extent" members of a leisure class, that they "move in a limbo between earlier parental domination and future integration with the social structure through the bonds of work and marriage."[21] In the end, then, the leisure of the adolescent produces a set of values, which, in turn, leads to delinquency.

Belief

Unlike the cultural deviance theory, the control theory assumes the existence of a common value system within the society or group whose norms are being violated. If the deviant is committed to a value system different from that of conventional society, there is, within the context of the theory, nothing to explain. The question is, "Why does a man violate the rules in which he believes?" It is not, "Why do men differ in their beliefs about what constitutes good and desirable conduct?" The person is assumed to have been socialized (perhaps imperfectly) into the group whose rules he is violating; deviance is not a question of one group imposing its rules on the members of another group. In other words, we not only assume the deviant *has* believed the rules, we assume he believes the rules even as he violates them.

How can a person believe it is wrong to steal at the same time he is stealing? In the strain theory, this is not a difficult problem. . . . The motivation to deviance adduced by the strain theorist is so strong that we can well understand the deviant act even assuming the deviator believes strongly that it is wrong.[22] However, given the control theory's assumptions about motivation, if both the deviant and the nondeviant believe the deviant act is wrong, how do we account for the fact that one commits it and the other does not?

Control theories have taken two approaches to this problem. In one approach, beliefs are treated as mere words that mean little or nothing if the other forms of control are missing. "Semantic dementia," the dissociation between rational faculties and emotional control which is said to be characteristic of the psychopath, illustrates this way of handling the problem.[23] In short, beliefs, at least insofar as they are expressed in words, drop out of the picture; since they do not differentiate between deviants and nondeviants, they are in the same class as "language" or any other characteristic common to all members of the group. Since they represent no real obstacle to the commission of delinquent acts, nothing need be said about how they are handled by those committing such acts. The control theories that do not mention beliefs (or values), and many do not, may be assumed to take this approach to the problem.

The second approach argues that the deviant rationalizes his behavior so that he can at once violate the rule and maintain his belief in it. Donald R. Cressey has advanced this argument with respect to embezzlement[24] and Sykes and Matza have advanced it with respect to delinquency.[25] In both Cressey's and Sykes and Matza's treatments, these rationalizations (Cressey calls them "verbalizations," Sykes and Matza term them "techniques of neutralization") occur prior to the commission of the deviant act. If the neutralization is successful, the person is free to commit the acts) in question. Both in Cressey and in Sykes and Matza, the strain that prompts the effort at neutralization also provides the motive force that results in the subsequent deviant act. Their theories are thus, in this sense, strain theories. Neutralization is difficult to handle within the context of a theory that adheres closely to control theory assumptions, because in the control theory there is no special motivational force to account for the neutralization. This difficulty is especially noticeable in Matza's later treatment of this topic, where the motivational component, the "will to delinquency" appears after the moral vacuum has been created by the techniques of neutralization.[26] The question thus becomes: Why neutralize?

In attempting to solve a strain theory problem with control theory tools, the control theorist is thus led into a trap. He cannot answer the crucial question. The concept of neutralization assumes the existence of moral obstacles to the commission of deviant acts. In order plausibly to account for a deviant act, it is necessary to generate motivation to deviance that is at least equivalent in force to the resistance provided by these moral obstacles. However, if the moral obstacles are removed, neutralization and special motivation are no longer required. We therefore follow the implicit logic of control theory and remove these moral obstacles by hypothesis. Many persons do not have an attitude of respect toward the rules of society; many persons feel no moral obligation to conform regardless of personal advantage. Insofar as the values and beliefs of these persons are consistent with their feelings, and there should be a tendency toward consistency, neutralization is unnecessary; it has already occurred.

Does this merely push the question back a step and at the same time produce conflict with the assumption of a common value system? I think not. In the first place, we do not assume, as does Cressey, that neutralization occurs in order to make a specific criminal act possible.[27] We do not assume, as do Sykes and Matza, that neutralization occurs to make many delinquent acts possible. We do not assume, in other words, that the person constructs a system of rationalizations in order to justify commission of acts he *wants* to commit. We assume, in contrast, that the beliefs that free a man to commit deviant acts are *unmotivated* in the sense that he does not construct or adopt them in order to facilitate the attainment of illicit ends. In the second place, we do not assume, as does Matza, that "delinquents concur in the conventional assessment of delinquency."[28] We assume, in contrast, that there is *variation* in the extent to which people believe they should obey the rules of society, and, furthermore, that the less a person believes he should obey the rules, the more likely he is to violate them.[29]

In chronological order, then, a person's beliefs in the moral validity of norms are, for no teleological reason, weakened. The probability that he will commit delinquent acts is therefore increased. When and if he commits a delinquent act, we may justifiably use the weakness of his beliefs in explaining it, but no special motivation is required to explain either the weakness of his beliefs or, perhaps, his delinquent act.

The keystone of this argument is of course the assumption that there is variation in belief in the moral validity of social rules. This assumption is amenable to direct empirical test and can thus survive at least until its first confrontation with data. For the present, we must return to the idea of a common value system with which this section was begun.

The idea of a common (or, perhaps better, a single) value system is consistent with the fact, or presumption, of variation in the strength of moral beliefs. We have not suggested that delinquency is based on beliefs counter to conventional morality; we have not suggested that delinquents do not believe delinquent acts are wrong. They may well believe these acts are wrong, but the meaning and efficacy of such beliefs are contingent upon other beliefs and, indeed, on the strength of other ties to the conventional order.[30]

❧ Relations Among the Elements

In general, the more closely a person is tied to conventional society in any of these ways, the more closely he is likely to be tied in the other ways. The person who is attached to conventional people is, for example, more likely to be involved in conventional activities and to accept conventional notions of desirable conduct. Of the six possible combinations of elements, three seem particlarly important and will therefore be discussed in some detail.

Attachment and Commitment

It is frequently suggested that attachment and commitment (as the terms are used here) tend to vary inversely. Thus, according to delinquency research, one of the lower-class adolescent's "problems" is that he is unable to sever ties to parents and peers, ties that prevent him from devoting sufficient time and energy to educational and occupational aspirations. His attachments are thus seen as getting in the way of conventional commitments.[31] According to stratification research, the lower-class boy who breaks free from these attachments is more likely to be upwardly mobile.[32] Both research traditions thus suggest that those bound to *conformity* for instrumental reasons are less likely to be bound to conformity by emotional ties to conventional others. If the unattached compensate for lack of attachment by commitment to achievement, and if the uncommitted make up for their lack of commitment by becoming more attached to persons, we could conclude that neither attachment nor commitment will be related to delinquency.

Actually, despite the evidence apparently to the contrary, I think it is safe to assume that attachment to conventional others and commitment to achievement tend to vary together. The common finding that middle-class boys are likely to choose instrumental values over those of family and friendship while the reverse is true of lower-class boys cannot, I think, be properly interpreted as meaning that middle-class boys are less attached than lower-class boys to their parents and peers. The zero-sum methodological model that produces such findings is highly likely to be misleading.[33] Also, although many of the characteristics of the upwardly mobile alluded to by Seymour M. Lipset and Reinhard Bendix could be accounted for as consequences rather than causes of mobility, a methodological critique of these studies is not necessary to conclude that we may expect to find a positive relation between attachment and commitment in the data to be presented here. The present study and the one study Lipset and Bendix cite as disagreeing with their general conclusion that the upwardly mobile come from homes in which interpersonal relations were unsatisfactory are both based on high school samples.[34] As Lipset and Bendix note, such studies necessarily focus on aspirations rather than actual mobility. For the present, it seems, we must choose between studies based on hopes for the occupational future and those based on construction or reconstruction of the familial past. Interestingly enough, the former are at least as likely to be valid as the latter.

Commitment and Involvement

Delinquent acts are events. They occur at specific points in space and time. For a delinquent act to occur, it is necessary, as is true of all events, for a series of causal chains to converge at a given moment in time. Events are difficult to predict, and specification of some of the conditions necessary for them to occur often leaves a large residue of indeterminacy. For example, to say that a boy is free of bonds to conventional society is not to say that he will necessarily commit delinquent acts; he may and he may not. All we can say with certainty is that he is *more likely* to commit delinquent acts than the boy strongly tied to conventional society.

76

It is tempting to make a virtue of this defect and espouse "probabilistic theory," since it, and it alone, is consistent with "the facts."[35] Nevertheless, this temptation should be resisted. The primary virtue of control theory is not that it relies on conditions that make delinquency possible while other theories rely on conditions that make delinquency possible while other theories rely on conditions that make delinquency necessary. On the contrary, with respect to their logical framework, these theories are superior to control theory, and, if they were as adequate empirically as control theory, we should not hesitate to advocate their adoption in preference to control theory.

But they are not as adequate, and we must therefore seek to reduce the indeterminacy within control theory. One area of possible development is with respect to the link between elements of the bond affecting the probability that one will be exposed to temptation.

The most obvious link in this connection is between educational and occupational aspirations (commitment) and involvement in conventional activities. We can attempt to show how commitment limits one's opportunities to commit delinquent acts and thus get away from the assumption implicit in many control theories that such opportunities are simply randomly distributed through the population in question.

Attachment and Belief

That there is a more or less straightforward connection between attachment to others and belief in the moral validity of rules appears evident. The link we accept here and which we shall attempt to document is described by Jean Piaget:

> It is not the obligatory character of the rule laid down by an individual that makes us respect this individual, it is the respect we feel for the individual that makes us regard as obligatory the rule he lays down. The appearance of the sense of duty in a child thus admits of the simplest explanation, namely that he receives commands from older children (in play) and from adults (in life), and that he respects older children and parents.[36]

In short, "respect is the source of law."[37] Insofar as the child respects (loves and fears) his parents, and adults in general, he will accept their rules. Conversely, insofar as this respect is undermined, the rules will tend to lose their obligatory character. It is assumed that belief in the obligatory character of rules will to some extent maintain its efficacy in producing conformity even if the respect which brought it into being no longer exists. It is also assumed that attachment may produce conformity even in the face of beliefs favorable to nonconformity. In short, these two sources of moral behavior, although highly and complexly related, are assumed to have an independent effect that justifies their separation.

◉ The Bond to What?

Control theorists sometimes suggest that attachment to any object outside one's self, whether it be the home town, the starry heavens, or the family dog, promotes moral behavior.[38] Although it seems obvious that some objects are more important than others and that the important objects must be identified if the elements of the bond are to produce the consequences suggested by the theory, a priori rankings of the objects of attachment have proved peculiarly unsatisfactory. Durkheim, for example, concludes that the three groups to whom attachment is most important in producing morality are the family, the nation, and humanity. He further concludes that, of these, the nation is most important.[39] All of which, given much contemporary thinking on the virtues of patriotism,[40] illustrates rather well the difficulty posed by such questions as: Which is more important in the control of delinquency, the father or the mother, the family or the school?

Although delinquency theory in general has taken a stand on many questions about the relative importance of institutions (for example, that the school is more important than the family), control theory has remained decidedly eclectic, partly because each element of the bond directs attention to different institutions. For these reasons, I shall treat specification of the units of attachment as a problem in the empirical interpretation of control theory, and not attempt at this point to say which should be more or less important.

◉ Where Is the Motivation?

The most disconcerting question the control theorist faces goes something like this: "Yes, but why do they do it?" In the good old days, the control theorist could simply strip away the "veneer of civilization" and expose man's "animal impulses" for all to see. These impulses appeared to him (and apparently to his audience) to provide a plausible account of the motivation to crime and delinquency. His argument was *not* that delinquents and criminals alone are animals, but that we are all animals, and thus all naturally capable of committing criminal acts. It took no great study to reveal that children, chickens, and dogs occasionally assault and steal from their fellow creatures; that children, chickens, and dogs also behave for relatively long periods in a perfectly moral manner. Of course the acts of chickens and dogs are not "assault" or "theft," and such behavior is not "moral"; it is simply the behavior of a chicken or a dog. The chicken stealing corn from his neighbor knows nothing of the moral law; he does not *want* to violate rules; he wants merely to eat corn. The dog maliciously destroying a pillow or feloniously assaulting another dog is the moral equal of the chicken. No motivation to deviance is required to explain his acts. So, too, no special motivation to crime within the human animal was required to explain his criminal acts.

Times changed. It was no longer fashionable (within sociology, at least) to refer to animal impulses. The control theorist tended more and more to deemphasize the motivational component of his theory. He might refer in the beginning to "universal human needs," or some such, but the driving force behind crime and delinquency was rarely alluded to. At the same time, his explanations of crime and delinquency increasingly left the reader uneasy. What, the reader asked, is the control theorist assuming? Albert K. Cohen and. James F. Short answer the question this way:

> . . . it is important to point out one important limitation of both types of theory. They [culture conflict and social disorganization theories] are both *control* theories in the sense that they explain delinquency in terms of the *absence* of effective controls. They appear, therefore, to imply a model of motivation that assumes that the impulse to delinquency is an inherent characteristic of young people and does not itself need to be explained; it is something that erupts when the lid—i.e., internalized cultural restraints or external authority—is off.[41]

There are several possible and I think reasonable reactions to this criticism. One reaction is simply to acknowledge the assumption, to grant that one is assuming what control theorists have always assumed about the motivation to crime—that it is constant across persons (at least within the system in question): "There is no reason to assume that only those who finally commit a deviant act usually have the impulse to do so. It is much more likely that most people experience deviant impulses frequently. At least in fantasy; people are much more deviant than they appear."[42] There is certainly nothing wrong with *making* such an assumption. We are free to assume anything we wish to assume; the truth of our theory is presumably subject to empirical test.[43]

A second reaction, involving perhaps something of a quibble, is to defend the logic of control theory and to deny the alleged assumption. We can say the fact that control theory suggests the absence of something causes delinquency is not a proper criticism, since negative relations have as much claim to scientific acceptability as do positive relations.[44] We can also say that the present theory does not impute an inherent impulse to *delinquency* to anyone.[45] That, on the contrary, it denies the necessity of such an imputation: "The desires, and other passions of man, are in themselves no sin. No more are the actions, that proceed from those passions, till they know a law that forbids them."[46]

A third reaction is to accept the criticism as valid, to grant that a complete explanation of delinquency would provide the necessary impetus, and proceed to construct an explanation of motivation consistent with control theory. Briar and Piliavin provide situational motivation: "We assume these acts are prompted by short-term situationally induced desires experienced by all boys to obtain valued goods, to portray courage in the presence of, or be loyal to peers, to strike out at someone who is disliked, or simply to 'get kicks.'"[47] Matza, too, agrees that delinquency cannot be explained simply by removal of controls:

> Delinquency is only epiphenomenally action . . . . [It] is essentially infraction. It is rule-breaking behavior performed by juveniles aware that they are violating the law and of the nature of their deed, and made permissible by the neutralization of infractious [!] elements. Thus, Cohen and Short are fundamentally right when they insist that social control theory is incomplete unless it provides an impetus by which the potential for delinquency may be realized.[48]

The impetus Matza provides is a "feeling of desperation," brought on by the "mood of fatalism," "the experience of seeing one's self as effect" rather than cause. In a situation in which manliness is stressed, being pushed around leads to the mood of fatalism, which in turn produces a sense of desperation. In order to relieve his desperation, in order to cast off the mood of fatalism, the boy "makes things happen"—he commits delinquent acts.[49]

There are several additional accounts of "why they do it" that are to my mind persuasive and at the same time generally compatible with control theory.[50] But while all of these accounts may be compatible with control theory, they are by no means deducible from it. Furthermore, they rarely impute built-in, unusual motivation to the delinquent: he is attempting to satisfy the same desires, he is reacting to the same pressures as other boys (as is clear, for example, in the previous quotation from Briar and Piliavin). In other words, if included, these accounts of motivation would serve the same function in the theory that "animal impulses" traditionally served: they might add to its persuasiveness and plausibility, but they would add little else, since they do not differentiate delinquents from nondelinquents.

In the end, then, control theory remains what it has always been: a theory in which deviation is not problematic. The question "Why do they do it?" is simply not the question the theory is designed to answer. The question is, "Why don't we do it?" There is much evidence that we would if we dared.

Endnotes

[1] Emile Durkheim, *Suicide,* trans. John A. Spaulding and George Simpson (New York: The Free Press, 1951), p. 209.

[2] Books have been written on the increasing importance of interpersonal sensitivity in modern life. According to this view, controls from within have become less important than controls from without in *producing* conformity. Whether or not this observation is true as a description of historical trends, it is true that interpersonal sensitivity has become moe important in *explaining* conformity. Although logically it should also have become more important in explaining nonconformity, the opposite has been the case, once again showing that Cohen's observation that an explanation of conformity should be an explanation of deviance cannot be translated as "an explanation of conformity has to be an explanation of deviance." for the view that interpersonal sensitivity currently plays a greater role than formerly in producing conformity, see William J. Goode, "Norm Commitment and Conformity to Role-Status Obligations," *American Journal of Sociology,* LXVI (1960), 246–258. And, of course, also see David Riesman, Nathan Glazer, and Reuel Denney, *the Lonely Crowd* (Garden City, New York: Doubleday, 1950), especially Part I.

[3] The literature on psychopathy is voluminous. See William McCord and Joan McCord, *the Psychopath* (Princeton: D. Van Nostrand, 1964).

[4] John M. Martin and Joseph P. Fitzpatrick, *Delinquent Behavior* (New York: Random House, 1964), p. 130.

[5] *Ibid.* For additional properties of the psychopath, see McCord and McCord, *The Psychopath,* pp. 1–22.

[6]Barbara Wootton. *Social Science and Social Pathology* (New York: Macmillan, 1959), p. 250.

[7]"The logical untenability [of the position that there are forces in man 'resistant to socialization'] was ably demonstrated by Parsons over 30 years ago, and it is widely recognized that the position is empirically unsound because it assumes[!] some universal biological drive system distinctly separate from socialization and social context—a basic and intransigent human nature" (Judith Blake and Kingsley Davis, "Norms, Values, and Sanctions," *Handbook of Modern Sociology*, ed. Robert E. L. Faris [Chicago: Rand McNally, 1964], p. 471).

[8]Emile Durkheim, *Moral Education,* trans. Everett K. Wilson and Herman Schnurer (New York: The Free Press, 1961), p. 64.

[9]Although attachment alone does not exhaust the meaning of internalization, attachments and beliefs combined would appear to leave only a small residue of "internal control" not susceptible in principle to direct measurement.

[10]F. Ivan Nye, *Family Relationships and Delinquent Behavior* (New York: Wiley, 1958), pp 5–7.

[11]Albert J. Reiss, Jr., "Delinquency as the Failure of Personal and Social Controls," *American Sociological Review,* XVI (1951), 196–207. For example, "Our observations show . . . that delinquent recidivists are less often persons with mature ego ideals or nondelinquent social roles" (p. 204).

[12]Scott Briar and Irving Piliavin, "Delinquency, Situational Inducements, and Commitment to Conformity," *Social Problems,* XIII (1965), 41–42. The concept "stake in conformity" was introduced by Jackson Toby in his "Social Disorganization and Stake in Conformity: Complementary Factors in the Predatory Behavior of Hoodlums," *Journal of Criminal Law, Criminology and Police Science,* XLVIII (1957), 12–17. See also his "Hoodlum or Business Man: An American Dilemma," *The Jews,* ed. Marshall Sklare (New York: The Free Press, 1958), pp. 542–550. Throughout the text I occasionally use "stake in conformity" in speaking in general of the strength of the bond to conventional society. So used, the concept is somewhat broader than is true for either Toby or Briar and Piliavin, where the concept is roughly equivalent to what is here called "commitment."

[13]Thomas Hobbes, *Leviathan* (Oxford: Basil Blackwell, 1957), p. 195.

[14]Howard S. Becker, "Notes on the Concept of Commitment," *American Journal of Sociology,* LXVI (1960), 35–36.

[15]Arthur L. Stinchcombe, *Rebellion in a High School* (Chicago: Quadrangle, 1964), p. 5.

[16]Richard A. Cloward and Lloyd E. Ohlin, *Delinquency and Opportunity* (New York: The Free Press, 1960), p. 147, quoting Edwin H. Sutherland, ed., *The Professional Thief* (Chicago: University of Chicago Press, 1937), pp. 211–213.

[17]William James, *Psychology* (Cleveland: World Publishing Co., 1948), p. 186.

[18]Few activities appear to be so engrossing that they rule out contemplation of alternative lines of behavior, at least if estimates of the amount of time men spend plotting sexual deviations have any validity.

[19]*The Sutherland Papers,* ed. Albert K. Cohen et al. (Bloomington: Indiana University Press, 1956), p. 37.

[20]David Matza and Gresham M. Sykes, "Juvenile Delinquency and Subterranean Values," *American Sociological Review,* XXVI (1961), 712–719.

[21]*Ibid.,* p. 718.

[22]The starving man stealing the loaf of bread is the image evoked by most strain theories. In this image, the starving man's belief in the wrongness of his act is clearly not something that must be explained away. It can be assumed to be present without causing embarrassment to the explanation.

[23]McCord and McCord, *The Psychopath,* pp. 12–15.

[24]Donald R. Cressey, *Other People's Money* (New York: The Free Press, 1953).

[25]Gresham M. Sykes and David Matza, "Techniques of Neutralization: A Theory of Delinquency," *American Sociological Review,* XXII (1957), 664–670.

[26]David Matza, *Delinquency and Drift* (New York: Wiley, 1964), pp. 181–191.

[27]In asserting that Cressey's assumption is invalid with respect to delinquency, I do not wish to suggest that it is invalid for the question of embezzlement, where the problem faced by the deviator is fairly specific and he can reasonably be assumed to be an upstanding citizen. (Although even here the fact that the embezzler's nonshareable financial problem often results from some sort of hanky-panky suggests that "verbalizations" may be less necessary than might otherwise be assumed.)

[28]*Delinquency and Drift,* p. 43.

[29]This assumption is not, I think, contradicted by the evidence presented by Matza against the existence of a delinquent subculture. In comparing the attitudes and actions of delinquents with the picture painted by delinquent subculture theorists, Matza emphasizes—and perhaps exaggerates—the extent to which delinquents are tied to the conventional order. In implicitly comparing delinquents with a supermoral man, I emphasize—and perhaps exaggerate—the extent to which they are not tied to the conventional order.

[30]The position taken here is therefore somewhere between the "semantic dementia" and the "neutralization" positions. Assuming variation, the delinquent is, at the

extremes, freer than the neutralization argument assumes. Although the possibility of wide discrepancy between what the delinquent professes and what he practices still exists, it is presumably much rarer than is suggested by studies of articulate "psychopaths."

[31]The idea that the middle-class boy is less closely tied than the lower-class boy to his peers has been widely adopted in the literature on delinquency. The middle-class boy's "cold and rational" relations with his peers are in sharp contrast with the "spontaneous and warm" relations of the lower-class boy. See, for example, Albert K. Cohen, *Delinquent Boys* (New York: The Free Press, 1955), pp. 102–109.

[32]The evidence in favor of this proposition is summarized in Seymour M. Lipset and Reinhard Bendix, *Social Mobility in Industrial Society* (Berkeley: University of California Press, 1959), especially pp. 249–259. For example: "These [business leaders] show strong traits of independence, they are characterized by an inability to form intimate relations and are consequently often socially isolated men" (p. 251).

[33]Relations between measures of attachment and commitment are examined in Chapter VIII.

[34]*Social Mobility*, p. 253.

[35]Briar and Piliavin, "Situational Involvements," p. 45.

[36]Jean Piaget, *The Moral Judgment of the Child*, trans. Marjorie Gabain (New York: The Free Press, n.d.), p. 101.

[37]Ibid., p. 379.

[38]Durkheim, *Moral Education*, p. 83.

[39]*Ibid.*, pp. 73–79.

[40]In the end, Durkheim distinguishes between a patriotism that leads to concern for domestic problems and one that emphasizes foreign relations (especially that variety which puts "national sentiment in conflict with commitments of mankind").

[41]See their "Juvenile Delinquency," in *Contemporary Social Problems*, ed. Robert K. Merton and Robert A. Nisbet (New York: Harcourt, Brace and World, 1961), p. 106.

[42]Howard S. Becker, *Outsiders* (New York: The Free Press, 1963), p. 26. See also Kate Friedlander, *The Psycho-Analytic Approach to Juvenile Delinquency* (New York: International Universities Press, 1947), p. 7.

[43]Cf. Albert K. Cohen, *Deviance and Control* (Englewood Cliffs, N.J.: Prentice-Hall, 1966), pp. 59–62.

[44]I have frequently heard the statement "it's an absence of something explanation" used as an apparently damning criticism of a sociological theory. While the origins of this view are unknown to me, the fact that such a statement appears to have some claim to plausibility suggests one of the sources of uneasiness in the face of a control theory.

[45]The popular "it's-an-id-argument" dismissal of explanations of deviant behavior assumes that the founding fathers of sociology somehow proved that the blood of man is neither warm nor red, but spiritual. The intellectual trap springs shut on the counterassumption that innate aggressive-destructive impulses course through the veins, as it should. The solution is not to accept both views, but to accept neither.

[46]Thomas Hobbes, Leviathan, p. 83. Given the history of the sociological response to Hobbes, it is instructive to compare Hobbes' picture of the motivation behind the deviant act with that painted by Talcott Parsons. According to Parsons, the motive to deviate is a psychological trait or need that the deviant carries with him at all times. This need is itself deviant: it cannot be satisfied by conformity. Social controls enter merely as reality factors that determine the form and manner in which this need will be satisfied. If one path to deviant behavior is blocked, the deviant will continue searching until he finds a path that is open. Perhaps because this need arises from interpersonal conflict, and is thus socially derived, the image it presents of the deviant as fundamentally immoral, as doing evil because it is evil, has been largely ignored by those objecting to the control theorist's tendency to fall back on natural propensities as a source of the energy that results in the activities society defines as wrong. See Talcott Parsons, The Social System (New York: The Free Press, 1951), Chapter 7.

[47]Briar and Piliavin, "Situational Inducements," p. 36.

[48]Delinquency and Drift, p. 182.

[49]Matza warns us that we cannot take the fatalistic mood out of context and hope to find important differences between delinquents and other boys: "That the subcultural delinquent is not significantly different from other boys is precisely the point" (ibid., p. 89).

[50]For example: Carl Werthman, "The Function of Social Definitions in the Development of Delinquent Careers," Juvenile Delinquency and Youth Crime, Report of the President's Commission on Law Enforcement and Administration of Justice (Washington: USGPO, 1960, pp. 155–170; Jackson Toby, "Affluence and Adolescent Crime," ibid., pp. 132–144; James F. Short, Jr., and Fred L. Strodtbeck, Group Process and Gang Delinquency (Chicago: University of Chicago Press, 1965), pp. 248–264.

Outsiders—Defining Deviance

HOWARD BECKER

In this article, Howard Becker defines "outsiders" as individuals who break a rule agreed on by a group. Becker also claims that rule breakers may perceive a person who enforces the rule as an outsider. In other words, Becker argues, many different facets of deviant behavior are relative. This 1963 piece established an early foundation for what has become known as the interactionist theory of deviant behavior.

*A*ll social groups make rules and attempt, at some times and under some circumstances, to enforce them. Social rules define situation and the kinds of behavior appropriate to them, specifying some actions as "right" and forbidding others as "wrong." When a rule is enforced, the person who is supposed to have broken it may be seen as a special kind of person, one who cannot be trusted to live by the rules agreed on by the group. He is regarded as an *outsider.*

But the person who is thus labeled an outsider may have a different view of the matter. He may not accept the rule by which he is being judged and may not regard those who judge him as either competent or legitimately entitled to do so. Hence, a second meaning of the term emerges: the rule-breaker may feel his judges are *outsiders.*

In what follows, I will try to clarify the situation and process pointed to by this double-barreled term: the situations of rule-breaking and rule-enforcement and the processes by which some people come to break rules and others to enforce them.

Some preliminary distinctions are in order. Rules may be of a great many kinds. They may be formally enacted into law, and in this case the police power of the state may be used in enforcing them. In other cases, they represent informal agreements, newly arrived at or encrusted with the sanction of age and tradition; rules of this kind are enforced by informal sanctions of various kinds.

Similarly, whether a rule has the force of law or tradition or is simply the result of consensus, it may be the task of some specialized body, such as the police or the committee on ethics of a professional association, to enforce it; enforcement, on the other hand, may be everyone's job or, at least, the job of everyone in the group to which the rule is meant to apply.

Many rules are not enforced and are not, in any except the most formal sense, the kind of rules with which I am concerned. Blue laws, which remain on the statute books though they have not been enforced for a hundred years, are examples. (It is important to remember, however, that an unenforced law may be reactivated for various reasons and regain all its original force; as recently occurred with respect to the laws governing the opening of commercial establishments on Sunday in Missouri.) Informal rules may similarly die from lack of enforcement. I shall mainly be concerned with what we can call the actual operating rules of groups, those kept alive through attempts at enforcement.

Finally, just how far "outside" one is, in either of the senses I have mentioned, varies from case to case. We think of the person who commits a traffic violation or gets a little too drunk at a party as being, after all, not very different from the rest of us and treat his infraction tolerantly. We regard the thief as less like us and punish him severely. Crimes such as murder, rape, or treason lead us to view the violator as a true outsider.

In the same way, some rule-breakers do not think they have been unjustly judged. The traffic violator usually subscribes to the very rules he has broken. Alcoholics are often ambivalent, sometimes feeling that those who judge them do not understand them and at other times agreeing that compulsive drinking is a bad thing. At the extreme, some deviants (homosexuals and drug addicts are good examples) develop full-blown ideologies explaining why they are right and why those who disapprove of and punish them are wrong.

☻ Definitions of Deviance

The outsider—the deviant from group rules—has been the subject of much speculation, theorizing, and scientific study. What laymen want to know about deviants is: why do they do it? How can we account for their rule-breaking? What is there about them that leads them to do forbidden things?

Scientific research has tried to find answers to these questions. In doing so it has accepted the common-sense premise that there is something inherently deviant (qualitatively distinct) about acts that break (or seem to break) social rules. It has also accepted the common-sense assumption that the deviant act occurs because some characteristic of the person who commits it makes it necessary or inevitable that he should. Scientists do not ordinarily question the label "deviant" when it is applied to particular acts or people but rather take it as given. In so doing, they accept the values of the group making the judgment.

It is easily observable that different groups judge different things to be deviant. This should alert us to the possibility that the person making the judgment of deviance, the process by which that judgment is arrived at, and the situation in which it is made may all be intimately involved in the phenomenon of deviance. To the degree that the common-sense view of deviance and the scientific theories that begin with its premises assume that acts that break rules are inherently deviant and thus take for granted the situations and processes of judgment, they may leave out an important variable. If scientists ignore the variable character of the process of judgment, they may by that omission limit the kinds of theories that can be developed and the kind of understanding that can be achieved.[1]

Our first problem, then, is to construct a definition of deviance. Before doing this, let us consider some of the definitions scientists now use, seeing what is left out if we take them as a point of departure for the study of outsiders.

The simplest view of deviance is essentially statistical, defining as deviant anything that varies too widely from the average. When a statistician analyzes the results of an agricultural experiment, he describes the stalk of corn that is exceptionally tall and the stalk that is exceptionally short as deviations from the mean or average. Similarly, one can describe anything that differs from what is most common as a deviation. In this view, to be left-handed or redheaded is deviant, because most people are right-handed and brunette.

So stated, the statistical view seems simple-minded, even trivial. Yet it simplifies the problem by doing away with many questions of value that ordinarily arise in discussions of the nature of deviance. In assessing any particular case, all one need do is calculate the distance of the behavior involved from the average. But it is too simple a solution. Hunting with such a definition, we return with a mixed bag—people who are excessively fat or thin, murderers, redheads, homosexuals, and traffic violators. The mixture contains some ordinarily thought of as deviants and others who have broken no rule at all. The statistical definition of deviance, in short, is too far removed from the concern with rule-breaking which prompts scientific study of outsiders.

A less simple but much more common view of deviance identifies it as something essentially pathological, revealing the presence of a "disease." This view rests, obviously, on a medical analogy. The human organism, when it is working efficiently and experiencing no discomfort, is said to be "healthy." When it does not work efficiently, a disease is present. The organ or function that has become deranged is said to be pathological. Of course, there is little disagreement about what constitutes a healthy state of the organism. But there is much less agreement when one uses the notion of pathology analogically, to describe kinds of behavior that are regarded as deviant. For people do not agree on what constitutes healthy behavior. It is difficult to find a definition that will satisfy even such a select and limited group as psychiatrists; it is impossible to find one that people generally accept as they accept criteria of health for the organism.[2]

Sometimes people mean the analogy more strictly, because they think of deviance as the product of mental disease. The behavior of a homosexual or drug addict is regarded as the symptom of a mental disease just as the diabetic's difficulty in getting bruises to heal is regarded as a symptom of his disease. But mental disease resembles physical disease only in metaphor:

> Starting with such things as syphilis, tuberculosis, typhoid fever, and carcinomas and fractures, we have created the class "illness." At first, this class was composed of only a few items, all of which shared the common feature of reference to a state of disordered structure or function of the human body as a physiochemical machine. As time went on, additional items were added to this class. They were not added, however, because they were newly discovered bodily disorders. The physician's attention had been deflected from this criterion and had become focused instead on disability and suffering as new criteria for selection. Thus, at first slowly, such things as hysteria, hypochondriasis, obsessive-compulsive neurosis, and depression were added to the category of illness. Then, with increasing zeal, physicians and especially psychiatrists began to call "illness" (that is, of course, "mental illness") anything and everything in which they could detect any sign of malfunctioning, based on no matter what norm. Hence, agoraphobia is illness because one should not be afraid of open spaces. Homosexuality is illness because heterosexuality is the social norm.

Divorce is illness because it signals failure of marriage. Crime, art, unde-sired political leadership, participation in social affairs, or withdrawal from such participation—all these and many more have been said to be signs of mental illness.[3]

The medical metaphor limits what we can see much as the statistical view does. It accepts the lay judgment of something as deviant and, by use of analogy, locates its source within the individual, thus preventing us from seeing the judgment itself as a critical part of the phenomenon.

Some sociologists also use a model of deviance based essentially on the medical notions of health and disease. They look at a society, or some part of a society, and ask whether there are any processes going on in it that tend to reduce its stability, thus lessening its chance of survival. They label such processes deviant or identify them as symptoms of social disorganization. They discriminate between those features of society which promote stability (and thus are "functional") and those which disrupt stability (and thus are "dysfunctional"). Such a view has the great virtue of pointing to areas of possible trouble in a society of which people may not be aware.[4]

But it is harder in practice than it appears to be in theory to specify what is functional and what dysfunctional for a society or social group. The ques-tion of what the purpose or goal (function) of a group is and, consequently, what things will help or hinder the achievement of that purpose, is very often a political question. Factions within the group disagree and maneuver to have their own definition of the group's function accepted. The function of the group or organization, then, is decided in political conflict, not given in the nature of the organization. If this is true, then it is likewise true that the questions of what rules are to be enforced, what behavior regarded as deviant, and which people labeled as outsiders must also be regarded as political.[5] The functional view of deviance, by ignoring the political aspect of the phenomenon, limits our understanding.

Another sociological view is more relativistic. It identifies deviance as the failure to obey group rules. Once we have described the rules a group enforces on its members, we can say with some precision whether or not a person has violated them and is thus, on this view, deviant.

This view is closest to my own, but it fails to give sufficient weight to the ambiguities that arise in deciding which rules are to be taken as the yard-stick against which behavior is measured and judged deviant. A society has many groups, each with its own set of rules, and people belong to many groups simultaneously. A person may break the rules of one group by the

91

very act of abiding by the rules of another group. Is he, then, deviant? Proponents of this definition may object that while ambiguity may arise with respect to the rules peculiar to one or another group in society, there are some rules that are very generally agreed to by everyone, in which case the difficulty does not arise. This, of course, is a question of fact, to be settled by empirical research. I doubt there are many such areas of consensus and think it wiser to use a definition that allows us to deal with both ambiguous and unambiguous situations.

☻ Deviance and the Responses of Others

The sociological view I have just discussed defines deviance as the infraction of some agreed-upon rule. It then goes on to ask who breaks rules, and to search for the factors in their personalities and life situations that might account for the infractions. This assumes that those who have broken a rule constitute a homogeneous category, because they have committed the same deviant act.

Such an assumption seems to me to ignore the central fact about deviance: it is created by society. I do not mean this in the way it is ordinarily understood, in which the causes of deviance are located in the social situation of the deviant or in "social factors" which prompt his action. I mean, rather, that *social groups create deviance by making the rules whose infraction constitutes deviance,* and by applying those rules to particular people and labeling them as outsiders. From this point of view, deviance is *not* a quality of the act the person commits, but rather a consequence of the application by others of rules and sanctions to an "offender." The deviant is one to whom that label has successfully been applied; deviant behavior is behavior that people so label.[6]

Since deviance is, among other things, a consequence of the responses of others to a person's act, students of deviance cannot assume that they are dealing with a homogeneous category when they study people who have been labeled deviant. That is, they cannot assume that these people have actually committed a deviant act or broken some rule, because the process of labeling may not be infallible; some people may be labeled deviant who in fact have not broken a rule. Furthermore, they cannot assume that the category of those labeled deviant will contain all those who actually have broken a rule, for many offenders may escape apprehension and thus fail to be included in the population of "deviants" they study. Insofar as the category lacks homogeneity and fails to include all the cases that belong in it, one cannot reasonably expect to find common factors of personality or life situation that will account for the supposed deviance.

What, then, do people who have been labeled deviant have in common? At the least, they share the label and the experience of being labeled as outsiders. I will begin my analysis with this basic similarity and view deviance as the product of a transaction that takes place between some social group and one who is viewed by that group as a rule-breaker. I will be less concerned with the personal and social characteristics of deviants than with the process by which they come to be thought of as outsiders and their reactions to that judgment.

Malinowski discovered the usefulness of this view for understanding the nature of deviance many years ago, in his study of the Trobriand Islands:

> One day an outbreak of wailing and a great commotion told me that a death had occurred somewhere in the neighborhood. I was informed that Kima'i, a young lad of my acquaintance, of sixteen or so, had fallen from a coco-nut palm and killed himself. . . . I found that another youth had been severely wounded by some mysterious coincidence. And at the funeral there was obviously a general feeling of hostility between the village where the boy died and that into which his body was carried for burial.
>
> Only much later was I able to discover the real meaning of these events. The boy had committed suicide. The truth was that he had broken the rules of exogamy, the partner in his crime being his maternal cousin, the daughter of his mother's sister. This had been known and generally disapproved of but nothing was done until the girl's discarded lover, who had wanted to marry her and who felt personally injured, took the initiative. This rival threatened first to use black magic against the guilty youth, but this had not much effect. Then one evening he insulted the culprit in public—accusing him in the hearing of the whole community of incest and hurling at him certain expressions intolerable to a native.
>
> For this there was only one remedy; only one means of escape remained to the unfortunate youth. Next morning he put on festive attire and ornamentation, climbed a coco-nut palm and addressed the community, speaking from among the palm leaves and bidding them farewell. He explained the reasons for his desperate deed and also launched forth a veiled accusation against the man who had driven him to his death, upon which it became the duty of his clansmen to avenge him. Then he wailed

aloud, as is the custom, jumped from a palm some sixty feet high and was killed on the spot. There followed a fight within the village in which the rival was wounded; and the quarrel was repeated during the funeral. . . .

If you were to inquire into the matter among the Trobrianders, you will find . . . that the natives show horror at the idea of violating the rules of exogamy and that they believe that sores, disease and even death might follow clan incest. This is the i'deal of native law, and in moral matters it is easy and pleasant strictly to adhere to the ideal—when judging the conduct of others or expressing an opinion about conduct in general.

When it comes to the application of morality and ideals to real life, however, things take on a different complexion. In the case described it was obvious that the facts would not tally with the ideal of conduct. Public opinion was neither outraged by the knowledge of the crime to any extent, nor did it react directly—it had to be mobilized by a public statement of the crime and by insults being hurled at the culprit by an interested party. Even then he had to carry out the punishment himself. . . . Probing further into the matter and collecting concrete information, I found that the breach of exogamy—as regards intercourse and not marriage—is by no means a rare occurrence, and public opinion is lenient, though decidedly hypocritical. If the affair is carried on *sub rosa* with a certain amount of decorum, and if no one in particular stirs up trouble—"public opinion" will gossip, but not demand any harsh punishment. If, on the contrary, scandal breaks out—everyone turns against the guilty pair and by ostracism and insults one or the other may be driven to suicide.[7]

Whether an act is deviant, then, depends on how other people react to it. You can commit clan incest and suffer from no more than gossip as long as no one makes a public accusation; but you will be driven to your death if the accusation is made. The point is that the response of other people has to be regarded as problematic. Just because one has committed an infraction of a rule does not mean that others will respond as though this had happened. (Conversely, just because one has not violated a rule does not mean that he may not be treated, in some circumstances, as though he had.)

The degree to which other people will respond to a given act as deviant varies greatly. Several kinds of variation seem worth noting. First of all, there is variation over time. A person believed to have committed a given "deviant" act may at one time be responded to much more leniently than he would be at some other time. The occurrence of "drives" against various kinds of deviance illustrates this clearly. At various times, enforcement officials may decide to make an all-out attack on some particular kind of deviance, such as gambling, drug addiction, or homosexuality. It is obviously much more dangerous to engage in one of these activities when a drive is on than at any other time. (In a very interesting study of crime news in Colorado newspapers, Davis found that the amount of crime reported in Colorado newspapers showed very little association with actual changes in the amount of crime taking place in Colorado. And, further, that peoples' estimate of how much increase there had been in crime in Colorado was associated with the increase in the amount of crime news but not with any increase in the amount of crime.)[8]

The degree to which an act will be treated as deviant depends also on who commits the act and who feels he has been harmed by it. Rules tend to be applied more to some persons than others. Studies of juvenile delinquency make the point clearly. Boys from middle-class areas do not get as far in the legal process when they are apprehended as do boys from slum areas. The middle-class boy is less likely, when picked up by the police, to be taken to the station; less likely when taken to the station to be booked; and it is extremely unlikely that he will be convicted and sentenced.[9] This variation occurs even though the original infraction of the rule is the same in the two cases. Similarly, the law is differentially applied to Negroes and whites. It is well known that a Negro believed to have attacked a white woman is much more likely to be punished than a white man who commits the same offense; it is only slightly less well known that a Negro who murders another Negro is much less likely to be punished than a white man who commits murder.[10] This, of course, is one of the main points of Sutherland's analysis of white-collar crime: crimes committed by corporations are almost always prosecuted as civil cases, but the same crime committed by an individual is ordinarily treated as a criminal offense.[11]

Some rules are enforced only when they result in certain consequences. The unmarried mother furnishes a clear example. Vincent[12] points out that illicit sexual relations seldom result in severe punishment or social censure for the offenders. If, however, a girl becomes pregnant as a result of such activities the reaction of others is likely to be severe. (The illicit pregnancy is also an interesting example of the differential enforcement of rules on different categories of people. Vincent notes that unmarried fathers escape the severe censure visited on the mother.)

Why repeat these commonplace observations? Because, taken together, they support the proposition that deviance is not a simple quality, present in some kinds of behavior and absent in others. Rather, it is the product of a process which involves responses of other people to the behavior. The same behavior may be an infraction of the rules at one time and not at another; may be an infraction when committed by one person, but not when committed by another; some rules are broken with impunity, others are not. In short, whether a given act is deviant or not depends in part on the nature of the act (that is, whether or not it violates some rule) and in part on what other people do about it.

Some people may object that this is merely a terminological quibble, that one can, after all, define terms any way he wants to and that if some people want to speak of rule-breaking behavior as deviant without reference to the reactions of others they are free to do so. This, of course, is true. Yet it might be worthwhile to refer to such behavior as *rule-breaking behavior* and reserve the term *deviant* for those labeled as deviant by some segment of society. I do not insist that this usage be followed. But it should be clear that insofar as a scientist uses "deviant" to refer to any rule-breaking behavior and takes as his subject of study only those who have been *labeled* deviant, he will be hampered by the disparities between the two categories.

If we take as the object of our attention behavior which comes to be labeled as deviant, we must recognize that we cannot know whether a given act will be categorized as deviant until the response of others has occurred. Deviance is not a quality that lies in behavior itself, but in the interaction between the person who commits an act and those who respond to it.

☺ Whose Rules?

I have been using the term "outsiders" to refer to those people who are judged by others to be deviant and thus to stand outside the circle of "normal" members of the group. But the term contains a second meaning, whose analysis leads to another important set of sociological problems: "outsiders," from the point of view of the person who is labeled deviant, may be the people who make the rules he had been found guilty of breaking.

Social rules are the creation of specific social groups. Modern societies are not simple organizations in which everyone agrees on what the rules are and how they are to be applied in specific situations. They are, instead, highly differentiated along social class lines, ethnic lines, occupational lines, and cultural lines. These groups need not and, in fact, often do not share the same rules. The problems they face in dealing with their environment, the history and traditions they carry with them, all lead to the evolution of different sets of rules. Insofar as the rules of various groups conflict and contradict one another, there will be disagreement about the kind of behavior that is proper in any given situation.

Italian immigrants who went on making wine for themselves and their friends during Prohibition were acting properly by Italian immigrant standards, but were breaking the law of their new country (as, of course, were many of their Old American neighbors). Medical patients who shop around for a doctor may, from the perspective of their own group, be doing what is necessary to protect their health by making sure they get what seems to them the best possible doctor; but, from the perspective of the physician, what they do is wrong because it breaks down the trust the patient ought to put in his physician. The lower-class delinquent who fights for his "turf" is only doing what he considers necessary and right, but teachers, social workers, and police see it differently.

While it may be argued that many or most rules are generally agreed to by all members of a society, empirical research on a given rule generally reveals variation in people's attitudes. Formal rules, enforced by some specially constituted group, may differ from those actually thought appropriate by most people.[13] Factions in a group may disagree on what I have called actual operating rules. Most important for the study of behavior ordinarily labeled deviant, the perspectives of the people who engage in the behavior are likely to be quite different from those of the people who condemn it. In this latter situation, a person may feel that he is being judged according to rules he has had no hand in making and does not accept, rules forced on him by outsiders.

To what extent and under what circumstances do people attempt to force their rules on others who do not subscribe to them? Let us distinguish two cases. In the first, only those who are actually members of the group have any interest in making and enforcing certain rules. If an orthodox Jew disobeys the laws of kashruth only other orthodox Jews will regard this as a transgression; Christians or nonorthodox Jews will not consider this deviance and would have no interest in interfering. In the second case, members of a group consider it important to their welfare that members of certain other groups obey certain rules. Thus, people consider it extremely important that those who practice the healing arts abide by certain rules; this is the reason the state licenses physicians, nurses, and others, and forbids anyone who is not licensed to engage in healing activities.

To the extent that a group tries to impose its rules on other groups in the society, we are presented with a second question: Who can, in fact, force others to accept their rules and what are the causes of their success? This is, of course, a question of political and economic power. . . . Here it is enough to note that people are in fact always *forcing* their rules on others, applying them more or less against the will and without the consent of those others. By and large, for example, rules are made for young people by their elders. Though the youth of this country exert a powerful influence culturally—the mass media of communication are tailored to their interests, for instance— many important kinds of rules are made for our youth by adults. Rules regarding school attendance and sex behavior are not drawn up with regard to the problems of adolescence. Rather, adolescents find themselves surrounded by rules about these matters which have been made by older and more settled people. It is considered legitimate to do this, for youngsters are considered neither wise enough nor responsible enough to make proper rules for themselves.

In the same way, it is true in many respects that men make the rules for women in our society (though in America this it changing rapidly). Negroes find themselves subject to rules made for them by whites. The foreign-born and those otherwise ethnically peculiar often have their rules made for them by the Protestant Anglo-Saxon minority. The middle class makes rules the lower class must obey—in the schools, the courts, and elsewhere.

Differences in the ability to make rules and apply them to other people are essentially power differentials (either legal or extralegal). Those groups whose social position gives them weapons and power are best able to enforce their rules. Distinctions of age, sex, ethnicity, and class are all related to differences in power, which accounts for differences in the degree to which groups so distinguished can make rules for others.

In addition to recognizing that deviance is created by the responses of people to particular kinds of behavior, by the labeling of that behavior as deviant, we must also keep in mind that the rules created and maintained by such labeling are not universally agreed to. Instead, they are the object of conflict and disagreement, part of the political process of society.

Endnotes

[1] Cf. Donald R. Cressey, "Criminological Research and the Definition of Crimes," *American Journal of Sociology*, LVI (May, 1951), 546–551.

[2]See the discussion in C. Wright Mills, "The Professional Ideology of Social Pathologists," *American Journal of Sociology*, XLIX (September, 1942), 165–180.

[3]Thomas Szasz, *The Myth of Mental Illness* (New York: Paul B. Hoeber, Inc., 1961), pp. 44–45; see also Erving Goffman, "The Medical Model and Mental Hospitalization," in *Asylums: Essays on the Social Situation of Mental Patients and Other Inmates* (Garden City: Anchor Books, 1961), pp. 321–386.

[4]See Robert K. Merton, "Social Problems and Sociological Theory," in Robert K. Merton and Robert A. Nisbet, editors, *Contemporary Social Problems* (New York: Harcourt, Brace and World, Inc., 1961), pp. 697–717; and Talcott Parsons, *The Social System* (New York: The Free Press of Glencoe, 1951), pp. 249–325.

[5]Howard Brotz similarly identifies the question of what phenomena are "functional" or "dysfunctional" as a political one in "Functionalism and Dynamic Analysis," *European Journal of Sociology*, 11 (1961), 170–179.

[6]The most important earlier statements of this view can be found in Frank Tannenbaum, *Crime and the Community* (New York: McGraw-Hill Book Co., Inc., 1951), and F. M. Lemert, *Social Pathology* (New York: McGraw-Hill Book Co., Inc., 1951). A recent article stating a position very similar to mine is John Kitsuse, "Societal Reaction to Deviance: Problems of Theory and Method," *Social Problems*, 9 (Winter, 1962), 247–256.

[7]Bronislaw Malinowski, *Crime and Custom in Savage Society* (New York: Humanities Press, 1926), pp. 77–80. Reprinted by permission of Humanities Press and Routledge & Kegan Paul, Ltd.

[8]F. James Davis, "Crime News in Colorado Newspapers," *American Journal of Sociology*, LVII (January, 1952), 325–330.

[9]See Albert K. Cohen and James F. Short, Jr., "Juvenile Delinquency," in Merton and Nisbet, *op. cit.*, p. 87.

[10]See Harold Garfinkel, "Research Notes on Inter- and Intra-Racial Homicides," *Social Forces*, 27 (May, 1949), 369–381.

[11]Edwin H. Sutherland, "White Collar Criminality," *American Sociological Review*, V (February, 1940), 1–12.

[12]Clark Vincent, *Unmarried Mothers* (New York: The Free Press of Glencoe, 1961), pp. 3–5.

[13]Arnold M. Rose and Arthur E. Prell, "Does the Punishment Fit the Crime?—A Study in Social Valuation," *American Journal of Sociology*, LXI (November, 1955), 247–259.

Questions

1. Why does Becker discount the statistical, pathological, and functional views of deviant behavior?

2. If Becker is correct in saying that those who label individuals as deviant are not infallible, what are the implications for label theory?

3. Becker contends that deviant behavior is an interaction between an individual and a group. What does he mean by this statement? Can you think of any examples from your campus that illustrate this point? Explain.

4. According to the theoretical framework developed in this article, "Those groups whose social position gives them weapons and power are best able to enforce their rules." When has this been true in American society? What about in other societies? Finally, cite cases in which the "rules" seem not to favor the powerful. That is, what kinds of behavior are defined as deviant that the powerful would rather have defined as normal? How might this situation arise?

The Poverty of the Sociology of Deviance: Nuts, Sluts, and Preverts

Alexander Liazos

Regis College

The author critically examines sociologists' study of deviance, and identifies three shortcomings. First, defining certain types of behavior as deviant stigmatizes the behavior. Second, the economic and political elite generally ignore deviant behavior. Third, sociology overlooks the role of power in deviance and fails to address how or why a particular behavior is defined as deviant.

C. Wright Mills left a rich legacy to sociology. One of his earliest, and best, contributions was "The Professional Ideology of Social Pathologists". (1943). In it, Mills argues that the small-town, middle-class background of writers of social problems textbooks blinded them to basic problems of social structure and power, and led them to emphasize melioristic, patchwork types of solutions to America's "problems," ranging from rape in rural orderly the structure of small-town America; anything else was pathology and disorganization. Moreover, these "problems," "ranging from rape in rural districts to public housing," were not explored systematically and theoretically; they were not placed in some larger political, historical, and social context. They were merely listed and decried.[1]

Since Mills wrote his paper, however, the field of social problems, social disorganization, and social pathology has undergone considerable changes. Beginning in the late 1940's and the 1950's, and culminating in the 1960's, the field of "deviance" has largely replaced the social problems orientation.

"The Poverty of the Sociology of Deviance: Nuts, Sluts, and Preverts," by Alexander Liazos, reprinted from *Social Problems*, vol. 20, 1972, pp. 103–120.

This new field is characterized by a number of features which distinguish it from the older approach.[2]

First, there is some theoretical framework, even though it is often absent in edited collections (the Rubington and Weinberg (1968) edited book is an outstanding exception). Second, the small-town morality is largely gone. Writers claim they will examine the phenomena at hand—prostitution, juvenile delinquency, mental illness, crime, and others—objectively, not considering them as necessarily harmful and immoral. Third, the statements and theories of the field are based on much more extensive, detailed, and theoretically-oriented research than were those of the 1920's and 1930's. Fourth, writers attempt to fit their theories to some central theories, concerns, and problems found in the general field of sociology; they try to transcend mere moralizing.

The "deviant" has been humanized; the moralistic tone is no longer ever-present (although it still lurks underneath the explicit disavowals); and theoretical perspectives have been developed. Nevertheless, all is not well with the field of "deviance." Close examination reveals that writers of this field still do not try to relate the phenomena of "deviance" to larger social, historical, political, and economic contexts. The emphasis is still on the "deviant" and the "problems" he presents to himself and others, not on the society within which he emerges and operates.

I examined 16 textbooks in the field of "deviance," eight of them readers, to determine the state of the field. (They are preceded by an asterisk in the bibliography.) Theoretically, eight take the labelling-interactionist approach; three more tend to lean to that approach; four others argue for other orientations (anomie, structural-functional, etc.) or, among the readers, have an "eclectic" approach; and one (McCaghy, et al., 1968) is a collection of biographical and other statements by "deviants" themselves, and thus may not be said to have a theoretical approach (although, as we shall see, the selection of the types of statements and "deviants" still implies an orientation and viewpoint). A careful examination of these textbooks revealed a number of ideological biases. These biases became apparent as much from what these books leave unsaid and unexamined, as from what they do say. The field of the sociology of deviance, as exemplified in these books, contains three important theoretical and political biases.

1. All writers, especially those of the labelling school, either state explicitly or imply that one of their main concerns is to *humanize* and *normalize*

the "deviant," to show that he is essentially no different from us. But by the very emphasis on the "deviant" and his identity problems and sub-culture, the opposite effect may have been achieved. The persisting use of the label "deviant" to refer to the people we are considering is an indi-cation of the feeling that these people are indeed different.

2. By the overwhelming emphasis on the "dramatic" nature of the usual types of "deviance"—prostitution, homosexuality, juvenile delin-quency, and others—we have neglected to examine other, more serious and harmful forms of "deviance." I refer to *covert institutional violence* (defined and discussed below) which leads to such things as poverty and exploitation, the war in Vietnam, unjust tax laws, racism and sexism, and so on, which cause psychic and material suffering for many Americans, black and white, men and women.

3. Despite explicit statements by these authors of the importance of *power* in the designation of what is "deviant," in their substantive analyses they show a profound unconcern with power and its implications. The really powerful, the upper classes and the power elite, those Gouldner (1968) calls the "top dogs," are left essentially unexamined by these sociologists of deviance.

◉ I.

Always implicit, and frequently explicit, is the aim of the labelling school to humanize and normalize the "deviant." Two statements by Becker and Matza are representative of this sentiment.

> In the course of our work and for who knows what private reasons, we fall into deep sympathy with the people we are studying, so that while the rest of society views them as unfit in one or another respect for the deference ordinarily accorded a fellow citizen, we believe that they are at least as good as anyone else, more sinned against than sinning (Becker, 1967:100–101).

> The growth of the sociological view of deviant phenomena involved, as major phases, the replacement of a correctional stance by an *appreciation* of the deviant subject, the tacit purging of a conception of pathology by a new stress on human *diversity,* and the erosion of a simple distinction

between deviant and conventional phenomena, resulting from intimate familiarity of the world as it is, which yielded a more sophisticated view stressing *complexity* (Matza, 1969:10).

For a number of reasons, however, the opposite effect may have been achieved; and "deviants" still seem different. I began to suspect this reverse effect from the many essays and papers I read while teaching the "deviance" course. The clearest example is the repeated use of the word "tolerate." Students would write that we must not persecute homosexuals, prostitutes, mental patients, and others, that we must be "tolerant" of them. But one tolerates only those one considers less than equal, morally inferior, and weak; those equal to oneself, one accepts and respects; one does not merely allow them to exist, one does not "tolerate" them.

The repeated assertion that "deviants" are "at least as good as anyone else" may raise doubts that this is in fact the case, or that we believe it. A young woman who grew up in the South in the 1940's and 1950's told Quinn (1954:146): "'You know, I think from the fact that I was told so often that I must treat colored people with consideration, I got the feeling that I could mistreat them if I wanted to.'" Thus with "deviants," if in fact they are as good as we are, we would not need to remind everyone of this fact; we would take it for granted and proceed from there. But our assertions that "deviants" are not different may raise the very doubts we want to dispel. Moreover, why would we create a separate field of sociology for "deviants" if there were not something different about them? May it be that even we do not believe our statements and protestations?

The continued use of the word "deviant" (and its variants), despite its invidious distinctions and connotations, also belies our explicit statements on the equality of the people under consideration. To be sure, some of the authors express uneasiness over the term. For example, we are told,

> In our use of this term for the purpose of sociological investigation, we emphasize that we do not attach any value judgement, explicitly or implicitly, either to the word "deviance" or to those describing their behavior or beliefs in this book (McCaghy, *et al.*, 1968:v).

Lofland (1969:2, 9–10) expresses even stronger reservations about the use of the term, and sees clearly the sociological, ethical, and political problems raised by its continued use. Yet, the title of his book is *Deviance and Identity*. Szasz (1970: xxv–xxvi) has urged that we abandon use of the term:

Words have lives of their own. However much sociologists insist that the term "deviant" does not diminish the worth of the person or group so categorized, the implication of inferiority adheres to the word. Indeed, sociologists are not wholly exempt from blame: they describe addicts and homosexuals as deviants, but never Olympic champions or Nobel Prize winners. In fact, the term is rarely applied to people with admired characteristics, such as great wealth, superior skills, or fame—whereas it is often applied to those with despised characteristics, such as poverty, lack of marketable skills, or infamy.

The term "social deviants" . . . does not make sufficiently explicit—as the terms "scapegoat" or "victim" do—that majorities usually categorize persons or groups as "deviant" in order to set them apart as inferior beings and to justify their social control, oppression, persecution, or even complete destruction.

Terms like victimization, persecution, and oppression are more accurate descriptions of what is really happening. But even Gouldner (1968), in a masterful critique of the labelling school, while describing social conflict, calls civil-rights and anti-war protesters "political deviants." He points out clearly that these protesters are resisting openly, not slyly, conditions they abhor. Gouldner is discussing political struggles; oppression and resistance to oppression; conflicts over values, morals, interests, and power; and victimization. Naming such protesters "deviants," even if *political* deviants, is an indication of the deep penetration within our minds of certain prejudices and orientations.

Given the use of the term, the definition and examples of "deviant" reveal underlying sentiments and views. Therefore, it is important that we redefine drastically the entire field, especially since it is a flourishing one: "Because younger sociologists have found deviance such a fertile and exciting field for their own work, and because students share these feelings, deviance promises to become an even more important area of sociological research and theory in the coming years" (Douglas, 1970a:3).

The lists and discussions of "deviant" acts and persons reveal the writers' biases and sentiments. These are acts which, "like robbery, burglary or rape [are] of a simple and dramatic predatory nature. . . ." (The President's Commission on Law Enforcement and the Administration of Justice, in Dinitz, *et al.,* 1969:105). All 16 texts, without exception, concentrate on actions and persons of a "dramatic predatory nature," on "preverts." This is true of both the labelling and other schools. The following are examples from the latter:

> Ten different types of deviant behavior are considered: juvenile delinquency, adult crime, prison sub-cultures, homosexuality, prostitution, suicide, homicide, alcoholism, drug addiction and mental illness (Rushing, 1969: preface).

> Traditionally, in American sociology the study of deviance has focused on criminals, juvenile delinquents, prostitutes, suicides, the mentally ill, drug users and drug addicts, homosexuals, and political and religious radicals (Lefton, et al., 1968:v).

> Deviant behavior is essentially violation of certain types of group norms; a deviant act is behavior which is proscribed in a certain way. [It must be] in a disapproved direction, and of sufficient degree to exceed the tolerance limit of the community . . . [such as] delinquency and crime, prostitution, homosexual behavior, drug addiction, alcoholism, mental disorders, suicide, marital and family maladjustment, discrimination against minority groups, and, to a lesser degree, role problems of old age (Clinard, 1968:28).

Finally, we are told that these are some examples of deviance every society must deal with: ". . . mental illness, violence, theft, and sexual misconduct, as well as . . . other similarly difficult behavior" (Dinitz, et al., 1969:3).

The list stays unchanged with the authors of the labelling school.

> . . . in Part I, "The Deviant Act," I draw rather heavily on certain studies of homicide, embezzlement, "naive" check forgery, suicide and a few other acts . . . in discussing the assumption of deviant identity (Part II) and the assumption of normal identity (Part III), there is heavy reference to certain studies of paranoia, "mental illness" more generally, and Alcoholics Anonymous and Synanon (Lofland, 1969:34).

> Homicide, suicide, alcoholism, mental illness, prostitution, and homosexuality are among the forms of behavior typically called deviant, and they are among the kinds of behavior that will be analyzed (Lofland, 1969:1). Included among my respondents were political radicals of the fat left and the far right, homosexuals, militant blacks, convicts and mental hospital patients, mystics, narcotic addicts, LSD and Marijuana users, illicit drug dealers, delinquent boys, racially mixed couples, hippies, health-food users, and bohemian artists and village eccentrics (Simmons, 1969:10).

Simmons (1969:27, 29, 31) also informs us that in his study of stereo-types of "deviants" held by the public, these are the types he gave to people: homosexuals, beatniks, adulterers, marijuana smokers, political radicals, alcoholics, prostitutes, lesbians, ex-mental patients, atheists, ex-convicts, intellectuals, and gamblers. In Lemert (1967) we find that except for the three introductory (theoretical) chapters, the substantive chapters cover the following topics: alcohol drinking, four; check forgers, three; stuttering, two; and mental illness, two. Matza (1969) offers the following list of "deviants" and their actions that "must be appreciated if one adheres to a naturalistic perspective": paupers, robbers, motorcycle gangs, prostitutes, drug addicts, promiscuous homosexuals, thieving Gypsies, and "free love" Bohemians (1969:16). Finally, Douglas' collection (1970a) covers these forms of "deviance": abortion, nudism, topless barmaids, prostitutes, homo-sexuals, violence (motorcycle and juvenile gangs), shoplifting, and drugs.

The omissions from these lists are staggering. The covert, institutional forms of "deviance" (part II, below) are nowhere to be found. Reading these authors, one would not know that the most destructive use of violence in the last decade has been the war in Vietnam, in which the U.S. has heaped unprecedented suffering on the people and their land; more bombs have been dropped in Vietnam than in the entire World War II. Moreover, the robbery of the corporate world—through tax breaks, fixed prices, low wages, pollution of the environment, shoddy goods, etc.—is passed over in our fascination with "dramatic and predatory" actions. Therefore, we are told that "while they certainly are of no greater social importance to us than such subjects as banking and accounting [or military violence], subjects such as marijuana use and motorcycle gangs are of far greater interest to most of us. While it is only a coincidence that our scientific interests corre-spond with the emotional interest in deviants, it is a happy coincidence and, I believe, one that should be encouraged" (Douglas, 1970a:5). And Matza (1969:17), in commenting on the "appreciative sentiments" of the "natura-listic spirit," elaborates on the same theme: "We do not for a moment wish that we could rid ourselves of deviant phenomena. We are intrigued by them. They are an intrinsic, ineradicable, and vital part of human society."

An effort is made to transcend this limited view and substantive concern with dramatic and predatory forms of "deviance." Becker (1964:3) claims that the new (labelling) deviance no longer studies only "delinquents and drug addicts, though these classical kinds of deviance are still kept under observation." It increases its knowledge "of the processes of deviance by studying physicians, people with physical handicaps, the mentally deficient, and others whose doings were formerly not included in the area." The powerful "deviants" are still left untouched, however. This is still true with another aspect of the new deviance. Becker (1964:4) claims that in the labelling perspective "we focus attention on the ether people involved in the process. We pay attention to the role of the non-deviant as well as that of the deviant." But we see that it is the ordinary non-deviants and the low-level agents of social control who receive attention, not the powerful ones (Gouldner, 1968).

In fact, the emphasis is more on the *subculture* and *identity* of the "deviants" themselves rather than on their oppressors and persecutors. To be sure, in varying degrees all authors discuss the agents of social control, but the fascination and emphasis are on the "deviant" himself. Studies of prisons and prisoners, for example, focus on prison subcultures and prisoner rehabilitation; there is little or no consideration of the social, political, economic, and power conditions which consign people to prisons. Only now are we beginning to realize that most prisoners are *political prisoners*—that their "criminal" actions (whether against individuals, such as robbery, or conscious political acts against the state) result largely from current social and political conditions, and are not the work of "disturbed" and "psychopathic" personalities. This realization came about largely because of the writings of political prisoners themselves: Malcolm X (1965), Eldridge Cleaver (1968), and George Jackson (1970), among others.[3]

In all these books, notably those of the labelling school, the concern is with the "deviant's" subculture and identity: his problems, motives, fellow victims, etc. The collection of memoirs and apologies of "deviants" in their own words (McCaghy, *et al.*, 1968) covets the lives and identities of prevert deviants: "prostitutes, nudists, abortionists, criminals, drug users, homosexuals, the mentally ill, alcoholics, and suicides. For good measure, some "militant deviants" are thrown in: Black Muslims, the SDS, and a conscientious objector. But one wonders about other types of "deviants": how do those who perpetrate the covert institutional violence in our society view themselves? Do they have identity problems? How do they justify their actions? How did the robber barons of the late 19th century steal, fix laws, and buy politicians six days of the week and go to church on Sunday? By what process can people speak of body counts and kill ratios with cool objectivity? On these and similar questions, this book (and all others)[4] provides no answers; indeed, the editors seem unaware that such questions should or could be raised.

Becker (1964), Rubington and Weinberg (1968), Matza (1969), and Bell (1971) also focus on the identity and subculture of "prevert deviants." Matza, in discussing the assumption of "deviant identity," uses as examples, and elaborates upon, thieves and marijuana users. In all these books, there are occasional references to and questions about the larger social and political structure, but these are not explored in any depth; and the emphasis remains on the behavior, identity, and rehabilitation of the "deviant" himself. This bias continues in the latest book which, following the fashions of the times, has chapters on hippies and militant protesters (Bell, 1971).

Even the best of these books, Simmons' *Deviants* (1969), is not free of the overwhelming concentration of the "deviant" and his identity. It is the most sympathetic and balanced presentation of the lives of "deviants": their joys, sorrows, and problems with the straight world and fellow victims. Simmons demystifies the processes of becoming "deviant" and overcoming "deviance." He shows, as well as anyone does, that these victims *are* just like us; and the differences they possess and the suffering they endure are imposed upon them. Ultimately, however, Simmons too falls prey to the three biases shown in the work of others: a) the "deviants" he considers are only of the "prevert" type; b) he focuses mostly on the victim and his identity, not on the persecutors; and c) the persecutors he does discuss are of the middle-level variety, the agents of more powerful others and institutions.

Because of these biases, there is an implicit, but very clear, acceptance by these authors of the current definitions of "deviance." It comes about because they concentrate their attention on those who have been *successfully labelled as "deviant,"* and not on those who break laws, fix laws, violate ethical and moral standards, harm individuals and groups, etc., but who either are able to hide their actions, or, when known, can deflect criticism, labelling, and punishment. The following are typical statements which reveal this bias.

". . . no act committed by members of occupational groups such as white-collar crimes, however unethical, should be considered as crime unless it is punishable by the state in some way" (Clinard, 1968:269). Thus, if some people can manipulate laws so that their unethical and destructive acts are not "crimes," we should cater to their power and agree that they are not criminals.

Furthermore, the essence of the labelling school encourages this bias, despite Becker's (1963:14) assertion that ". . . insofar as a scientist uses 'deviant' to refer to any rule-breaking behavior and takes as his subjects of study only those who have been *labelled* deviant, he will be hampered by the disparities between the two categories." But as the following statements from Becker and others show, this is in fact hat the labelling school does do.

Deviance is "created by society . . . *social groups create deviance by making the rules whose infraction constitutes deviance,* and by applying those rules to particular people and labelling them as outsiders" (Becker, 1963:8–9). Clearly, according to this view, in cases where no group has labelled another, no matter what the other group or individuals have done, there is nothing for the sociologist to study and dissect.

> Rules are not made automatically. Even though a practice may be harmful in an objective sense to the group in which it occurs, the harm needs to be discovered and pointed out. People must be made to feel that something ought to be done about it (Becker, 1963:162).

> What is important for the social analyst is not what people are by his lights or by his standards, but what it is that people construe one another and themselves to be for what reasons and with what consequences (Lofland, 1969:35).

> . . . deviance is in the eyes of the beholder. For deviance to become a social fact, somebody must perceive an act, person, situation, or event as a departure from social norms, must categorize that perception, must report the perception to others, must get them to accept this definition of the situation, and must obtain a response that conforms to this definition. Unless all these requirements are met, deviance as a social fact does not come into being (Rubington and Weinberg, 1968:v).

The implication of these statements is that the sociologist accepts current, successful definitions of what is "deviant" as the only ones worthy of his attention. To be sure, he may argue that those labelled "deviant" are not really different from the rest of us, or that there is no act intrinsically "deviant," erc. By concentrating on cases of successful labelling, however, he will not penetrate beneath the surface to look for other forms of "deviance"—undetected stealing, violence, and destruction. When people are not powerful enough to make the "deviant" label stick on others, we overlook these cases. But is it not as much a *social fact,* even though few of us pay much attention to it, that the corporate economy kills and maims more, is more violent, than any violence committed by the poor (the usual subjects of studies of violence)? By what reasoning and necessity is the "violence" of the poor in the ghettoes more worthy of our attention than the military bootcamps which numb recruits from the horrors of killing the "enemy" ("Oriental human beings," as we learned during the Calley trial)? But because these acts are not labelled "deviant," because they are covert, institutional, and normal, their "deviant" qualities are overlooked and they do not become part of the province of the sociology of deviance. Despite their best liberal intentions, these sociologists seem to perpetuate the very notions they think they debunk, and others of which they are unaware.

❧ II.

As a result of the fascination with "nuts, sluts, and preverts," and their identities and subcultures, little attention has been paid to the unethical, illegal, and destructive actions of powerful individuals, groups, and institutions in our society. Because these actions are carried out quietly in the normal course of events, the sociology of deviance does not consider them as part of its subject matter. This bias is rooted in the very conception and definition of the field. It is obvious when one examines the treatment, or, just as often, lack of it, of the issues of violence, crime, and white-collar crime.

Discussions of violence treat only one type: the "dramatic and predatory" violence committed by individuals (usually the poor and minorities) against persons and property. For example, we read, "crimes involving violence, such as criminal homicide, assault, and forcible rape, are concentrated in the slums" (Clinard, 1968: 123). Wolfgang, an expert on violence, has developed a whole theory on the "subculture of violence" found among the lower classes (e.g., in Rushing, 1969:233–40). And Douglas (1970a: part 4, on violence) includes readings on street gangs and the Hell's Angels. Thompson (1966), in his book on the Hell's Angels, devotes many pages to an exploration of the Angels' social background. In addition, throughout the book, and especially in his concluding chapter, he places the Angels' violence in the perspective of a violent, raping, and destructive society, which refuses to confront the reality of the Angels by distorting, exaggerating, and romanticizing their actions. But Douglas reprints none of these pages; rather, he offers us the chapter where, during a July 4 weekend, the Angels were restricted by the police within a lakeside area, had a drunken weekend, and became a tourist sideshow and circus.

In short, violence is presented as the exclusive property of the poor in the slums, the minorities, street gangs, and motorcycle beasts. But if we take the concept *violence* seriously, we see that much of our political and economic system thrives on it. In violence, a person is *violated*—there is harm done to his person, his psyche, his body, his dignity, his ability to govern himself (Garver, in Rose, 1969:6). Seen in this way, a person can be violated in many ways; physical force is only one of them. As the readings in Rose (1969) show, a person can be violated by a system that denies him a decent job, or consigns him to a slum, or causes him brain damage by near-starvation during childhood, or manipulates him through the mass media, and so on endlessly.

Moreover, we must see that *covert institutional violence* is much more destructive than overt individual violence. We must recognize that people's lives are violated by the very normal and everyday workings of institutions. We do not see such events and situations as violent because they are not dramatic and predatory; they do not make for fascinating reading on the lives of preverts; but they kill, maim, and destroy many more lives than do violent individuals.

Here are some examples. Carmichael and Hamilton (1967:4), in distinguishing between *individual* and *institutional* racism, offer examples of each:

> When white terrorists bomb a black church and kill five black children, that is an act of individual racism, widely deplored by most segments of the society. But when in that same city—Birmingham, Alabama—five hundred black babies die each year because of lack of proper food, shelter, and medical facilities, and thousands more are destroyed and maimed physically, emotionally and intellectually because of conditions of poverty and discrimination in the black community, that is a function of institutional racism.

Surely this is violence; it is caused by normal, quiet workings of institutions run by respectable members of community. Many whites also suffer from the institutional workings a profit-oriented society and economy; poor health, dead-end jobs, slum using, hunger in rural areas, and so are daily realities in their lives. This is surely much worse violence than any committed by the Hell's Angels or street gangs. Only these groups get stigmatized and analyzed by sociologists of deviance, however, while those good people who live in luxurious homes (fixing tax laws for their benefit) off profits derived from exploitative economic system—they are pillars of their community.

Violence is committed daily by the government, very often by lack of action. The same system that enriches businessmen farmers with billions of dollars through farm subsidies cannot be bothered to appropriate a few millions to deal with lead poisoning in the slums. Young children

> . . . get it by eating the sweet-tasting chips of peeling tenement walls, painted a generation ago with leaded paint.
>
> According to the Department of Health, Education, and Welfare, 400,000 children are poisoned each year, about 30,000 in New York City alone. About 3,200 suffer permanent brain damage, 800 go blind or become so mentally retarded that they require hospitalization for the rest of their lives, and approximately 200 die.
>
> The tragedy is that lead poisoning is totally man-made and totally preventable. It is caused by slum housing. And there ate now blood tests that can detect the disease, and medicines to cure it. Only a lack of purpose sentences 200 black children to die each year (Newfield, 1971).[5]

Newfield goes on to report that on May 20, 1971, a Senate-House conference eliminated $5 million from an appropriations budget. In fact, 200 children had been sentenced to death and thousands more to maiming and suffering.

Similar actions of violence are committed daily by the government and corporations; but in these days of misplaced emphasis, ignorance, and manipulation we do not see the destruction inherent in these actions. Instead, we get fascinated, angry, and misled by the violence of the poor and the powerless. We see the violence committed during political rebellions in the ghettoes (called "riots" in order to dismiss them), but all along we ignored the daily violence committed against the ghetto residents by the institutions of the society: schools, hospitals, corporations, the government. Check any of these books on deviance, and see how much of this type of violence is even mentioned, much less explored and described.

It may be argued that some of this violence is (implicitly) recognized in discussions of "white-collar" crime. This is not the case, however. Of the 16 books under consideration, only three pay some attention to white-collar crime (Cohen, 1966; Clinard, 1968; Dinitz, et al., 1969); and of these, only the last covers the issue at some length. Even in these few discussions, however, the focus remains on the *individuals* who commit the actions (on their greediness, lack of morality, etc.), not on the economic and political institutions within which they operate. The selection in Dinitz, et al. (1969: 99–109), from the President's Commission on Law Enforcement and the Administration of Justice, at least three times (pp. 101, 103, 108) argues that white-collar crime is "pervasive," causes "financial burdens" ("probably far greater than those produced by traditional common law theft offenses"), and is generally harmful. At least in these pages, however, there is no investigation of the social, political, and economic conditions which make the pervasiveness, and lenient treatment, of white-collar crime possible.

The bias against examining the structural conditions behind white-collar crime is further revealed in Clinard's suggestions on how to deal with it (in his chapter on "The Prevention of Deviant Behavior"). The only recommendation in three pages of discussion (704–7) is to teach everyone more "respect" for the law. This is a purely moralistic device; it pays no attention to the structural aspects of the problem, to the fact that even deeper than white-collar crime is ingrained a whole network of laws, especially tax laws, administrative policies, and institutions which systematically favor a small minority. More generally, discussions on the prevention of "deviance" and crime do not deal with institutional violence, and what we need to do to stop it.[6]

But there is an obvious explanation for this oversight. The people committing serious white-collar crimes and executing the policies of violent institutions are respectable and responsible individuals, not "deviants;" this is the view of the President's Commission on Law Enforcement and the Administration of Justice.

> Significantly, the Antitrust Division does not feel that lengthy prison sentences are ordinarily called for [for white-collar crimes]. It "rarely recommends jail sentences greater than 6 months—recommendations of 30-day imprisonment are most frequent" (Dinitz, et al., 1969:105).

> Persons who have standing and roots in a community, and are prepared for and engaged in legitimate occupations, can be expected to be particularly susceptible to the threat of criminal prosecution. Criminal proceedings and the imposition of sanctions have a much sharper impact upon those who have not been hardened by previous contact with the criminal justice system (in Dinitz, et al., 1969:104).

At the same time, we are told elsewhere by the Commission that white-collar crime is pervasive and widespread; "criminal proceedings and the imposition of sanctions" do not appear to deter it much.

The executives convicted in the Electrical Equipment case were respectable citizens. "Several were deacons or vestrymen of their churches." The rest also held prestigious positions: president of the Chamber of Commerce, bank director, little-league organizer, and so on (Dinitz, et al.,

1969:107). Moreover, "generally . . . in cases of white-collar crime, neither the corporations as entities nor their responsible officers are invested with deviant characters . . ." (Cohen, 1966:30). Once more, there is quiet acquiescence to his state of affairs. There is no attempt to find out why those who steal millions and whose actions violate lives are not "invested with deviant characters." There is no consideration given to the possibility that, as responsible intellectuals, it is our duty to explore and expose the structural causes for corporate and other serious crimes, which make for much more suffering than does armed robbery. We seem satisfied merely to observe what is, and have the causes unexamined.

In conclusion, let us look at another form of institutional "deviance." The partial publication of the Pentagon papers (June 1971) made public the conscious lying and manipulation by the government to quiet opposition to the Vietnam war. But lying pervades both government and economy. Deceptions and outright lies abound in advertising (see Henry, 1963). During the 1968 campaign, Presidential candidate Nixon blessed us with an ingenious form of deception. McGinniss (1969:149–50) is recording a discussion that took place before Nixon was to appear on live TV (to show spontaneity) the day before the election and answer, unrehearsed, questions phoned in by the viewing audience.

> "I understand Paul Keyes has been sitting up for two days writing questions," Roger Ailes said.
>
> "Well, not quite," Jack Rourke said. He seemed a little embarrassed.
>
> "What is going to happen?"
>
> "Oh . . ."
>
> "It's sort of semiforgery, isn't it?" Ailes said. "Keyes has a bunch of questions Nixon wants to answer. He's written them in advance to make sure they're properly worded. When someone calls in with something similar, they'll use Keyes' question and attribute it to the person who called. Isn't that it?"
>
> "More or less," Jack Rourke said.

In short, despite the supposedly central position of social structure in the sociological enterprise, there is general neglect of it in the field of "deviance." Larger questions, especially if they deal with political and economic issues, are either passed over briefly or overlooked completely. The focus on the actions of "nuts, sluts, and preverts" and the related slight of the criminal and destructive actions of the powerful, are instances of this avoidance.

❂ III.

Most of the authors under discussion mention the importance of power in labelling people "deviant." They state that those who label (the victimizers) are more powerful than those they label (the victims). Writers of the labelling school make this point explicitly. According to Becker (1963:17), "who can . . . force others to accept their rules and what are the causes of their success? This is, of course, a question of political and economic power." Simmons (1969:131) comments that historically, "those in power have used their positions largely to perpetuate and enhance their own advantages through coercing and manipulating the rest of the populace." And Lofland (1969:19) makes the same observation in his opening pages:

> It is in the situation of a very powerful party opposing a very weak one that the powerful party sponsors the *idea* that the weak party is breaking the rules of society. The very concepts of "society" and its "rules" are appropriated by powerful parties and made synonymous with their interests (and, of course, believed in by the naive, e.g., the undergraduate penchant for the phrases "society says. . . ," "society expects. . . ," "society does. . .").

But this insight is not developed. In none of the 16 books is there an extensive discussion of how power operates in the designation of deviance. Instead of a study of power, of its concrete uses in modern, corporate America, we are offered rather fascinating explorations into the identities and subcultures of "deviants," and misplaced emphasis on the middle-level agents of social control. Only Szasz (1961, 1963, and notably 1970) has shown consistently the role of power in one area of "deviance," "mental illness." Through historical and contemporary studies, he has shown that those labelled "mentally ill" (crazy, insane, mad, lunatic) and institutionalized have always been the powerless: women, the poor, peasants, the aged, and others. Moreover, he has exposed repeatedly the means used by powerful individuals and institutions in employing the "mental illness" label to discredit, persecute, and eliminate opponents. In short, he has shown the political element in the "mental illness" game.

In addition, except for Szasz, none of the authors seems to realize that the stigma of prostitution, abortion, and other "deviant" acts unique to women comes about in large part from the powerlessness of women and their status in society. Moreover, to my knowledge, no one has bothered to ask why there have always been women prostitutes for men to satisfy their sexual desires, but very few men prostitutes for women to patronize. The very word *prostitute* we associate with women only, not men. Both men and women have been involved in this "immoral" act, but the stigma has been carried by the women alone.

All 16 books, some more extensively than others, discuss the ideology, modes of operation, and views of *agents of social control,* the people who designate what is to be "deviant" and those who handle the people so designated. As Gouldner (1968) has shown, however, these are the lower and middle level officials, not those who make basic policy and decisions. This bias becomes obvious when we look at the specific agents discussed.

For example, Simmons (1969:18) tells us that some of "those in charge at every level" are the following: "university administrators, patrolmen, schoolmasters, and similar public employees. . . ." Do university administrators and teachers run the schools alone? Are they teaching and enforcing their own unique values? Do teachers alone create the horrible schools in the slums? Are the uniformity, punctuality, and conformity teachers inculcate their own psychological hang-ups, or do they represent the interests of an industrial technological-corporate order? In another sphere, do the police enforce their own laws?

Becker (1963:14) has shown consistent interest in agents of social control. However, a close examination reveals limitations. He discusses "moral crusaders" like those who passed the laws against marijuana. The moral crusader, "the prototype of the rule creator," finds that "the existing rules do not satisfy him because there is some evil which profoundly disturbs him." But the only type of rule creator Becker discusses is the moral crusader, no other. The political manipulators who pass laws to defend their interests and persecute dissenters are not studied. The "unconventional sentimentality," the debunking motif Becker (1964:4–5) sees in the "new deviance" is directed toward the police, the prison officials, the mental hospital personnel, the "average" person and his prejudices. The basic social, political, and economic structure, and those commanding it who guide the labelling and persecution, are left untouched. We have become so accustomed to debunking these low-level agents that we do not even know how to begin to direct our attention to the ruling institutions and groups (for an attempt at such an analysis, see Liazos, 1970).

In a later paper, Becker (1967) poses an apparently insoluble dilemma. He argues that, in studying agents of social control, we are always forced to study subordinates. We can never really get to the top, to those who "really" run the show, for if we study X's superior Y, we find Z above him, and so on endlessly. Everyone has somebody over him, so there is no one at the top. But this is a clever point without substance. In this hierarchy some have more power than others and some are at the top; they may disclaim their position, of course, but it is our job to show otherwise. Some people in this society do have more power than others: parents over children, men over women; some have considerable power over others: top administrators of institutions, for one; and some have a great deal of power, those Domhoff (1967) and others have shown to be the ruling class. It should be our task to explore and describe this hierarchy, its bases of strength, its uses of the "deviant" label to discredit its opponents in order to silence them, and to find ways to eliminate this hierarchy.

Discussions of the police reveal the same misplaced emphasis on lower and middle level agents of social control. In three of the books (Matza, 1969:182–95; Rubington and Weinberg, 1968:ch. 7; Dinitz, et al., 1969:40–47), we are presented with the biases and prejudices of policemen; their modes of operation in confronting delinquents and others; the pressures on them from various quartets; etc. In short, the focus is on the role and psychology of the policeman.

All these issues about the policeman's situation need to be discussed, of course; but there is an even more important issue which these authors avoid. We must ask, who passes the laws the police enforce? Whose agents are they? Why do the police exist? Three excellent papers (Cook, 1968; A. Silver, in Bordua, 1967; T. Hayden, in Rose, 1969) offer some answers to these questions. They show, through a historical description of the origins of police forces, that they have always been used to defend the status quo, the interests of the ruling powers. When the police force was created in England in the early 1800's, it was meant to defend the propertied classes from the "dangerous classes" and the "mob."[7] With the rise of capitalism and industrialism, there was much unrest from the suffering underclass; the professional police were meant to act as a buffer zone for the capitalist elite.

Similarly, in America during the early part of this century, especially in the 1930's, police were used repeatedly to attack striking workers and break their strikes. During the Chicago "police riot" of 1968, the police were not merely acting out their aggressions and frustrations; as Hayden shows, they acted with the consent, direction, and blessing of Mayor Daley and the Democratic party (which party represents the "liberal" wing of the American upper class).

It must be stressed that the police, like all agents of social control, are doing someone else's work. Sometimes they enforce laws and prejudices of "society," the much maligned middle class (on sex, marijuana, etc.); but at other times it is not "society" which gives them their directives, but specific interested groups, even though, often, "society" is manipulated to express its approval of such actions. Above all, we must remember that *"in a fundamentally unjust society, even the most impartial, professional, efficient enforcement of the laws by the police cannot result in justice"* (Cook, 1968:2). More generally, in an unjust and exploitative society, no matter how "humane" agents of social control are, their actions necessarily result in repression.

Broad generalization is another device used by some of these authors to avoid concrete examination of the uses of power in the creation and labelling of "deviance." Clairborne (1971) has called such generalization *"schlock."* The following are some of the tactics he thinks are commonly used in writing popular *schlock* sociology (some sociologists of deviance use similar tactics, as we shall see).

The Plausible Passive:

"New scientific discoveries are being made every day. . . . These new ideas are being put to work more quickly. . . ." [Toffler, in *Future Shock,* is] thereby rather neatly obscuring the fact that scientists and engineers (mostly paid by industry) are making the discoveries and industrialists (often with the aid of public funds) are putting them to work. An alternative to the Plausible Passive is the Elusive Impersonal: "Buildings in New York literally disappear overnight." What Toffler is trying to avoid saying is that contractors and real estate speculators *destroy* buildings overnight (Clairborne, 1971:118).

Rampant Reification, by which "conceptual abstractions are transformed into causal realities," also abounds. Toffler

speaks of the "roaring current of change" as "an elemental force" and of "that great, growling engine of change—technology." Which of course completely begs the question of what fuels the engine and whose hand is on the throttle. One does not cross-examine an elemental force, let alone suggest that it may have been engendered by monopoly profits (especially in defense and aerospace) or accelerated by government incentives (e.g., open or concealed subsidies, low capital gains tax, accelerated depreciation—which Nixon is now seeking to reinstitute) (Clairborne, 1971:118).

There are parallels in the sociology of deviance. Clinard (1968:ch. 4) argues that urbanization and the slum are breeding grounds for "deviant behavior." But these conditions are reified, not examined concretely. He says about urbanization and social change:

> Rapid social and cultural change, disregard for the importance of stability of generations, and untempered loyalties also generally characterize urban life. New ideas are generally welcome, inventions and mechanical gadgets are encouraged, and new styles in such arts as painting, literature, and music are often approved (1968:90).

But the slum, urbanization, and change are not reified entities working out their independent wills. For example, competition, capitalism, and the profit motive—all encouraged by a government controlled by the upper classes—have had something to do with the rise of slums. There is a general process of urbanization, but at given points in history it is fed by, and gives profits to, specific groups. The following are a few historical examples: the land enclosure policies and practices of the English ruling classes in the 17th and 18th centuries; the building of cheap housing in the 19th century by the owners of factory towns; and the profits derived from "urban renewal" (which has destroyed neighborhoods, created even more crowded slums, etc.) by the building of highways, luxury apartments, and stores.

Another favorite theme of *schlock* sociology is that "All Men Are Guilty." That means nothing can be done to change things. There is a variation of this theme in the sociology of deviance when we are told that a) all of us are deviant in some way, b) all of us label some others deviant, and c) "society" labels. Such statements preclude asking concrete questions: does the "deviance" of each of us have equal consequences for others? Does the labelling of each of us stick, and with what results?

For example, Simmons (1969:124) says:

> . . . I strongly suspect that officials now further alienate more culprits than they recruit back into conventional society, and I think they imprison at least as many people in deviance as they rehabilitate. We must remember that, with a sprinkling of exceptions, officials come from, are hired by, and belong to the dominant majority.

Who is that dominant majority? Are they always the numerical majority? Do they control the labelling and correctional process all by themselves? These questions are not raised.

Another case of *schlock* is found in Matza's discussion (lack of it, really) of "Leviathan" (1969, especially ch. 7). It is mentioned as a potent force in the labelling and handling of "deviance." But, vainly, one keeps looking for some exploration into the workings of "Leviathan." It remains a reified, aloof creature. What is it? Who controls it? How does it label? Why? Matza seems content to try to mesmerize us by mentioning it constantly (Leviathan is capitalized throughout); but we are never shown how it operates. It hovers in the background, it punishes, and its presence somehow cowers us into submission. But it remains a reified force whose presence is accepted without close examination.

The preceding examples typify much of what is wrong with the sociology of deviance: the lack of specific analysis of the role of power in the labelling process; the generalizations which, even when true, explain little; the fascination with "deviants"; the reluctance to study the "deviance" of the powerful.

◉ IV.

I want to start my concluding comments with two disclaimers.

a) I have tried to provide some balance and perspective in the field of "deviance," and in doing so I have argued against the exclusive emphasis on *nuts, sluts,* and *preverts* and their identities and subcultures. I do not mean, however, that the usually considered forms of "deviance" are unworthy of our attention. Suicide, prostitution, madness, juvenile delinquency, and others *are* with us; we cannot ignore them. People do suffer when labelled and treated as "deviant" (in *this* sense, "deviants" *are* different from conformists). Rather, I want to draw attention to phenomena which also belong to the field of "deviance."[8]

b) It is because the sociology of deviance, especially the labelling approach, contains important, exciting, and revealing insights, because it tries to humanize the "deviant," and because it is popular, that it is easy to overlook some of the basic ideological biases still pervading the field. For this reason, I have tried to explore and detail some of these biases. At the same time, however, I do not mean to dismiss the contributions of the field as totally negative and useless. In fact, in my teaching I have been using two of the books discussed here, Simmons (1969) and Rubington and Weinberg (1968).

The argument can be summarized briefly. (1) We should not study only, or predominantly, the popular and dramatic forms of "deviance." Indeed, we should banish the concept of "deviance" and speak of oppression, conflict, persecution, and suffering. By focusing on the dramatic forms, as we do now, we perpetuate most people's beliefs and impressions that such "deviance" is the basic cause of many of our troubles, that these people (criminals, drug addicts, political dissenters, and others) are the real "troublemakers"; and, necessarily, we neglect conditions of inequality, powerlessness, institutional violence, and so on, which lie at the bases of our tortured society. (2) Even when we do study the popular forms of "deviance," we do not avoid blaming the victim for his fate; the continued use of the term "deviant" is one due to this blame. Nor have we succeeded in normalizing him; the focus on the "deviant" himself, on his identity and subculture, has tended to confirm the popular prejudice that he is different.

Endnotes

[1]Bend and Vogenfanger (1964) examined social problems textbooks of the early 1960's; they found there was little theory or emphasis on social structure in them.

[2]What I say below applies to the "labelling-interactionist" school of deviance of Becker, Lemert, Erikson, Matza, and others: to a large degree, however, most of my comments also apply to the other schools.

[3]The first draft of this paper was completed in July, 1971. The killing of George Jackson at San Quentin on August 21, 1971, which many people see as a political murder, and the Attica prisoner rebellion of early September, 1971, only strengthen the argument about political prisoners. Two things became clear: a) Not only a few "radicals," but many prisoners (if not a majority) see their fate as the outcome of political forces and decisions, and themselves as political prisoners (see Fraser, 1971). Robert Chrisman's argument (in Fraser, 1971) points to such a conclusion clearly: "To maintain that all black offenders are, by their actions, politically correct, is dangerous romanticism. Black antisocial behavior must be seen in and of its own terms and corrected for enhancement of the black community." But there is a political aspect, for black prisoners' condition "derives from the political inequity of black people in America. A black prisoner's crime may or may not have been a political action against the state, but the state's action against him is always political." I would stress that the same is true of most white prisoners, for they come mostly from the exploited poorer

classes and groups. b) The state authorities, the political rulers, by their deeds if not their words, see such prisoners as political men and threats. The death of George Jackson, and the brutal crushing of the Attica rebellion, attest to the authorities' realization, and fear, that here were no mere riots with prisoners letting off steam, but authentic political actions, involving groups and individuals conscious of their social position and exploitation.

[4]With the exception of E. C. Hughes, in Becker (1964).

[5]As Gittlin and Hollander (1970) show, the children of poor whites also suffer from lead poisoning.

[6]Investigation of the causes and prevention of institutional violence would probably be biting the hand that feeds the sociologist, for we read that the government and foundations (whose money comes from corporate profits) have supported research on "deviant behavior," especially its prevention. "This has meant particularly that the application of sociological theory to research has increased markedly in such areas as delinquency, crime, mental disorder, alcoholism, drug addiction and discrimination" (Clinard, 1968:742). That's where the action is, not on white-collar crime, nor on the covert institutional violence of the government and economy.

[7]See Rude (1966) on the role of mobs of poor workers and peasants in 18th and 19th century England and France.

[8]The question of "what deviance is to the deviant" Gordon Fellman, private communication), not what the labelling, anomie, and other schools, or the present radical viewpoint say about such a person, is not dealt with here. I avoid this issue not because I think it unimportant, rather because I want to concentrate on the political, moral, and social issues raised by the biases of those presently writing about the "deviant."

References

Becker, Howard S. 1963. Outsiders. New York: Free Press.

_____. 1964. (ed.) The Other Side. New York: Free Press.

_____. 1967. "Whose side are we on?" Social Problems 14: 239–247 (reprinted in Douglas, 1970a, 99–111; references to this reprint).

Bell, Robert R. 1971. Social Deviance: A Substantive Analysis. Homewood, Illinois: Dorset.

Bend, Emil and Martin Vogenfanger. 1964. "A new look at Mills critique," in Mass Society in Crisis. Bernard Rosenberg, Israel Gerver, F. William Howton (eds.). New York: Macmillan, 1964, 111–122.

Bordua, David (ed.) 1967. The Police. New York: Wiley.

Carmichael, Stokeley and Charles V. Hamilton. 1967. Black Power. New York: Random House.

Clairborne, Robert. 1971. "Future schlock." The Nation, Jan. 25, 117–120.

Cleaver, Eldridge. 1968. Soul On Ice. New York: McGraw-Hill.

Clinard, Marshall B. 1968. Sociology of Deviant Behavior. (3rd ed.) New York: Holt, Rinehart, and Winston.

Cohen, Albert K. 1966. Deviance and Control. Englewood Cliffs, N.J.: Prentice-Hall.

Cook, Robert M. 1968 "The police." The Bulletin of the American Independent Movement (New Haven, Conn.), 3:6, 1–6.

Dinitz, Simon, Russell R. Dynes, and Alfred C. Clarke (eds.) 1969. Deviance. New York: Oxford University Press.

Domhoff, William G. 1967. Who Rules America? Englewood Cliffs, NJ.: Prentice-Hall.

Douglas, Jack D. 1970a. (ed.) Observations of Deviance. New York: Random House.

_____. 1970b (ed.) Deviance and Respectability: The Social Construction of Moral Meanings. New York: Basic Books.

Fraser, C. Gerald. 1971. "Black prisoners finding new view of themselves as political prisoners:" New York Times, Sept. 16.

Gittlin, Todd and Nanci and Hollander. 1970. Uptown: Poor Whites in Chicago. New York: Harper and Row.

Gouldner, Alvin W. 1968. "The sociologist as partisan: Sociology and the welfare state." American Sociologist 3:2, 103–116.

Henry, Jules. 1963. Culture Against Man. New York: Random House.

Jackson, George. 1970. Soledad Brother. New York: Bantam Books.

Lefton, Mark, J. K. Skipper, and C. H. McCaghy (eds.) 1968. Approaches to Deviance. New York: Appleton-Century-Crofts.

Lemert, Edwin M. 1967. Human Deviance, Social Problems, and Social Control. Englewood Cliffs, N.J.: Prentice-Hall.

Liazos, Alexander. 1970. Processing for Unfitness: socialization of "emotionally disturbed" lower-class boys into the mass society. Ph.D. dissertation, Brandeis University.

Lofland, John. 1969. Deviance and Identity. Englewood Cliffs, NJ.: Prentice-Hall.

McCaghy, Charles H., J. K. Skipper, and M. Lefton (eds.) 1968. In Their Own Behalf: Voices from the Margin. New York: Appleton-Century-Crofts.

McGinniss, Joe. 1969. The Selling of the President, 1968. New York: Trident.

Malcolm X. 1965. The Autobiography of Malcolm X. New York: Grove.

Matza, David. 1969. Becoming Deviant. Englewood Cliffs, NJ.: Prentice-Hall.

Mills, C. Wright. 1943. "The professional ideology of social pathologists." American Journal of Sociology 49:165–180.

Newfield, Jack. 1971. "Let them eat lead." New York Times, June 16, p. 45.

Quinn, Olive W. 1954. "The transmission of racial attitudes among white southerners." Social Forces 33:1, 41–47 (reprinted in E. Schuler, et al., eds., Readings in Sociology, 2nd ed., New York: Crowell, 1960, 140–150).

Rose, Thomas (ed.) 1969. Violence in America. New York: Random House.

Rubington, Earl and M. S. Weinberg (eds.). 1968. Deviance: The Interactionist Perspective. New York: Macmillan.

Rude, George. 1966. The Crowd in History. New York: Wiley.

Rushing, William A. (ed.) 1969. Deviant Behavior and Social Processes. Chicago: Rand McNally.

Simmons, J. L. 1969. Deviants. Berkeley, Cal.: Glendessary.

Szasz, Thomas S. 1961. The Myth of Mental Illness. New York: Harper and Row.

————. 1963. Law, Liberty, and Psychiatry. New York: Macmillan.

————. 1970. The Manufacture of Madness. New York: Harper and Row.

Thompson, Hunter S. 1966. Hell's Angels. New York: Ballantine.

◉ ◉ ◉

Questions

1. According to the author, what role has the "labeling perspective" played in the study of other forms of deviance besides delinquency and drug addiction?

2. What does the author mean when he contends that all deviance is ultimately political in nature?

3. Alexander Liazos wrote this article in 1972. Based on the selection of topics in your deviance course, do you think his claim that the economic and political elite ignore deviance still applies?

4. If you think Liazos's claim about the economic and political elite no longer applies, what has caused changes in the topics studied in deviance courses? If you believe that his assertion still applies, explain your reasoning.

Stigma and Social Identity

ERVING GOFFMAN

In this reading, Erving Goffman introduces the concept of stigma—that notion that certain traits are deeply discrediting to individuals. He addresses how the concept of stigma can be conceptualized, how stigma affects the stigmatized person's sense of self and identity, and how "normal" individuals interact with stigmatized individuals. Goffman's concept of stigma, and the related stigma-management strategies he describes, is often perceived as the basis for what's known as the symbolic interactionist theoretical framework in sociology.

. . .

☺ Preliminary Conceptions

Society establishes the means of categorizing persons and the complement of attributes felt to be ordinary and natural for members of each of these categories. Social settings establish the categories of persons likely to be encountered there. The routines of social intercourse in established settings allow us to deal with anticipated others without special attention or thought. When a stranger comes into our presence, then, first appearances are likely to enable us to anticipate his category and attributes, his "social identity"— to use a term that is better than "social status" because personal attributes such as "honesty" are involved, as well as structural ones, like "occupation."

We lean on these anticipations that we have, transforming them into normative expectations, into righteously presented demands.

Typically, we do not become aware that we have made these demands or aware of what they are until an active question arises as to whether or not they will be fulfilled. It is then that we are likely to realize that all along we

"Stigma and Social Identity," by Erving Goffman, reprinted from *Stigma: Notes on the Management of Spoiled Identity*, 1963, pp. 2-19. Copyright © 1963 by Simon and Schuster, Inc.

had been making certain assumptions as to what the individual before us ought to be. Thus, the demands we make might better be called demands made "in effect," and the character we impute to the individual might better be seen as an imputation made in potential retrospect—a characterization "in effect," a *virtual social identity*. The category and attributes he could in fact be proved to possess will be called his *actual social identity*.

While the stranger is present before us, evidence can arise of his possessing an attribute that makes him different from others in the category of persons available for him to be, and of a less desirable kind—in the extreme, a person who is quite thoroughly bad, or dangerous, or weak. He is thus reduced in our minds from a whole and usual person to a tainted, discounted one. Such an attribute is a stigma, especially when its discrediting effect is very extensive; sometimes it is also called a failing, a shortcoming, a handicap. It constitutes a special discrepancy between virtual and actual social identity. Note that there are other types of discrepancy between virtual and actual social identity, for example the kind that causes us to reclassify an individual from one socially anticipated category to a different but equally well-anticipated one, and the kind that causes us to alter our estimation of the individual upward. Note, too, that not all undesirable attributes are at issue, but only those which are incongruous with our stereotype of what a given type of individual should be.

The term stigma, then, will be used to refer to an attribute that is deeply discrediting, but it should be seen that a language of relationships, not attributes, is really needed. An attribute that stigmatizes one type of possessor can confirm the usualness of another, and therefore is neither creditable nor discreditable as a thing in itself. For example, some jobs in America cause holders without the expected college education to conceal this fact; other jobs, however, can lead the few of their holders who have a higher education to keep this a secret, lest they be marked as failures and outsiders. Similarly, a middle class boy may feel no compunction in being seen going to the library; a professional criminal, however, writes:

> I can remember before now on more than one occasion, for instance, going into a public library near where I was living, and looking over my shoulder a couple of times before I actually went in just to make sure no one who knew me was standing about and seeing me do it.[1]

So, too, an individual who desires to fight for his country may conceal a physical defect, lest his claimed physical status be discredited; later, the same individual, embittered and trying to get out of the army, may succeed in gaining admission to the army hospital, where he would be discredited if discovered in not really having an acute sickness.[2] A stigma, then, is really a special kind of relationship between attribute and stereotype, although I don't propose to continue to say so, in part because there are important attributes that almost everywhere in our society are discrediting.

The term stigma and its synonyms conceal a double perspective: does the stigmatized individual assume his differentness is known about already or is evident on the spot, or does he assume it is neither known about by those present nor immediately perceivable by them? In the first case one deals with the plight of the *discredited,* in the second with that of the *discreditable.* This is an important difference, even though a particular stigmatized individual is likely to have experience with both situations. I will begin with the situation of the discredited and move on to the discreditable but not always separate the two.

Three grossly different types of stigma may be mentioned. First there are abominations of the body—the various physical deformities. Next there are blemishes of individual character perceived as weak will, domineering or unnatural passions, treacherous and rigid beliefs, and dishonesty, these being inferred from a known record of, for example, mental disorder, imprisonment, addiction, alcoholism, homosexuality, unemployment, suicidal attempts, and radical political behavior. Finally there are the tribal stigma of race, nation, and religion, these being stigma that can be transmitted through lineages and equally contaminate all members of a family.[3] In all of these various instances of stigma, however, including those the Greeks had in mind, the same sociological features are found: an individual who might have been received easily in ordinary social intercourse possesses a trait that can obtrude itself upon attention and turn those of us whom he meets away from him, breaking the claim that his other attributes have on us. He possesses a stigma, an undesired differentness from what we had anticipated. We and those who do not depart negatively from the particular expectations at issue I shall call the *normals.*

The attitudes we normals have toward a person with a stigma, and the actions we take in regard to him, are well known, since these responses are what benevolent social action is designed to soften and ameliorate. By definition, of course, we believe the person with a stigma is not quite human. On this assumption we exercise varieties of discrimination, through which we effectively, if often unthinkingly, reduce his life chances. We construct a stigma-theory, an ideology to explain his inferiority and account for the danger he represents, sometimes rationalizing an animosity based on other differences, such as those of social class.[4] We use specific stigma terms such as cripple, bastard, moron in our daily discourse as a source of metaphor and imagery, typically without giving thought to the original meaning.[5] We tend to impute a wide range of imperfections on the basis of the original one,[6] and at the same time to impute some desirable but undesired attributes, often of a supernatural cast, such as "sixth sense," or "understanding":[7]

> For some, there may be a hesitancy about touching or steering the blind, while for others, the perceived failure to see may be generalized into a gestalt of disability, so that the individual shouts at the blind as if they were deaf or attempts to lift them as if they were crippled. Those confronting the blind may have a whole range of belief that is anchored in the stereotype. For instance, they may think they are subject to unique judgment, assuming the blinded individual draws on special channels of information unavailable to others.[8]

Further, we may perceive his defensive response to his situation as a direct expression of his defect, and then see both defect and response as just retribution for something he or his parents or his tribe did, and hence a justification of the way we treat him.[9]

Now turn from the normal to the person he is normal against. It seems generally true that members of a social category may strongly support a standard of judgment that they and others agree does not directly apply to them. Thus it is that a businessman may demand womanly behavior from females or ascetic behavior from monks, and not construe himself as someone who ought to realize either of these styles of conduct. The distinction is between realizing a norm and merely supporting it. The issue of stigma does not arise here, but only where there is some expectation on all sides that those in a given category should not only support a particular norm but also realize it.

Also, it seems possible for an individual to fail to live up to what we effectively demand of him, and yet be relatively untouched by this failure; insulated by his alienation, protected by identity beliefs of his own, he feels that he is a full-fledged normal human being, and that we are the ones who are not quite human. He bears a stigma but does not seem to be impressed or repentant about doing so. This possibility is celebrated in exemplary tales about Mennonites, Gypsies, shameless scoundrels, and very orthodox Jews.

In America at present, however, separate systems of honor seem to be on the decline. The stigmatized individual tends to hold the same beliefs about identity that we do; this is a pivotal fact. His deepest feelings about what he is may be his sense of being a "normal person," a human being like anyone else, a person, therefore, who deserves a fair chance and a fair break.[10] (Actually, however phrased, he bases his claims not on what he thinks is due *everyone,* but only everyone of a selected social category into which he unquestionably fits, for example, anyone of his age, sex, profession, and so forth.) Yet he may perceive, usually quite correctly, that whatever others profess, they do not really "accept" him and are not ready to make contact with him on "equal grounds."[11] Further, the standards he has incorporated from the wider society equip him to be intimately alive to what others see as his failing, inevitably causing him, if only for moments, to agree that he does indeed fall short of what he really ought to be. Shame becomes a central possibility, arising from the individual's perception of one of his own attributes as being a defiling thing to possess, and one he can readily see himself as not possessing.

The immediate presence of normals is likely to reinforce this split between self-demands and self, but in fact self-hate and self-derogation can also occur when only he and a mirror are about:

> When I got up at last . . . and had I learned to walk again, one day I took a hand glass and went to a long mirror to look at myself, and I went alone. I didn't want anyone . . . to know how I felt when I saw myself for the first time. But there was no noise, no outcry; I didn't scream with rage when I saw myself. I just felt numb. That person in the mirror *couldn't* be me. I felt inside like a healthy, ordinary, lucky person—oh, not like the one in the mirror! Yet when I turned my face to the mirror there were my own eyes looking back, hot with shame . . . when I did not cry or make any sound, it became impossible that I should speak of it to anyone, and the confusion and the panic of my discovery were locked inside me then and there, to be faced alone, for a very long time to come.[12]

> Over and over I forgot what I had seen in the mirror. It could not penetrate into the interior of my mind and become an integral part of me. I felt as if it had nothing to do with me; it was only a disguise. But it was not the kind of disguise which is put on voluntarily by the person who wears it, and which is intended to confuse other people as to one's identity. My disguise had been put on me without my consent or knowledge like the ones in fairy tales, and it was I myself who was confused by it, as to my own identity. I looked in the mirror, and was horror-struck because I did not recognize myself. In the place where I was standing, with that persistent romantic elation in me, as if I were a favored fortunate person to whom everything was possible, I saw a stranger, a little, pitiable, hideous figure,

and a face that became, as I stared at it, painful and blushing with shame. It was only a disguise, but it was on me, for life. It was there, it was there, it was real. Every one of those encounters was like a blow on the head. They left me dazed and dumb and senseless everytime, until slowly and stubbornly my robust persistent illusion of well-being and of personal beauty spread all through me again, and I forgot the irrelevant reality and was all unprepared and vulnerable again.[13]

The central feature of the stigmatized individual's situation in life can now be stated. It is a question of what is often, if vaguely, called "acceptance." Those who have dealings with him fail to accord him the respect and regard which the uncontaminated aspects of his social identity have led them to anticipate extending, and have led him to anticipate receiving; he echoes this denial by finding that some of his own attributes warrant it.

How does the stigmatized person respond to his situation? In some cases it will be possible for him to make a direct attempt to correct what he sees as the objective basis of his failing, as when a physically deformed person undergoes plastic surgery, a blind person eye treatment, an illiterate remedial education, a homosexual psychotherapy. (Where such repair is possible, what often results is not the acquisition of fully normal status, but a transformation of self from someone with a particular blemish into someone with a record of having corrected a particular blemish.) Here proneness to "victimization" is to be cited, a result of the stigmatized person's exposure to fraudulent servers selling speech correction, skin lighteners, body stretchers, youth restorers (as in rejuvenation through fertilized egg yolk treatment), cures through faith, and poise in conversation. Whether a practical technique or fraud is involved, the quest, often secret, that results provides a special indication of the extremes to which the stigmatized can be willing to go, and hence the painfulness of the situation that leads them to these extremes. One illustration may be cited:

> Miss Peck [a pioneer New York social worker for the hard of hearing] said that in the early days the quacks and get-rich-quick medicine men who abounded saw the League [for the hard of hearing] as their happy hunting ground, ideal for the promotion of magnetic head caps, miraculous vibrating machines, artificial eardrums, blowers, inhalers, massagers, magic oils, balsams, and other guaranteed, sure-fire, positive, and permanent cure-alls for incurable deafness. Advertisements for such hokum (until the 1920's when the American Medical Association moved in with an investigation campaign) beset the hard of hearing in the pages of the daily press, even in reputable magazines.[14]

The stigmatized individual can also attempt to correct his condition indirectly by devoting much private effort to the mastery of areas of activity ordinarily felt to be closed on incidental and physical grounds to one with his shortcoming. This is illustrated by the lame person who learns or re-learns to swim, ride, play tennis, or fly an airplane, or the blind person who becomes expert at skiing and mountain climbing.[15] Tortured learning may be associated, of course, with the tortured performance of what is learned, as when an individual, confined to a wheelchair, manages to take to the dance floor with a girl in some kind of mimicry of dancing.[16] Finally, the person with a shameful differentness can break with what is called reality, and obstinately attempt to employ an unconventional interpretation of the character of his social identity.

The stigmatized individual is likely to use his stigma for "secondary gains," as an excuse for ill success that has come his way for other reasons:

> For years the scar, harelip or misshapen nose has been looked on as a handicap, and its importance in the social and emotional adjustment is unconsciously all embracing. It is the "hook" on which the patient has hung all inadequacies, all dissatisfactions, all procrastinations and all unpleasant duties of social life, and he has come to depend on it not only as a reasonable escape from competition but as a protection from social responsibility.
>
> When one removes this factor by surgical repair, the patient is cast adrift from the more or less acceptable emotional protection it has offered and soon he finds, to his surprise and discomfort, that life is not all smooth sailing even for those with unblemished, "ordinary" faces. He is unprepared to cope with this situation without the support of a "handicap," and he may turn to the less simple, but similar, protection of the behavior patterns of neurasthenia, hysterical conversion, hypochondriasis or the acute anxiety states.[17]

He may also see the trials he has suffered as a blessing in disguise especially because of what it is felt that suffering can teach one about life and people:

> But now, far away from the hospital experience, I can evaluate what I have learned. [A mother permanently disabled by polio writes.] For it wasn't only suffering: it was also learning through suffering. I know my awareness of people has deepened and increased, that those who are close to me can count on me to turn all my mind and heart and attention to their problems. I could not have learned *that* dashing all over a tennis court.[18]

Correspondingly, he can come to re-assess the limitations of normals, as a multiple sclerotic suggests:

> Both healthy minds and healthy bodies may be crippled. The fact that "normal" people can get around, can see, can hear, doesn't mean that they are seeing or hearing. They can be very blind to the things that spoil their happiness, very deaf to the pleas of others for kindness; when I think of them I do not feel any more crippled or disabled than they. Perhaps in some small way I can be the means of opening their eyes to the beauties around us: things like a warm handclasp, a voice that is anxious to cheer, a spring breeze, music to listen to, a friendly nod. These people are important to me, and I like to feel that I can help them.[19]

And a blind writer:

> That would lead immediately to the thought that there are many occurrences which can diminish satisfaction in living far more effectively than blindness, and that lead would be an entirely healthy one to take. In this light, we can perceive, for instance, that some inadequacy like the inability to accept human love, which can effectively diminish satisfaction of living almost to the vanishing point, is far more a tragedy than blindness. But it is unusual for the man who suffers from such a malady even to know he has it and self pity is, therefore, impossible for him.[20]

And a cripple:

> As life went on, I learned of many, many different kinds of handicap, not only the physical ones, and I began to realize that the words of the crippled girl in the extract above [words of bitterness] could just as well have been spoken by young women who had never needed crutches, women who felt inferior and different because of ugliness, or inability to bear children, or helplessness in contacting people, or many other reasons.[21]

The responses of the normal and of the stigmatized that have been considered so far are ones which can occur over protracted periods of time and in isolation from current contact between normals and stigmatized.[22] This book, however, is specifically concerned with the issue of "mixed contacts"—the moments when stigmatized and normal are in the same "social situation," that is, in one another's immediate physical presence, whether in a conversation-like encounter or in the mere co-presence of an unfocused gathering.

The very anticipation of such contacts can of course lead normals and the stigmatized to arrange life so as to avoid them. Presumably this will have larger consequences for the stigmatized, since more arranging will usually be necessary on their part:

> Before her disfigurement [amputation of the distal half of her nose] Mrs. Dover, who lived with one of her two married daughters, had been an independent, warm and friendly woman who enjoyed traveling, shopping, and visiting her many relatives. The disfigurement of her face, however, resulted in a definite alteration in her way of living. The first two or three years she seldom left her daughter's home, preferring to remain in her room or to sit in the backyard. "I was heartsick," she said; "the door had been shut on my life."[23]

Lacking the salutary feed-back of daily social intercourse with others, the self-isolate can become suspicious, depressed, hostile, anxious, and bewildered. Sullivan's version may be cited:

> The awareness of inferiority means that one is unable to keep out of consciousness the formulation of some chronic feeling of the worst sort of insecurity, and this means that one suffers anxiety and perhaps even something worse, if jealousy is really worse than anxiety. The fear that others can disrespect a person because of something he shows means that he is always insecure in his contact with other people; and this insecurity arises, not from mysterious and somewhat disguised sources, as a great deal of our anxiety does, but from something which he knows he cannot fix. Now that represents an almost fatal deficiency of the self-system, since the self is unable to disguise or exclude a definite formulation that reads, "I am inferior. Therefore people will dislike me and I cannot be secure with them."[24]

When normals and stigmatized do in fact enter one another's immediate presence, especially when they there attempt to sustain a joint conversational encounter, there occurs one of the primal scenes of sociology; for, in many cases, these moments will be the ones when the causes and effects of stigma must be directly confronted by both sides.

The stigmatized individual may find that he feels unsure of how we normals will identify him and receive him.[25] An illustration may be cited from a student of physical disability:

> Uncertainty of status for the disabled person obtains over a wide range of social interactions in addition to that of employment. The blind, the ill, the deaf, the crippled can never be sure what the attitude of a new acquaintance will be, whether it will be rejective or accepting, until the contact has been made. This is exactly the position of the adolescent, the light-skinned

Negro, the second generation immigrant, the socially mobile person and the woman who has entered a predominantly masculine occupation.[26]

This uncertainty arises not merely from the stigmatized individual's not knowing which of several categories he will be placed in, but also, where the placement is favorable, from his knowing that in their hearts the others may be defining him in terms of his stigma:

> And I always feel this with straight people—that whenever they're being nice to me, pleasant to me, all the time really, underneath they're only assessing me as a criminal and nothing else. It's too late for me to be any different now to what I am, but I still feel this keenly, that that's their only approach, and they're quite incapable of accepting me as anything else.[27]

Thus in the stigmatized arises the sense of not knowing what the others present are "really" thinking about him.

Further, during mixed contacts, the stigmatized individual is likely to feel that he is "on,"[28] having to be self-conscious and calculating about the impression he is making, to a degree, and in areas of conduct which he assumes others are not.

Also, he is likely to feel that the usual scheme of interpretation for everyday events has been undermined. His minor accomplishments, he feels, may be assessed as signs of remarkable and noteworthy capacities in the circumstances. A professional criminal provides an illustration:

> "You know, it's really amazing you should read books like this, I'm staggered I am. I should've thought you'd read paper-backed thrillers, things with lurid covers, books like that. And here you are with Claud Cockburn, Hugh Klare, Simone de Beauvoir, and Lawrence Durrell!"
>
> You know, he didn't see this as an insulting remark at all: in fact, I think he thought he was being honest in telling me how mistaken he was. And that's exactly the sort of patronizing you get from straight people if you're a criminal. "Fancy that!" they say. "In some ways you're just like a human being!" I'm not kidding, it makes me want to choke the bleeding life out of them.[29]

A blind person provides another illustration:

> His once most ordinary deeds—walking nonchalantly up the street, locating the peas on his plate, lighting a cigarette—are no longer ordinary. He becomes an unusual person. If he performs them with finesse and assurance they excite the same kind of wonderment inspired by a magician who pulls rabbits out of hats.[30]

At the same time, minor failings or incidental impropriety may, he feels, be interpreted as a direct expression of his stigmatized differentness. Ex-mental patients, for example, are sometimes afraid to engage in sharp interchanges with spouse or employer because of what a show of emotion might be taken as a sign of. Mental defectives face a similar contingency:

> It also happens that if a person of low intellectual ability gets into some sort of trouble the difficulty is more or less automatically attributed to "mental defect" whereas if a person of "normal intelligence" gets into a similar difficulty, it is not regarded as symptomatic of anything in particular.[31]

A one-legged girl, recalling her experience with sports, provides other illustrations:

> Whenever I fell, out swarmed the women in droves, clucking and fretting like a bunch of bereft mother hens. It was kind of them, and in retrospect I appreciate their solicitude, but at the time I resented and was greatly embarrassed by their interference. For they assumed that no routine hazard to skating—no stick or stone—upset my flying wheels. It was a foregone conclusion that I fell because I was a poor, helpless cripple.[32]

> Not one of them shouted with outrage, "That dangerous wild bronco threw her!"—which, God forgive, he did technically. It was like a horrible ghostly visitation of my old roller-skating days. All the good people lamented in chorus, "That poor, poor girl fell off!"[33]

When the stigmatized person's failing can be perceived by our merely directing attention (typically, visual) to him—when, in short, he is a discredited, not discreditable, person—he is likely to feel that to be present among normals nakedly exposes him to invasions of privacy,[34] experienced most pointedly perhaps when children simply stare at him.[35] This displeasure in being exposed can be increased by the conversations strangers may feel free to strike up with him, conversations in which they express what he takes to be morbid curiosity about his condition, or in which they proffer help that he does not need or want.[36] One might add that there are certain classic formulae for these kinds of conversations: "My dear girl, how did you get your quiggle"; "My great uncle had a quiggle, so I feel I know all about your problem"; "You know I've always said that Quiggles are good family men and look after their own poor"; "Tell me, how do you manage to bathe with a quiggle?" The implication of these overtures is that the stigmatized individual is a person who can be approached by strangers at will, providing only that they are sympathetic to the plight of persons of his kind.

Given what the stigmatized individual may well face upon entering a mixed social situation, he may anticipatorily respond by defensive cowering. This may be illustrated from an early study of some German unemployed during the Depression, the words being those of a 43-year-old mason:

> How hard and humiliating it is to bear the name of an unemployed man. When I go out, I cast down my eyes because I feel myself wholly inferior. When I go along the street, it seems to me that I can't be compared with an average citizen, that everybody is pointing at me with his finger. I instinctively avoid meeting anyone. Former acquaintances and friends of better times are no longer so cordial. They greet me indifferently when we meet. They no longer offer me a cigarette and their eyes seem to say, "You are not worth it, you don't work."[37]

A crippled girl provides an illustrative analysis:

> When . . . I began to walk out alone in the streets of our town . . . I found then that wherever I had to pass three or four children together on the sidewalk, if I happened to be alone, they would shout at me, . . . Sometimes they even ran after me, shouting and jeering. This was something I didn't know how to face, and it seemed as if I couldn't bear it. . . .
>
> For awhile those encounters in the street filled me with a cold dread of all unknown children . . .
>
> One day I suddenly realized that I had become so self-conscious and afraid of all strange children that, like animals, they knew I was afraid, so that even the mildest and most amiable of them were automatically prompted to derision by my own shrinking and dread.[38]

Instead of cowering, the stigmatized individual may attempt to approach mixed contacts with hostile bravado, but this can induce from others its own set of troublesome reciprocations. It may be added that the stigmatized person sometimes vacillates between cowering and bravado, racing from one to the other, thus demonstrating one central way in which ordinary face-to-face interaction can run wild.

I am suggesting, then, that the stigmatized individual—at least the "visibly" stigmatized one—will have special reasons for feeling that mixed social situations make for anxious unanchored interaction. But if this is so, then it is to be suspected that we normals will find these situations shaky too. We will feel that the stigmatized individual is either too aggressive or too shame-faced, and in either case too ready to read unintended meanings into our actions. We ourselves may feel that if we show direct sympathetic concern for his condition, we may be overstepping ourselves; and yet if we actually forget that he has a failing we are likely to make impossible demands of him or unthinkingly slight his fellow-sufferers. Each potential source of discomfort for him when we are with him can become something we sense he is aware of, aware that we are aware of, and even aware of our state of awareness about his awareness; the stage is then set for the infinite regress of mutual consideration that Meadian social psychology tells us how to begin but not how to terminate.

Given what both the stigmatized and we normals introduce into mixed social situations, it is understandable that all will not go smoothly. We are likely to attempt to carry on as though in fact he wholly fitted one of the types of person naturally available to us in the situation, whether this means treating him as someone better than we feel he might be or someone worse than we feel he probably is. If neither of these tacks is possible, then we may try to act as if he were a "non-person," and not present at all as someone of whom ritual notice is to be taken. He, in turn, is likely to go along with these strategies, at least initially.

In consequence, attention is furtively withdrawn from its obligatory targets, and self-consciousness and "other-consciousness" occurs, expressed in the pathology of interaction—uneasiness.[39] As described in the case of the physically handicapped:

> Whether the handicap is overtly and tactlessly responded to as such or, as is more commonly the case, no explicit reference is made to it, the underlying condition of heightened, narrowed, awareness causes the interaction to be articulated too exclusively in terms of it. This, as my informants described it, is usually accompanied by one or more of the familiar signs of discomfort and stickiness: the guarded references, the common everyday words suddenly made taboo, the fixed stare elsewhere, the artificial levity, the compulsive loquaciousness, the awkward solemnity.[40]

In social situations with an individual known or perceived to have a stigma, we are likely, then, to employ categorizations that do not fit, and we and he are likely to experience uneasiness. Of course, there is often significant movement from this starting point. And since the stigmatized person is likely to be more often faced with these situations than are we, he is likely to become the more adept at managing them.

· · ·

Endnotes

[1]T. Parker and R. Allerton, *The Courage of His Convictions* (London: Hutchinson & Co. 1962), p. 109.

[2]In this connection see the review by M. Melzer, "Countermanipulation through Malingering," in A. Biderman and H. Zimmer, eds., *The Manipulation of Human Behavior* (New York: John Wiley & Sons, 1961), pp. 277–304.

[3]In recent history, especially in Britain, low class status functioned as an important tribal stigma, the sins of the parents, or at least their milieu, being visited on the child, should the child rise improperly far above his initial station. The management of class stigma is of course a central theme in the English novel.

[4]D. Riesman, "Some Observations Concerning Marginality," *Phylon,* Second Quarter, 1951, 122.

[5]The case regarding mental patients is presented by T. J. Scheff in a forthcoming paper.

[6]In regard to the blind, see E. Henrich and L. Kriegel, eds., *Experiments in Survival* (New York: Association for the Aid of Crippled Children, 1961), pp. 152 and 186; and H. Chevigny, *My Eyes Have a Cold Nose* (New Haven, Conn.: Yale University Press, paperbound, 1962), p. 201.

[7]In the words of one blind woman, "I was asked to endorse a perfume, presumably because being sightless my sense of smell was super-discriminating." See T. Keitlen (with N. Lobsenz), *Farewell to Fear* (New York: Avon, 1962), p. 10.

[8]A. G. Gowman, *The War Blind in American Social Structure* (New York: American Foundation for the Blind, 1957), p. 198.

[9]For examples, see Macgregor et al., *op. cit.,* throughout.

[10]The notion of "normal human being" may have its source in the medical approach to humanity or in the tendency of large-scale bureaucratic organizations, such as the nation state, to treat all members in some respects as equal. Whatever its origins, it seems to provide the basic imagery through which laymen currently conceive of themselves. Interestingly, a convention seems to have emerged in popular life-story writing where a questionable person proves his claim to normalcy by citing his acquisition of a spouse and children, and, oddly, by attesting to his spending Christmas and Thanksgiving with them.

[11]A criminal's view of this nonacceptance is presented in Parker and Allerton, *op. cit.,* pp. 110–111.

[12]K. B. Hathaway, *The Little Locksmith* (New York: Coward-McCann, 1943), p. 41, in Wright, *op. cit.,* p. 157.

[13]*Ibid.,* pp. 46–47. For general treatments of the self-disliking sentiments, see K. Lewin, *Resolving Social Conflicts,* Part III (New York: Harper & Row, 1948); A.

Kardiner and L. Ovesey, *The Mark of Oppression: A Psychosocial Study of the American Negro* (New York: W. W. Norton & Company, 1951); and E. H. Erikson, *Childhood and Society* (New York: W. W. Norton & Company, 1950).

[14]F. Warfield, *Keep Listening* (New York: The Viking Press, 1957), p. 76. See also H. von Hentig, *The Criminal and His Victim* (New Haven, Conn.: Yale University Press, 1948), p. 101.

[15]Keitlen, *op. cit.,* Chap. 12, pp. 117-129 and Chap. 14, pp. 137–149. See also Chevigny, *op. cit.,* pp. 85–86.

[16]Henrich and Kriegel, *op. cit.,* p. 49.

[17]W. Y. Baker and L. H. Smith, "Facial Disfigurement and Personality," *Journal of the American Medical Association,* CX11 (1939), 303. Macgregor et al., *op. cit.,* p. 57 ff., provide an illustration of a man who used his big red nose for a crutch.

[18]Henrich and Kriegel, *op. cit.,* p. 19.

[19]*Ibid.,* p. 35.

[20]Chevigny, *op. cit.,* p. 154.

[21]F. Carling, *And Yet We Are Human* (London: Chatto & Windus, 1962), pp. 23–24.

[22]For one review, see G. W. Allport, *The Nature of Prejudice* (New York: Anchor Books, 1958).

[23]Macgregor et al., *op. cit.,* pp. 91–92.

[24]From *Clinical Studies in Psychiatry,* H. S. Perry, M. L. Gawel, and M. Gibbon, eds. (New York: W. W. Norton & Company, 1956), p. 145.

[25]R. Barker, "The Social Psychology of Physical Disability," *Journal of Social Issues,* IV (1948), 34, suggests that stigmatized persons "live on a social-psychological frontier," constantly facing new situations. See also Macgregor et al., *op. cit.,* p. 87, where the suggestion is made that the grossly deformed need suffer less doubt about their reception in interaction than the less visibly deformed.

[26]Barker, *op. cit.,* p. 33.

[27]Parker and Allerton, *op. cit.,* p. 111.

[28]This special kind of self-consciousness is analyzed in S. Messinger et al., "Life as Theater: Some Notes on the Dramaturgic Approach to Social Reality," *Sociometry,* XXV (1962), 98–110.

[29]Parker and Allerton, *op. cit.,* p. 111.

[30]Chevigny, *op. cit.,* p. 140.

[31]L. A. Dexter, "A Social Theory of Mental Deficiency," *American Journal of Mental Deficiency,* LXII (1958), 923. For another study of the mental defective as a stigmatized person, see S. E. Perry, "Some Theoretical Problems of Mental Deficiency and Their Action Implications," *Psychiatry,* XVII (1954), 45–73.

141

[32]Baker, *Out on a Limb* (New York: McGraw-Hill Book Company, n.d.), p. 22.

[33]*Ibid.*, p. 73.

[34]This theme is well treated in R. K. White, B. A. Wright, and T. Dembo, "Studies in Adjustment to Visible Injuries: Evaluation of Curiosity by the Injured," *Journal of Abnormal and Social Psychology*, XLIII (1948), 13–28.

[35]For example, Henrich and Kriegel, *op. cit.*, p. 184.

[36]See Wright, *op. cit.*, "The Problem of Sympathy," pp. 233–237.

[37]S. Zawadski and P. Lazarsfeld, "The Psychological Consequences of Unemployment," *Journal of Social Psychology*, VI (1935), 239.

[38]Hathaway, *op. cit.*, pp. 155–157, in S. Richardson, "The Social Psychological Consequences of Handicapping," unpublished paper presented at the 1962 American Sociological Association Convention, Washington, D.C., 7–8.

[39]For a general treatment, see E. Goffman, "Alienation from Interaction," *Human Relations*, X (1957), 47–60.

[40]F. Davis, "Deviance Disavowal: The Management of Strained Interaction by the Visibly Handicapped," *Social Problems*, IX (1961), 123. See also White, Wright, and Dembo, *op. cit.*, pp. 26–27.

◉ ◉ ◉

Questions

1. Define "stigma."

2. What is the difference between "discredited" and "discreditable"? Give examples that fit each category.

3. What three kinds of stigma does Goffman discuss? How are these kinds of stigma related to the concepts of *discredited* and *discreditable*?

4. How do "mixed contacts" affect stigma management?

On Being Sane in Insane Places

D. L. ROSENHAN
Stanford University

This work cuts across several lines, including labeling theory and the role of institutions in treating the mentally ill. The article describes the author's attempt to study mentally ill individuals more closely; in particular, the ways in which "normal" individuals and professional staff interact with those diagnosed with mental illness. To conduct the study, Rosenhan had "pseudo-patients" (mentally healthy individuals) check into various psychiatric hospitals and record their experiences. This research provides a rich account of the powerlessness, depersonalization, and labeling that occur in mental institutions. The author also explains how institutional structure and environment contribute to these problems.

If sanity and insanity exist, how shall we know them?

The question is neither capricious nor itself insane. However much we may be personally convinced that we can tell the normal from the abnormal, the evidence is simply not compelling. It is commonplace, for example, to read about murder trials wherein eminent psychiatrists for the defense are contradicted by equally eminent psychiatrists for the prosecution on the matter of the defendant's sanity. More generally, there are a great deal of conflicting data on the reliability, utility, and meaning of such terms as "sanity," "insanity," "mental illness," and "schizophrenia".[1] Finally, as early as 1934, Benedict suggested that normality and abnormality are not universal.[2] What is viewed as normal in one culture may be seen as quite aberrant in another. Thus, notions of normality and abnormality may not be quite as accurate as people believe they are.

To raise questions regarding normality and abnormality is in no way to question the fact that some behaviors are deviant or odd. Murder is deviant.

"On Being Sane in Insane Places," by D.L. Rosenhan, reprinted from *Science*, vol. 179, January 1973, pp. 250–258.

So, too, are hallucinations. Nor does raising such questions deny the existence of the personal anguish that is often associated with "mental illness." Anxiety and depression exist. Psychological suffering exists. But normality and abnormality, sanity and insanity, and the diagnoses that flow from them may be less substantive than many believe them to be.

At its heart, the question of whether the sane can be distinguished from the insane (and whether degrees of insanity can be distinguished from each other) is a simple matter: do the salient characteristics that lead to diagnoses reside in the patients themselves or in the environments and contexts in which observers find them? From Bleuler, through Kretchmer, through the formulators of the recently revised *Diagnostic and Statistical Manual* of the American Psychiatric Association, the belief has been strong that patients present symptoms, that those symptoms can be categorized, and, implicitly, that the sane are distinguishable from the insane. More recently, however, this belief has been questioned. Based in part on theoretical and anthropological considerations, but also on philosophical, legal, and therapeutic ones. The view has grown that psychological categorization of mental illness is useless at best and downright harmful, misleading, and pejorative at worst. Psychiatric diagnoses, in this view, are in the minds of the observers and are not valid summaries of characteristics displayed by the observed.[3–5]

Gains can be made in deciding which of these is more nearly accurate by getting normal people (that is, people who do not have, and have never suffered, symptoms of serious psychiatric disorders) admitted to psychiatric hospitals and then determining whether they were discovered to be sane, and, if so, how. If the sanity of such pseudopatients were always detected, there would be prima facie evidence that a sane individual can be distinguished from the insane context in which he is found. Normality (and presumably abnormality) is distinct enough that it can be recognized wherever it occurs, for it is carried within the person. If, on the other hand, the sanity of the pseudopatients were never discovered, serious difficulties would arise for those who support traditional modes of psychiatric diagnosis. Given that the hospital staff was not incompetent, that the pseudopatient had been behaving as sanely as he had been outside of the hospital, and that it had never been previously suggested that he belonged in a psychiatric hospital, such an unlikely outcome would support the view that psychiatric diagnosis betrays little about the patient but much about the environment in which an observer finds him.

This article describes such an experiment. Eight sane people gained secret admission to 12 different hospitals.[6] Their diagnostic experiences constitute the data of the first part of this article; the remainder is devoted to a description of their experiences in psychiatric institutions. Too few psychiatrists and psychologists, even those who have worked in such hospitals, know what the experience is like. They rarely talk about it with former patients, perhaps because they distrust information coming from the previously insane. Those who have worked in psychiatric hospitals are likely to have adapted so thoroughly to the settings that they are insensitive to the impact of that experience. And while there have been occasional reports of researchers who submitted themselves to psychiatric hospitalization,[7] these researchers have commonly remained in the hospitals for short periods of time, often with the knowledge of the hospital staff. It is difficult to know the extent to which they were treated like patients or like research colleagues. Nevertheless, their reports about the inside of the psychiatric hospital have been valuable. This article extends those efforts.

❂ Pseudopatients and Their Settings

The eight pseudopatients were a varied group. One was a psychology graduate student in his 20's. The remaining seven were older and "established." Among them were three psychologists, a pediatrician, a psychiatrist, a painter, and a housewife. Three pseudopatients were women, five were men. All of them employed pseudonyms, lest their alleged diagnoses embarrass them later. Those who were in mental health professions alleged another occupation in order to avoid the special attentions that might be accorded by staff, as a matter of courtesy or caution, to ailing colleagues.[8] With the exception of myself (I was the first pseudopatient and my presence was known to the hospital administrator and chief psychologist and, so far as I can tell, to them alone), the presence of pseudopatients and the nature of the research program was not known to the hospital staffs.[9]

The settings were similarly varied. In order to generalize the findings, admission into a variety of hospitals was sought. The 12 hospitals in the sample were located in five different states on the East and West coasts. Some were old and shabby, some were quite new. Some were research-oriented, others not. Some had good staff-patient ratios, others were quite understaffed. Only one was a strictly private hospital. All of the others were supported by state or federal funds or, in one instance, by university funds.

After calling the hospital for an appointment, the pseudopatient arrived at the admissions office complaining that he had been hearing voices. Asked what the voices said, he replied that they were often unclear, but as far as he could tell they said "empty," "hollow," and "thud." The voices were unfamiliar and were of the same sex as the pseudopatient. The choice of these symptoms was occasioned by their apparent similarity to existential symptoms. Such symptoms are alleged to arise from painful concerns about the perceived meaninglessness of one's life. It is as if the hallucinating person were saying, "My life is empty and hollow." The choice of these symptoms was also determined by the *absence* of a single report of existential psychoses in the literature.

Beyond alleging the symptoms and falsifying name, vocation, and employment, no further alterations of person, history, or circumstances were made. The significant events of the pseudopatient's life history were presented as they had actually occurred. Relationships with parents and siblings, with spouse and children, with people at work and in school, consistent with the aforementioned exceptions, were described as they were or had been. Frustrations and upsets were described along with joys and satisfactions. These facts are important to remember. If anything, they strongly biased the subsequent results in favor of detecting sanity, since none of their histories or current behaviors were seriously pathological in any way.

Immediately upon admission to the psychiatric ward, the pseudopatient ceased simulating *any* symptoms of abnormality. In some cases, there was a brief period of mild nervousness and anxiety, since none of the pseudopatients really believed that they would be admitted so easily. Indeed, their shared fear was that they would be immediately exposed as frauds and greatly embarrassed. Moreover, many of them had never visited a psychiatric ward; even those who had, nevertheless had some genuine fears about what might happen to them. Their nervousness then, was quite appropriate to the novelty of the hospital setting, and it abated rapidly.

Apart from that short-lived nervousness, the pseudopatient behaved on the ward as he "normally" behaved. The pseudopatient spoke to patients and staff as he might ordinarily. Because there is uncommonly little to do on a psychiatric ward, he attempted to engage others in conversation. When asked by staff how he was feeling, he indicated that he was fine, that he no longer experienced symptoms. He responded to instructions from atten-dants, to calls for medication (which was not swallowed), and to dining-hall instructions. Beyond such activities as were available to him on the admis-sions ward, he spent his time writing down his observations about the ward, its patients, and the staff. Initially these notes were written "secretly," but as it soon became clear that no one much cared, they were subsequently writ-ten on standard tablets of paper in such public places as the dayroom. No secret was made of these activities.

The pseudopatient, very much as a true psychiatric patient, entered a hospital with no foreknowledge of when he would be discharged. Each was told that he would have to get out by his own devices, essentially by convincing the staff that he was sane. The psychological stresses associated with hospitalization were considerable, and all but one of the pseudopa-tients desired to be discharged almost immediately after being admitted. They were, therefore, motivated not only to behave sanely, but to be paragons of cooperation. That their behavior was in no way disruptive is confirmed by nursing reports, which have been obtained on most of the patients. These reports uniformly indicate that the patients were "friendly," "cooperative," and "exhibited no abnormal indications."

☻ The Normal Are Not Detectably Sane

Despite their public "show" of sanity, the pseudopatients were never detected. Admitted, except in one case, with a diagnosis of schizophrenia,[10] each was discharged with a diagnosis of schizophrenia "in remission." The label "in remission" should in no way be dismissed as a formality, for at no time during any hospitalization had any question been raised about any pseudopatient's simulation. Nor are there any indications in the hospital records that the pseudopatient's status was suspect. Rather, the evidence is strong that, once labeled schizophrenic, the pseudopatient was to be discharged, he must naturally be "in remission"; but he was not sane, nor, in the institution's view, had he ever been sane.

The uniform failure to recognize sanity cannot be attributed to the qual-ity of the hospitals, for, although there were considerable variations among them, several are considered excellent. Nor can it be alleged that there was simply not enough time to observe the pseudopatients. Length of hospitalization ranged from 7 to 52 days, with an average of 19 days. The pseudopatients were not, in fact, carefully observed, but this failure clearly speaks more to traditions within psychiatric hospitals than to lack of opportunity.

Finally, it cannot be said that the failure to recognize the pseudopatients' sanity was due to the fact that they were not behaving sanely. While there was clearly some tension present in all of them, their daily visitors could detect no serious behavioral consequences—nor, indeed, could other patients. It was quite common for the patients to "detect" the pseudopatients' sanity. During the first three hospitalizations, when accurate counts were kept, 35 of a total of 118 patients on the admissions ward voiced their suspicions, some vigorously. "You're not crazy. You're a journalist, or a professor [referring to the continual note-taking]. You're checking up on the hospital." While most of the patients were reassured by the pseudopatient's insistence that he had been sick before he came in but was fine now, some continued to believe that the pseudopatient was sane throughout his hospitalization.[11] The fact that the patients often recognized normality when staff did not raises important questions.

Failure to detect sanity during the course of hospitalization may be due to the fact that physicians operate with a strong bias toward what statisticians call the type 2 error.[5] This is to say that physicians are more inclined to call a healthy person sick (a false positive, type 2), than a sick person healthy (a false negative, type 1). The reasons for this are not hard to find: it is clearly more dangerous to misdiagnose illness than health. Better to err on the side of caution, to suspect illness even among the healthy.

But what holds for medicine does not hold equally well for psychiatry. Medical illnesses, while unfortunate, are not commonly pejorative. Psychiatric diagnoses, on the contrary, carry with them personal, legal, and social stigmas.[12] It was therefore important to see whether the tendency toward diagnosing the sane insane could be reversed. The following experiment was arranged at a research and teaching hospital whose staff had heard these findings but doubted that such an error could occur in their hospital. The staff was informed that at some time during the following 3 months, one or more pseudopatients would attempt to be admitted into the psychiatric hospital. Each staff member was asked to rate each patient who presented himself at admissions or on the ward according to the likelihood that the patient was a pseudopatient. A 10-point scale was used, with a 1 and 2 reflecting high confidence that the patient was a pseudopatient.

Judgments were obtained on 193 patients who were admitted for psychiatric treatment. All staff who had had sustained contact with or primary responsibility for the patient—attendants, nurses, psychiatrists, physicians, and psychologists—were asked to make judgments. Forty-one patients were alleged, with high confidence, to be pseudopatients by at least one member of the staff. Twenty-three were considered suspect by at least one psychiatrist. Nineteen were suspected by one psychiatrist *and* one other staff member. Actually, no genuine pseudopatient (at least from my group) presented himself during this period.

The experiment is instructive. It indicates that the tendency to designate sane people as insane can be reversed when the stakes (in this case, prestige and diagnostic acumen) are high. But what can be said of the 19 people who were suspected of being "sane" by one psychiatrist and another staff member? Were these people truly "sane," or was it rather the case that in the course of avoiding the type 2 error the staff tended to make more errors of the first sort—calling the crazy "sane"? There is no way of knowing. But one thing is certain: any diagnostic process that lends itself so readily to massive errors of this sort cannot be a very reliable one.

☻ The Stickiness of Psychodiagnostic Labels

Beyond the tendency to call the healthy sick—a tendency that accounts better for diagnostic behavior on admission than it does for such behavior after a lengthy period of exposure—the data speak to the massive role of labeling in psychiatric assessment. Having once been labeled schizophrenic, there is nothing the pseudopatient can do to overcome the tag. The tag profoundly colors others' perceptions of him and his behavior.

From one viewpoint, these data are hardly surprising, for it has long been known that elements are given meaning by the context in which they occur. Gestalt psychology made this point vigorously, and Asch[13] demonstrated that there are "central" personality traits (such as "warm" versus "cold") which are so powerful that they markedly color the meaning of other information in forming an impression of a given personality.[14] "Insane," "schizophrenic," "manic-depressive," and "crazy" are probably among the most powerful of such central traits. Once a person is designated abnormal, all of his other behaviors and characteristics are colored by that label.

Indeed, that label is so powerful that many of the pseudopatients' normal behaviors were overlooked entirely or profoundly misinterpreted. Some examples may clarify this issue.

Earlier I indicated that there were no changes in the pseudopatient's personal history and current status beyond those of name, employment, and where necessary, vocation. Otherwise, a veridical description of personal history and circumstances was offered. Those circumstances were not psychotic. How were they made consonant with the diagnosis of psychosis? Or were those diagnoses modified in such a way as to bring them into accord with the circumstances of the pseudopatient's life, as described by him?

As far as I can determine, diagnoses were in no way affected by the relative health of the circumstances of a pseudopatient's life. Rather, the reverse occurred: the perception of his circumstances was shaped entirely by the diagnosis. A clear example of such translation is found in the case of a pseudopatient who had had a close relationship with his mother but was rather remote from his father during his early childhood. During adolescence and beyond, however, his father became a close friend, while his relationship with his mother cooled. His present relationship with his wife was characteristically close and warm. Apart from occasional angry exchanges, friction was minimal. The children had rarely been spanked. Surely there is nothing especially pathological about such a history. Indeed, many readers may see a similar pattern in their own experiences, with no markedly deleterious consequences. Observe, however, how such a history was translated in the psychopathological context, this from the case summary prepared after the patient was discharged.

> This white 39-year-old male . . . manifests a long history of considerable ambivalence in close relationships, which begins in early childhood. A warm relationship with his mother cools during his adolescence. A distant relationship to his father is described as becoming very intense. Affective stability is absent. His attempts to control emotionality with his wife and children are punctuated by angry outbursts and, in the case of the children, spankings. And while he says that he has several good friends, one senses considerable ambivalence embedded in those relationships also. . . .

The facts of the case were unintentionally distorted by the staff to achieve consistency with a popular theory of the dynamics of a schizophrenic reaction.[15] Nothing of an ambivalent nature had been described in relations with parents, spouse, or friends. To the extent that ambivalence could be inferred, it was probably not greater than is found in all human relationships. It is true the pseudopatient's relationships with his parents changed over time, but in the ordinary context that would hardly be remarkable—indeed, it might very well be expected. Clearly, the meaning ascribed to his verbalizations (that is, ambivalence, affective instability) was determined by the diagnosis: schizophrenia. An entirely different meaning would have been ascribed if it were known that the man was "normal."

All pseudopatients took extensive notes publicly. Under ordinary circumstances, such behavior would have raised questions in the minds of observers, as, in fact, it did among patients. Indeed, it seemed so certain that the notes would elicit suspicion that elaborate precautions were taken to remove them from the ward each day. But the precautions proved needless. The closest any staff member came to questioning these notes occurred when one pseudopatient asked his physician what kind of medication he was receiving and began to write down the response. "You needn't write it," he was told gently. "If you have trouble remembering, just ask me again."

If no questions were asked of the pseudopatients, how was their writing interpreted? Nursing records for three patients indicate that the writing was seen as an aspect of their pathological behavior. "Patient engages in writing behavior" was the daily nursing comment on one of the pseudopatients who was never questioned about his writing. Given that the patient is in the hospital, he must be psychologically disturbed. And given that he is disturbed, continuous writing must be a behavioral manifestation of that disturbance, perhaps a subset of the compulsive behaviors that are sometimes correlated with schizophrenia.

One tacit characteristic of psychiatric diagnosis is that it locates the sources of aberration within the individual and only rarely within the complex of stimuli that surrounds him. Consequently, behaviors that are stimulated by the environment are commonly misattributed to the patient's disorder. For example, one kindly nurse found a pseudopatient pacing the long hospital corridors. "Nervous, Mr. X?" she asked. "No, bored," he said.

The notes kept by pseudopatients are full of patient behaviors that were misinterpreted by well-intentioned staff. Often enough, a patient would go "berserk" because he had, wittingly or unwittingly, been mistreated by, say, an attendant. A nurse coming upon the scene would rarely inquire even cursorily into the environmental stimuli of the patient's behavior. Rather, she assumed that his upset derived from his pathology, not from his present interactions with other staff members. Occasionally, the staff might assume that the patient's family (especially when they had recently visited) or other patients had stimulated the outburst. But never were the staff found to assume that one of themselves or the structure of the hospital had anything to do with a patient's behavior. One psychiatrist pointed to a group of patients who were sitting outside the cafeteria entrance half an hour before lunchtime. To a group of young residents he indicated that such behavior was characteristic of the oral-acquisitive nature of the syndrome. It seemed not to occur to him that there were very few things to anticipate in a psychiatric hospital besides eating.

A psychiatric label has a life and an influence of its own. Once the impression has been formed that the patient is schizophrenic, the expectation is that he will continue to be schizophrenic. When a sufficient amount of time has passed, during which the patient has done nothing bizarre, he is considered to be in remission and available for discharge. But the label endures beyond discharge, with the unconfirmed expectation that he will behave as a schizophrenic again. Such labels, conferred by mental health professionals, are as influential on the patient as they are on his relatives and friends, and it should not surprise anyone that the diagnosis acts on all of them as a self-fulfilling prophecy. Eventually, the patient himself accepts the diagnosis, with all of its surplus meanings and expectations, and behaves according.[5]

The inferences to be made from these matters are quite simple. Much as Zigler and Phillips have demonstrated that there is enormous overlap in the symptoms presented by patients who have been variously diagnosed,[16] so there is enormous overlap in the behaviors of the sane and the insane. The sane are not "sane" all of the time. We lose our tempers "for no good reason." We are occasionally depressed or anxious, again for no good reason. And we may find it difficult to get along with one or another person—again for no reason that we can specify. Similarly, the insane are not always insane. Indeed, it was the impression of the pseudopatients while living with them that they were sane for long periods of time—that the bizarre behaviors upon which their diagnoses were allegedly predicated constituted only a small fraction of their total behavior. If it makes no sense to label ourselves permanently depressed on the basis of an occasional depression, then it takes better evidence than is presently available to label all patients insane or schizophrenic on the basis of bizarre behaviors or cognitions. It seems more useful, as Mischel[17] has pointed out, to limit our discussions to *behaviors*, the stimuli that provoke them, and their correlates.

It is not known why powerful impressions of personality traits, such as "crazy" or "insane," arise. Conceivably, when the origins of and stimuli that give rise to a behavior are remote or unknown, or when the behavior strikes us as immutable, trait labels regarding the *behavior* arise. When, on the other hand, the origins and stimuli are known and available, discourse is limited to the behavior itself. Thus, I may hallucinate because I am sleeping, or I may hallucinate because I have ingested a peculiar drug. These are termed sleep-induced hallucinations, or dreams, and drug-induced hallucinations, respectively. But when the stimuli to my hallucinations are unknown, that is called craziness, or schizophrenia—as if that inference were somehow as illuminating as the others.

☻ The Experience of Psychiatric Hospitalization

The term "mental illness" is of recent origin. It was coined by people who were humane in their inclinations and who wanted very much to raise the station of (and the public's sympathies toward) the psychologically disturbed from that of witches and "crazies" to one that was akin to the physically ill. And they were at least partially successful, for the treatment of the mentally ill has improved considerably over the years. But while treatment has improved, it is doubtful that people really regard the mentally ill in the same way that they view the physically ill. A broken leg is something one recovers from, but mental illness allegedly endures forever.[18] A broken leg does not threaten the observer, but a crazy schizophrenic? There is by now a host of evidence that attitudes toward the mentally ill are characterized by fear, hostility, aloofness, suspicion, and dread.[19] The mentally ill are society's lepers.

That such attitudes infect the general population is perhaps not surprising, only upsetting. But that they affect the professionals—attendants, nurses, physicians, psychologists, and social workers—who treat and deal with the mentally ill is more disconcerting, both because such attitudes are self-evidently pernicious and because they are unwitting. Most mental health professionals would insist that they are sympathetic toward the mentally ill, that they are neither avoidant nor hostile. But it is more likely that an exquisite ambivalence characterizes their relations with psychiatric patients, such that their avowed impulses are only part of their entire attitude. Negative attitudes are there too and can easily be detected. Such attitudes should not surprise us. They are the natural offspring of the labels patients wear and the places in which they are found.

Consider the structure of the typical psychiatric hospital. Staff and patients are strictly segregated. Staff have their own living space, including their dining facilities, bathrooms, and assembly places. The glassed quarters that contain the professional staff, which the pseudopatients came to call "the cage," sit out on every dayroom. The staff emerge primarily for caretaking purposes—to give medication, to conduct a therapy or group meeting, to instruct or reprimand a patient. Otherwise, staff keep to themselves, almost as if the disorder that afflicts their charges is somehow catching.

So much is patient-staff segregation the rule that, for four public hospitals in which an attempt was made to measure the degree to which staff and patients mingle, it was necessary to use "time out of the staff cage" as the operational measure. While it was not the case that all time spent out of the cage was spent mingling with patients (attendants, for example, would occasionally emerge to watch television in the dayroom), it was the only way in which one could gather reliable data on time, for measuring.

The average amount of time spent by attendants outside of the cage was 11.3 percent (range, 3 to 52 percent). This figure does not represent only time spent mingling with patients, but also includes time spent on such chores as folding laundry, supervising patients while they shave, directing ward cleanup, and sending patients to off-ward activities. It was the relatively rare attendant who spent time talking with patients or playing games with them. It proved impossible to obtain a "percent mingling time" for nurses, since the amount of time they spent out of the cage was too brief. Rather, we counted instances of emergence from the cage. On the average, daytime nurses emerged from the cage 11.5 times per shift, including instances when they left the ward entirely (range, 4 to 39 times). Late afternoon and night nurses were even less available, emerging on the average 9.4 times per shift (range, 4 to 41 times). Data on early morning nurses, who arrived usually after midnight and departed at 8 a.m., are not available because patients were asleep during most of this period.

Physicians, especially psychiatrists, were even less available. They were rarely seen on the wards. Quite commonly, they would be seen only when they arrived and departed, with the remaining time being spent in their offices or in the cage. On the average, physicians emerged on the ward 6.7 times per day (range, 1 to 17 times). It proved difficult to make an accurate estimate in this regard, since physicians often maintained hours that allowed them to come and go at different times.

The hierarchical organization of the psychiatric hospital has been commented on before,[20] but the latent meaning of that kind of organization is worth noting again. Those with the most power have least to do with patients, and those with the least power are most involved with them. Recall, however, that the acquisition of role-appropriate behaviors occurs mainly through the observation of others, with the most powerful having the most influence. Consequently, it is understandable that attendants not only spend more time with patients than do any other members of the staff—that is required by their station in the hierarchy—but also, insofar as they learn from their superiors' behavior, spend as little time with patients as they can. Attendants are seen mainly in the cage, which is where the models, the action, and the power are.

I turn now to a different set of studies, these dealing with staff response to patient-initiated contact. It has long been known that the amount of time a person spends with you can be an index of your significance to him. If he initiates and maintains eye contact, there is reason to believe that he is considering your requests and needs. If he pauses to chat or actually stops and talks, there is added reason to infer that he is individuating you. In four hospitals, the pseudopatient approached the staff member with a request which took the following form: "Pardon me, Mr. [or Dr. or Mrs.] X, could you tell me when I will be eligible for grounds privileges?" (or " . . . when I will be presented at the staff meeting?" or ". . . when I am likely to be discharged?"). While the content of the question varied according to the appropriateness of the target and the pseudopatient's (apparent) current needs the form was always a courteous and relevant request for information. Care was taken never to approach a particular member of the staff more than once a day, lest the staff member become suspicious or irritated. In examining these data, remember that the behavior of the pseudopatients was neither bizarre nor disruptive. One could indeed engage in good conversation with them.

The data for these experiments are shown in Table 1, separately for physicians (column 1) and for nurses and attendants (column 2). Minor differences between these four institutions were overwhelmed by the degree to which staff avoided continuing contacts that patients had initiated. By far, their most common response consisted of either a brief response to the question, offered while they were "on the move" and with head averted, or no response at all.

The encounter frequently took the following bizarre form: (pseudopatient) "Pardon me, Dr. X. Could you tell me when I am eligible for grounds privileges?" (physician) "Good morning, Dave. How are you today?" (Moves off without waiting for a response.)

It is instructive to compare these data with data recently obtained at Stanford University. It has been alleged that large and eminent universities are characterized by faculty who are so busy that they have no time for students. For this comparison, a young lady approached individual faculty members who seemed to be walking purposefully to some meeting or teaching engagement and asked them the following six questions.

1) "Pardon me, could you direct me to Encina Hall?" (at the medical school: ". . . to the Clinical Research Center?").

2) "Do you know where Fish Annex is?" (there is no Fish Annex at Stanford).

3) "Do you teach here?"

4) "How does one apply for admission to the college?" (at the medical school: ". . . to the medical school?")

5) "Is it difficult to get in?"

6) "Is there financial aid?"

Without exception, as can be seen in Table 1, (column 3), all of the questions were answered. No matter how rushed they were, all respondents not only maintained eye contact, but stopped to talk. Indeed, many of the respondents went out of their way to direct or take the questioner to the office she was seeking, to try to locate "Fish Annex," or to discuss with her the possibilities of being admitted to the university.

Similar data, also shown in Table 1 (columns 4, 5, and 6) were obtained in the hospital. Here too, the young lady came prepared with six questions. After the first question, however, she remarked to 18 of her respondents (column 4), "I'm looking for a psychiatrist," and to 15 others (column 5), "I'm looking for an internist." Ten other respondents received no inserted

TABLE 1 *Self-initiated contact by pseudopatients with psychiatrists and nurses and attendants, compared to contact with other groups*

| Contact | Psychiatric hospitals | | University campus (nonmedical) | University medical center Physicians | | |
	(1) Psychiatrists	(2) Nurses and attendants	(3) Faculty	(4) "Looking for a psychiatrist"	(5) "Looking for an internist"	(6) No additional comment
Responses						
Moves on, head averted (%)	71	88	0	0	0	0
Makes eye contact (%)	23	10	0	11	0	0
Pauses and chats (%)	2	2	0	11	0	10
Stops and talks (%)	4	0.5	100	78	100	90
Mean number of questions answered (out of 6)	*	*	6	3.8	4.8	4.5
Respondents (No.)	13	47	14	18	15	10
Attempts (No.)	185	1283	14	18	15	10

* Not applicable.

157

comment (column 6). The general degree of cooperative responses is considerably higher for these university groups than it was for pseudopatients in psychiatric hospitals. Even so, differences are apparent within the medical school setting. Once having indicated that she was looking for a psychiatrist, the degree of cooperation elicited was less than when she sought an internist.

☻ Powerlessness and Depersonalization

Eye contact and verbal contact reflect concern and individuation; their absence, avoidance and depersonalization. The data I have presented do not do justice to the rich daily encounters that grew up around matters of depersonalization and avoidance. I have records of patients who were beaten by staff for the sin of having initiated verbal contact. During my own experience, for example, one patient was beaten, in the presence of other patients for having approached an attendant and told him, "I like you." Occasionally, punishment meted out to patients for misdemeanors seemed so excessive that it could not be justified by the most radical interpretations of psychiatric canon: Nevertheless, they appeared to go unquestioned. Tempers were often short. A patient who had not heard a call for medication would be roundly excoriated, and the morning attendants would often wake patients with, "Come on, you m——f——s, out of bed!"

Neither anecdotal nor "hard" data can convey the overwhelming sense of powerlessness which invades the individual as he is continually exposed to the depersonalization of the psychiatric hospital. It hardly matters *which* psychiatric hospital—the excellent public ones and the very plush private hospital were better than the rural and shabby ones in this regard, but, again, the features that psychiatric hospitals had in common overwhelmed by far their apparent differences.

Powerlessness was evident everywhere. The patient is deprived of many of his legal rights by dint of his psychiatric ommitment.[21] He is shorn of credibility by virtue of his psychiatric label. His freedom of movement is restricted. He cannot initiate contact with the staff, but may only respond to such overtures as they make. Personal privacy is minimal. Patient quarters and possessions can be entered and examined by any staff member, for whatever reason. His personal history and anguish is available to any staff member (often including the "grey lady" and "candy striper" volunteer) who chooses to read his folder, regardless of their therapeutic relationship to him. His personal hygiene and waste evacuation are often monitored. The water closets may have no doors.

At times, depersonalization reached such proportions that pseudopatients had the sense that they were invisible, or at least unworthy of account. Upon being admitted, I and other pseudopatients took the initial physical examinations in a semipublic room, where staff members went about their own business as if we were not there.

On the ward, attendants delivered verbal and occasionally serious physical abuse to patients in the presence of other observing patients, some of whom (the pseudopatients) were writing it all down. Abusive behavior on the other hand, terminated quite abruptly when other staff members were known to be coming. Staff are credible witnesses. Patients are not.

A nurse unbuttoned her uniform to adjust her brassiere in the presence of an entire ward of viewing men. One did not have the sense that she was being seductive. Rather, she didn't notice us. A group of staff persons might point to a patient in the dayroom and discuss him animatedly, as if he were not there.

One illuminating instance of depersonalization and invisibility occurred with regard to medications. All told, the pseudopatients were administered nearly 2100 pills, including Elavil, Stelazine, Compazine, and Thorazine, to name but a few. (That such a variety of medications should have been administered to patients presenting identical symptoms is itself worthy of note.) Only two were swallowed. The rest were either pocketed or deposited in the toilet. The pseudopatients were not alone in this. Although I have no precise records on how many patients rejected their medications, the pseudopatients frequently found the medications of other patients in the toilet before they deposited their own. As long as they were cooperative, their behavior and the pseudopatients' own in this matter, as in other important matters, went unnoticed throughout.

Reactions to such depersonalization among pseudopatients were intense. Although they had come to the hospital as participant observers and were fully aware that they did not "belong," they nevertheless found themselves caught up in and fighting the process of depersonalization. Some examples: a graduate student in psychology asked his wife to bring his textbooks to the hospital so he could "catch up on his homework"—this despite the elaborate precautions taken to conceal his professional association. The same student, who had trained for quite some time to get into the hospital, and who had looked forward to the experience, "remembered" some drag races that he had wanted to see on the weekend and insisted that he be discharged by that time. Another pseudopatient attempted a romance with a nurse. Subsequently, he informed the staff that he was applying for admission to graduate school in psychology and was very likely to be admitted, since a graduate professor was one of his regular hospital visitors. The same person began to engage in psychotherapy with other patients—all of this as a way of becoming a person in an impersonal environment.

❧ The Sources of Depersonalization

What are the origins of depersonalization? I have already mentioned two. First are attitudes held by all of us toward the mentally ill—including those who treat them—attitudes characterized by fear, distrust, and horrible expectations on the one hand, and benevolent intentions on the other. Our ambivalence leads, in this instance as in others, to avoidance.

Second, and not entirely separate, the hierarchical structure of the psychiatric hospital facilitates depersonalization. Those who are at the top have least to do with patients, and their behavior inspires the rest of the staff. Average daily contact with psychiatrists, psychologists, residents, and physicians combined ranged from 3.9 to 25.1 minutes, with an overall mean of 6.8 (six pseudopatients over a total of 129 days of hospitalization). Included in this average are time spent in the admissions interview, ward meetings in the presence of a senior staff member, group and individual psychotherapy contacts, case presentation conferences, and discharge meetings. Clearly, patients do not spend much time in interpersonal contact with doctoral staff. And doctoral staff serve as models for nurses and attendants.

There are probably other sources. Psychiatric installations are presently in serious financial straits. Staff shortages are pervasive, staff time at a premium. Something has to give, and that something is patient contact. Yet, while financial stresses are realities, too much can be made of them. I have the impression that the psychological forces that result in depersonalization are much stronger than the fiscal ones and that the addition of more staff would not correspondingly improve patient care in this regard. The incidence of staff meetings and the enormous amount of record-keeping on patients, for example, have not been as substantially reduced as has patient contact. Priorities exist, even during hard times. Patient contact is not a significant priority in the traditional psychiatric hospital, and fiscal pressures do not account for this. Avoidance and depersonalization may.

Heavy reliance upon psychotropic medication tacitly contributes to depersonalization by convincing staff that treatment is indeed being conducted and that further patient contact may not be necessary. Even here, however, caution needs to be exercised in understanding the role of psychotropic drugs. If patients were powerful rather than powerless, if they were viewed as interesting individuals rather than diagnostic entities, if they were socially significant rather than social lepers, if their anguish truly and wholly compelled our sympathies and concerns, would we not *seek* contact with them, despite the availability of medications? Perhaps for the pleasure of it all?

☻ The Consequences of Labeling and Depersonalization

Whenever the ratio of what is known to what needs to be known approaches zero, we tend to invent "knowledge" and assume that we understand more than we actually do. We seem unable to acknowledge that we simply don't know. The needs for diagnosis and remediation of behavioral and emotional problems are enormous. But rather than acknowledge that we are just embarking on understanding, we continue to label patients "schizophrenic," "manic-depressive," and "insane," as if in those words we had captured the essence of understanding. The facts of the matter are that we have known for a long time that diagnoses are often not useful or reliable, but we have nevertheless continued to use them. We now know that we cannot distinguish insanity from sanity. It is depressing to consider how that information will be used.

Not merely depressing, but frightening. How many people, one wonders, are sane but not recognized as such in our psychiatric institutions? How many have been needlessly stripped of their privileges of citizenship, from the right to vote and drive to that of handling their own accounts? How many have feigned insanity in order to avoid the criminal consequences of their behavior, and, conversely, how many would rather stand trial than live interminably in a psychiatric hospital—but are wrongly thought to be mentally ill? How many have been stigmatized by well-intentioned, but nevertheless erroneous, diagnoses? On the last point, recall again that a "type 2 error" in psychiatric diagnosis does not have the same consequences it does in medicate diagnosis. A diagnosis of cancer that has been found to be in error is cause for celebration. But psychiatric diagnoses are rarely found to be in error. The label sticks, a mark of inadequacy forever.

Finally, how many patients might be "sane" outside the psychiatric hospital but seem insane in it—not because craziness resides in them, as it were, but because they are responding to a bizarre setting, one that may be unique to institutions which harbor nether people? Goffman[4] calls the process of socialization to such institutions "mortification"—an apt metaphor that includes the processes of depersonalization that have been described here. And while it is impossible to know whether the pseudopatients' responses to these processes are characteristic of all inmates—they were, after all, not real patients—it is difficult to believe that these processes of socialization to a psychiatric hospital provide useful attitudes or habits of response for living in the "real world."

◉ Summary and Conclusions

It is clear that we cannot distinguish the sane from the insane in psychiatric hospitals. The hospital itself imposes a special environment in which the meanings of behavior can easily be misunderstood. The consequences to patients hospitalized in such an environment—the powerlessness, depersonalization, segregation, mortification, and self-labeling—seem undoubtedly countertherapeutic.

I do not, even now, understand this problem well enough to perceive solutions. But two matters seem to have some promise. The first concerns the proliferation of community mental health facilities, of crisis intervention centers, of the human potential movement, and of behavior therapies that, for all of their own problems, tend to avoid psychiatric labels, to focus on specific problems and behaviors, and to retain the individual in a relatively nonpejorative environment. Clearly, to the extent that we refrain from sending the distressed to insane places, our impressions of them are less likely to be distorted. (The risk of distorted perceptions, it seems to me, is always present, since we are much more sensitive to an individual's behaviors and verbalizations than we are to the subtle contextual stimuli that often promote them. At issue here is a matter of magnitude. And, as I have shown, the magnitude of distortion is exceedingly high in the extreme context that is a psychiatric hospital.)

The second matter that might prove promising speaks to the need to increase the sensitivity of mental health workers and researchers to the *Catch 22* position of psychiatric patients. Simply reading materials in this area will be of help to some such workers and researchers. For others, directly experiencing the impact of psychiatric hospitalization will be of enormous use. Clearly, further research into the social psychology of such total institutions will both facilitate treatment and deepen understanding.

I and the other pseudopatients in the psychiatric setting had distinctly negative reactions. We do not pretend to describe the subjective experiences of true patients. Theirs may be different from ours, particularly with the passage of time and the necessary process of adaptation to one's environment. But we can and do speak to the relatively more objective indices of treatment within the hospital. It could be a mistake, and a very unfortunate one, to consider that what happened to us derived from malice or stupidity on the part of the staff. Quite the contrary, our overwhelming impression of them was of people who really cared, who were committed and who were uncommonly intelligent. Where they failed, as they sometimes did painfully, it would be more accurate to attribute those failures to the environment in which they, too, found themselves than to personal callousness. Their perceptions and behavior were controlled by the situation, rather than being motivated by a malicious disposition. In a more benign environment, one that was less attached to global diagnosis, their behaviors and judgments might have been more benign and effective.

References and Notes

[1] P. Ash, *J. Abnorm. Soc. Psychol.* 44, 272 (1949); A. T. Beck, *Amer. J. Psychiat.* 119, 210 (1962); A. T. Boisen, *Psychiatry* 2, 233, (1938); N. Kreitman, *J. Ment. Sci.* 107, 876 (1961); N. Kreitman, P. Sainsbury, J. Morrisey, J. Towers, J. Scrivener, *ibid.*, p. 887; H. O. Schmitt and C. P. Fonda, *J. Abnorm. Soc. Psychol.* 52, 262 (1956); W. Seeman, *J. Nerv. Ment. Dis.* 118, 541 (1953). For an analysis of these artifacts and summaries of the disputes, see J. Zubin, *Annu. Rev. Psychol.* 18, 373 (1967); L. Philips and J. G. Draguns, *ibid.* 22, 447 (1971).

[2] R. Benedict, *J. Gen. Psychol.* 10, 59 (1934).

[3] See in this regard H. Becker, *Outsiders: Studies in the Sociology of Deviance* (Free Press, New York, 1963); B. M. Braginsky, D. D. Braginsky, K. Ring, *Methods of Madness: The Mental Hospital as a Last Resort* (Holt, Rinehart & Winston, New

York, 1969); G. M. Crocetti and P. V. Lemkau, *Amer. Sociol. Rev.* 30, 577 (1965); E. Goffman, Behavior in Public Places (Free Press, New York, 1964); R. D. Laing, *The Divided Self: A Study of Sanity and Madness* (Quadrangle, Chicago, 1960); D. L. Phillips, *Amer. Sociol. Rev.* 28, 963 (1963); T. R. Sarbin, *Psychol. Today* 6, 18 (1972); E. Schur, *Amer. J. Sociol.* 75, 309 (1969); T. Szasz, *Law, Liberty and Psychiatry* (Macmillan, New York, 1963); *The Myth of Mental Illness: Foundations of a Theory of Mental Illness* (Hoeber-Harper, New York, 1963). For a critique of some of these issues, see W. R. Gove, *Amer. Sociol. Rev.* 35, 873 (1970).

[4]G. E. Goffman, *Asylums* (Doubleday, Garden City, N.Y., 1961).

[5]T. J. Scheff, *Being Mentally Ill: A Sociological Theory* (Aldine, Chicago, 1966).

[6]Data from a ninth pseudopatient are not incorporated in this report because, although his sanity went undetected, he falsified aspects of his personal history, including his marital status and parental relationships. His experimental behaviors therefore were not identical to those of the other pseudopatients.

[7]A. Barry, *Bellevue Is a State of Mind* (Harcourt Brace Jovanovich, New York, 1971); J. Belknap, *Human Problems of a State Mental Hospital* (McGraw-Hill, New York, 1956); W. Caudill, F. C. Redlich, H. R. Gilmore, E. B. Brody, *Amer. J. Orthopsychiat.* 22, 314 (1952); A. R. Goldman, R. H. Bohr, T. A. Steinberg, *Prof. Psychol.* 1, 427 (1970); unauthored, *Roche Report* 1 (No. 13), 8 (1971).

[8]Beyond the personal difficulties that the pseudopatient is likely to experience in the hospital, there are legal and social ones that, combined, require considerable attention before entry. For example, once admitted to a psychiatric institution, it is difficult, if not impossible, to be discharged on short notice, state law to the contrary notwithstanding. I was not sensitive to these difficulties at the outset of the project, nor to the personal and situational emergencies that can arise, but later a writ of habeas corpus was prepared for each of the entering pseudopatients and an attorney was kept "on call" during every hospitalization. I am grateful to John Kaplan and Robert Bartels for legal advice and assistance in these matters.

[9]However distasteful such concealment is, it was a necessary first step to examining these questions. Without concealment, there would have been no way to know how valid these experiences were; nor was there any way of knowing whether whatever detections occurred were a tribute to the diagnostic acumen of the staff or to the hospital's rumor network. Obviously, since my concerns are general ones that cut across individual hospitals and staffs, I have respected their anonymity and have eliminated clues that might lead to their identification.

[10]Interestingly, of the 12 admissions, 11 were diagnosed as schizophrenic and one, with the identical symptomology, as manic-depressive psychosis. This diagno-

sis has a more favorable prognosis, and it was given by the only private hospital in our sample. On the relations between social class and psychiatric diagnosis, see A. deB. Holingshead and F. C. Redlich, *Social Class and Mental Illness: A Community Study* (Wiley, New York, 1958).

[11]It is possible, of course, that patients have quite broad latitudes in diagnosis and therefore are inclined to call many people sane, even those whose behavior is patently aberrant. However, although we have no hard data on this matter, it was our distinct impression that this was not the case. In many instances, patients not only singled us out for attention, but came to imitate our behaviors and styles.

[12]J. Cumming and E. Cumming, *Community Ment. Health* 1, 135 (1965); A. Farina and K. Ring, *J. Abnorm. Psychol.* 70, 47 (1965); H. E. Freekkman and O. G. Simmons, *The Mental Patient Comes Home* (Wiley, New York, 1963); W. J. Johannsen, *Ment. Hygiene* 53, 218 (1969); A. S. Linsky, *Soc. Psychol.* 5, 166 (1970).

[13]See Asch, *J. Abnorm. Soc. Psychol.* 41, 258 (1946); *Social Psychology* (Prentice-Hall, New York, 1952).

[14]See also I. N. Mensh and J. Wishner, *Psychol. Rev.* 67, 96 (1960); J. S. Bruner and R. Tagiuri, in *Handbook of Social Psychology*, G. Lindzey, Ed. (Addison Wesley, Cambridge, Mass., 1954), vol. 2, pp. 634–654; J. S. Bruner, D. Shapiro, R. Tagiuri, in *Person Perception and Interpersonal Behavior*, R. Tagiuri and L. Petrullo, Eds. (Stanford Univ. Press, Stanford, Calif., 1958), pp. 277–288.

[15]For an example of a similar self-fulfilling prophecy, in this instance dealing with the "central" trait of intelligence, see R. Rosenthal and L. Jacobson, *Pygmalion in the Classroom* (Holt, Rinehart & Winston, New York, 1968).

[16]E. Zigler and L. Phillips, *J. Abnorm. Soc. Psychol.* 63, 69 (1961). See also R. K. Freudenberg and J. P. Robertson, *A.M.A. Arch. Neurol. Psychiatr.* 76, 14 (1956).

[17]W. Mischel, *Personality and Assessment* (Wiley, New York, 1968).

[18]The most recent and unfortunate instance of this tenet is that of Senator Thomas Eagleton.

[19]T. R. Sarbin and J. C. Mancuso. *J. Clin. Consult. Psychol.* 35, 159 (1970); T. R. Sarbin, *ibid.* 31, 447 (1967); J. C. Nunnally, Jr., *Popular Conceptions of Mental Health* (Holt, Rinehart & Winston, New York, 1961).

[20]A. H. Stanton and M. S. Schwartz, *The Mental Hospital: A Study of Institutional Participation in Psychiatric Illness and Treatment* (Basic, New York, 1954).

[21]D. B. Wexler and S. E. Scoville, *Ariz. Law Rev.* 13, 1 (1971).

[22]I thank W. Mischel, E. Orne, and M. S. Rosenhan for comments on an earlier draft of this manuscript.

☻ ☻ ☻

Questions

1. How successful were "normal" individuals at checking into psychiatric hospitals?

2. Once the pseudo-patients were in the hospital and began to behave normally, how many of them were judged "not crazy" by the hospital staff? What does this number say about the power of the labels that professional staff apply to patients?

3. How did the structure and organization of the hospital contribute to the depersonalization of the patients?

4. What are some consequences of labeling a person as mentally ill?

5. This study was conducted in the late 1960s and early 1970s. How might the experiences of the mentally ill in everyday society be similar today? How might these experiences be different? Based on your own experiences and observations, how has the impact of being labeled as mentally ill changed during the decades since this article was published?

Pornography and Violence Against Women

EDWARD DONNERSTEIN
University of Wisconsin

Does pornography increase violence against women? Given the widespread availability of pornography, this question directly bears on women's safety in today's world. In this article, Edward Donnerstein summarizes several classic experiments in which randomly assigned male undergraduate students viewed erotic films under different conditions. The goal? To see whether viewing such films actually increased the men's aggressiveness toward women.

Recently, the National Institute of Mental Health designated that an understanding of the conditions that lead to sexual attacks against women is a major problem area and requires an increased focus. While there are many potential avenues of investigation, one that seems to be of current concern is the role of media effects in the possible elicitation of such aggressive acts, particularly in the area of pornography. Although the 1970 Presidential Commission on Obscenity and Pornography concluded that there was no evidence of a relationship between exposure to erotic forms of presentations and subsequent aggression (particularly sexual crimes), recent criticisms of these findings[1-3] have led a number of investigators to reexamine this issue. Specifically, research by a number of individuals in the social-psychological area has indicated that under appropriate conditions exposure to erotic forms of media presentations can facilitate subsequent aggressive behavior.[4-8] While this research has been directed at the effects of erotic media presentations on behavior, the issue of whether such presentations can in some manner be related to increased aggressive attacks against women has been only recently of concern.[8,9] It is generally believed by a large proportion of the population that many sexual materials can precipitate violent sexual crimes, such as rape.[10] Basic research directed at

"Pornography and Violence Against Women," by Edward Donnerstein, reprinted from *Annals of the New York Academy of Sciences*, vol. 347, 1980, pp. 277–288.

examining this concern, in regard to erotic forms of media and other presentations that depict women as victims of aggression, is an important goal of social research. The present series of studies was designed to examine this issue.

◉ Brief Historical Background

What are the effects of erotic or pornographic materials on antisocial behavior? An examination of recent research and reports in the area would suggest that the effects are, if anything, nonharmful. For example:

> It is concluded that pornography is an innocuous stimulus which leads quickly to satiation and that the public concern over it is misplaced.[11]

> If a case is to be made against "pornography" in 1970, it will have to made on the grounds other than demonstrated effects of a damaging personal or social nature. Empirical research designed to clarify the question has found no reliable evidence to date that exposure to explicit sexual materials plays a significant role in the causation of delinquent or criminal sexual behavior among youth or adults.[10]

However, recent criticisms of these findings by a number of investigators[2,3] have led to a reexamination of the issue of erotic exposure and subsequent aggressive behavior. While some individuals, like Cline,[2] have argued that there are major methodological and interpretation problems with the pornography commission report, others[12] believe that the observations might be premature. The major reason for this concern comes, in part, from a recent series of experimental studies that suggests that the relationship between exposure to erotic materials and subsequent aggressive behavior is more complex than first believed. The brief review of this research that follows summarizes the current state of this issue.

Aggression-Enhancing Effects of Erotic Exposure

A number of studies in which subjects have been angered, and later exposed to some form of erotic stimulation, have revealed increased aggressive behavior.[4,13] In fact, there is evidence to suggest that the facilitative effects are greater than those attributed to aggressive films.[4,14] Such findings have been interpreted in terms of a general arousal model, stating that under conditions where aggression is a dominant response any source of emotional arousal will tend to increase aggressive behavior.[15] In accordance with this model, aggressive behavior, in subjects who have previously been angered, has been shown to be increased by exposure to arousing sources such as aggressive or erotic films,[4] physical exercise,[16] and noise.[17] It would seem that because of their arousing properties erotic stimuli can have aggression-facilitating effects under certain conditions. Although there has been research indicating that erotic stimuli might increase aggression without prior anger arousal,[18] the majority of evidence to date would suggest that prior anger arousal is an important condition for a facilitative effect of erotic exposure.

Aggression-Inhibiting Effects of Erotic Exposure

A second group of studies[19,20] have shown that exposure to erotic stimuli can actually reduce subsequent aggression. A number of explanations have been suggested for this effect: erotic stimuli are somehow incompatible, in their emotional state, with aggression;[19,21] the level of anger arousal is inappropriate for an aggressive response;[20] or erotic exposure shifts attention away from previous anger arousal.[6] Whatever the explanation, there is sound evidence to suggest that under certain conditions erotic stimuli can reduce subsequent aggressive behavior.

A Reconciliation of the Research

While at first glance such results seem somewhat contradictory, recent studies by Donnerstein et at.[6] and Baron and Bell[7] seem to have resolved this controversy. It is now believed that as erotic stimuli become more arousing, they give rise to increases in aggressive behavior. At a low level of arousal, however, such stimuli act to distract a subject's attention away from previous anger[6] or act as an incompatible response with aggression,[7] thus reducing subsequent aggressive behavior. The evidence for this curvilinear relationship between sexual arousal and aggression seems fairly well established. In fact, Baron[22] has shown that this type of relationship also occurs when females are exposed to mild and highly erotic stimuli.

The Issue of Erotic Stimuli and Aggression against Women

While the current theorizing on the relationship of erotic stimuli and aggression seems fairly conclusive, it is interesting to note that all of the aforementioned studies were concerned with same-sex, primarily male-to-male, aggression. Yet, the social implications of this research would be more applicable by an examination of male aggression toward females. For, as noted by the U. S. Commission on Obscenity and Pornography:

> It is often asserted that a distinguishing characteristic of sexually explicit materials is the degrading and demeaning portrayal of the role and the status of the human female. It has been argued that erotic materials describe the female as a mere sexual object to be exploited and manipulated sexually.[10]

In recent years there has been an increasing concern about the relationship of pornography and violence against women. Writers in both the popular media and the scientific community have addressed this issue. Generally, they have taken for granted that pornography and aggression against women are tightly linked:

> We are somewhat educated now as to the effects of rape on women, but we know less about the effects of pornography . . . we can admit that pornography is sexist propaganda, no more and no less. Pornography is the theory, and rape is the practice.[22]

> Pornography is the undiluted essence of anti-female propaganda . . . does one need scientific methodology in order to conclude that the anti-female propaganda that permeates our nation's cultural output promotes a climate in which acts of sexual hostility directed against women are not only tolerated but ideologically encouraged?[23]

> Even when they do not overtly depict scenes of violence and degradation of women at the hands of men, such as rape, beatings, and subordination, the tone is consistently anti-feminist. . . . The intention would seem to be simply to degrade women, and it is noteworthy that in many cases of rape the men involved either act in the same manner. . . .[24]

However, what is the evidence regarding the relationship of pornography and aggression against women?

Some studies have attempted to determine whether or not erotica has a differential effect on aggression against men and against women. The general conclusion has been that no differential effects occur. Thus, in one series of studies, Mosher[25,26] found no increase in "sex-calloused" attitudes, aggressive verbal remarks, or exploitive sexual behavior toward females. More recent research by Jaffe *et al.*[5] and Baron and Bell[27] have also indicated that erotic exposure does not differentially affect men's aggression toward males or females.

There are a number of problems with the research that has examined the link between pornography and male aggression toward females. First, there is strong evidence that prior or subsequent anger instigation is critically important in facilitating aggression following erotic exposure. Given the fact that males are usually hesitant about aggressing against females,[28] and that in the above research subjects were not even instigated by their potential victim, it would seem unlikely that a differential facilitation in aggression would occur. In fact, except for the Jaffe *et al* study,[5] researchers found that exposing nonangered individuals to erotic films intended to *reduce* aggression or maintain it at a level comparable to that of subjects exposed to a neutral film.[19]

Second, previous researchers have found that only under conditions of high sexual arousal does a facilitative effect in aggression occur. Exposure to mild sexually arousing stimuli seems to reduce aggression, even in previously angered individuals.[19,7,6] Again, except for Jaffe *et al.,*[5] the research that has examined the relationship of erotic stimuli and aggression toward females has employed milder forms of sexually arousing stimuli.

It would seem, therefore, that an appropriate test of the effects of erotic stimuli on aggression toward females would need to employ both some form of anger instigation and high levels of sexual arousal. This particular combination of important factors, which seems to account for the facilitative effects of erotic stimuli on aggression, has not, until recently, been investigated in those studies in which females are the victims of aggression from males.

◉ *Experiment I*

A recent study by Donnerstein and Barrett[8] was designed to examine these issues using the theory and data of past research in the erotic stimuli-aggression area as a framework. Male subjects were exposed to either a neutral or highly arousing erotic film. The type of erotic stimuli employed was similar to those used in previous studies that have indicated facilitative effects for aggression.[4,13] In addition, prior to stimulus exposure subjects were either angered or treated in a neutral manner by a male or female target of aggression. Both aggressive behavior, in the form of electric shock, and physiological reactions of the subject were observed.

Since the procedures in the studies in this series were all similar, a few words regarding the methodology employed are presented. All subjects were male undergraduates who volunteered for the study as part of receiving extra credit in their course work. They believed that they were interacting with another male or female subject in a study on the effects of stress and performance. Our male subjects were first given an opportunity to write an essay with the understanding that the essay would be evaluated by the "other subject" via the delivery of electric shock. If the subject was in a condition where they were to be angered, they received a large number of shocks plus a negative written evaluation of their essay from the other male or female subject. Nonangered subjects received only one shock and a very positive evaluation. This type of procedure is very common in the literature and produces both physiological responses and self-reports that indicate that subjects have, in fact, been angered. Following this procedure, subjects were then given an opportunity to deliver shock to the "subject" who had evaluated their assay. No shock was actually delivered, but subjects assumed that they were in fact administering various levels of shock to this person. At various times in the studies, physiological responses of the subjects in the form of blood pressure, were measured. It should be noted that in addition to various consent forms that were signed by the subject, a complete debriefing as to the nature of the study was given to the subjects at the end of the session.

With this experimental procedure in mind, the first study in this series made a number of predictions based upon previous research in the area: (1) exposure to erotic films should increase aggressive behavior in angered individuals, while (2) no facilitation in aggressive behavior should occur for nonangered subjects. Of more immediate interest, however, were the following questions: (1) Would exposure to erotic stimuli differentially affect aggression toward males and females in subjects who have previously been instigated to aggress? (2) Might there be an increase in aggression toward females even without prior instigation due to implied sexually aggressive cues in the erotic films? and (3) What are the physiological patterns that emerge during film exposure? This third question was of special interest, in that from a theoretical perspective, the interaction of anger arousal and erotic-film-exposure arousal have been employed in an explanatory manner in this area.[4] To date, however, such results were based upon interactions with only male targets of aggression. There is a suggestion from prior research[29] that although males display less aggression toward females following provocation, physiological arousal is maintained at a high level. It seemed important, in terms of past research in this area, to examine further not only the arousal component of anger instigation from males to females, but also its interaction with highly arousing sexual stimuli. Donnerstein and Barrett[8] also examined the effects of anger, erotic stimuli, and sex on a more prosocial or rewarding response. Since it was expected that less social restraints would be present with this reward response than with the shock response toward females, subjects were given an opportunity in this study to administer rewards (money) to their target. The major results for this first study are presented in Tables 1 and 2. With regard to aggression, as measured by the intensity and durations of shocks administered to the male or female, two interactions were found. The first, anger X sex of target, indicated that angered subjects were more aggressive than nonangered subjects and that subjects angered by a male were more aggressive than those angered by a female. The second, anger X films, indicated that under nonanger conditions there were no effects for the films shown, but, when subjects were angry the erotic film increased aggression. Thus, when subjects were exposed to highly arousing erotic stimuli there was a possibility for aggression to be facilitated. More important to the discussion is the fact that no differential aggression was observed toward females as a function of film exposure. In fact, as has been the case in past studies,[29] less

TABLE 1 *Mean Intensity* X Duration as a Function of Experimental Conditions*

	Means	
Condition	Anger	No Anger
Anger X Sex of Target		
Male	1.86_a	0.95_c
Female	1.55_b	1.13_c
Anger X Films		
Erotic	1.90_a	0.93_c
Neutral	1.45_b	1.15_c

*Means with a different subscript differ from each other at the 0.05 level by Duncan's procedure.

173

TABLE 2 *Mean Change* In Blood Pressure as a Function of Experimental Conditions after Film Exposure*

	Film	
Condition	**Erotic**	**Neutral**
	Mean Blood Pressure	
Anger		
Males	1.8$_b$	-0.2$_b$
Females	9.4$_a$	-3.1$_c$
No Anger		
Males	8.2$_a$	-3.9$_c$
Females	7.2$_a$	-3.9$_c$
	Systolic Blood Pressure	
Anger		
Males	2.8$_b$	-1.4$_b$
Females	11.3$_a$	-4.8$_c$
No Anger		
Males	11.2$_a$	-5.6$_c$
Females	8.6$_a$	-6.2$_c$

*Means with different subscripts differ from each other at the 0.05 level by Duncan's procedure.

aggression was administered to the female targets. Does this imply, therefore, that erotic films do not influence aggression towards females as suggested by the pornography commission?[10] The physiological data obtained in this study would suggest that perhaps another process was operating with angered subjects. The blood pressure data indicated that higher levels of arousal were obtained with a female rather than a male target after erotic exposure, and that this arousal was still present after aggressing. It might have been expected, therefore, that aggression would have been higher toward females than males. Results, however, tended to indicate just the opposite. Under anger conditions females were aggressed against less than males. It is interesting to note that Taylor and Epstein[29] also found increased physiological arousal in male subjects who were less aggressive toward a female target under attack conditions. One possible explanation for this type of finding, suggested by Dengerink,[28] is that aggression towards females is generally disapproved of, and that this fear of disapproval could act to inhibit aggression. Further evidence that males were inhibited from acting aggressively toward female targets in this study was suggested by the reward data. Under anger conditions a reduction in reward was found for females. It would seem reasonable to suggest that in the context of this study changes in rewarding behavior would carry less social restraints than delivery of a noxious stimulus toward a female. If these results were a function of inhibitions toward aggressing against females, then conditions allowing for a reduction in inhibitions might reveal differential aggression toward males and females as a function of erotic exposure.

❀ &xperiment II

The purpose of this experiment was to create a condition in which male subjects would be less inhibited or restrained against aggressing toward a female, in order to examine the effects that erotic exposure would have upon such aggression. While there are many potential strategies to reduce aggressive inhibitions (e.g., aggressive models), the present study adopted a situation similar to that employed by Geen, Stonner, and Shope.[30] These investigators found that when subjects were given two opportunities to aggress against an anger instigator, aggression was higher than in a condition in which subjects were not given this initial aggression opportunity. Furthermore, subjects in the double aggression condition reported less restraints against aggressing than individuals in all other conditions. Additional support for this increase in aggression, following an initial opportunity to aggress, has been provided by a number of investigators (e.g., Reference 31). In the context of the present experiment, it was hypothesized that allowing male subjects an initial opportunity to aggress against a female would act to reduce any aggression inhibitions present. If erotic films are capable of facilitating aggression against females, then the present experiment, by incorporating both anger instigation and highly erotic films in addition to a reduction in inhibitions, should allow for a more judicious test of this possibility.

In this study, male subjects were angered by a male or female target prior to being placed into one of three film conditions. Before being given an opportunity to aggress, subjects viewed either a highly erotic film, aggressive film, or no film. After having one opportunity to aggress against the male or female target, subjects waited 10 minutes and were given a second opportunity to aggress.

The results of the present study, as seen in Figure 1, would suggest that highly erotic films can act to increase aggressive responses against females

FIGURE 1 *Mean shock intensity as a function of film conditions, sex of target, and time of aggression.*

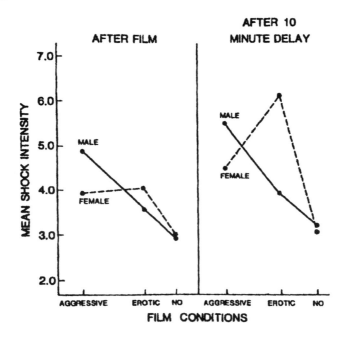

under certain conditions. When male subjects were given an opportunity to aggress immediately following film exposure, it was found that highly erotic films did increase aggression beyond that of the no-film controls. This finding corroborates those of other investigators[6,4] who have found that highly arousing erotica can act as a facilitator of aggression in previously angered individuals. In addition, it was found that during this initial aggression opportunity there was no differential aggression toward males or females. These results are also supportive of previous studies (e.g., References 27, 8, 5) that have indicated no sex-of-target effects following erotic exposure. However, when male subjects were given a second opportunity to aggress against the target, 10 minutes later, aggressive responses were increased against female targets. This finding of an increase in aggression against women in the delayed condition is the first demonstration that this effect can, in fact, occur.

◉ $\mathcal{E}$xperiment III

It has been suggested that a major problem with the conclusion of the pornography commission report[10] was the lack of research on "porno-violence," or aggressive content in erotic forms of materials.[2] This lack of research was surprising given the results of the National Commission on the Causes and Prevention of Violence,[32] dealing with media aggression and its effect on subsequent aggressive behavior.

Given the nature of most erotic films, in which women are depicted in a submissive, passive role, any subtle aggressive content could act to increase aggression against females because of their association with observed aggression. As noted in the work of Berkowitz,[33] one important determinant of whether an aggressive response is made is the presence of aggressive cues. Not only objects, but individuals can take on aggressive-cue value if they have been associated with observed violence. Thus, in the context of the present research, the viewing of more sexually aggressive films might facilitate aggression towards females because of the aggression-elicit-ing stimulus properties of the female target from her repeated association with observed violence. This increase in aggression should be especially true for previously angered individuals who are already predisposed to aggress. In the research discussed up to this point the films employed did not contain acts of aggression. If they do, perhaps the results would have differed with respect to female victims.

In order to examine this issue, male subjects in the present study[34] were angered or treated in a neutral manner by a male or female. They were then shown one of three films. Two of the films were highly erotic but differed in aggressive content. While one film was entirely nonaggressive, the other depicted the rape of a women by a man who breaks into her house and forces her at gunpoint into sexual activity. The third film was a neutral (nonerotic and nonaggressive) presentation.

The major results are presented in Figure 2. Two interactions occurred which deserve attention. The first, anger X film, indicated that both the erotic and aggressive-erotic film increased aggression, primarily in angered individuals. The largest increase occurred, however, for subjects exposed to the aggressive-erotic film. The second interaction, sex of target X film, indi-cated that while both types of erotic films increased aggression against a male, only the aggressive-erotic film facilitated aggression against a female, and this level of aggression was higher than that directed against a male.

177

FIGURE 2 *Mean shock intensity as a function of sex of target by films, and anger by films.*

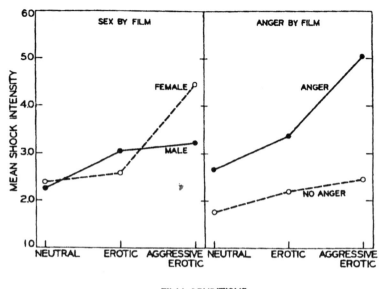

FILM CONDITIONS

Why would aggression be increased against the female after exposure to the aggressive-erotic film? One potential explanation is that the females' association with the victim in the film made her an aggressive stimulus that could elicit aggressive responses (e.g., Reference 33). The combination of anger and arousal from the film heightened this response and led to the highest level of aggression against the female. But, even under nonanger conditions aggression was increased. This was not the case for subjects paired with a male. Under nonanger, the aggressive-erotic film did not influence aggression against the male target. It would seem, then, that the female's association with observed violence was an important contributor to the aggressive responses toward her. If this is the case then it would be expected that films that depict violence against women, even without sexual content, could act as a stimulus for aggressive acts toward women. It seems important, therefore, for future research to begin a systematic investigation into the context of women's association with violence in the media.

◉ Conclusion and Implications

It was the intention of the present research to examine the effects that certain media presentations have on aggression against women. Results from these investigation suggest that films of both an erotic *and* aggressive nature can be a mediator of aggression toward women. In addition to the theoretical implications of these results, there is a more applied question that has been the concern of the present paper. When it is found that (1) 50% of university females report some form of sexual aggression,[35] (2) 39% of the sex offenders questioned indicate that pornography had something to do with the crime they committed,[36] and (3) the incidence of rape and other sexual assaults have increased then the question of what conditions precipitate such actions should be examined. The present research suggests that specific types of media account for part of these actions. Given the increase in sexual and other forms of violence against women depicted in the media, a concern over such presentations seems warranted. There is ample evidence that the observation of violent forms of media can facilitate aggressive response (e.g., Reference 37), yet to assume that the depiction of sexual-aggression could not have a similar effect, particularly against females, would be misleading. Given the findings of the present studies, it seems important for future investigations to begin a systematic examination of the role of the media in aggression against women.

References

[1]Berkowitz, L. 1971. Sex and violence: we can't have it both ways. Psychology Today.

[2]Cline, V. B. 1974. Another view: pornography effects, the state of the art. *In* Where Do You Draw the Line? V. B. Cline, Ed. Brigham Young University Press. Provo, Utah.

[3]Dienstbier, R. A. 1977. Sex and violence: Can research have it both ways? Comm. 27: 176–188.

[4]Zillmann, D. 1971. Excitation transfer in communication-mediated aggressive behavior. J. Exp. Soc. Psychol. 7: 419–434.

[5]Jaffw, Y., N. Malamuth, J. Feingold & S. Feshbach. 1974. Sexual arousal and behavioral aggression. J. Pers. Soc. Psychol. 30: 759–764.

[6]Donnerstein, E., M. Donnerstein & R. Evans. 1975. Erotic stimuli and aggression: facilitation or inhibition., J. Pers. Soc. Psychol. 32: 237–244.

[7]Baron, R. A. & P. A. Bell. 1977. Sexual arousal and aggression by males: effects of type of erotic stimuli and prior provocation. J. Pers. Soc. Psychol. 35: 79–87.

[8]Donnerstein, E. & G. Barrett. 1978. The effects of erotic stimuli on male aggression towards females. J. Pers. Soc. Psychol. 36: 180–188.

[9]Donnerstein, E. & J. Hallam. 1978 The facilitating effects of erotica on aggression toward females. J. Pers. Soc. Psychol. 36: 1270–1277.

[10]Presidential Commission on Obscenty and Pornography. 1971. U.S. Government Printing Office. Washington, D.C.

[11]Howard, J. L., M. B. Liptzin & C. B. Reifler. 1973. Is pornography a problem? J. Soc. Issues 29: 133–145.

[12]Loebert, R. M. & N. S. Schwarzberg. 1977. Effects of mass media. Annu. Rev. Psychol. 28: 141–173.

[13]Meyer, T. P. 1972. The effects of sexually arousing and violent films on aggressive behavior. J. Sex. Res. 8: 324–333.

[14]Zillmann, D., J. L. Hoyt & K. D. Day. 1974. Strength and duration of the effects of aggressive, violent, and erotic communications on subsequent aggressive behavior. Comm. Res. 1: 286–306.

[15]Bandura, A. 1973. Aggression: A Social Learning Analysis. Prentice-Hall, Inc. Englewood Cliffs, N.J.

[16]Zillmann, D., A. Katcher & B. Milavsky. 1972. Excitation transfer from physical exercise to subsequent aggressive behavior. J. Exp. Soc. Psychol. 8: 247–259.

[17]Donnerstein, E. & D. W. Wilson. 1976. Effects of noise and perceived control on ongoing and subsequent aggressive behavior. J. Pers. Soc. Psychol. 34: 774–781.

[18]Malamuth, N. M., S. Fesbach & Y. Jaffe. 1977. Sexual arousal and aggression: recent experiments and theoretical issues. J. Soc. Issues 33: 110–133.

[19]Baron, R. A. 1974. The aggression-inhibiting influence of heightened sexual arousal. J. Pers. Soc. Psychol. 30: 318–322.

[20]Frodi A. 1977. Sexual arousal, situational restrictiveness, and aggressive behavior. J. Res. in Pers. 11: 48–58.

[21]Zillmann, D. & B. S. Sapolsky. 1977. What mediates the effect of mild erotica on annoyance and hostile behavior in males? J. Pers. Soc. Psychol. 35: 587–596.

[22]Mprgan, R. 1978. Going Too Far. Vintage Press, Inc. New York, N.Y.

[23]Brownmiller, S. 1975. Against Our Will. Bantam Books, Inc. New York, N.Y.

[24]Eysenck, H. J. & H. Nias. 1978. Sex, Violence, and the Media. Spector. London, England.

[25]Mosher, D. L. 1971. Pornographic films, male verbal aggression against women, and guilt. In Technical Report of the Commission on Obscenity and Pornography 8. U.S. Government Printing Office. Washington, D.C.

[26]Mosher, D. L. 1971. Psychological reactions to pornographic films. In Technical Report of the Commission on Obscenity and Pornography 8. U.S. Government Printing Office. Washington, D.C.

[27]Baron, R. A. & P. A. Bell. 1973. Effects of heightened sexual arousal on physical aggression. Proc. 81st Ann. Conv. of the Amer. Psych. Assoc. 8: 171–172.

[28]Dengerink, H. A. 1976. Personality variables as mediators of attack-instigated aggression. In Perspectives on Aggression. R. Geen & E. O'Neal, Eds. Academic Press Inc. New York. N.Y.

[29]Taylor, S. P. & S. Epstein. 1967. Aggression as a function of the interaction of the sex of the aggressor and the sex of the victim. Pers. 35: 474–486.

[30]Geen, R. G., D. Stonner & G. L. Shope. 1975. The facilitation of aggression by aggression: a study of response inhibition and disinhibition. J. Pers. Soc. Psychol. 31: 721–726.

[31]Geen, R. G. & M. B. Quanty. 1977. The facilitation of aggression by aggression: a study of response inhibition and disinhibition. J. Pers. Soc. Psychol. 31: 721–726.

[32]National Commission on the Causes and Prevention of Violence. 1969. U.S. Government Printing Office. Washington. D.C.

[33]Berkowitz, L. 1974. Some determinants of impulsive aggression: the role of mediated associations with reinforcements for aggression. Psych. Rev. 81: 165–176.

[34]Donnerstein, E. 1979. Pornography commission revisited: aggressive-erotica and violence against women. (Submitted for publication.)

[35]Kanin, E. G. & S. R. Parcell. 1977. Sexual aggression: a second look at the offended female. Arch. Sex. Behav. 6: 67–76.

[36]Walker, E. C. 1971. Erotic stimuli and the aggressive sexual offender. Technical Report of Commission on Obscenity and Pornography 8. U.S. Government Printing Office. Washington, D.C.

[37]Geen, R. G. 1978. Some effects of observing violence upon the behavior of the observer. In Progress in Experimental Personality Research. B. Maher, Ed. 8. Academic Press. Inc. New York, N.Y.

Questions

1. Under what conditions did the viewing of erotic films increase violence against both men and women?

2. Under what conditions did such viewing increase violence against women only?

3. Why would anger facilitate the violent effect of pornography?

4. What was the effect of erotic-aggressive films?

5. These studies were conducted in laboratories with undergraduate students. Do you think these findings hold true for the general population?

6. Given what you have learned from this article, do you think we should change any of the laws regarding the sale of pornography? Why or why not?

Prostitution Control in America: Rethinking Public Policy

Ronald Weitzer

George Washington University

Prostitution is illegal throughout the United States—except in Las Vegas, Nevada. In this selection, Ronald Weitzer examines three alternative approaches to prostitution: decriminalization, legalization, and a two-track model. Based on three criteria—public preferences, efficiency of resource utilization, and harm reduction—Weitzer recommends that the United States adopt the two-track model of social control of prostitution.

✿ Problems with Current Policy

Prostitution control in America involves the commitment of substantial criminal justice resources—with little impact on the sex trade or on collateral problems such as victimization of prostitutes and effects on host communities.

Criminal Justice System Costs

There are approximately 90,000 annual arrests in the United States for violations of prostitution laws (Bureau of Justice Statistics, annual), in addition to an unknown number of arrests of prostitutes under disorderly conduct or loitering statutes. The fiscal costs are substantial. A study of the country's sixteen largest cities found that they spent a total of $120 million in 1985 enforcing prostitution laws (Pearl, 1987). Data are unavailable on the costs of prostitution control nationwide, but extrapolating from the above figure

"Prostitution Control in America: Rethinking Public Policy," by Ronald Weitzer, reprinted from *Crime, Law and Social Change*, vol. 32, 1999, pp. 83–102.

on just a few cities, there is no question that the total expenditure is considerable.

What are the benefits of these expenditures? A San Francisco Crime Committee (1971: 20) concluded in 1971 that spending on prostitution control "buys essentially nothing of a positive nature," and Atlanta's Task Force on Prostitution (1986) concluded that this spending was a "waste" that burdened the courts and lowered police morale. Moreover, law enforcement has little effect on the amount of prostitution, offers little protection to prostitutes at risk, and gives little relief to communities besieged by street prostitution. At best, the problem is *contained* within a particular area where prostitutes are occasionally subjected to the revolving door of arrest, fines, brief jail time, and release or *displaced* into another locale, begetting the same revolving-door dynamic. Containment is the norm throughout the United States; displacement requires sustained police intervention, which is rare. Instead, law enforcement typically consists of periodic arrests and occasional, sweeping crackdowns on prostitutes. Containment may be acceptable to residents of neighborhoods free of street prostitution, but is aggravating to many residents of prostitution zones.

Victimization

Street prostitutes are at considerable risk of violence from customers, exploitation from pimps, and drug and health problems. A survey of 200 street prostitutes in San Francisco found that two-thirds had been assaulted by customers and pimps and 70 percent had been raped by customers (Silbert and Pines, 1982). Other studies report similar rates of victimization among street prostitutes (Barnard, 1993; Davis, 2000; Farley and Barkan, 1998; James and Meyerling, 1977). However, all of these studies relied on convenience samples (women who contacted service agencies or were interviewed in jail or on the streets), not random samples, which likely skews the results toward that part of the population experiencing the most victimization. This means that the high victimization rates reported are probably lower for street prostitutes as a whole. Having said that, all evidence indicates that street prostitutes are indeed vulnerable to abuse and that prevailing methods of prostitution control in most cities offer little protection against such victimization.

Workers involved in upscale prostitution, such as escorts and call girls, are relatively free of victimization (Perkins, 1991: 290). They are not immune to violence, but it is not the occupational hazard that it is for street workers.

Community Impact

It is street prostitution—not the more clandestine, indoor varieties of sex work—that generates the lion's share of citizen complaints about prostitution in America. A wide variety of sources (e.g., Clark, 1993; Persons, 1996) and my extensive search of newspaper articles in Lexis/Nexis (Weitzer, 2000) identified a set of common claims made by residents of neighborhoods with street prostitution.

Unlike the antiprostitution reformers of the 19th and early 20th centuries, who made much of the immorality and sinfulness of prostitution as well as the exploitation of "fallen" women (Hobson, 1987; Pivar, 1973), neighborhood groups in contemporary America are driven less by moral indignation than by *overt street behavior* on the part of prostitutes, pimps, and customers. Stress is placed on the *tangible environmental effects* of sexual commerce on the street.

The degree to which prostitutes, pimps, and customers cause commotion in public places varies across time and place. Still, the public visibility of the enterprise increases the likelihood that it will have some adverse effect on the surrounding community. Similarities across cities in the manifestation of street prostitution produce similar complaints among residents. Standard complaints center on conduct such as streetwalkers' brazen flagging down of customers' cars, arguing and fighting with people on the street, visible drug use, performing sex acts in public, and littering with used condoms and syringes (both unsightly trash and a public health hazard). Children are frequently mentioned in the litany of grievances: they witness transactions and sex acts being consummated; they sometimes discover discarded condoms and syringes; and they are occasionally approached by prostitutes or customers.

Customers are scorned in these communities as much as the prostitutes (Persons, 1996). Not only do they contribute to traffic congestion in their ritual cruising of prostitution strolls, they also harass and proposition women whom they mistake for prostitutes. Many communities have targeted the customers (by recording their license plate numbers, videotaping, etc.) more than the prostitutes, because the johns are seen as more vulnerable to public identification and shaming.

185

Residents define street prostitution not as a mere nuisance or "victimless crime" but instead as eroding the quality of life and contributing to neighborhood decay and street disorder (cf. Kelling and Coles, 1996; Skogan, 1990; Wilson and Kelling, 1982). As a coalition of twenty-eight neighborhood and business groups in San Francisco declared, street prostitution "poses a very serious threat to the integrity of San Francisco's business and residential communities" (Coalition, 1996).

No data exist on the magnitude of the problems due to street prostitution in American cities (aside from arrest rates and residents' claims that the problem is serious), but the literature on this topic indicates that street prostitution can present a real problem for host communities.

⊛ Alternative Policies

Soliciting for purposes of prostitution, pimping, and other prostitution-related activities are crimes throughout the United States, and this criminalization policy is seldom questioned. Rarely have policy makers shown a willingness to rethink the status quo and experiment with novel approaches.[1] No national commission of inquiry has examined prostitution, with the result that almost no public debate has taken place. Alternatives to the current policy of blanket criminalization are evaluated below.

Decriminalization

Decriminalization would remove all criminal penalties and result in a laissez-faire approach in which prostitution would be left unregulated. Prostitutes' rights groups, like COYOTE (Call Off Your Old Tired Ethics),[2] favor full decriminalization of adult prostitution because they define it as work, like any other work, and because decriminalization is the only policy that recognizes prostitutes' "right" to use their bodies as they wish. Regulations are opposed because they would allow government interference with this right and because they would only perpetuate the stigmatization of prostitutes (e.g., if restricted to brothels or red light districts).

There is virtually no public support for decriminalization. A 1983 survey found that only 7 percent of the public thought "there should be no laws against prostitution" (Merit, 1983). Policy makers are almost universally opposed to decriminalization, making this a nonstarter in any serious discussion of policy alternatives (Parnas, 1981). Moreover, the logic behind decriminalization is shaky. Freed of regulation, prostitutes arguably would enjoy advantages unavailable to purveyors of other commercial services (Skolnick and Dombrink, 1978: 201; Decker, 1979: 463). A major Canadian commission held that prostitution should enjoy no special immunity from the law: "it is difficult to see how some degree of regulation could be avoided" in light of "the special risks inherent in the activity of prostitution" (Special Committee, 1985: 518). Taken to its extreme, decriminalization would permit prostitutes and their customers to engage in sexual exchanges without restriction, except for extant prohibitions on public nudity and sex.

Although decriminalization is roundly dismissed by the American public and policy makers, its advocates sometimes manage to get it onto the public agenda. A recent example illustrates the fate of a decriminalization proposal, in a city known for its tolerance. A Task Force on Prostitution was formed by San Francisco's Board of Supervisors in 1994 to explore alternatives to existing methods of prostitution control. Members included representatives of community and business groups, the National Lawyer's Guild, National Organization for Women, prostitutes' rights groups, the police department, and the district attorney's office. From the beginning, the prostitutes' advocates and their sympathizers set the agenda and dominated the proceedings, which led to chronic infighting. Supervisor Terence Hallinan was the driving force behind the panel but unsatisfied with the result: "I didn't ride herd on this task force. I would have liked a better balance. . . . Instead of coming up with good, practical solutions, they spent months fighting about decriminalization and legalization."[3] After a majority of the members voted to recommend a policy of decriminalization in January 1995,[4] the six community and business representatives resigned. One of the latter later proclaimed that the departure of community members shredded the legitimacy of the panel and troubled the remaining members: "They were upset as hell because the task force lost credibility without the citizens' groups participating."[5] While the comment is not made from a disinterested position, the task force report itself expresses regret that consensus was not achieved on its main recommendation.

The panel's endorsement of decriminalization reflected the interests of prostitutes' advocates and their allies and doomed the report's prospect for serious consideration in official circles. The city's Board of Supervisors promptly shelved the report. It is possible, however, that a less radical recommendation would have been received more favorably by city officials;

Supervisor Hallinan and even some community leaders had floated the possibility of legalization (zoning into red light areas) when the task force was first proposed.

*L*egalization

Legalization spells *regulation* of some kind: licensing or registration, confining prostitutes to red light districts, state-restricted brothels, mandatory medical exams, special business taxes, etc. Implicit in the idea of legalization is the principle of harm reduction: that is, that regulation is necessary to reduce some of the problems associated with prostitution. The American public is divided on the issue, with support for legalization ranging from a quarter to half the population in most polls (Gallup, 1991, 1996; Harris, 1978, 1990; Merit, 1983; Weitzer, 2000). This support has not, however, translated into popular pressure for legal change anywhere in the country, in part because most citizens see it as far removed from their personal interests and because policy makers are largely silent on the issue (Weitzer, 1991).

Some advocates of legalization cite with approval Nevada's legal brothels. Confined to small-scale operations in rural areas of the state (and prohibited in Las Vegas and Reno due to opposition from the gambling industry), this model hardly solves the problem of street prostitution in urban areas. Streetwalkers flourish in Las Vegas and Reno, despite the existence of legal brothels in counties adjacent to these cities. What is needed is some kind of specifically urban solution to an essentially urban problem.

Since Nevada legalized brothels in 1971, no other state has seriously considered legalization. Legislators fear being branded as "condoning" prostitution, and see no political advantages in any kind of liberalization. The exceptions seem to prove the rule of futility. For example, bills to permit licensing of prostitutes and brothels were introduced in the California State Assembly in the 1970s, to no avail (Jennings, 1976; Parnas, 1981). In 1992 New York City Councilor Julia Harrison offered a resolution for licensing prostitutes, restricting legal brothels to certain parts of the city, and requiring HIV tests of the workers. The purpose was "to eliminate the pestilence of street activity in residential neighborhoods," as the resolution declared. Harrison told me that she got the "highest praise from the community" in her district, Flushing, but her proposal met with stiff opposition in the city council and never made it out of committee.[6]

A major determinant of the success of legalization is the willingness of prostitutes to comply with the regulations. Those who have pimps may not be allowed to work in most regulated systems, particularly if it means a dilution of the pimps' control over their employees. Where legalization includes stipulations as to who can and cannot engage in the sex trade, certain types of individuals will be excluded from the legal regime, forcing them to operate illicitly. Where underage or diseased or migrant prostitutes are ineligible, they would have no recourse but to work in the shadows of the regulated system. Moreover, every conceivable form of legalization would be rejected by some or many eligible prostitutes, who would see no benefits in abiding by the new restrictions and would resent the infringement on their freedom. It is precisely on these grounds that prostitutes' rights groups denounce licensing, mandatory health checks, and legal brothel systems. A possible exception would be zoning street prostitution into a suitable locale: away from residential areas but in places that are safe and unintimidating for prostitutes and customers alike. Many streetwalkers would be satisfied with this kind of arrangement, but others would not. Red light districts in industrial zones have been proposed, but most streetwalkers would reject confinement to these areas because they typically lack places of refuge and sustenance, such as restaurants, coffee shops, bars, parks, and cheap hotels—all of which are facilitative of street prostitution (Cohen, 1980). Even if an acceptable locale could be found, there is no guarantee that street prostitution would be confined to that area; market saturation in the designated zone would push some workers into less competitive locales. Moreover, while zoning presumably would remove street prostitution from residential areas, it would not necessarily remedy other problems associated with street work, such as violence and drug abuse.

Would a system of legal prostitution attract an influx of prostitutes into the host city? If limited to one or a few cities in the United States, the answer would be affirmative. Were it more widespread, each locale would hold less attraction to outside workers.

More fundamentally, would legalization, in any of its forms, institutionalize and officially condone prostitution and make it more difficult for workers to leave the business? Government officials, feminists, and prostitutes' rights advocates alike object to legalization on precisely these grounds. Whether legalization would indeed make it more difficult for workers to leave prostitution than is the case under criminalization would depend in part on whether the workers were officially labeled as prostitutes—via registration, licensing, special commercial taxes, a registry for mandatory health checks—or whether their identities would remain unknown to the authorities, as might be the case if legalization took the form of zoning.

A final consideration is the willingness and capacity of municipal authorities to actively regulate the sex trade and compel compliance with the rules. American officials are almost universally unprepared to assume this responsibility. Why would any American city assume the added burden of planning, launching, and managing a system of legal prostitution when the benefits are doubtful and when the logistical, resource, and moral costs would be envisioned as unacceptably high? Whatever the possible merits (health, safety, etc.) of any particular model of legalization, it is therefore imperative to consider its feasibility in the United States. Advocates face almost impossible odds trying to marshall support from legislators and the wider population. Proposals for legalization, while occasionally floated, will remain nonstarters in this country for the foreseeable future. A third policy alternative may have broader appeal.

A Two-Track Model

Policy makers often fail to draw the crucial distinction between street and off-street prostitution, partly because both types are criminalized by law throughout the United States. But since prostitution manifests itself in fundamentally different ways on the street and in indoor venues, it is only sensible to treat the two differently. One model would (1) *target resources exclusively toward the control of street prostitution* and (2) *relax controls on indoor prostitution* such as escort agencies, massage parlors, call girls, and brothels. A few blue-ribbon panels have recommended changes either consistent with or close to this two-track model. A San Francisco commission noted that whereas street prostitution has significant adverse consequences for public order and public health, the situation is quite the opposite for indoor prostitution—a situation warranting a dual approach (San Francisco Committee, 1971). An Atlanta task force went a step further in recommending that law enforcement be directed against street prostitution rather than off-street prostitution and that city officials provide more assistance to neighborhoods affected by prostitution, in the form of greater liaison between neighborhood associations and the authorities and redevelopment of communities to discourage street prostitution and other crime (Atlanta Task Force, 1986). And a landmark Canadian commission argued that abating street prostitution would require legislation allowing prostitutes to work somewhere else. It recommended (1) allowing unobtrusive street solicitation, (2) punishment of obnoxious behavior by streetwalkers (offensive language, disturbing the peace, disrupting traffic), and (3) permitting one or two prostitutes to work out of their residence (Special Committee, 1985). (The third proposal was endorsed by a recent Canadian task force [Working Group, 1998: 71]). Indoor work by one or two prostitutes was seen as preferable to work on the streets or in brothels since it gives the workers maximum autonomy and shields them against exploitation by pimps and other managers. The commission also recommended giving provincial authorities the option of legalizing small, non-residential brothels, subject to appropriate controls.

In all three cases, government officials rejected the recommendations without explanation in San Francisco and Atlanta, and in Canada on the grounds that it would condone prostitution. Some Australian states, however, have recently implemented the two-track approach, i.e., decriminalizing brothels and increasing enforcement against street prostitution (Sullivan, 1997).

⊂rack One: Jndoor ⪢rostitution

Some cities already have an informal policy of de facto decriminalization of indoor prostitution—essentially ignoring call girls, escort agencies, and massage parlors unless a complaint is made, which is seldom. Police in other cities, however, devote substantial time and resources to this side of the sex trade, where it accounts for as much as half the prostitution arrests or consumes up to half the vice budgets. One study of sixteen cities found that indoor prostitution accounted for between a quarter and a third of all prostitution arrests in Baltimore, Memphis, and Milwaukee, and half the arrests in Cleveland.[7] Some cities (like Houston and Philadelphia) have shifted their emphasis from the street to indoor prostitution, ostensibly to go after the "big fish."[8] Some other police departments devote an entire branch to combatting outcall and escort services, e.g., the Pandering Unit in Detroit and the Ad Vice Unit in Los Angeles.

Efforts against indoor prostitution typically involve elaborate, time-consuming undercover operations to entrap the women. Such stings require considerable planning, and large-scale operations can last a year or two, becoming rather costly affairs. The Heidi Fleiss case in Los Angeles is only the most notorious recent example. There have been some federal actions as well. In 1990, for example, federal agents launched raids on more than forty upscale escort agencies in twenty-three cities. The sting was the culmination of a two-year undercover investigation, costing $2.5 million.[9]

An officer attached to the Ad Vice unit in Los Angeles justified his work with rather twisted logic: "We're trying to keep it from becoming rampant on our streets" (A&E, 1997). In fact, crackdowns on indoor prostitution can have the opposite result—increasing the number of streetwalkers—thus unintentionally exacerbating the most obtrusive side of the prostitution trade. Closures of massage parlors and other indoor venues have had precisely this effect in some cities (Cohen, 1980: 81; Larsen, 1992; Lowman, 1992; Pearl, 1985), and a New Orleans vice officer noted that, "Whenever we focus on indoor investigations, the street scene gets insane."[10]

The success of a policy of nonenforcement regarding indoor prostitution would require that it be implemented without fanfare. A public announcement that a city had decided to take a "hands off" approach to this variety of sex work might serve as a magnet drawing legions of indoor workers and clients into the locale. But in cities where it is not already standard practice, an unwritten policy of nonenforcement might be a sensible innovation. It would free up resources for the more pressing problems on the street, and might have the effect of pushing some streetwalkers indoors, as one commission reasoned: "Keeping prostitutes off the streets may be aided by tolerating them off the streets" (San Francisco Committee, 1971: 44). Such an effect is far from certain, however. As a general rule, there is little mobility between the different ranks of prostitution (Benson and Matthews, 1995; Heyl, 1979), and each type has unique attractions to the workers. Advantages of street work include greater flexibility in working conditions than the more restrictive indoor work, rapid turnover of customers and lower time-commitment per trick, and the freedom and excitement of street hustling. Regarding the latter, "Many prostitutes say they prefer the constant action on the street. . . . They enjoy the game aspect of the transaction and the intensity of life as a streetwalker, in contrast to work in a massage parlor or house" (James, 1973: 148). Some clients also prefer streetwalkers: advantages include easy access, anonymity, low cost, choice of women, and the thrill of cruising for sex on the streets—though other clients are attracted to indoor venues because they are safer and more discreet (Campbell, 1998). Moreover, indoor work may not be an option for those streetwalkers who lack the social skills and physical attractiveness that may be required by such establishments or their clients. Indoor and outdoor prostitution serve different markets (Reynolds, 1986). Having said that, greater police intervention on the street has at least some potential to induce some streetwalkers indoors, perhaps into massage parlors.

Compared to street prostitution, there is relatively little public opposition to indoor prostitution, provided it remains inconspicuous. Escort agencies and call girls are typically ignored by community groups, and even massage parlors and brothels arouse little concern relative to streetwalking—again, provided they remain discreet. In San Francisco, a leader of the neighborhood group Save Our Streets told me that most residents of his community would not be bothered by indoor prostitution: "My gut feeling is that, yes, that would be OK. No one has voiced concern over massage parlors" in the area.[11] And a Washington, D.C., neighborhood activist remarked that "people wouldn't be too upset if prostitution went indoors."[12] Community groups rarely mobilize against indoor prostitution, and it appears that the general population is less concerned about this side of the trade. A 1988 survey of residents of Toledo, Ohio (a conservative, working-class city) found that 28 percent supported legal "government-controlled brothels" and 19 percent supported decriminalization of "private call-girl prostitution" (McCaghy and Cernkovich, 1991). No national public opinion polls have asked about specific types of prostitution; instead, they ask vague questions about "legalization" or legal "regulation." Findings of a national Canadian survey may approximate American patterns: while only 11 percent of the population found street prostitution acceptable, a higher number accepted designated red light districts (28 percent), brothels (38 percent), escort and call girl services (43 percent), and prostitution on private premises (45 percent) (Peat Marwick, 1984). Clearly, the *visibility* of prostitution shapes its public acceptability.

Is there a class bias in the two-track approach? Does it favor the higher class, indoor sector and unfairly target the lower-echelon streetwalkers? Inherent in any two-track approach are disparate effects on actors associated with each track, and with respect to prostitution there are legitimate grounds for differential treatment: (1) certain other types of commercial enterprise are prohibited on the streets, and there is no compelling reason why street prostitution should be permitted and (2) "this kind of policy may not be considered too inequitable if the costs inflicted on society by the street prostitutes are greater . . . than from those working in hotels" and other indoor venues (Reynolds, 1986: 194). The legal principle on which this proposal rests is that the criminal law should not interfere with the conduct of consenting adults, provided that this conduct does not *harm* the legally protected interests of others. Whereas street prostitution often involves violence against prostitutes, ancillary crime, disorderly behavior in public, and other adverse effects on host neighborhoods, indoor prostitution is in accord with the harm-reduction principle (Caughey, 1974; Comment, 1977). As the San Francisco Committee on Crime (1971: 38) flatly concluded, "continued criminalization of private, non-visible prostitution cannot be warranted by fear of associated crime, drug abuse, venereal disease, or protection of minors." The Canadian commission (1985: 515) agreed: "The concern with the law is not what takes place in private, but the public manifestation of prostitution." Similarly, harms to prostitutes themselves are pronounced for street workers but much less so for workers in brothels and massage parlors and call girls and escorts (Bryan, 1966, Exner et al., 1977, Farley and Davis, 1978; Reynolds, 1986). As a recent Canadian task force noted, "the two objectives of harm reduction and violence prevention could most likely occur if prostitution was conducted indoors" (Working Group, 1998: 35). The policy implication is clear: "reassign police priorities to those types of prostitution that inflict the greatest costs" (Reynolds, 1986: 192), namely, street prostitution.

Track Two: Restructuring Street Prostitution Control

One advantage of the two-track model is that resources previously devoted to the control of indoor prostitution can be transferred to where they are most needed: the street-level sex trade. Under this model, a policy of *more frequent arrests* of streetwalkers and johns would replace the current norm of sporadic, half-hearted enforcement. This is just the first step, however. What happens after arrest is equally important.

Most prostitution arrests in the United States require that offenders be caught in the act of solicitation, a labor-intensive form of control that limits enforcement efforts. In this legal context it would be naive to think that the "oldest profession" can be wholly eradicated from any major American city. The costs to the prostitute (fines, jail time) could be enhanced, but not dramatically for a misdemeanor offense. Moreover, stiffer penalties have the unfortunate side-effect of forcing prostitutes back onto the streets to recoup their losses, essentially becoming an added cost of doing business. Other, very different approaches are worth considering. A San Diego Task Force (1993), a British parliamentary committee (Benson and Matthews, 1996), and the Association of Chief Police Officers in Britain (Bennetto, 1996) have called for community service sanctions for prostitutes, and New York City has recently experimented with this penalty. If the policy of fining prostitutes simply encourages reoffending to recover losses, community service may open up avenues for a different line of work for at least some of the individuals who truly aspire to reintegration into conventional society. *Community service sanctions are superior to fines or incarceration for this population,* and any policy of intensified arrests should be coupled with a shift toward community service sanctions.

A third reform in the control of street-level prostitution is the need for a more *comprehensive program of meaningful job training and other needed services for those who want to leave prostitution* but eschew low-paying, dead-end jobs. It is not known what percentage of street prostitutes want to leave prostitution, but for those who do, resources are scarce (and even scarcer for sex workers who do not want to leave the industry, but need services). Services to women in the sex industry are woefully inadequate (Weiner, 1996; Seattle Women's Commission, 1995). For example, in Seattle,

> Existing services are not prepared to deal with the unique issues of sex industry women [e.g., stigma, sexual trauma, emotional problems]. . . . Nor do women have the backup resources of family and education needed to reorganize their lives. (Boyer, Chapman, and Marshall, 1993: 20)

Getting prostitutes off the streets requires positive incentives and assistance in the form of housing, job training, counseling, and drug treatment, but the dominant approach is overwhelmingly coercive rather than rehabilitative. Past experience abundantly shows the failure of narrowly punitive intervention. Without meaningful alternatives to prostitution there is little opportunity for a career change.

What about the customers? Traditionally, the act of patronizing a prostitute was not a crime in the United States. This was largely due to the tremendous status disparity between male clients and "women of ill repute." Prostitutes were outcasts whereas patrons were seen as valuable members of society, even if they occasionally dabbled in deviant sexual liaisons. As Abraham Flexner wrote in 1920, the customer "discharges important social and business relations, is a father or brother responsible for the maintenance of others, has commercial or industrial duties to meet. He cannot be imprisoned without damaging society" (quoted in Little, 1995: 38–39). This justification for gender discrimination persists in some quarters today. The renowned Model Penal Code reflects this double standard: The code stipulates that prostitution should be treated as a misdemeanor, while patronizing a prostitute should be punished as a mere violation—an infraction punishable by a fine rather than incarceration. The disparity was defended even as late as 1980, in the official commentary on the code:

> Authorization of severe penalties [jail time] for such misconduct [patronizing] is wholly unrealistic. Prosecutors, judges, and juries would be prone to nullify severe penalties in light of the common perception of extramarital intercourse as a widespread practice. . . . This level of condemnation [a violation and fine] would seem far more in keeping with popular understanding than would more severe sanctions. Furthermore, the lenient treatment of customers reflects the orientation of the offense toward the merchandizers of sexual activity. (American Law Institute, 1980: 468)

The prevalence of extramarital sex, a "popular understanding" favoring the clients, and the notion that the law should target sellers, not buyers, of vice are all invoked to justify lenient treatment of clients. Most state penal codes now treat patronizing as a misdemeanor, not a mere violation as the Model Penal Code recommended.

Since the 1960s, the act of patronizing or soliciting a prostitute has been criminalized by all states, though many state laws continue to punish patronizing less severely than prostitution (Posner and Silbaugh, 1996: 156). And in most cities, enforcement against customers is either sporadic or lacking altogether. Although the double standard has eroded to some extent, it is still only in the exceptional jurisdiction where prostitutes and their patrons are treated equally. Elsewhere, gender bias persists in both arrest rates and penalties (Bernat, 1985; Lowman, 1990). Nationally, of the approximately 90,000 prostitution arrests every year, roughly one-third are males (Bureau of Justice Statistics, annual), which breaks down to about 20 percent male prostitutes and 10 percent male customers. In light of the fact that customers greatly outnumber prostitutes, the gender disparity in arrests appears even more disproportional. Gender bias is also evident in sanctions. In Seattle from 1991 to 1993, for example, 2,508 prostitutes were arrested for solicitation while only 500 customers were arrested for patronizing (Seattle Women's Commission, 1995). And in 1993, 69 percent of the prostitutes charged with solicitation were convicted whereas only 9 percent of the customers were convicted, largely because they were offered pre-trial diversion. Indeed, in most cities first-time arrested customers are routinely offered diversion rather than prosecution. And those customers who are prosecuted and convicted are less likely than prostitutes to receive fines or jail time (Lowman, 1990). In Vancouver between 1991 and 1995, for example, only 0.5 percent of convicted customers were jailed and 9 percent fined; the remainder received absolute or conditional discharges. Convicted prostitutes were treated more harshly: 29 percent were jailed and 32 percent were given suspended sentences (Atchison et al., 1998).

An argument can be made for paying more attention to the *demand side* of prostitution. First, sheer numbers would seem to justify greater control of the customers, who are far more numerous than prostitutes. A major 1992 survey found that 16 percent of American men ages 18–59 said they had ever paid for sex (Laumann et al., 1994). A question on something as stigmatized as one's personal involvement in prostitution is likely to yield some underreporting; still, it is clear that a significant proportion of the male population has had such encounters.

Second, demand-side prostitution controls can pay much higher dividends than supply-side controls. Prostitutes are dependent on this work for their livelihood and not easily deterred by sanctions. Customers, who have a greater stake in conventional society, are more fearful of arrest and punishment and more vulnerable than prostitutes to public shaming and stigmatization (Persons, 1996). A British study found that arrested customers were unconcerned about fines but very worried about damage to their reputations if their activities were made public (Matthews, 1993: 14–15). A corollary is that customers are much less likely to recidivate after their first arrest. For example, in Washington, D.C., only 7 percent of the 563 males (mostly customers, some male prostitutes) arrested for prostitution offenses from 1990 to 1992 had previously been arrested for such an offense, whereas this was true of 47 percent of the 847 females arrested for prostitution offenses.[13] Similar findings were reported in Vancouver, Canada: 2 percent of the arrested customers and 49 percent of the arrested prostitutes were recidivists (Lowman, 1990).

The large number of patrons and their greater susceptibility to deterrence are arguably good grounds for intensifying enforcement against them. Indeed, the customers may be uniquely qualified for deterrence:

> It is exactly in such situations, when the perpetrator is enmeshed in society and where the act is not central and integrated in his way of life, that punishment and deterrence have a positive effect. . . . With a unilateral

197

criminalization of the customers, we believe that a portion of the prostitution market will disappear. (Finstad and Hoigard, 1993: 222)

Others claim that cracking down on customers may even eradicate prostitution from a locale: "If communities really desire to eliminate prostitution, and not its side effects, customer control would be an obvious strategy to pursue" (Boles and Tatro, 1978: 76). And there appears to be substantial public support for targeting customers in some fashion, including public shaming. A 1995 national poll found that half of the public believed the media should disseminate the names and pictures of men convicted of soliciting prostitutes (*Newsweek*, 1995). Residents of neighborhoods with street prostitution are especially likely to favor such controls (Weitzer, 2000). As a member of one civic association noted, "These guys are the weak link in this chain. He's the one with the most to lose; that's why he's got to be kept out" (Gray, 1991: 25).

Though most cities continue to target their enforcement efforts against prostitutes rather than their customers, a few cities have begun to redirect control efforts toward the customers. One particularly innovative program is the "johns' school"—a program designed to educate and rehabilitate arrested customers. Since 1995, when San Francisco launched its First Offenders Prostitution Program for customers, several other cities have followed suit, including Buffalo, Las Vegas, Nashville, St. Paul, and some Canadian and British cities. San Francisco's school is a joint effort by the district attorney's office, the police department, the public health department, community leaders, and former prostitutes. The men avoid an arrest record and court appearance by paying a $500 fee, attending the school, and not reoffending for one year after the arrest. Every aspect of the all-day course is designed to *shame, educate, and deter* the men from future contact with prostitutes. The lectures are designed for maximum shock value: the men are frequently asked how they would feel if their mothers, wives, or daughters were "prostituted," and why they were "using" and "violating" prostitutes by patronizing them. The audience is also exposed to a graphic slide show on sexually transmitted diseases, horror stories about the wretched lives of prostitutes and their oppression by pimps, and information about the adverse impact of street prostitution on neighborhoods.

Unlike other shaming sanctions—such as printing customers' names or photos in local newspapers or on cable TV shows—where humiliation or "stigmatizing shaming" (Braithwaite, 1989) of the offender is a goal, shaming in the johns' schools occurs in the context of a day of reeducation about the various harms of prostitution. This is closer to the "reintegrative sham-ing" model (Braithwaite, 1989) linking punishment to rehabilitation, though this ends once the class concludes. A measure of rehabilitation is recidivism: of the nearly 2,200 graduates of San Francisco's school from March 1995 to February 1999, only eighteen were subsequently rearrested for solicitation. Toronto's program reports low recidivism as well.[14]

Low recidivism, or "specific deterrence" among the graduates of the johns' schools does not necessarily mean that the program is also having a larger "general deterrent" effect (on the never-arrested population of prospective johns), since in most cities with johns' schools, the number of johns on the streets is thus far unabated. Moreover, it is difficult to tell whether nonrecidivism is due to the school experience per se or to the arrest. Official statistics show low recidivism among previously arrested customers generally (including those who had not attended a johns school), suggesting that the arrest is the decisive deterrent.

Customers are also the focus of another innovative program. Inspired by drug forfeiture laws, a growing number of cities have passed ordinances empowering police to confiscate customers' cars when caught in the act of soliciting sexual favors on the street. Portland, Detroit, New York, Chicago, Washington, San Diego, Milwaukee, and Philadelphia are only a few of the cities where such laws have been enacted. After a car is seized a civil hear-ing is held to determine if there are grounds for forfeiture. Forfeited cars are sold at auction or retained as city property.

The laws vary substantially. Some are lenient with first-time offenders; others treat first-timers and repeat offenders the same. Most cities eventually return the car if the arrested driver is not the owner—if the car belongs to the driver's wife, employer, or a rental company. But some cities confiscate vehicles even if the owner was uninvolved in the crime. In St. Paul, Minnesota, for instance, an auto dealer's car taken on a test drive was used to solicit a prostitute and was seized by the police. (The Supreme Court ruled in *Bennis v. Michigan* in March, 1996 that confiscation of property, even if the owner was not involved in the crime, is not unconstitutional.) Finally, in some cities (Oakland, California, Portland, Oregon, Washington, D.C.), a person may be acquitted of the criminal offense of soliciting a pros-titute but lose his car in the civil case (where the standard of proof is lower), while in other cities the policy is to return the car if the criminal case fails.

Portland's 1989 forfeiture law has been the inspiration for other cities. Police seized 1,089 vehicles from 1990 through 1993, 52 of which (5 percent) were eventually forfeited; more recently, police have seized around 350 cars per year, only a few of which have been forfeited.[15] Most were first-time arrestees, who were allowed to sign a release agreement stipulating that they would refrain from any future street solicitation or automatically forfeit their car. The result is that the number of repeat offenders is almost nil. Between 1989 and May 1993, only 1 percent of the arrestees had been rear-rested.[16]

The benefits of forfeiture laws may not be limited to their deterrent value but may also provide revenue for the police department. In Detroit, for instance, the proceeds have been used to buy police equipment and pay for officers' overtime. And even when cars are returned to their owners, some cities (e.g., Portland) recover the costs of police time, towing, and storage by charging a fee for the returned car. This is tantamount to a fine levied on all seized cars, whether or not the drivers are found guilty.

The forfeiture policy raises some obvious problems. Loss of a car penal-izes not only the perpetrator but other family members who depend on it, and the punishment may not fit the crime. Permanent loss of a car worth perhaps thousands of dollars seems disproportionately harsh for a misde-meanor offense, and arguably violates the Eighth Amendment's prohibition on excessive fines. Moreover, there is a wide disparity in the value of the cars seized, from the worthless to the expensive. Such unequal punishment may violate the equal protection clause of the Fourteenth Amendment.

The car seizure policy and the johns' schools show that some cities (albeit a minority) have begun to take customers more seriously than in the past. Moreover, the two programs are more imaginative than the arrest-and-fine approach and put more emphasis on deterring arrestees from recidivating. It remains to be seen whether sustained efforts to attack the demand for street prostitutes will pay dividends in reducing demand, as some analysts claim. But even if it does not have this effect, it can be justi-fied by the principle that law enforcement should be gender neutral.

◉ Conclusion

The two-track model outlined here has advantages over both the current policy of blanket criminalization and the alternatives of decriminalization and legalization. It is arguably superior to the other approaches in satisfying key tests: public preferences regarding the proper focus of law enforcement, efficient use of criminal justice resources, and the harm-reduction principle.

Essential ingredients of the policy include (1) redirecting control efforts from indoor to street prostitution, (2) gender-neutral law enforcement, and (3) providing support services and assistance for persons who want to leave prostitution. Most effective implementation of the policy would require changes in all three areas simultaneously.

Endnotes

[1]There has been more debate in official circles in Britain and Canada, where a number of cities have considered legalization.

[2]Founded in 1973 by former prostitute Margo St. James, COYOTE is the premier prostitutes' rights group in the United States, and is affiliated with several lesser known organizations (Weitzer, 1991). Although COYOTE claims to represent all prostitutes, it has been closely aligned with upper-echelon call girls, not streetwalkers.

[3]*San Francisco Examiner,* December 6, 1995.

[4]"The Task Force therefore recommends that the City stop enforcing and prosecuting prostitution crimes" (San Francisco Task Force, 1996: 6).

[5]Interview, April 29, 1997.

[6]Interview, June 7, 1993.

[7]Julie Pearl study, on file with *Hastings Law Journal.*

[8]Interviews with vice officers in these cities by Julie Pearl; transcripts on file with *Hastings Law Journal.*

[9]*San Francisco Chronicle,* April 6, 1990.

[10]Vice sergeant interviewed by Julie Pearl, May 1985; transcript on file at *Hastings Law Journal.*

[11]Interview, July 9, 1993.

[12]Interview, July 27, 1993.

[13]Figures provided by the U.S. Attorney's Office, Washington, D.C.

[14]Personal communication from Sergeant Doug Mottram, Metropolitan Toronto Police, August 7, 1997.

[15]Interview with Sergeant Steve Larson, Portland Police Department, September 24, 1997.

[16]*Newsday,* May 12, 1993.

References

A&E [Arts and Entertainment Network], "Red Light Districts," Videotape, 1997.

American Law Institute, *Model Penal Code and Commentaries, Part II, Sections 240.0 to 251.4,* (Philadelphia: American Law Institute, 1980).

Atchison, C., L. Fraser and J. Lowman, "Men Who Buy Sex," in J. Elias, V. Bullough, V. Elias and G. Brewer (eds.), *Prostitution,* (Amherst: Prometheus, 1998).

Atlanta Task Force on Prostitution, *Findings and Recommendations,* (Mayor's Office: Atlanta, Georgia, 1986).

Barnard, M., "Violence and Vulnerability: Conditions of Work for Street Working Prostitutes," *Sociology of Health and Illness* 1993, 15, 683–705.

Bennetto, J., "Community Work the Best Penalty for Vice, say Police," *The Independent* [London], October 21, 1996.

Benson, C. and R. Matthews, "Street Prostitution: Ten Facts in Search of a Policy," *International Journal of the Sociology of Law* 1995, 23, 395–415.

Benson, C. and R. Matthews, *Report of the Parliamentary Group on Prostitution,* (London: Middlesex University, 1996).

Bernat, F., "New York State's Prostitution Statute: Case Study of the Discriminatory Application of a Gender Neutral Law," in C. Schweber and C. Feinman (eds.), *Criminal Justice Politics and Women,* (New York: Haworth, 1985).

Boles, J. and C. Tatro, "Legal and Extralegal Methods of Controlling Female Prostitution: A Cross-Cultural Comparison," *International Journal of Comparative and Applied Criminal Justice* 1978, 2, 71–85.

Boyer, D., L. Chapman and B. Marshall, *Survival Sex in King County: Helping Women Out,* Report submitted to the King County Women's Advisory Board, March 1993.

Braithwaite, J., *Crime, Shame, and Reintegration,* (Cambridge: Cambridge University Press, 1989).

Bryan, J., "Occupational Ideologies and Individual Attitudes of Call Girls," *Social Problems* 1996, 13, 441–450.

Bureau of Justice Statistics, *Sourcebook of Criminal Justice Statistics,* (Washington, D.C.: Government Printing Office, annual).

Campbell, R., "Invisible Men: Making Visible Male Clients of Female Prostitutes in Merseyside," in J. Elias, V. Bullough, V. Elias and G. Brewer (eds.), *Prostitution,* (Amherst: Prometheus, 1998).

Caughey, M., "The Principle of Harm and its Application to Laws Criminalizing Prostitution," *Denver Law Journal* 1974, 51, 235–262.

Clark, C., "Prostitution," *Congressional Quarterly Researcher* 1993, 3, 505–527.

Coalition of San Francisco Business and Neighborhood Communities Impacted by Prostitution, *Resolution,* 1996.

Comment, "Privacy and Prostitution," *Iowa Law Review* 1977, 63, 248–265.

Cohen, B., *Deviant Street Networks: Prostitution in New York City,* (Lexington, MA: Lexington, 1980).

Davis, N.J., "From Victims to Survivors: Working with Recovering Street Prostitutes," in R. Weitzer (ed.), *Sex for Sale: Prostitution, Pornography, and the Sex Industry,* (New York: Routledge, 2000).

Decker, J., *Prostitution: Regulation and Control,* (Littleton, CO: Rothman, 1979).

Exner, J.E., J. Wylie, A. Leura and T. Parrill, "Some Psychological Characteristics of Prostitutes," *Journal of Personality Assessment* 1977, 41, 474–485.

Farley, F. and S. Davis, "Masseuses, Men, and Massage Parlors," *Journal of Sex and Marital Therapy* 1978, 4, 219–225.

Farley, M. and H. Barkan, "Prostitution, Violence, and Posttraumatic Stress Disorder," *Women and Health* 1998, 27, 37–49.

Finstad, L. and C. Hoigard, "Norway," in N. Davis (ed.), *Prostitution: An International Handbook on Trends, Problems, and Policies,* (Westport, CT: Greenwood, 1993).

Gallup Organization, *Gallup Poll Monthly.* No. 313. October 1991.

_____. Public Opinion Online, Lexis/Nexis. Gallup poll, May 28–29, 1996.

Gray, K., "Prostitution Opponents Aim to Seize Johns' Cars," *Newsday,* December 5, 1991, p. 25.

Harris poll, Public Opinion Online, Lexis/Nexis. N = 1,513, November 30–December 10, 1978.

Harris poll, Public Opinion Online, Lexis/Nexis. N = 2,254. January 11–February 11, 1990.

Heyl, B., "Prostitution: An Extreme Case of Sex Stratification," in F. Adler and R. Simon (eds.), *The Criminology of Deviant Women,* (Boston: Houghton Mifflin, 1979).

Hobson, B.M., *Uneasy Virtue,* (New York: Basic Books, 1987).

James, J., "Prostitute-Pimp Relationships," *Medical Aspects of Human Sexuality* 1973, 7, 147–160.

Jennings, M.A., "The Victim as Criminal: A Consideration of California's Prostitution Law," *California Law Review* 1976, 64, 1235–1284.

Kelling, G. and C. Coles, *Fixing Broken Windows,* (New York: Free Press, 1996).

Larsen, E.N., "The Politics of Prostitution Control: Interest Group Politics in Four Canadian Cities," *International Journal of Urban and Regional Research* 1992, 16, 169–189.

Laumann, E., J. Gagnon, R. Michael and S. Michaels, *The Social Organization of Sexuality: Sexual Practices in the United States*, (Chicago: University of Chicago Press, 1994).

Little, C., *Deviance and Control*, (Itasca, IL: Peacock, 1995).

Lowman, J., "Notions of Formal Equality Before the Law: The Experience of Street Prostitutes and their Customers," *Journal of Human Justice* 1990, 1, 55–76.

Lowman, J., "Street Prostitution Control," *British Journal of Criminology* 1992, 32, 1–17.

McCaghy, C. and S. Cernkovich, "Changing Public Opinion toward Prostitution Laws," Paper presented at the World Congress of Sexology, Amsterdam, 1991.

Matthews, R., *Kerb-Crawling, Prostitution, and Multi-Agency Policing*, Paper no. 43, (London: Home Office, 1993).

Merit Audits and Surveys, *Merit Report*. October 15–20, 1983.

Milman, B., "New Rules for the Oldest Profession: Should We Change our Prostitution Laws?" *Harvard Women's Law Journal* 1980, 3, 1–82.

Newsweek poll, Public Opinion Online. Lexis/Nexis. N = 753, January 26–27, 1995.

Pearl, J., "The Highest Paying Customer: America's Cities and the Costs of Prostitution Control," *Hastings Law Journal* 1987, 38, 769–800.

Peat Marwick and Partners, *A National Population Study of Prostitution and Pornography*, Report no. 6., (Ottawa: Department of Justice, 1984).

Perkins, R., *Working Girls*, (Canberra: Australian Institute of Criminology, 1991).

Persons, C., "Sex in the Sunlight: The Effectiveness, Efficiency, Constitutionality, and Advisability of Publishing Names and Pictures of Prostitutes' Patrons," *Vanderbilt Law Review* 1996, 49, 1525–1575.

Pivar, D., *Purity Crusade*, (Westport, CT: Greenwood, 1973).

Posner, R. and K. Silbaugh, *A Guide to America's Sex Laws*, (Chicago: University of Chicago Press, 1996).

Reynolds, H., *The Economics of Prostitution*, (Springfield: Charles Thomas, 1986).

San Diego Prostitution Task Force, *Report*, (San Diego City Council, October 1993).

San Francisco Committee on Crime, *A Report on Non-Victim Crime in San Francisco, Part 2: Sexual Conduct, Gambling, Pornography*, (Mayor's Office, 1971).

San Francisco Task Force on Prostitution, *Final Report*, (San Francisco Board of Supervisors, March 1996).

Seattle Women's Commission, *Project to Address the Legal, Political, and Service Barriers Facing Women in the Sex Industry.* Report to the Major and City Council, (Seattle: July 1995).

Silbert, M. and A. Pines, "Victimization of Street Prostitutes," *Victimology* 1982, 7, 122–133.

Skogan, W., *Disorder and Decline,* (New York: Free Press, 1990).

Skolnick, J. and J. Dombrink, "The Legalization of Deviance," *Criminology* 1978, 16, 193–208.

Special Committee on Pornography and Prostitution, *Pornography and Prostitution in Canada,* (Ottawa: Dept. of Supply and Services, 1985).

Sullivan, B., *The Politics of Sex: Prostitution and Pornography in Australia since 1945,* (New York: Cambridge University Press, 1997).

Weiner, A., "Understanding the Social Needs of Streetwalking Prostitutes," *Social Work* 1996, 41, 97–105.

Weitzer, R., "Prostitutes' Rights in the United States: The Failure of a Movement," *Sociological Quarterly* 1991, 32, 23–41.

Weitzer, R., "The Politics of Prostitution in America," in R. Weitzer (ed.), *Sex for Sale: Prostitution, Pornography, and the Sex Industry,* (New York: Routledge, 2000).

Wilson, J.Q. and G. Kelling, "Broken Windows," *Atlantic Monthly* March 1982, 29–38.

Working Group [Federal/Provincial Territorial Working Group on Prostitution], *Report and Recommendations in Respect of Legislation, Policy, and Practices Concerning Prostitution-Related Activities,* (Ottawa: Department of Justice, 1998).

❧ ❧ ❧

Questions

1. What is the "two-track" model of prostitution control? How does this model differ from current methods of control?

2. What changes would be necessary to allow implementation of the two-track model? Are these changes politically or practically feasible? Explain your thinking.

3. What are some possible negative consequences of implementing the two-track model?

4. Weitzer recommends gender-neutral law-enforcement strategies and the provision of support services for persons who want to leave prostitution. Are these recommendations inherent in the two-track model that he describes? Would these changes also prove effective under current conditions, which criminalize prostitution?

5. Which social-control strategy would you adopt if your primary concern were harm reduction? What if your main concern were resource utilization?

6. Of the three models discussed, which do you think your community would most likely adopt? Why?

"Becoming" Lesbian, Gay, and Bisexual

ROBERT E. OWENS, JR.

In the United States, people continue to debate whether sexual orientation is genetically inherited ("nature") or socially learned ("nurture"). Yet there are a few unquestionable facts. First, sexual identification and awareness often emerge during adolescence and constitute "rites of passage" for young people. Second, the social roles, customs, attitudes, and behaviors associated with being gay are socially constructed and learned—just as those associated with being heterosexual are learned. In this selection, Robert Owens Jr. details a process by which young people "become" lesbian, gay, or bisexual. He also explores how adolescents cope with the confusion and stigma associated with being nonheterosexual.

> Dear God, I am fourteen years old. . . . [L]et me know what is happening to me.
>
> Alice Walker, *The Color Purple*

Although many educators and professionals deny the existence of queer kids, the process of becoming lesbian, gay, or bisexual is very much an adolescent rite of passage. Sexual identification is not embraced immediately upon self-recognition and there is a gradual process of "coming out" to oneself. Most individuals pass from awareness to positive self-identity between ages thirteen and twenty, and a positive lesbian, gay, or bisexual identity is being established earlier today than in the past.[1] Relatively few middle school youths self-identify as lesbian, gay, or bisexual in contrast to as high as 6 to 7 percent of older high school males who describe themselves as primarily homosexual.[2]

This [reading] describes a "generic" pattern of becoming. Many individual variations exist. The process seems to differ for men and women. In general, on issues of relational expectations, sexual awareness, and equality,

"'Becoming' Lesbian, Gay, and Bisexual," by Robert E. Owens Jr., reprinted from *Queer Kids: The Challenges and Promise for Lesbian, Gay and Bisexual Youth*, Robert E. Owens Jr. (Ed.), 1998, pp. 15–38. Copyright © 1998 by Haworth Press, Inc.

young lesbians have more in common with young heterosexual women and young gays have more in common with young heterosexual men than young lesbians and gay men have with each other.[3] It is possible that being male or female is more important overall than being gay or lesbian. As has been observed, "Female homosexuality is to be understood as a unique female phenomenon, rather than a state which is either the same as or the reverse of male homosexuality."[4]

Even with these differences, the questions asked along the journey are surprisingly similar.

> *Am I really lesbian (or gay)?*
> *Why me?*
> *What will my parents think?*
> *Am I the only one?*
> *Should I tell my best friend ?*

In general, over a period of years and against a backdrop of stigmatization, lesbian, gay, and bisexual youths gradually accept the label homosexual or bisexual for themselves as they interact with the sexual-minority community and increasingly disclose their sexual orientation.[5]

This [reading] will describe a four-step process of "becoming." From their initial feelings of being different, gay, lesbian, and bisexual individuals gradually become aware of their same-sex attractions, engage in same-sex erotic behavior and dating, and finally self-identify as lesbian, gay, or bisexual.

☻ Feeling Different

Seventy percent or more of lesbian, gay, and bisexual adolescents and adults report feeling different at an early age, often as early as age four or five.[6] A fourteen-year-old gay male writes in his school paper,

> [T]here was always something I knew was a little bit different about me. I didn't know exactly what that might have been. It was just something that was there and I learned to accept it. . . .

Seventeen-year-old Kenneth recalls, "I've known I was different since I was five or six."[7] For some lesbian, gay, and bisexual adults the feeling of difference centered on a vague attraction to, or curiosity about, their own gender.

For most youths, these feelings are not sexual as we will see later in this section.[8] Early childhood experiences may later be interpreted in light of sexual orientation identification.

Many sexual-minority youths state that before they even knew what the difference was they were convinced of its importance. Linda recalls, "Quietly I knew."[9] From second grade on Tony knew instinctively that he was unlike other boys. They knew it too and targeted Tony for ridicule. Philip, a high schooler with deafness, recalls, "I didn't know what it was . . . but I just knew I was different."[10] In contrast to reports from lesbians and gays, only about 10 percent of heterosexual adults report feeling different or odd as a child.[11]

Many lesbian and gay adults report that as children they felt like an "outsider" within their peer group and their family. They describe isolation, low popularity, scant dating, and lack of interest in the other sex, little participation in same-sex games, and gender nonconformity.[12] Derek, an African-American teen, had physical relations with other boys from age five on. He reports engaging in prepubescent games such as *doctor* and *I'll show you mine if you'll* . . . with boys, but never with girls. Furtive mutual fondling also occurred with other boys.[13]

As children, some but certainly not a majority of gay and bisexual male youths found men to be "enigmatic and unapproachable"[14] and felt more comfortable with women and girls. In general, these youth did not enjoy rough or athletic activities, especially team sports, and the coercion to participate, preferring instead books, art, and fantasy play. Doug, a very bright child, enjoyed problem-solving tasks such as puzzles and word games. Some gay male youths attribute their sexuality to a failure to develop "masculine" characteristics and to being "feminized" through ostracism by boys and association with girls with whom they shared more interests.[15] Jim, a young white gay male, was an isolate in his class except for the occasional female friend. He was labeled a sissy by the other children.

Many gay males report that they were more sensitive than other boys and had their feelings hurt more easily; cried more easily; had more aesthetic interests; were drawn to other "sensitive" boys, girls, and adults; and felt and acted less aggressively than their peers.[16] A young student recalls,

> I never felt like I fit in. I don't know why for sure. I feel different. I thought it was because I was more sensitive.[17]

"I had a keener interest in the arts," recalls a young gay man. "I never learned to fight; I just didn't feel I was like other boys. I was very fond of pretty things like ribbons and flowers and music; I was indifferent to boys' games, . . . I was more interested in watching insects and reflecting on certain things. . . ."[18] Male youths may experience the dichotomy of being attracted to the very bullies who are tormenting him.

Approximately 70 percent of lesbian and gay adults report gender nonconforming behaviors in contrast to 16 percent and 3 percent for heterosexual females and males respectively.[19] These figures must be treated carefully because they are based on subject reports. In contrast, very few lesbian and gay adults exhibit gender or sex role inappropriate behaviors.[20]

The actual incidence of gender nonconformity is unknown and does not seem to be related to the amount of masculine or feminine behavior seen in an adult. "I was more masculine," recalls a young lesbian, "more independent, more aggressive, more outdoorish."[21] For the child who doesn't conform, whispers and innuendo about her or his sexual orientation may begin early. Parental admonitions to avoid another child who seems different can plant the seeds of homophobia early. Linda, a young lesbian, recalls her distaste for Barbie and learning in first grade to sneak on a pair of shorts under the dresses her mother made her wear to church.

Gender nonconformity seems to be related to socioeconomic status with the most exaggerated behavior found in lower income groups.[22] In general, those who are most different in gender behavior are the most pressured to change.[23] Malcolm, an African-American youth, was a devoutly religious child. Commenting on the boy's effeminate mannerisms, one congregant told Malcolm, "You're degrading God's name." To which the minister added, "You're a disgrace."[24] Often lesbian and gay children are teased for their gender nonconformity. The impact of teasing seems to be more severe for boys than for girls.[25] Miles, a very agile child, became awkward and less willing to try physical activity when at age five, someone stated that he ran "like a girl." "When the others called me names and stuff," recalls Malcolm, "I assumed they were right. I had very low self-esteem."[26] Boys may be viewed as weird and be rejected as undesirable playmates. For their part, some gay and bisexual boys reject play with other boys as unsafe and unenjoyable.[27]

At some level, both the child and the family recognize that a difference exists.[28] This recognition can lead to conflict within both the family and the individual. For me, it meant enrollment by my parents in Cub Scouts and Boy Scouts and an endless stream of failed attempts to play Little League. As for Malcolm, mentioned above, "I was embarrassing to them [his family], especially to my father." He continues,

> When we were in the projects and I would play with other kids, there were times when my mom would tell me to come in. She would say, "Those kids don't want you to play with them." She always made me feel like there was something wrong with me.[29]

For many individuals, feeling lesbian or gay is a natural part of themselves. Most lesbians, gays, and bisexuals state emphatically that they did not choose their sexual orientation and that they were not in control of their feelings. Kevin, now an adult, remembers that he had known he was gay, even before he heard the word or knew its meaning.[30] His older brothers' friends elicited very different feelings in him than in his brothers.

❧ Awareness of Same-Sex Attractions

Sexual awareness usually begins in early adolescence. Awareness is not a sudden event but a gradual sensitivity and consciousness, a growing realization that "I might be homosexual." Most individuals develop feelings and awareness before they ever have a label for them. For some youths, awareness is better described as confusion. Labeling of these feelings may become very frightening.[31] Edmund White in A Boy's Own Story (1982) recalled, "I see now that what I wanted was to be loved by men and to love them back but not to be a homosexual."[32] It is important to remember that while initial awareness may be met with some shock among self-identified youths, only 30 percent of lesbians and 20 percent of gay males report that they experienced negative feelings about themselves.[33] Dan realized he was gay when he was eleven. "It just gave me a sense of wholeness."[34]

The mean age for same-sex awareness and attractions is 10.9 to 13.2 years with a reported range of 10 to 18 years.[35] In a recent survey called Sex on Campus, 87 percent of lesbian college students and 63 percent of gay male college students report that they were aware of their sexual orientation by high school, although some knew their orientation in elementary school.

Recalling her confusion, Linda remembers that nobody felt as passionate about members of their own gender as she felt about two of her friends.[36] As a group, boys report being aware before girls. Approximately one-third of gay male youths report same-sex attractions prior to the onset of puberty.[37] In one study, a third of lesbian and gay teens claim that they knew they were homosexual prior to age ten.[38] Mickey, age eighteen, reports an awareness of such feelings at age four or five, concluding, "I've always wanted to touch and be touched by guys."[39] He began to realize that he was not heterosexual in seventh grade. Similarly, Andrew, a young white gay man, remembers noticing at age eight the beauty of his swimming instructor, an older boy of sixteen. Henry, a young college student, recalls, "What I wanted ever since I was five or six watching Marlo Thomas' boyfriend on television, was to have a man in my bed!"[40]

Often these early attractions are vague and impressionistic. One young gay teen recalled,

> My first memory of being attracted to men was a dream I had when I was six or seven. I was in a bathtub with a man in the middle of the forest. I remember this was a happy dream for me, and I dreamt it over and over again for years.[41]

More common is the fifth grade experience of Nathaniel, a middle-class African-American teen. "I was noticing guys," he recalls. "Not knowing that I was gay—just curious about guys."[42] Derek, also African American, recalls,

> In every grade, there was at least one boy that I had a certain fondness for. . . . And later on, . . . I recognized this as crushes. I wanted to spend as much time as I could with them.[43]

The vague same-sex attractions of childhood become eroticized in adolescence. The mean age for same-sex erotic fantasies among males is reported to be 13.9 years, for females somewhat later. "I had homosexual fantasies consistently," recalls Audrey, a young gay man. "If I had a heterosexual fantasy it was because I forced it upon myself."[44] At age fifteen, Mike began to collect photos of his best friend and to write his friend's name all over his notebooks. "It was like I was a junior high girl," he recalls. "I didn't know I had fallen in love with my best friend."[45] Norma Jean became aware of her sexual feelings while working as a store clerk.

> Some women runners kept coming by the store. . . . After they finished practicing, all of those gorgeous bodies would just pile into the store to get something to drink. I became very sexually excited about that. I made sure that I worked the nights they practiced.[46]

In his book *What the Dead Remember*, Harlan Green recalls from boyhood:

> I picked up the *Saturday Evening Post* . . . I turned the page and stopped
> . . . I breathed out, transfixed at what I saw . . . a picture of men and boys
> in black-and-white advertising Hanes or BVD's.[47]

Similarly, Darrell remembers scanning underwear ads closely in second grade, looking for an outline of what lay beneath. Erotic feelings can come from pictures, words, and voices that others might not consider erotic in the least.

Same-sex attractions are reported by many queer kids to have always been present, deep within the "natural self."[48] Richard, age nineteen, summarizes, "I have always been gay, although I did not know what that meant at the time."[49] In seventh grade, Amy, a young lesbian, recalls that she suddenly changed to a more gender-neutral manner of dress with the defense that "I just want to be myself."[50]

Gay male youths report that they first experienced an obsession to be near masculinity. Mickey, age eighteen, recalls,

> At eight I fell in love with Neal, this guy who rode my bus. . . . I guess he
> was fourteen. . . . I always wanted to sit with him or be next to him. . . . I
> spent my childhood fantasizing about men, not sexually . . , but just being
> close to them and having them hold me or hug me.[51]

Former NFL running back David Kopay recalls a high school football captain two years older than himself. At the time, David did everything possible to be close to this teammate.[52] At age eleven, Tony developed nonsexual "crushes" on other boys in his scout troop. A seventeen-year-old Chinese-American youth recalls, "In high school . . . I had a crush on a guy I didn't even know."[53] Cory became obsessed with Jessie when both were in seventh grade. He recalls,

> I started going crazy. He looked better every day. I did not do anything
> during that time; I just looked a lot. . . . I just couldn't go up to him and
> say, "Hey, Jessie, I'm horny for you."[54]

Although occasionally a peer, the object of the obsession is more often an older male, such as a teacher, scout leader, coach, or older cousin. As a child, Denny's interest in big league sports masked his secretive crushes on the players he admired. A former neighbor, now an adult gay man, confided in me that he had wanted to have sex with me since we met when he was age thirteen and I was thirty-four. "These are often cases of unrequited love," explains Paul Gibson, author of the 1989 DHHS report on adolescent suicide, "with the youth never revealing their true feelings."[55]

Some lesbians report that they were attracted to women in authority positions. Maria had a crush on her third grade teacher. Tara, enamored with her softball coach recalls, "I would fantasize about being a man, so I could kiss her."[56] Other lesbian girls are attracted to peers. Lynn, a lesbian student, developed a crush on her best friend with whom she often danced to recorded music in the dark, took long walks, and slept over.

The reverse of the "typical" heterosexual pattern may occur in which a lesbian or gay teen is drawn to members of the other sex as friends but sexually attracted to members of the same sex. Gay male teens may have many female friends but not be sexually attracted to females. "I was real attracted to pretty women," explains Elisa, "but I identified more with men. But there was no attraction between us."[57]

An erotically aroused teen may or may not have engaged in same-sex sexual behavior. In fact, same-sex feelings and attractions almost always precede same-sex behavior.[58] Usually, erotic feelings appear in the early teens, although some adults report that they had same-sex fantasies and arousal as early as late preschool. Scott, an adolescent, recalls sexual interests at age six or seven. Approximately 70 percent of lesbians and 95 percent of gay men report same-sex arousal by age nineteen. In contrast, only 6 percent of heterosexual women and 20 percent of heterosexual men report same-sex arousal by this age.[59]

Most gay and bisexual male adolescents report that they initially believed that all boys felt as they did about other males.[60] Eventually they learned otherwise and the inner conflict of self versus society began, along with its accompanying confusion. Having defined himself along societal expectations, a youth may be concerned about the discrepancy that is now developing. An increasing doubt grows as both males and females become aware of their inability to fulfill heterosexual expectations. At age thirteen, Martin, an African-American student, was struck by the realization that his sexual feeling and being gay were one in the same. Chris, an eighteen-year-old male, adds, "I was under the impression that since I was gay, I wouldn't be able to do anything substantial with my life."[61]

Initial realization may be accompanied by intense anxiety and an identity crisis. Mike, a gay middle school student, spent hours in the counselor's office with vague school-related problems. He refused to face the sexual issue and recalls, "I was convinced they'd kick me out of school and send me to jail."[62] "[S]uddenly all the feelings . . . came together," recalls eighteen-year-old Joanne, "and pointed to the label, lesbian. As a result, I walked around like a shell shock victim for days."[63] "I was frightened," explains Linda. "Although I'd become somewhat comfortable with my label as 'the weird one,' lesbianism was too weird."[64] At age thirteen, Michelle kept a dream journal and she dreamt that she and a female friend kissed. "I immediately stopped keeping my journal," she recalls.[65] A sixteen-year-old Chinese-American Texan confides, "It was a total shock. . . . I simply could not accept myself. All the confidence I had in me disappeared."[66]

Positive self-regard and the plans for a bright future may appear to be lost as a teen recognizes that she or he is a member of a despised minority. Conflict can occur between a teen's positive self-esteem and her or his own internalized homophobia with its negative connotations.

Although this conflict easily resolves for some, others incorporate familial and societal values of the homosexual as sick, wrong, and undesirable, a member of a despised minority. Paul became aware of his attraction to other boys and to male TV stars at age eleven. "When the feelings did not go away I became distraught; the problem seemed beyond my control," he recalls. "I spent whole days crying alone in my room, and my family and friends didn't know what to make of me."[67] A fourteen-year-old bisexual girl reports, "I'd been thinking about it but I didn't want to believe what I was thinking."[68] She had first begun to be attracted to both boys and girls at age eleven. Having "bought into" society's negative values and social conditioning, queer kids may begin to hate themselves intensely.

Many gay and bisexual male youths report, that sexual thoughts and feelings intrude on everything else.[69] They report being frightened by their awareness, threatened by the possibilities, and energized by the intensity of their feelings and the sense of the forbidden. "I knew I was clearly checking out the guys in the shower after soccer practice," a young gay man recalls. "This scared the shit out of me."[70] With little except negative feedback from home or school, these adolescents have no context within which to make sense of their feelings.

Myths and stereotypes of lesbians, gays, and bisexuals are a source of much of their confusion. A nineteen-year-old lesbian recalls, "I heard so many times, 'You look straight.' I thought that was stupid. . . . What's looking straight, what's looking gay?"[71] A young gay male or lesbian may try to fulfill the stereotype or be repelled by it. Lack of appropriate role models only exacerbates the situation.

The extreme loneliness of this period, as described by lesbian, gay, and bisexual adults, may be even more acute for younger adolescents who do not have the maturity to explore these complex feelings. This isolation may be made more harsh by a youth's active avoidance of other students suspected of being lesbian, gay, or bisexual. A queer kid can become the loneliest person in the high school.[72] Vulnerable and afraid of being revealed, a sexual-minority teen may be incapable of withstanding peer pressure to conform to a heterosexual standard that does not fit. Anti-homosexual jokes or ridicule are especially painful.

Youths may learn to hide their desires as wrong, believing that they will change or decrease. "Over the years, these tiny denials have a cumulative effect."[73] The youth may hate herself or himself for feeling a certain way but the sexual feelings continue to come. The result may be acting out, rebellion, dangerous sexual behavior, depression, and/or suicide.

In similar fashion, those youth who are very open about their sexual orientation may also experience isolation. Former "friends" may ridicule or stop associating. When Jill began to dress in a more "butch" manner, her phone fell silent as more and more girls she had considered friends avoided her. At school, she became an isolate.

The sense of isolation increases with the fear of discovery and rejection, especially for teens who belong to racial minorities. Many honestly believe that they are the only lesbian or gay student in their high school.[74]

Early recognition of sexual orientation by today's teens contrasts sharply with the lengthy process of self-acceptance and identification reported by many older lesbian, gay, and bisexual adults. Few resources or guides exist to facilitate this process for the young adolescent.

*C*oping *S*trategies

The three most common coping strategies for defending one's self against internalized and externalized homophobia, from least to most satisfactory for psychological adjustment, are repression of desires, suppression of homosexual impulses, and acceptance and disclosure to others.[75] Although each is discussed below as a distinct coping strategy, it is rare that instructions are so clear in real life. Instead, the behavior of each lesbian, gay, and bisexual adolescent evolves to best serve the individual and the immediate environment.

Few youths enter treatment to change their sexual orientation unless the family makes this demand. Most attempt home remedies, especially ones that deny same-sex attractions and emphasize heterosexual roles.[76]

Repression of Desires

By repressing unacceptable or disconcerting desires, the lesbian or gay teen attempts to prevent these desires from entering her or his consciousness. Unfortunately, this strategy offers the youth no opportunity to integrate sexual desires and sexual identity. Behavior and identity also become disconnected. Repressed or hidden feelings may work for a while but eventually emerge, often unexpectedly, resulting in panic, coping disruption, and disorganization. Some repressed teens may display acting out behavior.[77] The most common forms of repression are rationalization, relegation to insignificance, and compartmentalization.

Rationalization. The rationalization strategy uses the claim that the behavior was only for gratification and was a special case or situation.[78] Events are characterized as isolated incidents not to be repeated. Common rationalizations include:

> *We were both drunk.*
> *We just got high and. . . .*
> *It's just a phase; I'll grow out of it.*
> *I just needed some money.*
> *I was just lonely.*
> *All guys do it once.*

Relegation to insignificance. The insignificance strategy can be summarized as "No big deal."[79] Common types include:

> *It was just experimenting; so what.*
> *It was no big deal; we hardly touched.*
> *I was curious, that's all.*
> *It was just a favor for a friend, nothing more.*
> *He's the one who gave me head.*

Compartmentalization. In the compartmentalization strategy, sex and relationships become disconnected.[80] Sexual behavior is set aside as if it is unrelated to the person who engages in it. Common compartmentalization phrases include:

> *It just happened once.*
> *It's just something that happened; I'm not like that.*

I mess around; it doesn't mean nothing.
We're really good friends; that's it.
I love her, not all women.

Suppression of Homosexual Impulses

Unlike repression which tries to prevent same-sex desires, suppression tries to override them. The result is a moratorium on development that merely delays positive same-sex sexual identification until age thirty or forty but does not "cure" an individual.[81] Sexual orientation does not change. In general, the more heterosexual experience a person has had, the older the age at which she or he self-identifies as lesbian or gay.[82]

Youths employing this coping strategy are heavily invested in "the big lie" or "the big secret." Real fear of exposure and/or rejection exists. On the incorrect assumption that homosexuals possess the behavioral characteristics of the other sex, youth may attempt to remedy the situation by accentuating gender-typical behavior. This compensation can be noted in an accentuated male swagger or in male bodybuilding or female interest in clothing and cosmetics. Spontaneity may be suppressed as the youth attempts to control all behaviors and agonizes about all uncertainties.

A teen may become sexually active with the other sex, to the point of pregnancy in some extreme cases among women.[83] Meanwhile, fear may prevent same-sex experimentation, sexual maturation, and exploration of intimate relationships by a youth suppressing same-sex feeling. Peter, age seventeen, did not begin to question his sexuality until age sixteen and attempted to suppress his feelings, thus delaying identification of his true sexual feelings.[84] Withholding and suppressing personal information and interests in order to gain peer acceptance results in a false persona that is kept in place with vigilance and elaborate defenses.

As a result of delayed sexual identity, some individuals display adolescent-like behaviors when they finally come out even if well beyond adolescence. These might include intense but brief romantic involvements, frequent sexual experimentation, and over concern for one's own physical appearance.[85]

Withdrawal to celibacy or asexuality. Although relatively infrequent, a small percentage of gay male youths report that puberty was sexless and that they were deeply involved in masculine activities such as sports.[86] These teens

218

may look and act like other males and participate in male activities. They may crave male friendships deeply, but terminate or avoid close relations because of the temptations encountered. Likewise, masturbation may be avoided because of same-sex erotic feelings and fantasies. Often these young adults deny that they had sexual feelings and attractions as children.

Tran, who lettered in three sports, believed he was too busy for sex. Carlton competed in high school track, gymnastics, and swimming but had to be cautious with the feelings he could not totally suppress.

> I felt like I had to be ultra-careful in the dressing room. I couldn't let my eyes wander; I couldn't let anyone suspect the slightest thing. I found myself putting up more of a front in sports than anywhere else. I felt like it was such a proving ground—proving my manhood to my father, to the other guys, to myself.[87]

Tom had his paper route, football, Boy Scouts, and the band.

Females may also choose to remain asexual under the guise of saving themselves for marriage or for just the right man. These individuals may even avoid information pertaining to sexuality. Those who choose to remain asexual, whether male or female, may delay awareness and gradual self-acceptance.[88]

In some cases, individuals, particularly those from strict religious backgrounds, may use crossdressing or transexualism in an attempt to confront their true feelings of homoeroticism. Sometimes this behavior disappears when individuals become exposed to a gay peer group.[89] In some ethnic groups, especially among hispanics, cross-dressing behavior is more common among both lesbian and gay youths.

Overcoming obstructionism requires overwhelming alternative information or a traumatic event that forces the individual to be honest with her or his feelings. It is difficult to help a youth with sexual issues when for the youth there is no issue.

Denial and heterosexual dating and sex. "Passing" or "learning to hide" as a heterosexual is the most common adjustment.[90] Responding to peer and societal pressure, a teen may use heterosexual dating as an attempt to fit in or to change her or his sexual orientation. Approximately two-thirds of gay men and three-fourths of lesbians have engaged in heterosexual dating.[91] The increasing pressure on teens to date may have raised these values to 85 percent of today's youth.[92] These figures may be even higher in conservative areas, such as the South. Norma Jean, a poor, small town, Southern teen, felt she had no choice but to adopt a heterosexual persona. As for being an open lesbian, "It wasn't an option."[93] Vince, was muscular, played football, made fag jokes, had a regular girlfriend, attended a fundamentalist church, and sang in an evangelical choir. The outward signs were a perfect cover. He tried to be "The Best Heterosexual of the Year." Eric, a white twenty-one-year-old, recalls, "Hiding became an art."[94]

A youth may try to control any mannerisms or dress that might be perceived as gender inappropriate by peers. Lesbian and gay adolescents monitor themselves:

Is my voice too high?
Did I appear too happy when she entered the room?
Am I standing too close?

Malcolm describes the process:

I had to become more masculine. . . . I would make myself walk[,] . . . I would make my voice sound[,] . . . I would make myself sit a certain way. It was total insanity. I was not being me.[95]

Greg, a young African-American man, recalls, "Once when we were in Sunday school, the guys were ganging up on me about my eyelashes, saying they were entirely too long and beautiful for me to really be normal. I was so appalled . . . that I went home and cut my eyelashes off."[96] In addition to perpetuation of self-denial, this strategy can lead to problems of self-esteem because it fails to change sexual interests and desires.

Some teens attempt to cultivate a heterosexual role and to engage in antigay jokes and teasing. By teasing others suspected of similar feelings, a youth hopes to deflect suspicion from herself or himself.[97] In other words, the best defense is a good offense. Audrey told fag jokes and played pranks: "My social objective was to fit in," he explains, "and homosexuality definitely was not fitting in. I wanted to deny it in front of other people because I denied it to myself."[98] John, age sixteen, continues, "And the more nasty comments I made about gay people, the less gay I felt, like further and further away from this horrible thing."[99] "Once I beat up a guy for being a faggot," confesses another young gay man. "No one suspected me [of being gay]," he adds, "because I did sports and had a girlfriend."[100]

Heterosexual girlfriends and boyfriends become a screen for hiding the true self and a wall between a youth and self-awareness. This wall enabled at least one gay youth to confide, "I guess I'm homosexual until I find the right woman."[101] Nathaniel, a middle-class African-American high schooler, explains, "When I got Delta [his girlfriend], it was like a cover. I was having sex with a man but for security I got a girlfriend. . . ."[102] As part of the cover, members of the other gender may be pursued as "sport" but with little serious intentions. Trying desperately to fit in, a young man explains, "It [pursuing women] gave me something to do to tell the other guys who were always bragging."[103] Monica acted "boy-crazy," although she had no sexual interest in boys. For Lee, a lesbian high schooler, the most difficult part was pretending when "I really didn't care."[104]

A lesbian or gay youth actually may believe that she or he is heterosexual but uncomfortable. Sex may feel unnatural, lacking an emotional component.[105] "I was just going through the motions," explains Kimberly. "It was expected of me, so I did it."[106] Drew reports that heterosexual dating anxiety results in nausea and diarrhea before each date.

Heterosexual relationships are often of short duration for gay and bisexual male youths but over half involve some sexual contact with young women.[107] Sex with one or two girls is often sufficient to satisfy curiosity. Gay and bisexual males express a preference for friendship over romance with females. As one adolescent explains, "I was disappointed because it [dating and sex] was such hard work—not physically, I mean, but emotionally."[108]

In similar fashion, lesbians may have two or three sexual contacts in the context of heterosexual dating. "I never really wanted to be intimate with any guy," explains Georgina, in a comment that echoes the sentiment of many lesbian teens. "I always wanted to be their best friend."[109]

Young women may engage in promiscuous heterosexual behavior in an attempt to make themselves heterosexual or to prove to themselves that they really are not lesbian.[110] Lisa, a young lesbian, states that she never enjoyed sex with boys but did it "to prove I wasn't gay."[111] This tactic can be summed up as *I can't be a lesbian; I have a boyfriend.*

The benefits of this coping strategy tend to be short-lived. A fourteen year-old white gay male writes in his school paper,

> If there is anything I hate, it is having to be a fake. Unfortunately, I'm forced to do this every day of my life when I go to school.

"I fervently tried to take a more active interest in girls," notes Paul, "but I could tell that it was contrived."[112] Although she strenuously tried to be heterosexual in high school, Bonnie, a twenty-one-year-old bisexual, remembers, "I developed painful crushes on female teachers and straight girlfriends that left me feeling so pathetic and impotent."[113] Passing as a heterosexual negates a lesbian or gay youth's feelings and ultimately herself or himself. John, age nineteen recalls,

> I used to stand around with the guys and try to look interested in all their gas about this girl and that. . . . All the time I'd be thinking about one or the other of them. It seemed like I didn't belong.[114]

Fear of exposure becomes very real. Jack, age twenty-two and described as "straight-acting," recalls the panic at age thirteen or fourteen when "I saw a Bloomingdale ad for Calvin Klein underwear that I could not take my eyes off of."[115]

The overall result of this charade is psychological tension which may lead to depression, shame, fear of disclosure, and anxiety, although her or his surface demeanor may seem calm.[116] For example, covert gay college men experience more psychological tension, social problems, and isolation than openly gay men.[117] In short, those in hiding "have the most concern over self-esteem, self-acceptance, and status and feel the most social isolation, powerlessness, normlessness, and personal incompetence."[118] Paul, a gay college student, tried desperately as a teen to be heterosexual. "From seventh grade to tenth grade," he recalls, "while everyone's hormones were running rampant, I was attracted to no one; emotionally I was numb. I hadn't a clue about what it meant to be sexually attracted to someone."[119]

Healthy personalities develop when they are shared openly and honestly with others. Those in hiding have little opportunity to date or to develop same-sex relationships in a socially sanctioned context similar to that of heterosexual youth.

Redirection of energies into other areas (Compensation) Some queer kids become too busy to bother with sex.[120] The student who is class president, yearbook editor, school play lead, and tennis team captain is too busy for any dating, heterosexual or otherwise. Although effeminate-acting and disinterested in girls, Jacob, an African-American high school overachiever, was never questioned by his family about his sexual orientation. "He don't have time for girls . . ." his family rationalized. "He's doing his books."[121] A positive correlation of both delayed same-sex erotic behavior and self-identification with better grades exists among gay men.[122] In other words, those with later behavior and self-identification have higher grades.

In similar fashion, in ninth grade, Malcolm, a young African-American male, became a religious true-believer, an indefatigable pioneer in the Jehovah's Witnesses. He would hide in his room for hours reading the Bible and proselytize door to door for over 100 hours a month. "If I prayed all the time and stayed active in the church," he reasoned, "maybe somehow I could appease God . . . and he wouldn't be so angry at me. . . ."[123] When this strategy failed, Malcolm devoted himself to his studies and became an honor student.

Self-Acceptance and Disclosure to Others ("Coming Out")

Accepting one's homosexuality is the optimal strategy.[124] Unfortunately, society encourages lesbian and gay teens to adopt a repressive or suppressive strategy. As a consequence, lesbian and gay youths become subject to psychological stresses that can affect their well-being.

Awareness of sexual orientation may encourage some adolescents to gain limited exposure to the larger lesbian, gay, and bisexual community. First steps may be very tentative, such as calling a hot line or attending a youth group. A teen may attempt to get to know another lesbian or gay youth or adult. For this youth, the goal is usually explorational, not sexual or relational.[125]

Accepting oneself need not always be a traumatic process. Michael, age sixteen, remarks:

> I can bring love and happiness to someone's life . . . Different is not bad. . . .[126]

Another teen, a cocky fourteen-year-old, adds that although the thought of being gay was frightening, the possible terror of living life as a "pseudo-heterosexual" was indescribable.

☙ First Sexual Contacts and Dating

Same-sex erotic contact, such as body rubbing, manual genital contact, or oral genital contact, may begin around thirteen years for gay boys and fifteen for lesbian girls.[127] The mean age of first consensual orgasm is approximately sixteen years for today's young gay males, although some studies have placed the age much earlier.[128] Data vary with the definition of "first sexual contact" and with the age of both the subjects and the study itself. It is important to remember that many children, who, as adults, do not identify as lesbian or gay, engage in adolescent same-sex erotic behavior, and that such behavior is not a cause of homosexuality.

Frequently, the first same-sex kiss, whether sexual in nature or not, is significant. Nancy describes the "incredible feeling" when she and Connie brushed their lips together lightly for the first time. Neither Dan nor Steven, swim team buddies, said anything as they turned from their homework toward each other. "I remember thinking, oh God, don't let me be wrong; don't let me be wrong about this one thing in my entire life," Dan recalls.[129] The unplanned kiss was like a rush of air through his body. Others describe a feeling of "being home at last."

Both boys and girls engage in same-sex erotic behavior prior to self-identifying but the time between these two events differs greatly from about two-and-a-half years for males to four months on average for females.[130] Approximately two-thirds of gay male youths who reported that their sexuality felt natural very early welcomed puberty as a link between their attractions and sexual behavior. "Until then," reports a male student, "I had felt I could never fall in love, that I had no sexual feelings. . . ."[131] Often, there is an "ah-ha" or "eureka" when sexual arousal, imagery, fantasy, romantic notions, and sexual behavior come together. According to Linda, a young adult, she had "an undeniable feeling that this was . . . best for me."[132] A young gay man explains, "I didn't feel like I was cheating on Beth [his girlfriend] because the sex felt so different, so right."[133] John, a high school student continues, "I felt everything that I hadn't felt with a woman."[134] Although some lesbian, gay, and bisexual youths will still persist in their notion that they are similar sexually to others of their gender, they have great difficulty denying their attractions, and most explore and experiment with same-sex behaviors.

For some youths, same-sex erotic behavior is accompanied by shame and guilt. For example, although he had been engaging in sexual behavior for at least four years, Mike continued to promise not to transgress again and to ask God's help in making him stop. Those males with a history of rejection may begin to fear that such rejection will continue.[135] Same-sex sexual encounters are one more thing for which they may be ostracized by their peers. When Rob, age thirteen, agreed to perform oral sex on a very handsome athlete in his junior high, he had no idea that the ensuing "trap" would reveal his homosexuality to many of the boys in his scout troop and result in extreme embarrassment and isolation.

Lesbian and gay youths are more likely to engage in early sexual behavior of all types than are heterosexuals. As a group, lesbian and gay adults report earlier and more frequent same-sex contacts than do heterosexuals and more adolescent sexual behavior involving both sexes.[136] These trends are most evident among gay male youth.[137] Almost two-thirds of gay men masturbated with another boy before adolescence, more than double the figure reported by nongay men.[138]

In general, gay males behave sexually much like heterosexual males. Both are more likely than females to give in to sexual urges and to have serial partners. Unlike their heterosexual counterparts, however, gay males don't have socially sanctioned opportunities to learn a dating "script." Freed from the constraints that women place on male sexual assertiveness, however, gay males may experience a series of sexual encounters with little emotional attachment. In contrast, women, regardless of their sexual orientation, tend to value intimacy and attachment in their intimate relationships with others.

Sex role behaviors may become evident within same-sex relationships although they are not unique to lesbian and gay couples.[139] Male relationships may lack intimacy if both partners exhibit male sex role characteristics of competitiveness and independence. In contrast, female relationships may be very intimate while lacking individuality and autonomy. These tendencies can be counterbalanced over time with practice and patience.

As many as 70 percent of lesbian and gay teens may have had some *heterosexual* experience by adulthood.[140] In contrast, over 30 percent of self-identified lesbian and gay youths have no *same*-sex experience.[141] Heterosexual erotic behavior may continue despite a personal recognition of a lesbian, gay, or bisexual orientation by an individual. For some sexual-minority teens, heterosexual activity is part of their "cover."

In general, lesbians are more likely to continue to engage in heterosexual behaviors and relationships even after they come out to themselves. This difference reflects the positive relationship between self-worth and *success-with-boyfriends* found among junior and senior high school girls.

Emotionally vulnerable youth, especially males, may make sexual contact with other gay teens or adults under less than ideal conditions. Unfortunately, these furtive, solely sexual contacts may set a pattern for interactions with other gays. Dangerous settings, such as parks or rest areas after sunset, and the exploitive nature of the sexual encounters reinforce the worst gay stereotypes and may be internalized by a teen. For those queer kids still denying their feelings, such sexual encounters allow them to participate in sexual behavior devoid of an affectional component.

On the other hand, a naive youth may also misinterpret the intense feelings aroused by sex, the supportive environment, and physical affection as romantic love. Joseph, a gay student, concluded, "There's no simple answers; feelings are more important than sex."[142] Subsequent nonfulfillment of these feelings and the indifference of the other participant may convince the youth that love and intimacy are not possible within same-sex relationships.[143]

Other youths may welcome a mutual emotional commitment, nurture it, and develop mature feelings. Jacob, an African-American high school junior, met Warren, a senior, in a community choir. Jacob recalls,

> [W]e started to have sex. It started to be an emotional thing. He got to the point of telling me he loved me. That was the first time anybody ever said anything like that. It was kind of hard to believe that even after sex there are really feelings. We became good friends.[144]

For Christopher, age nineteen, expressing his sexual orientation for the first time confirmed and validated his feelings.

> Having repressed my sexuality for so long, it was an amazing experience to physically express it . . . It was . . . a giant step toward accepting who I am.[145]

For still others, sex and love may come together and be terrifying. "And that [emotion] scared the shit out of me . . ." confides a young gay man. "As I moved into eighth grade, it became more and more clear to me what it was all about, and it was sex, but with a twist, romance."[146] Still, it is important to remember that only 15 percent of self-identified lesbian teens and 25 percent of gay teens report negative feelings regarding their first same-sex erotic activity.[147]

Same-sex experiences are often the product of crushes, hero-worship and/or intimate friendships, especially for heterosexual youth.[148] Jeff's first experience at age twelve occurred at the urging of a high school neighbor. Another young man explains,

> Derek was my best friend. After soccer practice the fall of our junior year we celebrated both making the "A" team by getting really drunk. We were just fooling around and suddenly our pants were off. . . . I was so scared I stayed out of school for three days. . . .[149]

Beyond enjoyment, these erotic behaviors serve an information-gathering and comparison, reassurance, or experimentation function for queer kids.[150]

Among all males, the reported differences in the percentage of individuals engaging in same sex activity varies, especially with increasing age (Table 1). As would be expected, gay youths increasingly engage in same-sex sexual behavior while nongay youth demonstrate an opposite trend.[151]

Possibly as high as 60 percent of *all prepubescent* males and 33 percent of *all prepubescent* girls have some type of same-sex experience, while 33 percent and 17 percent respectively experience postpubescent orgasm with a same-sex partner.[152] Although other studies have reported lower percentages, the values are still higher than the percentage who will later identify as lesbian or gay.[153] Matthew, a student, observed, "Everyone is a bit gay, especially when you're young."[154] Only 2 percent of heterosexual men and almost no heterosexual women report predominantly homosexual activity as adolescents. In contrast 56 percent of gay men and 41 percent of adult lesbians had engaged in predominantly homosexual behavior.[155] The majority of heterosexual youth who engage in same-sex erotic behavior do not continue to do so in adulthood.

The quality of same-sex erotic behavior appears to differ among adolescents based on sexual orientation. Same-sex sexual activity by lesbians and gays may be more emotional, more planned, and less playful than same-sex activity among heterosexuals.[156] Lesbian and gay teens report a strong affectional component and feelings of love and desire. In contrast, the heterosexual activity by lesbian and gay youths may have an experimental quality.

TABLE 1 *Percentage of Males Engaging in Same-Sex Experiences*

	Sexual Orientation	
Age level	Nongay	Gay
During childhood (ages 5–9 yrs.)	5	40
During preadolescence (ages 10–12 yrs.)	25	60
During adolescence (ages 13–17 yrs.)	15	70
During early adulthood (ages 18–24 yrs.)	5	95

Adapted from Savin-Williams and Lenhart, 1990.

227

Among gay and bisexual male youths, there is a positive relationship between the age of onset of puberty and the age of first same-sex erotic activity.[157] In contrast, the age of first heterosexual activity among the same youths is more closely related to chronological age. Heterosexual encounters seem to begin around age fifteen regardless of the age of onset of puberty.

Must lesbian and gay youths state that they want committed same-sex relationships.[158] The more a youth has engaged in same-sex erotic behavior, the more she or he desires a romantic relationship. In our culture, the process of dating and forming relationships is an important developmental experience through which we define ourselves and gain self-confidence. Falling in love and forming long-term romantic relationships is related to higher self-esteem and self-acceptance.

Although societal supports are nonexistent, 90 percent of lesbians and nearly 70 percent of gay youth between the ages of fourteen and twenty-three have been involved in at least one same-sex relationship. Unfortunately, these are often secretive, short-lived, and covert.[159] Social pressures make it difficult to form and maintain same-sex romantic relationships. "[L]ove of a woman," explains Diane, "was never a possibility that I even realized could be."[160] "[L]ove was something I watched other [heterosexual] people experience and enjoy," continues Lawrence. "I was expected to be part of a world with which I had nothing in common."[161] John, age sixteen, adds, "I've gone through my whole life not getting to know about relationships, not learning about any of this stuff."[162] Vic, a college-age lesbian, concludes,

> I think that whole straight ceremony of dating is not accessible to queer youth. Dating implies a certain amount of choice, the freedom to pick and choose. Well, pick and choose from who? A bunch of people who have to flash each other secret signals to be recognized.[163]

◉ Self-Identification

Self-identification usually occurs in late adolescence between the ages of sixteen and twenty-one.[164] The mean age for openly gay young adult males to self-identify is 16.2 years, although some self-identifying occurs as early as age 14.[165] As some segments of society become more open, self-identification is occurring even earlier,[166] especially in large urban areas. There is much individual variation. Self-identification does not imply self-acceptance which is dependent on many things, including romantic relationships and acceptance by others.

The relative lateness of sexual identification for lesbians and gays as compared to heterosexuals can be attributed to homophobia, discrimination, and societal prohibitions. No doubt, confusion and fear account for the lapse of time between first becoming aware of erotic feelings and labeling them. Sixteen-year-old Andy was caught between self-hatred for cowardly remaining in the closet and the threat of harassment should he come out.

Although Victor, a seventeen-year-old bisexual, reminds us that, "Bisexuals are *not* waiting to make up their minds about their sexual identity,"[167] for many *youths*, self-identification as bisexual is a rest stop on the way to claiming a lesbian or gay identity. Bisexuality seems more accepted and maintains a link to the heterosexual majority. More African-Americans than European Americans choose this route because African-American communities seem to be more tolerant of bisexuality.[168] African-American teens may adopt a less heterosexual lifestyle than their white peers while being less willing to identify as lesbian or gay.

Initial feelings may gradually evolve into a sense of relief, of well-being, and "rightness." Naomi, age twenty, explains,

> [T]his feeling was so natural, I guess I trusted my own feelings enough not to believe anybody's negative ones. Because I felt that if what I'm doing is what they're saying is sick and bad, well they [the critics] must be sick and bad.[169]

This conscious recognition of sexuality is the beginning of self-acceptance.[170] A lesbian or gay teen may express self-anger at her or his earlier pattern of conformity.

Self-identification can be viewed as a two-step process in which a youth first accepts her or his sexual identity and then integrates that identity with her or his personality and self-concept. A twenty-year-old female student describes how it feels to be an integrated whole:

> I feel that I am the terrific person I am today because I'm a lesbian. I decided that I was gay when I was very young. After making that decision, which was the hardest thing I could ever face, I feel like I can do anything.[171]

Through acceptance, an adolescent begins to view the notion of "lesbianness," "gayness," or bisexuality in a positive way. "It's a real love and trust of women, and respect," states Brenda, age seventeen. "It's something inside me that I can't explain."[172] During this phase, a youth may make an initial disclosure or "come out" to a very trusted friend or family member. Disclosure seems very important for positive self-identification as lesbian or gay.[173]

Acceptance is followed by integration in which a young person identifies as lesbian or gay and proud. "My soul feels more comfortable," explains Shannon, age seventeen. "It feels right."[174] Integration and pride often are accompanied by a public self-disclosure known as "Coming out of the closet" or simply as "Coming out." Coming out is an adjusting between the real and the social self and as such, is a necessary process for healthy personality integration. Being known as lesbian or gay is an important step in identity formation.[175] Early self-disclosure seems to be related positively to high self-esteem. Michael, a student, explains the process:

> Contrary to . . . opinion, I didn't wake up one morning and say, "Gee, I think I'll be gay for the rest of my life. That'll be fun." Why would anyone choose a life filled with discrimination? The only choice I made was to come out of the closet.[176]

Coming out and the often accompanying anger and pride are important for identity stabilization.[177] Integration of sexual identity is a lifelong process.

Integration is enhanced through interaction with other lesbian and gay adults and involvement in the sexual-minority community.[178] Typically, youths come to prefer social interactions with other lesbians and/or gays. Self-identification with others becomes positive.

When compared to those still in sexual-identity turmoil, the well-integrated lesbian or gay male may have higher self-esteem and greater well-being, a greater capacity for and more confidence in love both in sexual relationships and in friendships, and increased productivity.[179] More energy is spent in living an open life and less on trying to hide it. Honest heterosexuals occasionally will express awe for the lesbian or gay adult who has come through this process and now knows who she or he is and faces the world confident and unafraid. The battle with homophobia and heterosexism and with their own internalized "demons" can leave the winners proud to proclaim "I am who I am!"

Unfortunately, not everyone can accept her or his own lesbian, gay, or bisexual identity. The road to a well-integrated, healthy, positive, cohesive identity is strewed with those who can not really accept themselves and continue to use all manner of subterfuge to hide their true identity.

◉ *C*onclusion

Sexual self-identification is part of the larger process of adolescent development, a confusing, sometimes contradictory, process in itself. For many
teens their sexuality is ambiguous and not clearly delineated. They may
begin to understand their feelings but not to clarify them. All the while these
processes are occurring within an atmosphere of adolescent conformity and
burgeoning independence. The adolescent question "Who am I?" becomes
entangled with a second question "What does it mean to be lesbian or
gay?"[180]

Most homosexuals accept their sexual orientation and "lead successful,
productive, non-neurotic lives as self-acknowledged gay men and
lesbians."[181] More than half would not change their sexual orientation if
such were possible, despite the negative attitudes of the larger society.[182]
The process of becoming has its own rewards. Questioning and exploring
can make an individual more sensitive to difference and more accepting of
it. Every issue from coming out to having children is there to be explored,
discussed, and decided. Erna, a young Navajo woman, concludes that, as a
result, "We are special, because we're able to deal with . . . life."[183]

Through the process of "becoming" lesbian, gay, or bisexual, the individual's range of possibilities increases, and the coping skills acquired to
transcend adversity give an individual the ability to find fulfillment. "I have
learned a lot more about myself," states Rachel, a sixteen-year-old
Midwesterner. "If I had a choice, I wouldn't change my sexual orientation."[184]

*E*ndnotes

[1] G. J. McDonald, "Individual differences in the coming-out process for gay men:
Implications for theoretical models," *Journal of Homosexuality*, (Volume 8,
1982).

P. K. Rector, "The acceptance of homosexual identity in adolescence: A
phenomenological study," *Dissertation Abstracts International*, (Volume 43,
1982).

[2] G. J. Remafedi, M. Resnick, R. Blum, and L. Harris, L. "Demography of sexual orientation in adolescents," *Pediatrics*, (Volume 89, 1992).

[3] Dailey, 1979; Peplau, Cochran, Rook, and Pedesky, 1978.

M. T. Saghir and E. Robins, "Clinical aspects of female homosexuality." In J. Marmor, Ed., *Homosexual behavior: A modern reappraisal.* (New York: Basic Books, 1980).

[4]M. Kirkpatrick and C. Morgan, "Psychodynamic psychotherapy of female homosexuality." In J. Marmor, Ed., *Homosexual behavior: A modern reappraisal.* (New York: Basic Books, 1981), p. 372–373.

[5]R. R. Troiden, "Homosexual identity formation," *Journal of Adolescent Health Care,* (Volume 9, 1988).

[6]A. P. Bell, M. S. Weinberg, and S. K. Hammersmith, *Sexual preference: Its development in men and women.* (Bloomington, IN: Indiana University Press, 1981a).

R. C. Savin-Williams, "Memories of childhood and early adolescent sexual feelings among gay and bisexual boys: A narrative approach." In R. C. Savin-Williams and K. M. Cohen, Eds., *The lives of lesbians, gays, amid bisexuals.* (Fort Worth, TX: Harcourt & Brace College Publishers, 1996c).

R. R. Troiden, "Becoming homosexual: A model of gay identity acquisition," *Psychiatry,* (Volume 42, 1979).

[7]A. Heron, Ed., *One teenager in ten.* (Boston, MA: Alyson, 1983), p. 115.

[8]Durby, 1994.

[9]L. Heal, "It happened on Main Street." In B. L. Singer, Ed., *Growing up gay/growing up lesbian.* (New York: The New Press, 1994), p. 9.

[10]P. J. Gorton, "Different from the others." In R. Luczak, Ed., *Eyes of desire: A deaf gay and lesbian reader.* (Boston, Alyson, 1993), p. 20.

[11]Bell, Weinberg, and Hammersmith, 1981a.

[12]R. Green, "Gender identity in childhood and later sexual orientation," *American Journal of Psychiatry,* (Volume 142, 1985).

G. B. MacDonald, "Exploring sexual identity: Gay people and their families," *Sex Education Coalition News,* (Volume 5, 1983).

R. Robertson, "Young gays." In J. Hart and J. Richardson, Eds., *The theory and practice of homosexuality.* (New York: Routledge & Kegan Paul, 1981).

B. Zuger, "Early effeminate behavior in boys," *Journal of Nervous and Mental Disorders,* (Volume 172, 1984).

R. C. Savin-Williams, *Gay and lesbian youth: Expressions of identity.* (Washington, DC: Hemisphere, 1990).

R. C. Savin-Williams, "Ethnic- and sexual-minority youth." In R. C. Savin-Williams and K. M. Cohen, Eds., *The lives of lesbians, gays, amid bisexuals.* (Fort Worth, TX: Harcourt & Brace College Publishers, 1996b).

[13]K. Chandler, *Passages of pride: Gay and lesbian youth come of age.* (New York: Times Books, 1995).

[14]Savin-Williams, 1996c, p. 100.

[15]Ibid.

[16]Bell, Weinberg, and Hammersmith, 1981a.

R. C. Friedman and L. O. Stern, "Juvenile aggressivity and sissiness in homosexual and heterosexual males," *Journal of the Academy of Psychoanalysis,* (Volume 8, 1980).

R. Green, "Childhood cross-gender behavior and subsequent sexual preference," *American Journal of Psychiatry,* (Volume 36, 1979).

[17]R. R. Troiden, "Becoming homosexual: A model of gay identity acquisition," *Psychiatry,* (Volume 42, 1979), p. 363.

[18]Bell, Weinberg, and Hammersmith, 1981a, p. 74.

[19]M. T. Saghir and E. Robins, *Male and female homosexuality.* (Baltimore, MD: Williams & Wilkins, 1973).

[20]I. Bieber, *Homosexuality: A psychoanalytic study.* (New York: Basic Books, 1962).

M. Eisner, *An investigation of the coming-out process, lifestyle, amid sex-role orientation of lesbians.* Unpublished doctoral dissertation, York University, Toronto (1982).

R. B. Evans, "Childhood parental relationships of homosexual men," *Journal of Consulting and Clinical Psychology,* (Volume 33, 1969).

E. A. McCauley and A. A. Ehrhardt, "Role expectations and definitions: A comparison of female transsexuals and lesbians," *Journal of Homosexuality,* (Volume 3, 1977).

C. Van Cleave, "Self-identification, self-identification discrepancy, an environmental perspective of women with same-sex preference." *Dissertation Abstracts International,* (Volume 38, 1978).

[21]Bell, Weinberg, and Hammersmith, 1981a, p. 148.

[22]S. O. Murray, *Social theory, homosexual realities.* (New York: Gai Sabre Books, 1984).

R. Parker, "Youth, identity, and homosexuality: The changing shape of sexual life in contemporary Brazil." In G. Herdt, Ed., *Gay and lesbian youth.* (Binghamton, NY: Harrington Park Press, 1989).

[23]R. Green, *The "sissy boy syndrome" and the development of homosexuality.* (New Haven, CT: Yale University Press, 1987).

Whitan, 1983.

[24]J. T. Sears, *Growing up gay in the South: Race, gender, and journeys of the spirit.* (Binghamton, NY: Harrington Park Press, 1991a), p. 50.

[25]R. C. Savin-Williams and R. E. Lenhart, "AIDS prevention among gay and lesbian youth: Psychosocial stress and health care intervention guidelines." In D. G. Ostrow, Ed., *Behavioral aspects of AIDS.* (New York: Plenum Medical Book Co., 1990).

[26]Sears, 1991a, p. 49.

[27]Savin-Williams, 1996c.

[28]E. Coleman, "Developmental stages of the coming-out process," *Journal of Homosexuality*, (Volume 7, 1982b).

[29]Sears, 1991a, p. 49.

[30]K. Jennings, "American dreams." In B. L. Singer, Ed., *Growing up gay/growing up lesbian.* (New York: The New Press, 1994).

[31]Sanders, 1980.

C. J. Strayer, "Research on homosexuality in the Netherlands," *The Netherlands' Journal of Sociology*, (Volume 12, 1976).

[32]E. White, *A boy's own story.* (New York: E.P. Dutton, 1982), p. 169.

[33]A. M. Boxer, *Betwixt and between: Developmental discontinuities of gay and lesbian youth.* Paper presented at the Society for Research on Adolescence, Alexandria, VA (1988, March).

[34]E. Bass and K. Kaufman, *Free your mind: The book for gay, lesbian, and bisexual youth—and their allies.* (New York: Harper Perennial, 1996), p. 24.

[35]Coleman, 1982b.

K. Jay and A. Young, *The gay report: Lesbians and gay men speak out about sexual experiences and lifestyles.* (New York: Simon & Schuster, 1979).

A. C. Kinsey, W. B. Pomeroy, and C. E. Martin, *Sexual behavior in the human male.* (Philadelphia, PA: W. B. Saunders, 1948).

H. Kooden, S. Morin, D. Riddle, M. Rogers, B. Sang, and F. Strassburger, *Removing the stigma. Final Report of the Task Force on the Status of Lesbian and Gay Male Psychologists.* (Washington, DC: American Psychological Association, 1979).

MacDonald, 1983; Rector, 1982.

R. A. Rodriguez, *Significant events in gay identity development: Gay men in Utah.* Paper presented at the annual meeting of the American Psychological Association, Atlanta, GA (1988, August).

G. Sanders, "Homosexuals in the Netherlands," *Alternative Lifestyles*, (Volume 3, 1980).

J. Spada, *The Spada Report: The newest survey of gay male sexuality.* (New York: New American Library, 1979).

Troiden, 1979.

[36]Heal, 1994.

[37]G. J. Remafedi, "Male homosexuality: The adolescent's perspective," *Pediatrics,* (Volume 79, 1987b).

[38]S. K. Telljohann and J. H. Price, "A qualitative examination of adolescent homosexuals' life experiences: Ramifications for secondary school personnel," *Journal of Homosexuality,* (Volume 26, 1993).

[39]Savin-Williams, 1996c, p. 97.

[40]Sears, 1991a, p. 112.

[41]Remafedi, 1987b, p. 328.

[42]J. T. Sears, "Black-gay or gay-black: Choosing identities and identifying choices." In G. Unks, Ed., *The gay teen.* (New York: Routledge, 1995), p. 142.

[43]Chandler, 1995, p. 6.

[44]Sears, 1991a, p. 352.

[45]P. Singer, "Breaking through," Rochester, NY, *Democrat and Chronicle,* (1993, July 4), p. D–1.

[46]Sears, 1991a, p. 84.

[47]J. Green, "This school is out," *The New York Times Magazine,* (1991, October 13), p. 18.

[48]Savin-Williams, 1996c.

[49]Ibid., p. 100.

[50]Chandler, 1995, p. 16.

[51]Savin-Williams, 1996c, p. 98.

[52]D. Kopay and P. D. Young, *The David Kopay Story: An extraordinary self-revelation.* (New York: Donald Fine, 1988).

[53]"Starting over: A Chinese teenager comes to a new home and comes out," *Crossroads,* (1996, Winter/Spring), p. 6.

[54]Sears, 1991a, p. 205.

[55]P. Gibson, "Report of the Secretary's 'Task Force on Youth Suicide.'" In M. Feinleib, Ed., *Prevention and intervention in youth suicide.* Washington, DC: U.S. Department of Health and Human Services, Public Health Services; Alcohol, Drug Abuse and Mental health Administration, (1989), pp. 3–131.

[56]Chandler, 1995, p. 82.

[57]Sears, 1991a. p. 290.

[58]Boxer, 1988.

A. H. Buss, *Self-consciousness and social anxiety.* (San Francisco, CA: W. H. Freeman, 1980).

McDonald, 1982; Remafedi, 1987b.

T. Roesler and R. Deisher, "Youthful male homosexuality," *Journal of the American Medical Association,* (Volume 219, 1972).

Savin-Williams, 1990.

[59]Bell, Weinberg, and Hammersmith, 1981a, 1981b.

[60]Savin-Williams, 1996c.

[61]S. Maguen, "Gay rural youth lack support from the community," *The Advocate,* (1992, November 17), p. 54.

[62]Singer, 1993, p. D–1.

[63]Heron, 1983, pp. 9–10.

[64]Heal, 1994, p. 10.

[65]Bass and Kaufman, 1996, p. 17.

[66]"Starting over," 1996, p. 6.

[67]P. D. Toth, "Realizing it's OK to be gay." Rochester, NY, *Times Union,* (1993, October 12), p. 15.

[68]S. Parsavand, "Discussion groups ease acceptance for gay high schoolers," *Schenectady Gazette,* (1993, December 5), p. A–1.

[69]D. A. Anderson, "Family and peer relations of gay adolescents." In S. C. Geinstein, Ed., *Adolescent psychiatry: Developmental and clinical studies,* Volume 14. (Chicago: The University of Chicago Press, 1987).

Savin-Williams, 1996c.

[70]R. C. Savin-Williams, "Dating and romantic relations among gay, lesbian, and bisexual youths." In R. C. Savin-Williams and K. M. Cohen, Eds., *The lives of lesbians, gays, and bisexuals.* (Fort Worth, TX: Harcourt & Brace College Publishers, 1996a), p. 170.

[71]M. Schneider, "Sappho was a right-on adolescent: Growing up lesbian," *Journal of Homosexuality,* (Volume 17, 1989), p. 118.

[72]J. L. Norton, "The homosexual and counseling," *Personnel and Guidance Journal,* (Volume 54, 1976).

[73]R. Fisher, *The gay mystique: Time myth and reality of male homosexuality.* (New York: Stein & Day, 1972), p. 249.

[74]B. L. Singer, Ed., *Growing up gay/growing up lesbian*. (New York: The New Press, 1994).

[75]Bell, Weinberg, and Hammersmith, 1981a.

V. C. Cass, "Homosexual identity formation: Testing a theoretical model," *Journal of Homosexuality*, (Volume 4, 1979).

J. A. Lee, "Going public: A study of the sociology of homosexual liberation," *Journal of Homosexuality*, (Volume 3, 1977).

A. K. Malyon, "The homosexual adolescent: Developing issues and social bias," *Child Welfare*, (Volume 60, 1981).

A. D. Martin, "Learning to hide: The socialization of the gay adolescent," *Adolescent Psychiatry*, (Volume 10, 1982).

K. Plummer, *The making of the modern homosexual*. (London: Hutchinson, 1981).

Reiche and Dannecker, 1977; Sanders, 1980; Troiden, 1979.

[76]Anderson, 1987.

[77]G. P. Mallon, "Gay and no place to go: Assessing the needs of gay and lesbian adolescents in out-of-home settings," *Child Welfare*, (Volume 71, 1992a).

[78]Cass, 1979; Plummer, 1981.

R. C. Savin-Williams and R. G. Rodriguez, "A developmental, clinical perspective on lesbian, gay male, and bisexual youths." In T. P. Gulotta, G. R. Adams, and R. Montemayor, Eds., *Adolescent sexuality*. (Newbury Park, CA: Sage, 1993).

C. A. Tripp, *The homosexual matrix*. (New York: McGraw-Hill, 1975).

Troiden, 1979.

[79]Cass, 1979; Reiche and Dannecker, 1977; Savin-Williams and Rodriguez, 1993; Troiden, 1979.

[80]C. DeMontflores and S. J. Schultz, "Coming out: Similarities and differences for lesbians and gay men," *Journal of Social Issues*, (Volume 34, 1978).

Malyon, 1981; Martin, 1982; Tripp, 1975.

[81]Malyon, 1981.

[82]Troiden and Goode, 1980.

[83]D. A. Anderson, "Lesbian and gay adolescents: Social and developmental considerations." In G. Unks, Ed., *The gay teen*. (New York: Routledge, 1995).

[84]Savin-Williams, 1996c.

[85]Ross-Reynolds, 1988.

[86]Cass, 1979; Lee, 1977.

G. Sanders, 1980.

[87]Sears, 1991a, p. 194.

[88]Savin-Williams, 1996c.

[89]E. S. Hetrick and A. D. Martin, "Developmental issues and their resolution for gay and lesbian adolescents," *Journal of Homosexuality*, (Volume 14, 1987).

[90]Bell, Weinberg, and Hammersmith, 1981; Cass, 1979; Martin, 1982; Lee, 1977.

R. Reich and M. Dannecker, "Male homosexuality in West Germany—A sociological investigation," *Journal of Sex Research*, (Volume 13, 1977).

G. Sanders, 1980.

M. S. Weinberg and C. J. Williams, *Male homosexuals: Their problems and adaptations.* (New York: Penguin, 1974).

[91]A. P. Bell and M. S. Weinberg, *Homosexualities: A study of diversity among men and women.* (New York: Simon & Shuster, 1978).

S. Schafer, "Sexual and social problems of lesbians," *Journal of Sex Research*, (Volume 12, 1976).

Spada, 1979.

R. R. Troiden and E. Goode, "Variables related to acquisition of gay identity," *Journal of Homosexuality*, (Volume 5, 1980).

Weinberg and Williams, 1974.

[92]B. S. Newman and P. O. Muzzonigro, "The effects of traditional family values on the coming out process of gay male adolescents," *Adolescence*, (Volume 28, 1993).

[93]Sears, 1991a, p. 82.

[94]L. D. Brimmer, *Being different: Lambda youth speak out.* (New York Franklin Watts, 1995), p. 37.

[95]Sears, 1991a, p. 52.

[96]L. Dime, *Joining the Tribe*, (New York: Anchor Books, 1995), p. 242.

[97]C. A. Rigg, "Homosexuality and adolescence," *Pediatric Annual*, (Volume 11, 1982).

[98]Sears, 1991a, p. 353.

[99]Due, 1995, p. 77.

[100]K. M. Cohen and R. C. Savin-Williams, "Developmental perspectives on coming out to self and others." In R. C. Savin-Williams and K. M. Cohen, Eds., *The lives*

of lesbians, gays, and bisexuals. (Fort Worth, TX: Harcourt & Brace College Publishers, 1996), p. 126.

[101]D. Boyer, "Male prostitution and homosexual identity." In G. Herdt, Ed., Gay and Lesbian Youth, (Binghamton, NY: Harrington Park Press, 1989), p. 169.

[102]Sears, 1991a, p. 132.

[103]Savin-Williams, 1996a, p. 173.

[104]Due, 1995, p. 108.

[105]G. Herdt and A. M. Boxer, Children of horizons: How gay and lesbian teens are leading a new way out of time closet. (Boston: Beacon Press, 1993).

[106]Sears, 1991a, p. 327.

[107]Herdt and Boxer, 1993.

G. J. Remafedi, "Adolescent homosexuality: Psycho-social and medical implications," Pediatrics, (Volume 79, 1987a).

Remafedi, 1987b; Roesler and Deisher, 1972; Savin-Williams, 1990; Sears, 1991a.

[108]Savin-Williams, 1996b, p. 172.

[109]Sears, 1991a, p. 327.

[110]M. S. Schneider and B. Tremble, "Training service providers to work with gay and lesbian adolescents: A workshop," Journal of Counseling and Development, (Volume 65, 1986).

[111]Heron, 1983, p. 76.

[112]Toth, 1993, October 12, p. 15.

[113]Bass and Kaufman, 1996, p. 33.

[114]J. Gover, "Gay youth in the family," Journal of Emotional and Behavioral Problems, (Volume 2, Number 4, 1993), p. 36.

[115]Savin-Williams, 1996c, p. 105.

[116]Weisberg and Williams, 1974.

[117]L. J. Braaten and C. D. Darling, "Overt and covert homosexual problems among male college students," Genetic Psychology Monographs, (Volume 71, 1965).

[118]F. L. Myrick, "Homosexual types: An empirical investigation," Journal of Sex Research, (Volume 10, 1974a), p. 234.

[119]Toth, 1993, October 12, p. 15.

[120]G. Sanders, 1980.

[121]Sears, 1995, p. 140.

122J. Harry, "Adolescent sexuality: Masculinity-femininity, and educational attainment," ERIC Document No. 237395, (1983a).

123Sears, 1991a, p. 52.

124Martin, 1982.

125Savin-Williams, 1990.

126Michael, "Different is not bad." In B. L. Singer, Ed., Growing up gay/growing up lesbian. (New York: The New Press, 1994), p. 60.

127J. A. Cook, A. M. Boxer, and G. Herdt, First homosexual and heterosexual experiences reported by gay and lesbian youth in an urban community. Paper presented at the annual meeting of the American Sociological Association. San Francisco, CA, (1989).

128S. M. Brady, "The relationship between differences in stages of homosexual identity formation and background characteristics, psychological well-being and homosexual adjustment," Dissertation Abstracts International, (Volume 45, 1985).

Rodriguez, 1988.

129Bass and Kaufman, 1996, p. 92.

130Sears, 1991a.

131R. A. Isay, "The development of sexual identity in homosexual men." In S. I. Greenspan and G. H. Pollack, Eds., The course of life: Volume IV, Adolescence. (Medison, CT: International Universities Press, 1991), p. 477.

132Heal, 1994, p. 12.

133Savin-Williams, 1996a, p. 175.

134Due, 1995, p. 74.

135Savin-Williams, 1996c.

136M. Manosevitz, "Early sexual behavior in adult homosexual and heterosexual males," Journal of Abnormal Psychology, (Volume 76, 1970).

137DeMonteflores and Schultz, 1978; Shafer, 1977; Remafedi, 1987a.

138Saghir and Robins, 1973.

139J. C. Gonsiorek, "Mental health issues of gay and lesbian adolescents," Journal of Adolescent Health Care, (Volume 9, 1988).

140Cook, Boxer, and Herdt, 1989.

141G. Ross-Reynolds, "Issues in counseling the 'homosexual' adolescent." In J. Grimes, Ed., Psychological approaches 10 problems of children and adolescents. (Des Moines, IA: Iowa Department of Education, 1982).

[142]M. Mac an Ghaill, "Schooling, sexuality and male power: Towards an emancipatory cirriculum," *Gender and Education*, (Volume 3, 1991), p. 298.

[143]Gover, 1993.

[144]Sears, 1991a, p. 127.

[145]Brimmer, 1995, p. 64.

[146]Savin-Williams, 1996c, p. 104.

[147]Boxer, 1988.

[148]C. L. Chng, "Adolescent homosexual behavior and the health educator," *Journal of School Health*, (Volume 61, 1980).

[149]Savin-Williams, 1996a, p. 171.

[150]M. Glasser, "Homosexuality in adolescence," *British Journal of Medical Psychology*, (Volume 50, 1977).

[151]Savin-Williams and Lenhart, 1990.

[152]J. Diepold and R. D. Young, "Empirical studies of adolescent sexual behavior: A critical review,"*Adolescence*, (Volume 14, 1979).

Kinsey, Pomeroy, and Martin, 1948.

A. C. Kinsey, W. B. Pomeroy, C. E. Martin, and R. H. Gebhard, *Sexual behavior in the human female.* (Philadelphia, PA: W.B. Saunders, 1953).

[153]R. E. Fay, C. F. Turner, A. D. Klassen, and J. H. Gagnon, "Prevalence and patterns of same-gender sexual contact among men," *Science*, (Number 243, 1989).

E. Goode and L. Haber, "Sexual correlates of homosexual experience: An exploratory study of college women," *Journal of Sex Research*, (Volume 13, 1977).

R. Sorenson, *Adolescent sexuality in contemporary society.* (New York: World Book, 1973).

[154]Mac an Ghaill, 1991, p. 298.

[155]Bell, Weinberg, and Hammersmith; 1981a.

A. P. Bell, M. S. Weinberg, and S. K. Hammersmith, *Sexual preference: Its development in men and women*, (Statistical appendix). (Bloomington, IN: Indiana University Press, 1981b).

[156]Isay, 1991.

[157]R. C. Savin-Williams, "An exploratory study of pubertal maturation timing and self-esteem among gay and bisexual male youths," *Developmental Psychology*, (Volume 31. 1995).

[158]D'Augehli, 1991.

J. Harry and W. B. DeVall, *The social organization of gay males*. (New York: Praeger, 1978).

Remafedi, 1987a; G. Sanders, 1980; Savin-Williams, 1990.

[159]Sears, 1991a.

[160]Stanley and Wolf, 1980, p. 47.

[161]W. Curtis, Ed., *Revelations: A collection of gay male coming-out stories*. (Boston, MA: Alyson, 1988), p. 109–110.

[162]Due, 1995, p. 74.

[163]Ibid., pp. 123–124.

[164]Rodriguez, 1988; Savin-Williams and Lenhart, 1990.

[165]Remafedi, 1987b; Rodriguez, 1988.

[166]D. Offer and A. M. Boxer, "Normal adolescent development: Empirical research findings." In M. Lewis, Ed., *Child and adolescent psychiatry: A comprehensive textbook*. (Baltimore, MD: Williams & Wilkins, 1991).

Rector, 1982.

[167]Chandler, 1995, p. 146.

[168]Sears, 1991a.

[169]Schneider, 1989, pp. 121–122.

[170]Isay, 1991.

[171]Schneider, 1989, p. 123.

[172]Ibid., p. 128.

[173]S. M. Jourard, *The transparent self*. (New York: Van Nostrand, 1971).

[174]Schneider, 1989, p. 128.

[175]Malyon, 1981.

[176]M. Sluchan, "Whose world is it anyway?" *The Weekly Pennsylvanian*, (1993, March 30), p. 4.

[177]Savin-Williams, 1990.

[178]Troiden, 1979.

[179]Isay, 1991.

[180]Schneider, 1989.

[181]Savin-Williams, 1990, p. 182.

[182]Remafedi, 1987b.

[183]E. Pahe, "Speaking up." In B. L. Singer, Ed., *Growing up gay/growing up lesbian*. (New York: The New Press, 1994), p. 234.

[184]A. Heron, Ed., *Two teenagers in twenty*. (Boston, MA: Alyson, 1994), p. 14.

❧ ❧ ❧

Questions

1. What are the four steps in becoming lesbian, gay, or bisexual? Is any one of these steps more problematic than the others? Explain.

2. At what age do the various stages tend to occur? How much variation is there in the timing or sequencing of becoming lesbian, gay, or bisexual?

3. How do the processes of becoming gay, lesbian, or bisexual compare with those of becoming heterosexual?

4. How do young people cope with the anxiety they experience when they become aware of their same-sex attraction?

5. How effective are nonheterosexual youths' coping strategies? Are these strategies more effective for lesbians, gays, or bisexuals, or are they equally effective for all three groups?

6. Do you think Owens's four steps are accurate? Would you add other steps? If so, what would they be?

Legalize It?: A Bulletin From the War on Drugs

Erich Goode

In this article, Erich Goode reviews evidence for and against the legalization of drugs in the United States. This evidence includes reviewing the impact of prohibition on alcohol consumption rates, the effect of legalizing marijuana in the Netherlands, and the depenalization of marijuana in several states. Although Goode harshly criticizes the war on drugs as a failure, he argues that legalization may not be a realistic or appropriate policy, and instead points to the promise of harm reduction programs.

The explosion of crack cocaine use in the mid-1980s set off a fierce debate in the United States. In the midst of calls to crack down on drug users and suppliers, a formerly politically unpalatable proposal emerged: drug legalization. Advocates argue that enforcing the drug laws has fattened the wallets of drug gangs, increased drug-related violence, corrupted law enforcement, dissuaded drug abusers from seeking medical help, and in the end failed to deter drug use. It is time, these critics claim, to legalize illicit drugs, stop arresting drug users and focus entirely on treatment.

It is true that the "war" approach to controlling drug abuse and its side effects has failed. But the hope that simply legalizing drugs will work is also unrealistic. The optimal strategy is a program focused largely—and pragmatically—on reducing the damage that both drug abuse and the war on drugs inflict on users and society at large.

Legalization proposals vary across a wide spectrum. Some plans call for regulating all psychoactive substances in the same way we currently regulate alcohol. The alcohol model would legalize the possession of any and all drugs, but the government would control how they can be sold. Others endorse dispensing certain substances by prescription to the drug-dependent. The most

Reprinted from *Contexts* 3:3, by permission of the Copyright Clearance Center. Copyright © 2004 by The University of California Press.

radical proposals call for no state control whatsoever. This laissez-faire model of full decriminalization is endorsed by libertarians. Other decriminalization approaches are limited to certain drugs—usually marijuana—in small quantities, and to possession, not sale or distribution. Advocates of these various models agree that law enforcement should not and cannot solve the problem of drug abuse. They argue that the current system causes harm, which some form of legalization would alleviate, and that drug use would not skyrocket under legalization.

"Harm reduction"—more a strategy for evaluating policies and their consequences than a specific proposal—is often confused with legalization. Harm reductionists are pragmatic rather than programmatic. They weigh costs and benefits, focus more on the health of the community than on individual rights, tend to be cautious or even pessimistic about some legalization models and argue that policy should be set on a drug-by-drug basis. According to this approach, the goal of drug policy is to reduce death, disease, predatory crime, and other costs, not to attain some idealized outcome.

❧ *£egalize £t?*

Would any form of drug legalization work better than the war on drugs? In what specific ways might legalization succeed or fail? While most of what is written on drug laws has been polemical, serious researchers have studied the possible consequences of changes to the law. Most focus on the practical effects of various policy proposals, leaving the moral issues to philosophers, politicians and pundits. One strategy is to look at the history of drug regulation.

Drug Policy and Drug Use, Past and Present

Journalist Edward Brecher described 19th-century America as "a dope fiend's paradise." For much of the 1800s, few jurisdictions controlled psychoactive substances. During the first half of the century, children were permitted to purchase and drink alcohol, politicians and the military distributed liquor, and work in rural planting fields and urban workshops was usually accompanied by more than one pull at the jug. Tax records indicate that in 1830, per-capita alcohol consumption was more than three times what it is today. As for narcotics, the problem of addiction has hardly improved from the days when these substances were legal. During the 19th century, under a laissez-faire policy, there were at least as many narcotic addicts as there are today. Historians estimate that at the end of the 19th century there were at least 300,000 opiate addicts, most of whom started using drugs to treat medical problems. That amounts to about 3.7 addicts per 1,000 people. Today, about 1 million people are addicted to heroin, which is approximately 3.55 per 1,000 people.

But a comparison between then and now should take into consideration more than numbers alone. Under a more or less laissez-faire 19th-century legal system, few addicts committed crimes to pay for their habit, the criminal-addict subculture was small and violent gangs did not distribute drugs. Today, our laws prohibit and penalize the possession and distribution of nearly all psychoactive substances for recreational purposes—and some for any reason. Each year, we arrest 1.5 million people for drug offenses, and between 300,000 and 400,000 drug offenders reside in state and federal prisons, more than the number of violent offenders. Today, about one-third of state prison inmates and half of federal inmates are serving time for drug crimes. There are more than 15 times as many people in state prisons for drug crimes now than there were in 1980, and the proportion of all state prisoners who are drug offenders has quadrupled. Likewise, federal prisons house four times more drug offenders now than in 1980, and the proportion of all federal prisoners who are drug offenders has doubled. Comparatively, the United States incarcerates more drug offenders (150 per 100,000 people) than the European Union does for all crimes put together (fewer than 100 per 100,000). It seems the social costs of drug use are higher than ever.

Perhaps the fear of arrest and imprisonment discourages potential users from taking up the joint, pipe or needle. Supporters of prohibition consider Reagan's war on drugs a success, because use—especially among adolescents and young adults, which had shot up during the permissive 1960s and 70s—declined significantly and spectacularly during the 1980s. (Ironically, the crack epidemic hit precisely when casual, recreational drug use declined.) Yet, beginning in the early 1990s, rates of recreational drug use increased again among young people. (After 2000, they declined a bit.) Another blow to advocates of a law enforcement approach is that today American schoolchildren are more than twice as likely to use marijuana—and almost four times as likely to use other illicit drugs—as are their European peers. Also, Reagan's drug war failed to curb supply. During his presidency, the purity of the two most dangerous illicit drugs—heroin and cocaine—increased, while their price declined. Methamphetamine, a powerful and once-popular stimulant commonly referred to as "speed," also made a strong comeback. Moreover, "club" drugs such as Ecstasy, GHB, and Rohypnol, which were not on anyone's radar screen a decade ago, are now widespread.

For these reasons, critics of the current system believe that drug prohibition has been a failure. Legalizers believe that enforcement of drug laws has untoward social side-effects. They argue that the prohibitions more than the drugs are responsible for the crime, violence and medical pathology. And they think the solution to the substance abuse problem is legalization. Under close scrutiny, however, the evidence does not always back up their claims.

Lessons from Alcohol Prohibition

Critics of the drug laws often point to national prohibition of alcohol in the United States as evidence that banning illicit substances does not work. Actually, Prohibition (1920–33) offers a complex lesson. Evidence on cirrhosis of the liver and hospital admissions for alcohol-related dementia indicates that alcohol consumption almost certainly declined during Prohibition—mainly among the heaviest drinkers. (Interestingly, these measures of heavy alcohol consumption began to decline before both state and federal prohibitions were imposed.) Tax records indicate that American adults drank an average of two gallons of absolute alcohol per year before Prohibition. During 1934, the first full year after Prohibition was repealed, this figure came to just under one gallon, suggesting that the experience of Prohibition deterred drinking even after it became legal again. The first lesson we learn from Prohibition is that criminalization can work—at least partially—to discourage use.

Deterrence aside, Prohibition proved a costly mistake. It enriched and empowered organized crime, increased murders, generated disrespect for the law, encouraged corruption among government officials, deprived the government of tax revenue and drove people to drink toxic "bootleg" substitutes. The second lesson of Prohibition is that outlawing illicit substances may generate damaging unanticipated consequences.

The fact is, most Americans did not regard alcohol consumption as a sin. When state referenda were held, voters chose to repeal rather than continue Prohibition by 15 million to 4 million votes. Alcohol was a part of the lives of many Americans—something that is untrue today of heroin, cocaine or speed. Hence, Prohibition offers a third lesson: behavior that is in the mainstream of American culture probably cannot be successfully prohibited. But behavior that runs against the grain may be an altogether different matter.

The Lesson of Marijuana Decriminalization

Possessing small amounts of marijuana has been decriminalized—or, to use a term coined by Robert MacCoun and Peter Reuter, "depenalized"—in 12 states. This means that, if apprehended with pot, users cannot be arrested, will not serve jail or prison time, and will have no criminal record. Instead, they may have their stash confiscated and be required to pay a small fine. (Marijuana possession in any quantity—approved scientific research excepted—remains illegal according to federal law.) Surveys as recent as an October, 2002 Time/CNN poll show that 7 out of 10 Americans favor assessing fines over jail time.

Most policy analysts believe—based on systematic before-and-after comparisons—that removing criminal penalties on small-quantity possession did not open a floodgate of marijuana use in the depenalized states. Year-by-year changes in use in the decriminalized states basically follow the same up-and-down patterns as the nation as a whole. Also, many law enforcement officials feel that decriminalization has saved the states money at relatively little risk to public health.

The Netherlands provides another case study of the consequences of legalizing marijuana. There, anyone beyond the age of 18 can walk into one of roughly 800 "coffee shops" and purchase up to five grams of marijuana or hashish, a bit less than a quarter of an ounce. No "hard" drugs may be sold in these shops, selling to minors is illegal, and blatant advertising is not permitted. Studies of marijuana use in the Netherlands do not provide clear-cut evidence either for or against legalization. On the one hand, use among Dutch youth increased rather dramatically after legalization. In 1984, only 15 percent of 18-to-20 year-olds had ever used marijuana; by 1996, 44 percent had. Similarly, the percentage of youth who had used the drug in the previous month more than doubled from 8 to 18 percent during that period. This evidence seems to support the prohibitionists' argument.

On the other hand, usage rates have increased only modestly during the past decade and appear to be leveling off. According to surveys, rates of Dutch high schoolers using cannabis, although lower than in Ireland, the United Kingdom, and France, are among the highest in Europe. Yet, they are still considerably below the rates for high school students in the United States, where most states continue to criminalize marijuana. Clearly, the *de facto* legalization of cannabis in the Netherlands has not brought about a torrent of marijuana and hashish consumption, and most Dutch citizens and officials favor the current laws. In short, the experiences of the Netherlands and the United States suggest that decriminalization would not produce significantly higher levels of marijuana use. It is entirely possible that, uniquely for marijuana, nearly everyone who wants to use the drug already does so.

The Economics of Drug Use

Legalizers typically argue that we need not worry about decriminalization making drugs cheaper and thus more enticing, because the relationship between the price of drugs and demand for them is weak or nonexistent. Economists, however, find that cost significantly influences demand for drugs. Elasticity—the variation in demand for goods as prices rise and fall—differs considerably from drug to drug. Demand for heroin drops only 0.2 to 0.3 percent for every 1 percent increase in price, but the demand for marijuana drops roughly 1 percent for every 1 percent increase in price. Cigarettes (a 0.4 percent decrease) and alcohol (a 0.7 percent decrease) fall somewhere in between.

Prohibition hugely increases the price of illicit drugs and therefore should discourage use. (Decriminalization retains penalties on distribution, sale and large-quantity possession. Hence, even in the decriminalized states, marijuana remains fairly expensive.) Legalization would lower prices, which would probably reduce the property crimes committed by addicts (their habits would be cheaper), but it would almost certainly increase rates of use. Prohibitionists predict that tens of millions of Americans would take up cocaine or heroin. This worst-case scenario is almost certainly wildly off the mark. Use would increase the most not among current nonusers, but among the heaviest current users. Studies indicate that if these drugs were cheaper and less difficult to acquire, addicts would use them in much greater volume.

When drugs are legal, the government can use taxes to raise prices and discourage use. Current state and federal taxes on legal drugs—alcohol and tobacco—are far too low, at less than 50 cents per drink and 1 dollar per pack of cigarettes, to significantly deter drinking and smoking. Not included in that dollar is the price markup charged by cigarette companies to pay off the $200 billion that they have agreed to pay the states in a legal settlement; in effect, this is taxation by another means. Since most drug-related deaths stem from alcohol (85,000 per year, according to the Centers for Disease Control) and tobacco (440,000 per year), increasing alcohol and cigarette taxes could save lives. Whether through prohibition or taxes, policies that raise costs are a powerful way to depress demand.

Of course, financial cost is not the only way in which prohibition might reduce use. Criminalization imposes other types of costs: the extra time and effort required to get drugs and the risk of incarceration. Proponents of "absolute deterrence" believe that enforcing drug laws yet more firmly can drastically reduce or eliminate illegal drug use by locking up users and dealers and scaring off would-be violators. From that perspective, the war on drugs has been a failure, because it has been insufficiently aggressive. But "stamping out" drug use is a fool's errand. "Stamping out"—or even drastically reducing—drug use is an unrealistic standard by which to judge the effectiveness of the drug laws. No one expects laws penalizing robbery, rape, or murder to "stamp out" those crimes.

"Relative deterrence"—a more moderate position—argues that, while prohibition cannot eliminate it, drug use would be more common in the absence of law enforcement. Imagine if any adult could freely purchase currently illegal drugs in licensed shops or markets, out of a catalogue or over the Internet. Drug use would surely increase. And it would rise significantly under almost any of the more radical forms of proposed legalization. Would such increased drug use be bad? It depends on the drug, and for some drugs, it depends on how the drug is used and who uses it. Apparently, for alcohol, a drink or two a day can actually stimulate good health. But for tobacco, any use is harmful, and the greater the use, the greater the harm. The story is a bit more complicated with heroin and cocaine. The way they are used today is harmful, and while legalization would eliminate some features of that harm, others would remain. Hence, higher levels of use would inevitably mean higher levels of harm.

On the other hand, the more similar a system of "legalization" is to the current system of prohibition, the more the black market would step in to provide an alternative supply of illegal drugs as it does today.

◉ Harm Reduction

Today, critics of the war on drugs are less likely to advocate legalization, and more likely to endorse some form of "harm reduction." There is a vast middle ground between strict criminal punishment and outright legalization. That territory should be explored, harm reductionists argue, to reduce deaths, disease, financial cost and crime. Find out what programs work to reduce harm, they urge, and adopt them. These advocates believe that better results will be achieved by being experimental, pragmatic and empirical.

The United States currently spends three times more money on law enforcement than on treatment and prevention. Harm reduction strategists suggest that we reverse the priority of these expenditures. They also advocate eliminating programs for drug eradication and crop substitution in source countries. Evidence gathered by the RAND Corporation indicates that these programs do not work. In addition, they are financially and politically costly. Tax dollars would be far better spent on more effective ways to combat addiction, such as treatment programs.

Needle exchange programs are another effective approach to reducing harm. They appear to lower rates of HIV transmission. Between 1988 and 1993, HIV rates decreased by 6 percent in major cities with needle exchange programs, and increased by 6 percent in cities without them. Critics of needle exchange have been unable to explain this phenomenon. These programs have been adopted nearly everywhere in the Western world. Yet they reach only 10 percent of intravenous drug users in the United States. In spite of favorable evaluations of the policy by expert panels—including the General Accounting Office and the Institute of Medicine of the National Academy of Sciences—and in spite of positive findings from the dozens of studies done to evaluate these programs, the federal government staunchly opposes needle exchange programs as "encouraging drug abuse." From a harm reduction perspective, such objections are counter-productive because the programs can help control a deadly epidemic.

Researchers have also conducted hundreds of studies of drug treatment. Overwhelmingly, these studies show that treatment works. Drug addicts and abusers who spend time in treatment programs—and the more time spent, the more this is true—tend to reduce their levels of drug abuse, commit less predatory crime, and live longer, healthier lives, than those who do not. Methadone maintenance has been studied particularly carefully. It cuts crime and saves lives. Equating the administration of methadone to heroin addicts with giving vodka to an alcoholic, as some critics do, is semantic hocus-pocus, harm reductionists argue. Even with cheating, enrollees significantly reduce their drug use and its byproducts, such as crime.

As with all policy research, the causal arrows are not always easy to draw, but most analysts are convinced from controlled studies that, over the long run, treatment is considerably more cost-effective than incarceration. Although failure rates are high, treatment programs reduce the total volume of illicit drug use and criminal behavior by roughly one-third to one-half. And a majority of drug abusers significantly reduce or abandon their use of illicit substances after a second, third, fourth, or fifth attempt at treatment— roughly comparable to the repeated failures following treatment for smoking.

Experimental programs that administer injected methadone are under way in the United Kingdom. Oral morphine is being tried in Austria, Australia, Switzerland and the Netherlands. In Germany, programs involving the use of codeine have been tried. Switzerland and the Netherlands have inaugurated injected heroin maintenance programs. Do they work? At this writing, we do not have definitive answers. But, if the goal is reducing harm and not simply drug use, American authorities should also be exploring such avenues.

◉ A Choice

The outright legalization of hard drugs is both politically impossible and potentially dangerous for our society. Debating drug legalization is at present little more than cocktail party chatter, what legal scholars Franklin Zimring and Gordon Hawkins refer to as a "sideshow." Public opinion polls show that fewer than 5 percent of Americans support the legalization of hard drugs. The prospects for harm reduction strategies look somewhat better. While these strategies face formidable political obstacles in the United States, they can be adopted pragmatically, one step at a time, in individual locales or jurisdictions. Such programs are being instituted in Western Europe. They should be studied and, if they work, emulated.

Yet even after the facts are in, moral issues cannot be circumvented. Decisions about public policy ultimately rest on morality and ideology, because all programs result in a "mixed bag" of results, some good, some less desirable. How do we weigh the outcomes? Debate over which mixed bag is the least bad can never be resolved on strictly scientific grounds.

Many concerned citizens oppose any program that appears to condone drug use, even if it saves lives, while many proponents of legalization or decriminalization—especially free market libertarians—favor fully decriminalizing drugs, even if that results in higher rates of drug-related fatalities.

Still, the sanctity of human life is a rhetorical "ace in the hole" for harm reduction proponents. It is time, they argue, to begin taking steps to save lives.

☺ ☺ ☺

Questions

1. What legalization models have been proposed?

2. What are the potential problems with each model?

3. What has been the effect of legalizing marijuana in the Netherlands?

4. What is Erich Goode's conclusion about the possibility of legalizing drugs in the United States? On what grounds does he make it?

5. Has reading this article changed your attitudes concerning the legal status of drugs? Why or why not?

Serial Murder: Popular Myths and Empirical Realities

JAMES ALAN FOX
JACK LEVIN

Serial murder has existed throughout recorded history. Most of us can recall some of the more publicized serial killers that have plagued Western Europe and the United States. Our limited knowledge leads us to assume that Jack the Ripper was the first serial killer. More contemporary serial murderers that have been widely known include Jeffrey Dahmer (cannibalized his victims), Kenneth Bianchi (the Hillside Strangler), Ted Bundy (sorrority girl killer), Danny Rolling (Gainesville/University of Florida killer), and Charles Manson (race-based murders). Of this group, only Charles Manson never killed any of his victims: He persuaded his followers to kill on his behalf. With so many prominent names in American society, it seems logical to conclude that serial killing is an epidemic, or at least frequently occurring. In fact, this is a myth. This is just one myth that exists regarding serial killers. In this selection, Jack Levin and James Fox explore 10 myths regarding serial killers.

Since the early 1980s, Americans have become more aware of and concerned about a particularly dangerous class of murderers, known as serial killers. Characterized by the tendency to kill repeatedly (at least three or four victims) and often with increasing brutality, serial killers stalk their victims, one at a time, for weeks, months, or years, generally not stopping until they are caught.

The term *serial killer* was first used in the early 1980s (see Jenkins, 1994), although the phenomenon of repeat killing existed, of course, throughout recorded history. In the late 1800s, for example, Hermann Webster Mudgett (aka H. H. Holmes) murdered dozens of attractive young women in his Chicago "house of death," and the infamous Jack the Ripper

Reprinted by permission from *Homicide: A Source book of Social Research*, edited by M. Dwayne Smith & Margaret A. Zahn. Copyright © 1998 by Sage Publications, Inc.

stalked the streets of London, killing five prostitutes. Prior to the 1980s, repeat killers such as Mudgett and Jack the Ripper were generally described as mass murderers. The need for a special classification for repeat killers was later recognized because of the important differences between multiple murderers who kill simultaneously and those who kill serially (Levin & Fox, 1985). *Mass killers*—those who slaughter their victims in one event—tend to target people they know (e.g., family members or coworkers), often for the sake of revenge, using an efficient weapon of mass destruction (e.g., a high-powered firearm). As we shall describe below, serial murderers are different in all these respects, typically killing total strangers with their hands to achieve a sense of power and control over others.

A rising concern with serial killing has spawned a number of media presentations, resulting in the perpetrators of this type of murder becoming a regular staple of U.S. popular culture. A steady diet of television and movie productions could lead viewers to believe that serial killing is a common type of homicide. An increasing interest in serial homicide, however, has not been limited solely to the lay public. During the past two decades, the number, as well as the mix, of scholars devoting their attention to this crime has dramatically changed. Until the early 1980s, the literature exploring aspects of multiple homicide consisted almost exclusively of bizarre and atypical case studies contributed by forensic psychiatrists pertaining to their court-assigned clients. More recently, there has been a significant shift toward social scientists examining the cultural and social forces underlying the late 20th-century rise in serial murder as well as law enforcement operatives developing research-based investigative tools for tracking and apprehending serial offenders.

Despite the shift in disciplinary focus, some basic assumptions of psychiatry appear to remain strong in the public mind. In particular, it is widely believed that the serial killer acts as a result of some individual pathology produced by traumatic childhood experiences. At the same time, a developing law enforcement perspective holds that the serial killer is a nomadic, sexual sadist who operates with a strict pattern to victim selection and crime scene behavior; this model has also contributed to myopic thinking in responding to serial murder. Unfortunately, these assumptions from both psychiatry and law enforcement may have retarded the development of new and more effective approaches to understanding this phenomenon. In an attempt to present a more balanced view, this chapter examines (serially, of course) several myths about serial killing/killers, some longstanding and others of recent origin, that have been embraced more on faith than on hard evidence.

❧ /Myth 1: 𝒯here is an 𝒮pidemic of 𝒮erial /Murder in the 𝒰nited 𝒮tates

Although interest in serial murder has unquestionably grown, the same may not necessarily be true for the incidence of this crime itself. Curiously enough, there may actually be more scholars studying serial murder than there are offenders committing it. Regrettably, it is virtually impossible to measure with any degree of precision the prevalence of serial murder today, or even less so to trace its long-term trends (see Egger, 1990, 1998; Kiger, 1990). One thing for certain, however, is that the problem is nowhere near epidemic proportions (Jenkins, 1994).

It is true that some serial killers completely avoid detection. Unlike other forms of homicide, such as spousal murder, many of the crimes committed by serial killers may be unknown to authorities. Because serial murderers usually target strangers and often take great care in covering up their crimes by disposing of their victims' bodies, many of the homicides may remain as open missing persons reports. Moreover, because the victims frequently come from marginal groups, such as persons who are homeless, prostitutes, and drug users, disappearances may never result in any official reports of suspicious activity.

Even more problematic than the issue of missing data in measuring the extent of serial murder, law enforcement authorities are often unable to identify connections between unsolved homicides separated through time or space (Egger, 1984, 1998). Even if communication between law enforcement authorities were improved (as it has become in recent years), the tendency for some serial killers to alter their *modus operandi* frustrates attempts to link seemingly isolated killings to the same individual.

The lack of any hard evidence concerning the prevalence of serial homicide has not prevented speculation within both academic and law enforcement fields. The "serial killer panic of 1983–85," as it has been described by Jenkins (1988), was fueled by some outrageous and unsupportable statistics promulgated by the U.S. Department of Justice to buttress its claim that the extent of serial murder was on the rise. Apparently, some government officials reasoned that because the number of unsolved homicides had surged from several hundred per year in the early 1960s to several thousand per year in the 1980s, the aggregate body count produced by serial killers could be as high as 5,000 annually (Fox & Levin, 1985; for commentary on homicide clearance rates, see Chapter 6 by Marc Riedel). Unfortunately, this gross exaggeration was endorsed in some academic publications as well (see Egger, 1984; Holmes & DeBurger, 1988).

More sober thinking on the prevalence issue has occurred in recent years (Egger, 1990, 1998; Holmes & Holmes, 1998). Although still subject to the methodological limitations noted above in the identification of serial crimes, Hickey (1997) has attempted the most exhaustive measurement of the prevalence and trends in serial murder. In contrast to the Justice Department's estimate of thousands of victims annually, Hickey (1997) enumerated only 2,526 to 3,860 victims slain by 399 serial killers between 1800 and 1995. Moreover, between 1975 and 1995, the highest levels in the two centuries, Hickey identified only 153 perpetrators and as many as 1,400 victims, for an average annual tally of far less than 100 victims. Although Hickey's data collection strategy obviously ignored undetected cases, the extent of the problem is likely less than 1% of homicides in the country. Of course, that as much as 1% of the nation's murder problem can potentially be traced to but a few dozen individuals reminds us of the extreme deadliness of their predatory behavior.

☻ Myth 2: Serial Killers are Unusual in Appearance and Lifestyle

As typically portrayed, television and cinematic versions of serial killers are either sinister-appearing creatures of the night or brilliant-but-evil master criminals. In reality, however, most tend to fit neither of these descriptions. Serial killers are generally White males in their late 20s or 30s who span a broad range of human qualities including appearance and intelligence.

Some serial killers are high school dropouts, and others might indeed be regarded as unappealing by conventional standards. At the same time, a few actually possess brilliance, charm, and attractiveness. Most serial killers, however, are fairly average, at least to the casual observer. In short, they are "extraordinarily ordinary"; ironically, part of the secret of their success is that they do not stand out in a crowd or attract negative attention to themselves. Instead, many of them look and act much like "the boy next door"; they hold full-time jobs, are married or involved in some other stable relationship, and are members of various local community groups. The one trait that tends to separate prolific serial killers from the norm is that they are exceptionally skillful in their presentation of self so that they appear beyond suspicion. This is part of the reason why they are so difficult to apprehend (Levin & Fox, 1985).

A related misconception is that serial killers, lacking stable employment or family responsibilities, are full-time predators who roam far and wide, often crossing state and regional boundaries in their quest for victims. Evidence to the contrary notwithstanding, serial killers have frequently been characterized as nomads whose compulsion to kill carries them hundreds of thousands of miles a year as they drift from state to state and region to region leaving scores of victims in their wake. This may be true of a few well-known and well-traveled individuals, but not for the vast majority of serial killers (Levin & Fox, 1985). According to Hickey (1997), only about a third of the serial killers in his database crossed state lines in their murder sprees. John Wayne Gacy, for example, killed all of his 33 young male victims at his Des Plaines, Illinois, home, conveniently burying most of them there as well. Gacy had a job, friends, and family but secretly killed on a part-time, opportunistic basis.

❧ Myth 3: Serial Killers are All Insane

What makes serial killers so enigmatic—so irrational to many casual observers—is that they generally kill not for love, money, or revenge but for the fun of it. That is, they delight in the thrill, the sexual satisfaction, or the dominance that they achieve as they squeeze the last breath of life from their victims. At a purely superficial level, killing for the sake of pleasure seems nothing less than "crazy."

The basis for the serial killer's pursuit of pleasure is found in a strong tendency toward sexual sadism (Hazelwood, Dietz, & Warren, 1992) and an interest reflected in detailed fantasies of domination (Prentky, Burgess, & Rokous, 1989). Serial killers tie up their victims to watch them squirm and torture their victims to hear them scream. They rape, mutilate, sodomize, and degrade their victims to feel powerful, dominant, and superior.

Many individuals may have fantasies about torture and murder but are able to restrain themselves from ever translating their sadistic dreams into reality. Those who do not contain their urges to kill repeatedly for no apparent motive are assumed to suffer from some extreme form of mental illness. Indeed, some serial killers have clearly been driven by psychosis, such as Herbert Mullen of Santa Cruz, California, who killed 13 people during a 4-month period to avert an earthquake—at least that is what the voices commanded him to do (the voices also ordered him to burn his penis with a cigarette).

In either a legal or a medical sense, however, most serial killers are not insane or psychotic (see Levin & Fox, 1985; Leyton, 1986). They know right from wrong, know exactly what they are doing, and can control their desire to kill—but choose not to. They are more cruel than crazy. Their crimes may be sickening, but their minds are not necessarily sick. Most apparently do not suffer from hallucinations, a profound thought disorder, or major depression. Indeed, those assailants who are deeply confused or disoriented are generally not capable of the level of planning and organization necessary to conceal their identity from the authorities and, therefore, do not amass a large victim count.

Many serial killers seem instead to possess a personality disorder known as sociopathy (or antisocial personality). They lack a conscience, are remorseless, and care exclusively for their own needs and desires. Other people are regarded merely as tools to be manipulated for the purpose of maximizing their personal pleasure (see Harrington, 1972; Magid & McKelvey, 1988). Thus, if given to perverse sexual fantasy, sociopaths simply feel uninhibited by societal rules or by conscience from literally chasing their dreams in any way necessary for their fulfillment (see Fox, 1989; Levin & Fox, 1985; Vetter, 1990).

Serial killers are not alone in their sociopathic tendencies. The American Psychiatric Association estimates that 3% of all males in our society could be considered sociopathic (for a discussion of the prevalence of antisocial personality disorder, see American Psychiatric Association, 1994). Of course, most sociopaths do not commit acts of violence; they may lie, cheat, or steal, but rape and murder are not necessarily appealing to them—unless they are threatened or they regard killing as a necessary means to some important end.

❂ Myth 4: All Serial Killers are Sociopaths

Although many serial killers tend to be sociopaths, totally lacking in concern for their victims, some actually do have a conscience but are able to neutralize or negate their feelings of remorse by rationalizing their behavior. They feel as though they are doing something good for society, or at least nothing that bad.

Milwaukee's cannibalistic killer, Jeffrey Dahmer, for example, actually viewed his crimes as a sign of love and affection. He told Tracy Edwards, a victim who managed to escape, that if he played his cards right, he too could give his heart to Jeff. Dahmer meant it quite literally, of course, but according to Edwards, he said it affectionately, not threateningly.

The powerful psychological process of *dehumanization* allows many serial killers to slaughter scores of innocent people by viewing them as worthless and therefore expendable. To the dehumanizer, prostitutes are seen as mere sex machines, gays are AIDS carriers, nursing home patients are vegetables, and homeless alcoholics are nothing more than human trash.

In a process related to this concept of dehumanization, many serial killers compartmentalize the world into two groups—those whom they care about versus everyone else. "Hillside Strangler" Kenneth Bianchi, for example, could be kind and loving to his wife and child as well as to his mother and friends yet be vicious and cruel to those he considered meaningless. He and his cousin started with prostitutes, but later, when they grew comfortable with killing, branched out to middle-class targets.

◉ /lyth 5: Serial Killers are Inspired by Pornography

Could Theodore Bundy have been right in his death row claim that pornography turned him into a vicious killer, or was he just making excuses to deflect blame? It should be no surprise that the vast majority of serial killers do have a keen interest in pornography, particularly sadistic magazines and films (Ressler, Burgess, & Douglas, 1988). Sadism is the source of their greatest pleasure, and so, of course, they experience it vicariously in their spare time, when not on the prowl themselves. That is, a preoccupation with pornography is a reflection, not the cause, of their own sexual desires. At most, pornography may reinforce sadistic impulses, but it cannot create them.

There is experimental evidence that frequent and prolonged exposure to violent pornography tends to desensitize "normal" men to the plight of victims of sexual abuse (Malamuth & Donnerstein, 1984). In the case of serial killers, however, it takes much more than pornography to create such an extreme and vicious personality.

● Myth 6: Serial Killers are Products of Bad Childhoods

Whenever the case of an infamous serial killer is uncovered, journalists and behavioral scientists alike tend to search for clues in the killer's childhood that might explain the seemingly senseless or excessively brutal murders. Many writers have emphasized, for example, Theodore Bundy's concerns about being illegitimate, and biographers of Hillside Strangler Kenneth Bianchi capitalized on his having been adopted.

There is a long tradition of research on the childhood correlates of homicidal proneness. For example, several decades ago, Macdonald (1963) hypothesized a triad of symptoms—enuresis, fire setting, and cruelty to animals—that were seen as reactions to parental rejection, neglect, or brutality. Although the so-called Macdonald's Triad was later refuted in controlled studies (see Macdonald, 1968), the connection between parental physical/sexual abuse or abandonment and subsequent violent behavior has remained a continuing focus of research (Sears, 1991). It is often suggested that because of such deep-rooted problems, serial killers suffer from a profound sense of powerlessness that they compensate for through extreme forms of aggression in which they exert control over others.

It is true that the biographies of most serial killers reveal significant physical and psychological trauma at an early age. For example, based on in-depth interviews with 36 incarcerated murderers, Ressler et al. (1988) found evidence of psychological abuse (e.g., public humiliation) in 23 cases and physical trauma in 13 cases. Hickey (1997) reported that among a group of 62 male serial killers, 48% had been rejected as children by a parent or some other important person in their lives. Of course, these same types of experiences can be found in the biographies of many "normal" people as well. More specifically, although useful for characterizing the backgrounds of serial killers, the findings presented by Ressler et al. and Hickey lack a comparison group drawn from non-offending populations for which the same operational definitions of trauma have been applied. Therefore, it is impossible to conclude that serial killers have suffered as children to any greater extent than others.

As a related matter, more than a few serial killers—from New York City's David Berkowitz to Long Island's Joel Rifkin—were raised by adoptive parents. In the adopted child syndrome, and individual displaces anger for birth parents onto adoptive parents as well as other authority figures. The syndrome is often expressed early in life in "provocative antisocial behavior" including fire setting, truancy, promiscuity, pathological lying, and stealing. Deeply troubled adopted children may, in fantasy, create imaginary play-mates who represent their antisocial impulses. Later, they may experience a dissociative disorder or even the development of an alter personality in which their murderous tendencies become situated (Kirschner, 1990, 1992).

The apparent overrepresentation of adoption in the biographies of serial killers has been exploited by those who are looking for simple explanations for heinous crimes, without fully recognizing the mechanisms behind or value of the link between adoption and criminal behavior. Even if adoption plays a role in the making of a serial murderer, the independent variable remains to be specified—that is, for example, rejection by birth parents, poor health and prenatal care of birth mother, or inadequate bonding to adoptive parents.

Some neurologists and a growing number of psychiatrists suggest that serial killers have incurred serious injury to the limbic region of the brain resulting from severe or repeated head trauma, generally during childhood. As an example, psychiatrist Dorothy Lewis and neurologist Jonathan Pincus, along with other colleagues, examined 15 murderers on Florida's death row and found that all showed signs of neurological irregularities (Lewis, Pincus, Feldman, Jackson, & Bard, 1986). In addition, psychologist Joel Norris (1988) reported excessive spinal fluid found in the brain scan of serial killer Henry Lee Lucas. Norris argued that this abnormality reflected the possible damage caused by an earlier blow or a series of blows to Lucas's head.

It is critical that we place in some perspective the many case studies that have been used in an attempt to connect extreme violence to neurological impairment. Absent from the case study approach is any indication of the prevalence of individuals who did not act violently despite a history of trauma. Indeed, if head trauma were as strong a contributor to serial murder as some suggest, then we would have many times more of these killers than we actually do.

It is also important to recognize that neurological impairment must occur in combination with a host of environmental conditions to place an individual at risk for extreme acts of brutality. Dorothy Lewis cautions, "The neuropsychiatric problems alone don't make you violent. Probably the environmental factors in and of themselves don't make you a violent person. But when you put them together, you create a very dangerous character" ("Serial Killers," 1992). Similarly, Ressler asserts that no single childhood problem indicates future criminality: "There are a whole pot of conditions that have to be met" for violence to be predictable (quoted in Meddis, 1987, p. 3A). Head trauma and abuse, therefore, may be important risk factors, but they are neither necessary nor sufficient to make someone a serial killer. Rather, they are part of a long list of circumstances—including adoption, shyness, disfigurement, speech impediments, learning and physical disabilities, abandonment, death of a parent, academic and athletic inadequacies—that may make a child feel frustrated and rejected enough to predispose, but not predestine, him or her toward extreme violence.

Because so much emphasis has been placed on early childhood, developmental factors in making the transition into adulthood and middle age are often overlooked. Serial killers tend to be in their late 20s and 30s, if not older, when they first show outward sings of murderous behavior. If only early childhood and biological predisposition were involved, why do they not begin killing as adolescents or young adults? Many individuals suffer as children, but only some of them continue to experience profound disappointment and detachment regarding family, friends, and work. For example, Danny Rolling, who murdered several college students in Gainesville, Florida, may have had a childhood filled with frustration and abuse, but his eight-victim murder spree did not commence until he was 36 years old. After experiencing a painful divorce, he drifted from job to job, from state to state, from prison to prison, and finally from murder to murder (Fox & Levin, 1996).

◉ Myth 7: Serial Killers can be Identified in Advance

Predicting dangerousness, particularly in an extreme form such as serial homicide, has been an elusive goal for those investigators who have attempted it. For example, Lewis, Lovely, Yeager, and Femina (1989) suggest that the interaction of neurological/psychiatric impairment and a history of abuse predicts violent crime, better even than previous violence itself. Unfortunately, this conclusion was based on retrospective "postdiction" with a sample of serious offenders, rather than a prospective attempt to predict violence within a general cross section.

It is often said that "hindsight is 20/20." This is especially true for serial murder. Following the apprehension of a serial killer, we often hear mixed reports that "he seemed like a nice guy, but there was something about him that wasn't quite right." Of course, there is often something about most people that may not seem "quite right." When such a person is exposed to be a serial murderer, however, we tend to focus on those warning signs in character and biography that were previously ignored. Even the stench emanating from Jeffrey Dahmer's apartment, which he had convincingly explained to the neighbors as the odor of spoiled meat from his broken freezer, was unexceptional until after the fact.

The methodological problems in predicting violence in advance are well known (Chaiken, Chaiken, & Rhodes, 1994). For a category of violence as rare as serial murder, however, the low base rate and consequent false-positive dilemma are overwhelming. Simply put, there are thousands of White males in their late 20s or 30s who thirst for power, are sadistic, and lack strong internal controls; most emphatically, however, the vast majority of them will never kill anyone.

◎ Myth 8: All Serial Killers are Sexual Sadists

Serial killers who rape, torture, sodomize, and mutilate their victims attract an inordinate amount of attention from the press, the public, and professionals as well. Although they may be the most fascinating type of serial killer, they are hardly the only type.

Expanding their analysis beyond the sexual sadist, Holmes and DeBurger (1988) were among the first to assemble a motivational typology of serial killing, classifying serial murderers into four broad categories: visionary (e.g., voices from God), mission-oriented (e.g., ridding the world of evil), hedonistic (e.g., killing for pleasure), and power/control-oriented (e.g., killing for dominance). Holmes and DeBurger further divided the hedonistic type into three subtypes: lust, thrill, and comfort (see also Holmes & Holmes, 1998).

Although we applaud Holmes and DeBurger for their attempt to provide some conceptual structure, we must also note a troubling degree of overlap among their types. For example, Herbert Mullen, believing that he was obeying God's commandment, "sacrificed" (in his mind) more than a dozen people to avert catastrophic earthquakes; his motivation was both "visionary" and "mission-oriented." Furthermore, the typology is somewhat misaligned: Both the "lust" and "thrill" subtypes are expressive motivations, whereas "comfort" (e.g., murder for profit or to eliminate witnesses) is instrumental or a means toward an end.

Modifying the Holmes-DeBurger framework, we suggest that serial murders can be reclassified into three categories, each with two subtypes:

1. Thrill
   a. Sexual sadism
   b. Dominance

2. Mission
   a. Reformist
   b. Visionary

3. Expedience
   a. Profit
   b. Protection

Most serial killings can be classified as thrill motivated, and the *sexual sadist* is the most common of all. In addition, a growing number of murders committed by hospital caretakers have been exposed in recent years; although not sexual in motivation, these acts of murder are perpetrated for the sake of *dominance* nevertheless.

A less common form of serial killing consists of mission-oriented killers who murder to further a cause. Through killing, the *reformist* attempts to rid the world of filth and evil, such as by killing prostitutes, gays, or homeless persons. Most self-proclaimed reformists are also motivated by thrill seeking but try to rationalize their murderous behavior. For example, Donald Harvey, who worked as an orderly in Cincinnati-area hospitals, confessed to killing 80 or more patients through the years. Although he was termed a mercy killer, Harvey actually enjoyed the dominance he achieved by playing God with the lives of other people.

In contrast to pseudoreformists, *visionary* killers, as rare as they may be, genuinely believe in their missions. They hear the voice of the devil or God instructing them to kill. Driven by these delusions, visionary killers tend to be psychotic, confused, and disorganized. Because their killings are impulsive and even frenzied, visionaries rarely remain on the street long enough to become prolific serial killers.

The final category of serial murder includes those who are motivated by the expedience of either profit or protection. The *profit-oriented* serial killer systematically murders as a critical element of the overall plan to dispose of victims to make money (e.g., Sacramento landlady Dorothea Puente murdered 9 elderly tenants to cash their social security checks). By contrast, the *protection-oriented* killer uses murder to cover up criminal activity (e.g., the Lewington brothers systematically robbed and murdered 10 people throughout Central Ohio).

◉ /\yth 9: Serial Killers Select Victims Who Somehow Resemble Their /\others

Shortly after the capture of Hillside Strangler Kenneth Bianchi, psychiatrists speculated that he tortured and murdered young women as an expression of hatred toward his mother, who had allegedly brutalized him as a youngster (Fox & Levin, 1994). Similarly, the execution of Theodore Bundy gave psychiatrists occasion to suggest that his victims served as surrogates for the real target he sought, his mother.

Although unresolved family conflicts may in some cases be a significant source of frustration, most serial killers have a more opportunistic or prag-matic basis for selecting their victims. Quite simply, they tend to prey on the most vulnerable targets—prostitutes, drug users, hitchhikers, and runaways, as well as older hospital patients (Levin & Fox, 1985). Part of the vulnera-bility concerns the ease with which these groups can be abducted or overtaken. Children and older persons are defenseless because of physical stature or disability; hitchhikers and prostitutes become vulnerable as soon as they enter the killer's vehicle; hospital patients are vulnerable in their total dependency on their caretakers.

Vulnerability is most acute in the case of prostitutes, which explains their relatively high rate of victimization by serial killers. A sexual sadist can cruise a red-light district, seeking out the woman who best fits his deadly sexual fantasies. When he finds her, she willingly complies with his wishes—until it is too late.

Another aspect of vulnerability is the ease with which the killers can avoid being detected following a murder. Serial killers of our time are often sly and crafty, fully realizing the ease with which they can prey on street-walkers and escape detection, much less arrest. Because the disappearance of a prostitute is more likely to be considered by the police, at least initially, as a missing person rather than a victim of homicide, the search for the body can be delayed weeks or months. Also, potential witnesses to abductions in red-light districts tend to be unreliable sources of information or distrustful of the police.

Frail older persons, particularly those in hospitals and nursing homes, represent a class of victims that is at the mercy of a different type of serial killer, called "angels of death." Revelations by a Long Island nurse who poisoned his patients in a failed attempt to be a hero by resuscitating them and of two Grand Rapids nurses aides who murdered older patients to form a lovers' pact have horrified even the most jaded observers of crime.

Not only are persons who are old and infirm vulnerable to the misdeeds of their caretakers who may have a particularly warped sense of mercy, but hospital homicides are particularly difficult to detect and solve. Death among older patients is not uncommon, and suspicions are rarely aroused. Furthermore, should a curiously large volume of deaths occur within a short time on a particular nurse's shift, hospital administrators feel in a quandary. Not only are they reluctant to bring scandal and perhaps lawsuits to their own facility without sufficient proof, but most of the potentially incriminating evidence against a suspected employee is long buried with the victim.

◉ Myth 10: Serial Killers Really Want to Get Caught

Despite the notion that serial killers are typically lacking in empathy and remorse, some observers insist that deeply repressed feelings of guilt may subconsciously motivate them to leave telltale clues for the police. Although this premise may be popular in media portrayals, most serial killers go to great lengths to avoid detection, such as carefully destroying crime scene evidence or disposing of their victims' bodies in hard-to-find dump sites.

There is an element of self-selection in defining serial killing. Only those offenders who have sufficient cunning and guile are able to avoid capture long enough to accumulate the number of victims necessary to be classified as serial killers. Most serial killers are careful, clever, and, to use the FBI's typology (see Ressler et al., 1988), organized. Of course, disorganized killers, because of their carelessness, tend to be caught quickly, often before they surpass the serial killer threshold of victim count.

Murders committed by a serial killer are typically difficult to solve because of lack of both motive and physical evidence. Unlike the usual homicide that involves an offender and a victim who know one another, serial murders are almost exclusively committed by strangers. Thus, the usual police strategy of identifying suspects by considering their possible motive, be it jealousy, revenge, or greed, is typically fruitless.

Another conventional approach to investigating homicides involves gathering forensic evidence—fibers, hairs, blood, and prints—from the scene of the crime. In the case of many serial murders, however, this can be rather difficult, if not impossible. The bodies of the victims are often found at desolate roadsides or in makeshift graves, exposed to rain, wind, and snow. Most of the potentially revealing crime scene evidence remains in the unknown killer's house or car.

Another part of the problem is that unlike those shown in the media, many serial killers do not leave unmistakable and unique "signatures" at their crime scenes. As a result, the police may not recognize multiple homicides as the work of the same perpetrator. Moreover, some serial killings, even if consistent in style, traverse jurisdictional boundaries. Thus, "linkage blindness" is a significant barrier to solving many cases of serial murder (Egger, 1984).

To aid in the detection of serial murder cases, the FBI operationalized in 1985 the Violent Criminal Apprehension Program (VICAP), a computerized database for the collection and collation of information pertaining to unsolved homicides and missing persons around the country. It is designed to flag similarities in unsolved crimes that might otherwise be obscure (Howlett, Haufland, & Ressler, 1986).

Although an excellent idea in theory, VICAP has encountered significant practical limitations. Complexities in the data collection forms have limited the extent of participation of local law enforcement agencies in completing VICAP questionnaires. More important, pattern recognition is far from a simple or straightforward task, regardless of how powerful the computer or sophisticated the software. Furthermore, even the emergence of a pattern among a set of crime records in the VICAP database does not ensure that the offender will be identified.

In addition to the VICAP clearinghouse, the FBI, on request, assembles criminal profiles of the unknown offenders, based on behavioral clues left at crime scenes, autopsy reports, and police incident reports. Typically, these profiles speculate on the killer's age, race, sex, marital status, employment status, sexual maturity, possible criminal record, relationship to the victim, and likelihood of committing future crimes. At the core of its profiling strategy, the FBI distinguishes between *organized nonsocial* and *disorganized asocial* killers. According to Hazelwood and Douglas (1980), organized killers typically are intelligent, are socially and sexually competent, are of high birth order, are skilled workers, live with a partner, are mobile, drive late model cars, and follow their crimes in the media. In contrast, disorganized killers generally are unintelligent, are socially and sexually inadequate, are of low birth order, are unskilled workers, live alone, are nonmobile, drive old cars or no car at all, and have minimal interest in the news reports of their crimes.

According to the FBI analysis, these types tend to differ also in crime scene characteristics (Ressler et al., 1988). Specifically, organized killers use restraints on the victim, hide or transport the body, remove the weapon from the scene, molest the victim prior to death, and are methodical in their style of killing. Operating differently, disorganized killers tend not to use restraints, leave the body in full view, leave a weapon at the scene, molest the victim after death, and are spontaneous in their manner of killing. The task of profiling involves, therefore, drawing inferences from the crime scene to the behavioral characteristics of the killer.

Despite the Hollywood hype that exaggerates the usefulness of criminal profiling, it is an investigative tool of some, albeit limited, value. Even when constructed by the most experienced and skillful profilers, such as those at the FBI, profiles are not expected to solve a case; rather, they provide an additional set of clues in cases found by local police to be unsolvable. Simply put, a criminal profile cannot identify a suspect for investigation, nor can it eliminate a suspect who does not fit the mold. An overreliance on the contents of a profile can misdirect a serial murder investigation, sometimes quite seriously (see, for example; Fox & Levin, 1996). Clearly, a criminal profile can assist in assigning subjective probabilities to suspects whose names surface through more usual investigative strategies (e.g., interviews of witnesses, canvassing of neighborhoods, and "tip" phone lines). There is, however, no substitute for old-fashioned detective work and, for that matter, a healthy and helpful dose of luck.

⊛ From Myth to Reality

The study of serial homicide is in its infancy, less than two decades old (O'Reilly-Fleming, 1996). The pioneering scholars noted the pervasiveness and inaccuracy of long-standing psychiatric misconceptions regarding the state of mind of the serial killer (see Levin & Fox, 1985; Leyton, 1986; Ressler et al., 1988). More recently, these unfounded images have been supplanted by newer myths, including those concerning the prevalence and apprehension of serial killers.

The mythology of serial killing has developed from a pervasive fascination with a crime about which so little is known. Most of the scholarly literature is based on conjecture, anecdote, and small samples, rather than rigorous and controlled research. The future credibility of this area of study will depend on the ability of criminologists to upgrade the standards of research on serial homicide. Only then will myths about serial murder give way to a reliable foundation of knowledge.

References

American Psychiatric Association. (1994), *Diagnostic and statistical manual of mental disorders* (4th ed.). Washington, DC: American Psychiatric Association.

Chaiken, J., Chaiken, M., and Rhodes, W. (1994). Predicting violent behavior and classifying violent offenders. In A. J. Reiss Jr. and J. A. Roth (Eds.), *Understanding and preventing violence* (Vol. 4, pp. 217–295). Washington, DC: National Academy Press.

Egger, S. A. (1984). A working definition of serial murder and the reduction of linkage blindness. *Journal of Police Science and Administration, 12,* 348–357.

Egger, S. A. (1990). *Serial murder: An elusive phenomenon.* Westport, CT: Praeger.

Egger, S. A. (1998). *The killers among us: An examination of serial murder and its investigation.* Upper Saddle River, NJ: Prentice Hall.

Fox, J. A. (1989, January 29). The mind of a murderer. *Palm Beach Post,* p. 1E.

Fox, J. A., and Levin, J. (1985, December 1). Serial Killers: How Statistics mislead us. *Boston Herald,* p. 45.

Fox, J. A., and Levin, J. (1994). *Overkill: Mass murder and serial killing exposed.* New York: Plenum.

Fox, J. A., and Levin, J. (1996). *Killer on campus.* New York: Avon Books.

Harrington, A. (1972). *Psychopaths.* New York: Simon and Schuster.

Hazelwood, R. R., Dietz, P. E., and Warren, J. (1992). The criminal sexual sadist. *FBI Law Enforcement Bulletin, 61,* 12–20.

Hazelwood, R. R., and Douglas, J. E. (1980). The lust murderer. *FBI Law Enforcement Bulletin, 49,* 1–5.

Hickey, E. W. (1997). *Serial murderers and their victims* (2nd ed.). Belmont, CA: Wadsworth.

Holmes, R. M., and DeBurger, J. (1988). *Serial murder.* Newbury Park, CA: Sage.

Holmes, R. M., and Holmes, S. T. (1998). *Serial murder* (2nd ed.). Thousand Oaks, CA: Sage.

Howlett, J. B., Haufland, K. A., and Ressler, R. J. (1986). The violent criminal apprehension program—VICAP: A progress report. *FBI Law Enforcement Bulletin*, 55, 14–22.

Jenkins, P. (1988). Myth and murder: The serial killer panic of 1983–85. *Criminal Justice Research Bulletin* (No. 3). Huntsville, TX: Sam Houston State University.

Jenkins, P. (1994). *Using murder: The social construction of serial homicide*. New York: Walter de Gruyter.

Kiger, K. (1990). The darker figure of crime: The serial murder enigma. In S. A. Egger (Ed.), *Serial murder: An elusive phenomenon* (pp. 35–52). New York: Praeger.

Kirschner, D. (1990). The adopted child syndrome: Considerations for psychotherapy. *Psychotherapy in Private Practice, 8*, 93–100.

Kirschner, D. (1992). Understanding adoptees who kill: Dissociation, patricide, and the psychodynamics of adoption. *International Journal of Offender Therapy & Comparative Criminology, 36*, 323–333.

Levin, J., and Fox, J. A. (1985). *Mass murder: America's growing menace*. New York: Plenum.

Lewis, D. O., Lovely, R., Yeager, C., and Femina, D. D. (1989). Toward a theory of the genesis of violence: A follow-up study of delinquents. *Journal of the American Academy of Child and Adolescent Psychiatry, 28*, 431–436

Lewis, D. O., Pincus, J. H., Feldman, M., Jackson, L., and Bard, B. (1986). Psychiatric, neurological, and psychoeducational characteristics of 15 death row inmates in the United States. *American Journal of Pscychiatry, 143*, 838–845.

Leyton, E. (1986). *Compulsive killers: The story of modern multiple murderers*. New York: New York University Press.

Macdonald, J. M. (1963). The threat to kill. *American Journal of Psychiatry, 120*, 125–130.

Macdonald, J. M. (1968). *Homicidal threats*. Springfield, IL: Charles C Thomas.

Magid, K., and McKelvey, C. A. (1988). *High risk: Children without a conscience*. New York: Bantam.

Malamuth, N. M., and Donnerstein, E. (1984). *Pornography and sexual aggression*. Orlando, FL: Academic Press.

Meddis, S. (1987, March 31). FBI: Possible to spot, help serial killers early. *USA Today*, p. 3A.

Norris, J. (1988). *Serial killers: The growing menace*. New York: Doubleday.

O'Reilly-Fleming, T. (1996). *Serial and mass murder: Theory, research and policy*. Toronto, Ontario: Canadian Scholars' Press.

Prentky, R. A., Burgess, A. W., and Rokous, F. (1989). The presumptive role of fantasy in serial sexual homicide. *American Journal of Psychiatry, 146,* 887–891.

Ressler, R. K., Burgess, A. W., and Douglas, J. E. (1988). *Sexual homicide: Patterns and motives.* Lexington, MA: Lexington Books.

Sears, D. J. (1991). *To kill again.* Wilmington, DE: Scholarly Resources Books.

Serial killers. (1992, October 18). NOVA. Boston: WGBHTV.

Vetter, H. (1990). Dissociation, psychopathy, and the serial murderer. In S. A. Egger (Ed.), *Serial murder: An elusive phenomenon* (pp. 73–92). New York: Praeger.

◎ ◎ ◎

Questions

1. In your opinion, which of the many myths seems to be most widely known?

2. Which of the myths is most difficult for you to accept? Which seems to be only marginally supported given the evidence provided by Levin and Fox? Explain.

3. Implied throughout the article, and directly addressed in some sections, is how society tends to be characterized in ways that support the emergence and existence of serial killers. Explain how society's structure and culture contribute to this process.

4. Research one of the serial killers listed in the abstract or in the article. Explain which myths seem to be true, and which myths seem to be false, regarding your chosen killer.

5. What is it about American society that makes us more likely to sensationalize serial killers, thus making it more likely to think the myths are true?

Fraternities and Rape on Campus

PATRICIA YANCEY MARTIN AND ROBERT A. HUMMER
Florida State University

In this reading, Patricia Yancey Martin and Robert Hummer analyze the social contexts of fraternities and their contribution to sexual assault and rape on college campuses. The authors pay particular attention to fraternity culture, including the values that are transmitted to fraternity members and the socialization processes associated with pledging. The authors conclude that cultures of masculinity and violence, coupled with a lack of institutional control, contribute to the problem of sex crimes on campuses.

Rapes are perpetrated on dates, at parties, in chance encounters, and in specially planned circumstances. That group structure and processes, rather than individual values or characteristics, are the impetus for many rape episodes was documented by Blanchard (1959) 30 years ago (also see Geis 1971), yet sociologists have failed to pursue this theme (for an exception, see Chancer 1987). A recent review of research (Muehlenhard and Linton 1987) on sexual violence, or rape, devotes only a few pages to the situational contexts of rape events, and these are conceptualized as potential risk factors for individuals rather than qualities of rape-prone social contexts.

Many rapes, far more than come to the public's attention, occur in fraternity houses on college and university campuses, yet little research has analyzed fraternities at American colleges and universities as rape-prone contexts (cf. Ehrhart and Sandler 1985). Most of the research on fraternities reports on samples of individual fraternity men. One group of studies compares the values, attitudes, perceptions, family socioeconomic status, psychological traits (aggressiveness, dependence), and so on, of fraternity and nonfraternity men (Bohrnstedt 1969; Fox, [Hodge, and Ward 1987; Kanin 1967; Lemire 1979; Miller 1973). A second group attempts to iden-

"Fraternities and Rape on Campus," by Patricia Yancey Martin and Robert A. Hummer, reprinted from *Gender and Society*, vol. 3, no. 4, 1989, pp. 457–473.

tify the effects of fraternity membership over time on the values, attitudes, beliefs, or moral precepts of members (Hughes and Winston 1987; Marlowe and Auvenshine 1982; Miller 1973; Wilder, Hoyt, Doren, Hauck, and Zettle 1978; Wilder, Hoyt, Surbeck, Wilder, and Carney 1986). With minor exceptions, little research addresses the group and organizational context of fraternities or the social construction of fraternity life (for exceptions, see Letchworth 1969; Longino and Karl 1973; Smith 1964).

. . . Ehrhart and Sandler (1985) identify over 50 cases of gang rapes on campus perpetrated by fraternity men, and their analysis points to many of the conditions that we discuss here. Their analysis is unique in focusing on conditions in fraternities that make gang rapes of women by fraternity men both feasible and probable. They identify excessive alcohol use, isolation from external monitoring, treatment of women as prey, use of pornography, approval of violence, and excessive concern with competition as precipitating conditions to gang rape (also see Merton 1985; Roark 1987).

The study reported here confirmed and complemented these findings by focusing on both conditions and processes. We examined dynamics associated with the social construction of fraternity life, with a focus on processes that foster the use of coercion, including rape, in fraternity men's relations with women. Our examination of men's social fraternities on college and university campuses as groups and organizations led us to conclude that fraternities are a physical and sociocultural context that encourages the sexual coercion of women. We make no claims that all fraternities are "bad" or that all fraternity men are rapists. Our observations indicated, however, that rape is especially probable in fraternities because of the kinds of organizations they are, the kinds of members they have, the practices their members engage in, and a virtual absence of university or community oversight. Analyses that lay blame for rapes by fraternity men on "peer pressure" are, we feel, overly simplistic (cf. Burkhart 1989; Walsh 1989). We suggest, rather, that fraternities create a sociocultural context in which the use of coercion in sexual relations with women is normative and in which the mechanisms to keep this pattern of behavior in check are minimal at best and absent at worst. We conclude that unless fraternities change in fundamental ways, little improvement can be expected.

276

❂ Methodology

Our goal was to analyze the group and organizational practices and conditions that create in fraternities an abusive social context for women. We developed a conceptual framework from an initial case study of an alleged gang rape at Florida State University that involved four fraternity men and an 18-year-old coed. The group rape took place on the third floor of a fraternity house and ended with the "dumping" of the woman in (the hallway of a neighboring fraternity house. According to newspaper accounts, the victim's blood-alcohol concentration, when she was discovered, was .349 percent, more than three times the legal limit for automobile driving and an almost lethal amount. One law enforcement officer reported that sexual intercourse occurred during the time (the victim was unconscious: "She was in a life-threatening situation" (*Tallahassee Democrat*, 1988b). When the victim was found, she was comatose and had suffered multiple scratches and abrasions. Crude words and a fraternity symbol had been written on her thighs (*Tampa Tribune*, 1988). When law enforcement officials tried to investigate the case, fraternity members refused to cooperate. This led, eventually, to a five-year ban of the fraternity from campus by the university and by the fraternity's national organization.

In trying to understand how such an event could have occurred, and how a group of over 150 members (exact figures are unknown because the fraternity refused to provide a membership roster) could hold rank, deny knowledge of the event, and allegedly lie to a grand jury, we analyzed newspaper articles about the case and conducted open-ended interviews with a variety of respondents about the case and about fraternities, rapes, alcohol use, gender relations, and sexual activities on campus. Our data included over 100 newspaper articles on the initial gang rape case; open-ended interviews with Greek (social fraternity and sorority) and non-Greek (independent) students (N = 20); university administrators (N = 8, five men, three women); and alumni advisers to Greek organizations (N = 6). Open-ended interviews were held also with judges, public and private defense attorneys, victim advocates, and state prosecutors regarding the processing of sexual assault cases. Data were analyzed using the grounded theory method (Glaser 1978; Martin and Turner 1986). In the following analysis, concepts generated from the data analysis are integrated with the literature on men's social fraternities, sexual coercion, and related issues.

◉ Fraternities and the Social Construction of Men and Masculinity

Our research indicated that fraternities are vitally concerned—more than with anything else—with masculinity (cf. Kanin 1967). They work hard to create a macho image and context and try to avoid any suggestion of "wimpishness," effeminacy, and homosexuality. Valued members display, or are willing to go along with, a narrow conception of masculinity that stresses competition, athleticism, dominance, winning, conflict, wealth, material possessions, willingness to drink alcohol, and sexual prowess vis-à-vis women.

Valued Qualities of Members

When fraternity members talked about the kind of pledges they prefer, a litany of stereotypical and narrowly masculine attributes and behaviors was recited and feminine or woman-associated qualities and behaviors were expressly denounced (cf. Merton 1985). Fraternities seek men who are "athletic," "big guys," good in intramural competition, "who can talk college sports." Males "who are willing to drink alcohol," "who drink socially," or "who can hold their liquor" are sought. Alcohol and activities associated with the recreational use of alcohol are cornerstones of fraternity social life. Nondrinkers are viewed with skepticism and rarely selected for membership.[1]

Fraternities try to avoid "geeks," nerds, and men said to give the fraternity a "wimpy" or "gay" reputation. Art, music, and humanities majors, majors in traditional women's fields (nursing, home economics, social work, education), men with long hair, and those whose appearance or dress violate current norms are rejected. Clean-cut, handsome men who dress well (are clean, neat, conforming, fashionable) are preferred. One sorority woman commented that "the top ranking fraternities have the best looking guys."

One fraternity man, a senior, said his fraternity recruited "some big guys, very athletic" over a two-year period to help overcome its image of wimpishness. His fraternity had won the interfraternity competition for highest grade-point average several years running but was looked down on as "wimpy, dancy, even gay." With their bigger, more athletic recruits, "our

278

reputation improved; we're a much more recognized fraternity now." Thus a fraternity's reputation and status depends on members' possession of stereotypically masculine qualities. Good grades, campus leadership, and community service are "nice" but masculinity dominance—for example, in athletic events, physical size of members, athleticism of members—counts most.

Certain social skills are valued. Men are sought who "have good personalities," are friendly, and "have the ability to relate to girls" (cf. Longino and Karl 1973). One fraternity man, a junior, said: "We watch a guy [a potential pledge] talk to women . . . we want guys who can relate to girls." Assessing a pledge's ability to talk to women is, in part, a preoccupation with homosexuality and a conscious avoidance of men who seem to have effeminate manners or qualities. If a member is suspected of being gay, he is ostracized and informally drummed out of the fraternity. A fraternity with a reputation as wimpy or tolerant of gays is ridiculed and shunned by other fraternities. Militant heterosexuality is frequently used by men to keep each other in line (Kimmel 1987).

Financial affluence or wealth, a male-associated value in American culture, is highly valued by fraternities. In accounting for why the fraternity involved in the gang rape that precipitated our research project had been recognized recently as "the best fraternity chapter in the United States," a university official said: "They were good-looking, a big fraternity, had lots of BMWs [expensive, German-made automobiles]." After the rape, newspaper stories described the fraternity members' affluence, noting the high number of members who owned expensive cars (*St. Petersburg Times,* 1988).

The Status and Norms of Pledgeship

A pledge (sometimes called an associate member) is a new recruit who occupies a trial membership status for a specific period of time. The pledge period (typically ranging from 10 to 15 weeks) gives fraternity brothers an opportunity to assess and socialize new recruits. Pledges evaluate the fraternity also and decide if they want to become brothers. The socialization experience is structured partly through assignment of a Big Brother to each pledge. Big Brothers are expected to teach pledges how to become a brother and to support them as they progress through the trial membership period. Some pledges are repelled by the pledging experience, which can entail physical abuse; harsh discipline; and demands to be subordinate, follow orders, and engage in demeaning routines and activities, similar to those used by the military to "make men out of boys" during boot camp.

Characteristics of the pledge experience are rationalized by fraternity members as necessary to help pledges unite into a group, rely on each other, and join together against outsiders. The process is highly masculinist in execution as well as conception. A willingness to submit to authority, follow orders, and do as one is told is viewed as a sign of loyalty, togetherness, and unity. Fraternity pledges who find the pledge process offensive often drop out. Some do this by openly quitting, which can subject them to ridicule by brothers and other pledges, or they may deliberately fail to make the grades necessary for initiation or transfer schools and decline to reaffiliate with the fraternity on the new campus. One fraternity pledge who quit the fraternity he had pledged described an experience during pledgeship as follows:

> This one guy was always picking on me. No matter what I did, I was wrong. One night after dinner, he and two other guys called me and two other pledges into the chapter room. He said, "Here, X, hold this 25 pound bag of ice at arms' length 'til I tell you to stop." I did it even though my arms and hands were killing me. When I asked if I could stop, he grabbed me around the throat and lifted me off the floor. I thought he would choke me to death. He cussed me and called me all kinds of names. He took one of my fingers and twisted it until it nearly broke. . . . I stayed in the fraternity for a few more days, but then I decided to quit. I hated it. Those guys are sick. They like seeing you suffer.

Fraternities' emphasis on toughness, withstanding pain and humiliation, obedience to superiors, and using physical force to obtain compliance contributes to an interpersonal style that de-emphasizes caring and sensitivity but fosters intragroup trust and loyalty. If the least macho or most critical pledges drop out, those who remain may be more receptive to, and influenced by, masculinist values and practices that encourage the use of force in sexual relations with women and the covering up of such behavior (cf. Kanin 1967).

Norms and Dynamics of Brotherhood

Brother is the status occupied by fraternity men to indicate their relations to each other and their membership in a particular fraternity organization or group. Brother is a male-specific status; only males can become brothers, although women can become "Little Sisters," a form of pseudomembership.

"Becoming a brother" is a rite of passage that follows the consistent and often lengthy display by pledges of appropriately masculine qualities and behaviors. Brothers have a quasi-familial relationship with each other, are normatively said to share bonds of closeness and support, and are sharply set off from nonmembers. Brotherhood is a loosely defined term used to represent the bonds that develop among fraternity members and the obligations and expectations incumbent upon them (cf. Marlowe and Auvenshine [1982] on fraternities' failure to encourage "moral development" in freshman pledges).

Some of our respondents talked about brotherhood in almost reverential terms, viewing it as the most valuable benefit of fraternity membership. One senior, a business-school major who had been affiliated with a fairly high-status fraternity throughout four years on campus, said:

> Brotherhood spurs friendship for life, which I consider its best aspect, although I didn't see it that way when I joined. Brotherhood bonds and unites. It instills values of caring about one another, caring about community, caring about ourselves. The values and bonds [of brotherhood] continually develop over the four years [in college] while normal friendships come and go.

Despite this idealization, most aspects of fraternity practice and conception are more mundane. Brotherhood often plays itself out as an overriding concern with masculinity and, by extension, femininity. As a consequence, fraternities comprise collectivities of highly masculinized men with attitudinal qualities and behavioral norms that predispose them to sexual coercion of women (cf. Kanin 1967; Merton 1985; Rapaport and Burkhart 1984). The norms of masculinity are complemented by conceptions of women and femininity that are equally distorted and stereotyped and that may enhance the probability of women's exploitation (cf. Ehrhart and Sandler 1985; Sunday 1981, 1986).

Practices of Brotherhood

Practices associated with fraternity brotherhood that contribute to the sexual coercion of women include a preoccupation with loyalty, group protection and secrecy, use of alcohol as a weapon, involvement in violence and physical force, and an emphasis on competition and superiority.

Loyalty, group protection, and secrecy. Loyalty is a fraternity preoccupation. Members are reminded constantly to be loyal to the fraternity and to their brothers. Among other ways, loyalty is played out in the practices of group protection and secrecy. The fraternity must be shielded from criticism. Members are admonished to avoid getting the fraternity in trouble and to bring all problems "to the chapter" (local branch of a national social fraternity) rather than to outsiders. Fraternities try to protect themselves from close scrutiny and criticism by the Interfraternity Council (a quasi-governing body composed of representatives from all social fraternities on campus), their fraternity's national office, university officials, law enforcement, the media, and the public. Protection of the fraternity often takes precedence over what is procedurally, ethically, or legally correct. Numerous examples were related to us of fraternity brothers' lying to outsiders to "protect the fraternity."

Group protection was observed in the alleged gang rape case with which we began our study. Except for one brother, a rapist who turned state's evidence, the entire remaining fraternity membership was accused by university and criminal justice officials of lying to protect the fraternity. Members consistently failed to cooperate even though the alleged crimes were felonies, involved only four men (two of whom were not even members of the local chapter), and the victim of the crime nearly died. According to a grand jury's findings, fraternity officers repeatedly broke appointments with law enforcement officials, refused to provide police with a list of members, and refused to cooperate with police and prosecutors investigating the case (*Florida Flambeau*, 1988).

Secrecy is a priority value and practice in fraternities, partly because full-fledged membership is premised on it (for confirmation, see Ehrhart and Sandler 1985; Longino and Kart 1973; Roark 1987). Secrecy is also a boundary-maintaining mechanism, demarcating in-group from out-group, us from them. Secret rituals, handshakes, and mottoes are revealed to pledge brothers as they are initiated into full brotherhood. Since only brothers are supposed to know a fraternity's secrets, such knowledge affirms membership in the fraternity and separates a brother from others. Extending secrecy tactics from protection of private knowledge to protection of the fraternity from criticism is a predictable development. Our interview indicated that individual members knew the difference between right and wrong, but fraternity norms that emphasize loyalty, group protection, and secrecy often overrode standards of ethical correctness.

Alcohol as weapon. Alcohol use by fraternity men is normative. They use it on weekdays to relax after class and on weekends to "get drunk," "get crazy," and "get laid." The use of alcohol to obtain sex from women is pervasive—in other words, it is used as a weapon against sexual reluctance. According to several fraternity men whom we interviewed, alcohol is the major tool used to gain sexual mastery over women (cf. Adams and Abarbanel 1988; Ehrhart and Sandler 1985). One fraternity man, a 21-year-old senior, described alcohol use to gain sex as follows: "There are girls that you know will fuck, then some you have to put some effort into it. . . . You have to buy them drinks or find out if she's drunk enough. . . ."

A similar strategy is used collectively. A fraternity man said that at parties with Little Sisters: "We provide them with 'hunch punch' and things get wild. We get them drunk and most of the guys end up with one." "'Hunch punch,'" he said, "is a girls' drink made up of overproof alcohol and powdered Kool-Aid, no water or anything, just ice. It's very strong. Two cups will do a number on a female." He had plans in the next academic term to surreptitiously give hunch punch to women in a "prim and proper" sorority because "having sex with prim and proper sorority girls is definitely a goal." These women are a challenge because they "won't openly consume alcohol and won't get openly drunk as hell." Their sororities have "standards committees" that forbid heavy drinking and easy sex.

In the gang rape case, our sources said that many fraternity men on campus believed the victim had a drinking problem and was thus an "easy make." According to newspaper accounts, she had been drinking alcohol on the evening she was raped; the lead assailant is alleged to have given her a bottle of wine after she arrived at his fraternity house. Portions of the rape occurred in a shower, and the victim was reportedly so drunk that her assailants had difficulty holding her in a standing position (*Tallahassee Democrat*, 1988a). While raping her, her assailants repeatedly told her they were members of another fraternity under the apparent belief that she was too drunk to know the difference. Of course, if she was too drunk to know who they were, she was too drunk to consent to sex (cf. Allgeier 1986; Tash 1988).

One respondent told us that gang rapes are wrong and can get one expelled, but he seemed to see nothing wrong in sexual coercion one-on-one. He seemed unaware that the use of alcohol to obtain sex from a woman is grounds for a claim that a rape occurred (cf. Tash 1988). Few women on campus (who also may not know these grounds) report date rapes, however, so the odds of detection and punishment are slim for fraternity men who use alcohol for "seduction" purposes (cf. Byington and Keeter 1988; Merton 1985).

Violence and physical force. Fraternity men have a history of violence (Ehrhart and Sandler 1985; Roark 1987). Their record of hazing, fighting, property destruction, and rape has caused them problems with insurance companies (Bradford 1986; Pressley 1987). Two university officials told us that fraternities "are the third riskiest property to insure behind toxic waste dumps and amusement parks." Fraternities are increasingly defendants in legal actions brought by pledges subjected to hazing (Meyer 1986; Pressley 1987) and by women who were raped by one or more members. In a recent alleged gang rape incident at another Florida university, prosecutors failed to file charges but the victim filed a civil suit against the fraternity nevertheless (*Tallahassee Democrat,* 1989).

Competition and superiority. Interfraternity rivalry fosters in-group identification and out-group hostility. Fraternities stress pride of membership and superiority over other fraternities as major goals. Interfraternity rivalries take many forms, including competition for desirable pledges, size of pledge class, size of membership, size and appearance of fraternity house, superiority in intramural sports, highest grade-point averages, giving the best parties, gaining the best or most campus leadership roles, and, of great importance, attracting and displaying "good looking women." Rivalry is particularly intense over members, intramural sports, and women (cf. Messner 1989).

⊛ Fraternities' Commodification of Women

In claiming that women are treated by fraternities as commodities, we mean that fraternities knowingly, and intentionally, use women for their benefit. Fraternities use women as bait for new members, as servers of brothers' needs, and as sexual prey.

Women as bait. Fashionably attractive women help a fraternity attract new members. As one fraternity man, a junior, said, "They are good bait."

Beautiful, sociable women are believed to impress the right kind of pledges and give the impression that the fraternity can deliver this type of woman to its members. Photographs of shapely, attractive coeds are printed in fraternity brochures and videotapes that are distributed and shown to potential pledges. The women pictured are often dressed in bikinis, at the beach, and are pictured hugging the brothers of the fraternity. One university official says such recruitment materials give the message: "Hey, they're here for you, you can have whatever you want," and, "we have the best looking women. Join us and you can have them too." Another commented: "Something's wrong when males join an all-male organization as the best place to meet women. It's so illogical."

Fraternities compete in promising access to beautiful women. One fraternity man, a senior, commented that "the attraction of girls [i.e., a fraternity's success in attracting women] is a big status symbol for fraternities." One university official commented that the use of women as a recruiting tool is so well entrenched that fraternities that might be willing to forgo it say they cannot afford to unless other fraternities do so as well. One fraternity man said, "Look, if we don't have Little Sisters, the fraternities that do will get all the good pledges." Another said, "We won't have as good a rush [the period during which new members are assessed and selected] if we don't have these women around."

In displaying good-looking, attractive, skimpily dressed, nubile women to potential members, fraternities implicitly, and sometimes explicitly, promise sexual access to women. One fraternity man commented that "part of what being in a fraternity is all about is the sex" and explained how his fraternity uses Little Sisters to recruit new members:

> We'll tell the sweetheart [the fraternity's term for Little Sister], "You're gorgeous; you can get him." We'll tell her to fake a scam and she'll go hang all over him during a rush party, kiss him, and he thinks he's done wonderful and wants to join. The girls think it's great too. It's flattering for them.

Women as servers. The use of women as servers is exemplified in the Little Sister program. Little Sisters are undergraduate women who are rushed and selected in a manner parallel to the recruitment of fraternity men. They are affiliated with the fraternity in a formal but unofficial way and are able, indeed required, to wear the fraternity's Greek letters. Little Sisters are not full-fledged fraternity members, however; and fraternity national offices and most universities do not register or regulate them. Each fraternity has an officer called Little Sister Chairman who oversees their organization and activities. The Little Sisters elect officers among themselves, pay monthly dues to the fraternity, and have well-defined roles. Their dues are used to pay for the fraternity's social events, and Little Sisters are expected to attend and hostess fraternity parties and hang around the house to make it a "nice place to be." One fraternity man, a senior, described Little Sisters this way: "They are very social girls, willing to join in, be affiliated with the group, devoted to the fraternity." Another member, a sophomore, said: "Their sole purpose is social—attend parties, attract new members, and 'take care' of the guys."

Our observations and interviews suggested that women selected by fraternities as Little Sisters are physically attractive, possess good social skills, and are willing to devote time and energy to the fraternity and its members. One undergraduate woman gave the following job description for Little Sisters to a campus newspaper:

> It's not just making appearances at all the parties but entails many more responsibilities. You're going to be expected to go to all the intramural games to cheer the brothers on, support and encourage the pledges, and just be around to bring some extra life to the house. [As a Little Sister] you have to agree to take on a new responsibility other than studying to maintain your grades and managing to keep your checkbook from bouncing. You have to make time to be a part of the fraternity and support the brothers in all they do. (*The Tomahawk*, 1988)

The title of Little Sister reflects women's subordinate status; fraternity men in a parallel role are called Big Brothers. Big Brothers assist a sorority primarily with the physical work of sorority rushes, which, compared to fraternity rushes, are more formal, structured, and intensive. Sorority rushes take place in the daytime and fraternity rushes at night so fraternity men are free to help. According to one fraternity member, Little Sister status is a benefit to women because it gives them a social outlet and "the protection of the brothers." The gender-stereotypic conceptions and obligations of these Little Sister and Big Brother statuses indicate that fraternities and sororities promote a gender hierarchy on campus that fosters subordination and dependence in women, thus encouraging sexual exploitation and the belief that it is acceptable.

Women as sexual prey. Little Sisters are a sexual utility. Many Little Sisters do not belong to sororities and lack peer support for refraining from unwanted sexual relations. One fraternity man (whose fraternity has 65 members and 85 Little Sisters) told us they had recruited "wholesale" in the prior year to "get lots of new women." The structural access to women that the Little Sister program provides and the absence of normative supports for refusing fraternity members' sexual advances may make women in this program particularly susceptible to coerced sexual encounters with fraternity men.

Access to women for sexual gratification is a presumed benefit of fraternity membership, promised in recruitment materials and strategies and through brothers' conversations with new recruits. One fraternity man said: "We always tell the guys that you get sex all the time, there's always new girls. . . . After I became a Greek, I found out I could be with females at will." A university official told us that, based on his observations, "no one [i.e., fraternity men] on this campus wants to have 'relationships.' They just want to have fun [i.e., sex]." Fraternity men plan and execute strategies aimed at obtaining sexual gratification, and this occurs at both individual and collective levels.

Individual strategies include getting a woman drunk and spending a great deal of money on her. As for collective strategies, most of our undergraduate interviewees agreed that fraternity parties often culminate in sex and that this outcome is planned. One fraternity man said fraternity parties often involve sex and nudity and can "turn into orgies." Orgies may be planned in advance, such as the Bowery Ball party held by one fraternity. A former fraternity member said of this party:

> The entire idea behind this is sex. Both men and women come to the party wearing little or nothing. There are pornographic pinups on the walls and usually porno movies playing on the TV. The music carries sexual overtones. . . . They just get schnockered [drunk] and, in most cases, they also get laid.

When asked about the women who come to such a party, he said: "Some Little Sisters just won't go. . . . The girls who do are looking for a good time, girls who don't know what it is, things like that."

Other respondents denied that fraternity parties are orgies but said that sex is always talked about among the brothers and they all know "who each other is doing it with." One member said that most of the time, guys have sex with their girlfriends "but with socials, girlfriends aren't allowed to come and it's their [members'] big chance [to have sex with other women]." The use of alcohol to help them get women into bed is a routine strategy at fraternity parties.

◉ Conclusions

In general, our research indicated that the organization and membership of fraternities contribute heavily to coercive and often violent sex. Fraternity houses are occupied by same-sex (all men) and same-age (late teens, early twenties) peers whose maturity and judgment is often less than ideal. Yet fraternity houses are private dwellings that are mostly off-limits to, and away from scrutiny of, university and community representatives, with the result that fraternity house events seldom come to the attention of outsiders. Practices associated with the social construction of fraternity brotherhood emphasize a macho conception of men and masculinity, a narrow, stereotyped conception of women and femininity, and the treatment of women as commodities. Other practices contributing to coercive sexual relations and the cover-up of rapes include excessive alcohol use, competitiveness, and normative support for deviance and secrecy (cf. Bogal-Allbritten and Allbritten 1985; Kanin 1967).

Some fraternity practices exacerbate others. Brotherhood norms require "sticking together" regardless of right or wrong; thus rape episodes are unlikely to be stopped or reported to outsiders, even when witnesses disapprove. The ability to use alcohol without scrutiny by authorities and alcohol's frequent association with violence, including sexual coercion, facilitates rape in fraternity houses. Fraternity norms that emphasize the value of maleness and masculinity over femaleness and femininity and that elevate the status of men and lower the status of women in members' eyes undermine perceptions and treatment of women as persons who deserve consideration and care (cf. Ehrhart and Sandier 1985; Merton 1985).

Androgynous men and men with a broad range of interests and attributes are lost to fraternities through their recruitment practices. Masculinity of a narrow and stereotypical type helps create attitudes, norms, and practices that predispose fraternity men to coerce women sexually, both individually and collectively (Allgeier 1986; Hood 1989; Sanday 1981, 1986). Male athletes on campus may be similarly disposed for the same reasons (Kirshenbaum 1989, Telander and Sullivan 1989).

Research into the social contexts in which rape crimes occur and the social constructions associated with these contexts illumine rape dynamics on campus. Blanchard (1959) found that group rapes almost always have a leader who pushes others into the crime. He also found that the leader's latent homosexuality, desire to show off to his peers, or fear of failing to prove himself a man are frequently an impetus. Fraternity norms and practices contribute to the approval and use of sexual coercion as an accepted tactic in relations with women. Alcohol-induced compliance is normative, whereas, presumably, use of a knife, gun, or threat of bodily harm would not be because the woman who "drinks too much" is viewed as "causing her own rape" (cf. Ehrhart and Sandler 1985).

Our research led us to conclude that fraternity norms and practices influence members to view the sexual coercion of women, which is a felony crime, as sport, a contest, or a game (cf. Sato 1988). This sport is played not between men and women but between men and men. Women are the pawns or prey in the interfraternity rivalry game; they prove that a fraternity is successful or prestigious. The use of women in this way encourages fraternity men to see women as objects and sexual coercion as sport. Today's societal norms support young women's right to engage in sex at their discretion, and coercion is unnecessary in a mutually desired encounter. However, nubile young women say they prefer to be "in a relationship" to have sex while young men say they prefer to "get laid" without a commitment (Muehlenhard and Linton 1987). These differences may reflect, in part, American puritanism and men's fears of sexual intimacy or perhaps intimacy of any kind. In a fraternity context, getting sex without giving emotionally demonstrates "cool" masculinity. More important, it poses no threat to the bonding and loyalty of the fraternity brotherhood (cf. Farr 1988). Drinking large quantities of alcohol before having sex suggests that "scoring" rather than intrinsic sexual pleasure is a primary concern of fraternity men.

Unless fraternities' composition, goals, structures, and practices change in fundamental ways, women on campus will continue to be sexual prey for fraternity men. As all-male enclaves dedicated to opposing faculty and administration and to cementing in-group ties, fraternity members eschew any hint of homosexuality. Their version of masculinity transforms women, and men with womanly characteristics, into the out-group. "Womanly men" are ostracized; feminine women are used to demonstrate members' masculinity. Encouraging renewed emphasis on their founding values (Longino and Kart 1973), service orientation and activities (Lemire 1979), or members' moral development (Marlowe and Auvenshine 1982) will have little effect on fraternities' treatment of women. A case for or against fraternities cannot be made by studying individual members. The fraternity qua group and organization is at issue. Located on campus along with many vulnerable women, embedded in a sexist society, and caught up in masculinist goals, practices, and values, fraternities' violation of women—including forcible rape—should come as no surprise.

Endnote
[1]Recent bans by some universities on open-keg parties at fraternity houses have resulted in heavy drinking before coming to a party and an increase in drunkenness among those who attend. This may aggravate, rather than improve, the treatment of women by fraternity men at parties.

References

Allgeier, Elizabeth. 1986. "Coercive Versus Consensual Sexual Interactions." G. Stanley Hall Lecture to American Psychological Association Annual Meeting, Washington, DC, August.

Adams, Aileen and Gail Abarbanel. 1988. *Sexual Assault on Campus: What Colleges Can Do*. Santa Monica, CA: Rape Treatment Center.

Blanchard, W. H. 1959. "The Group Process in Gang Rape." *Journal of Social Psychology* 49:259–66.

Bogal-Allbritten, Rosemarie B. and William L. Allbritten. 1985. "The Hidden Victims: Courtship Violence Among College Students." *Journal of College Student Personnel* 43:201–4.

Bohrnstedt, George W. 1969. "Conservatism, Authoritarianism and Religiosity of Fraternity Pledges." *Journal of College Student Personnel* 27:36–43.

Bradford, Michael. 1986. "Tight Market Dries Up Nightlife at University." *Business Insurance* (March 2): 2, 6.

Burkhart, Barry. 1989. Comments in Seminar on Acquaintance/Date Rape Prevention: A National Video Teleconference, February 2.

Burkhart, Barry R. and Annette L. Stanton. 1985. "Sexual Aggression in Acquaintance Relationships." Pp. 43–65 in *Violence to Intimate Relationships,* edited by G. Russell. Englewood Cliffs, NJ: Spectrum.

Byington, Diane B. and Karen W. Keeter. 1988. "Assessing Needs of Sexual Assault Victims on a University Campus." Pp. 23–31 in *Student Services: Responding to Issues and Challenges.* Chapel Hill: University of North Carolina Press.

Chancer, Lynn S. 1987. New Bedford, Massachusetts, March 6, 1983-March 22, 1984: The 'Before and After' of a Group Rape. *Gender & Society* 1:239–60.

Ehrhart, Julie K. and Bernice R. Sandler. 1985. *Campus Gang Rape: Party Games?* Washington, DC: Association of American Colleges.

Farr, K. A. 1988. "Dominance Bonding Through the Good Old Boys Sociability Network." *Sex Roles* 18:259–77.

Florida Flambeau. 1988. "Pike Members Indicted in Rape." (May 19): 1, 5.

Fox, Elaine, Charles Hodge, and Waller Ward. 1987. "A Comparison of Attitudes Held by Black and White Fraternity Members." *Journal of Negro Education* 56:521–34.

Geis, Gilbert. 1971. "Group Sexual Assaults." *Medical Aspects of Human Sexuality* 5:101–13.

Glaser, Barney G. 1978. *Theoretical Sensitivity: Advances in the Methodology of Grounded Theory.* Mill Valley, CA: Sociology Press.

Hood, Jane. 1989. "Why Our Society is Rape Prone." *New York Times,* May 16.

Hughes, Michael J. and Roger B. Winston, Jr. 1987. "Effects of Fraternity Membership on Interpersonal Values." *Journal of College Student Personnel* 45:405–11.

Kanin, Eugene J. 1967. "Reference Groups and Sex Conduct Norm Violations." *The Sociological Quarterly* 8:495–504.

Kimmel, Michael, ed., 1987. *Changing Men: New Directions in Research on Men and Masculinity.* Newbury-Park, CA: Sage.

Kirshenbaum, Jerry. 1989. "Special Report, An American Disgrace: A Violent and Unprecedented Lawlessness Has Arisen Among College Athletes in All Parts of the Country." *Sports Illustrated* (February 27): 16–19.

Lemire, David. 1979. "One Investigation of the Stereotypes Associated with Fraternities and Sororities." *Journal of College Student Personnel* 37:54–57.

Letchworth, G. E. 1969. "Fraternities Now and in the Future." *Journal of College Student Personnel* 10:118–22.

Longino, Charles F., Jr., and Cary S. Kart. 1973. "The College Fraternity: An Assessment of Theory and Research." *Journal of College Student Personnel* 31:118–25.

Marlowe, Anne F. and Dwight C. Auvenshine. 1982. "Greek Membership: Its Impact on the Moral Development of College Freshmen." *Journal of College Student Personnel* 40:53–57.

Martin, Patricia Yancey and Barry A. Turner. 1986. "Grounded Theory and Organizational Research." *Journal of Applied Behavioral Science* 22:141–57.

Merton, Andrew. 1985. "On Competition and Class: Return to Brotherhood." *Ms.* (September): 60–65, 121–22.

Messner, Michael. 1989. "Masculinities and Athletic Careers." *Gender & Society* 3:71–88.

Meyer, T. J. 1986. "Fight Against Hazing Rituals Rages on Campuses." *Chronicle of Higher Education* (March 12):34–36.

Miller, Leonard D. 1973. "Distinctive Characteristics of Fraternity Members." *Journal of College Student Personnel* 31:126–28.

Muehlenhard, Charlene L. and Melaney A. Linton. 1987. "Date Rape and Sexual Aggression in Dating Situations: Incidence and Risk Factors." *Journal of Counseling Psychology* 34:186–96.

Pressley, Sue Anne. 1987. "Fraternity Hell Night Still Endures." *Washington Post* (August 11):B1.

Rapaport, Karen and Barry R. Burkhart. 1984. "Personality and Attitudinal Characteristics of Sexually Coercive College Males." *Journal of Abnormal Psychology* 93:216–21.

Roark, Mary L. 1987. "Preventing Violence on College Campuses." *Journal of Counseling and Development* 65:367–70.

Sanday, Peggy Reeves. 1981. "The Socio-Cultural Context of Rape: A Cross-Cultural Study." *Journal of Social Issues* 37:5–27.

———. 1986. "Rape and the Silencing of the Feminine." Pp. 84–101 in *Rape,* edited by S. Tomaselli and R. Porter. Oxford: Basil Blackwell.

St. Petersburg Times. 1988. "A Greek Tragedy." (May 29):1F, 6F.

Sato, Ikuya. 1988. "Play Theory of Delinquency: Toward a General Theory of 'Action.'"

Symbolic Interaction 11:191–212.

Smith, T. 1964. "Emergence and Maintenance of Fraternal Solidarity." *Pacific Sociological Review* 7:29–37.

Tallahassee Democrat. 1988a. "FSU Fraternity Brothers Charged" (April 27):IA, 12A.

———. 1988b. "FSU Interviewing Students About Alleged Rape" (April 24):1D.

———. 1989. "Woman Sues Stetson in Alleged Rape" (March 19):3B.

Tampa Tribune. 1988. "Fraternity Brothers Charged in Sexual Assault of FSU Coed." (April 27):6B.

Tash. Gary B. 1988. "Date Rape." *The Emerald of Sigma Pi Fraternity* 75(4):1–2.

Telander, Rick and Robert Sullivan. 1989. "Special Report, You Reap What You Sow." *Sports Illustrated* (February 27):20–34.

The Tomahawk. 1988. "A Look Back at Rush, A Mixture of Hard Work and Fun" (April/May):3D.

Walsh, Claire. 1989. Comments in Seminar on Acquaintance/Date Rape Prevention: A National Video Teleconference, February 2.

Wilder, David H., Arlyne E. Hoyt, Dennis M. Doren, William E. Hauck, and Robert D. Zettle. 1978. "The Impact of Fraternity and Sorority Membership on Values and Attitudes." *Journal of College Student Personnel* 36:445–49.

Wilder, David H., Arlyne E. Hoyt, Beth Shuster Surbeck, Janet C. Wilder, and Patricia Imperatrice Carney. 1986. "Greek Affiliation and Attitude Change in College Students." *Journal of College Student Personnel* 44:510–19.

❧ ❧ ❧

Questions

1. In what respects does the social context of fraternities facilitate sexual assault and rape?

2. How are fraternity members socialized into cultures of masculinity and violence? Is the socialization process effective? Explain your response.

3. How do fraternities "commodify" women? How does commodification contribute to sexual assault and rape?

4. To what degree does a lack of institutional control contribute to the problems of sexual assault and rape on college campuses?

5. How could a fraternity, college, or university substantially reduce the risks discussed by Martin and Hummer?

6. Some people might argue that fraternities are not social contexts that promote, develop, or socialize males into a culture of masculinity and violence. Rather, men who join fraternities are predisposed to commit sexual violence; therefore, they select themselves into fraternity life. Can self-selectivity be a significant contributor to the problem of sexual violence on campuses? How are Martin and Hummer's findings suscep- tible to this counterargument? How are they not?

Convicted Rapists' Vocabulary of Motive: Excuses and Justifications

DIANA SCULLY AND JOSEPH MAROLLA
Virginia Commonwealth University

In this selection, the authors interview convicted rapists currently serving prison time for their crimes. They find that rapists can be classified into two groups: "admitters" and "deniers." From these two groups, the authors derive a typology of excuses and justifications that rapists use to explain their behavior. According to the authors, the use of excuses and justifications lets rapists think of themselves as non-rapists or ex-rapists.

Psychiatry has dominated the literature on rapists since "irresistible impulse" (Glueck, 1925:323) and "disease of the mind" (Glueck, 1925:243) were introduced as the causes of rape. Research has been based on small samples of men, frequently the clinicians' own patient population. Not surprisingly, the medical model has predominated: rape is viewed as an individualistic, idiosyncratic symptom of a disordered personality. That is, rape is assumed to be a psychopathologic problem and individual rapists are assumed to be "sick." However, advocates of this model have been unable to isolate a typical or even predictable pattern of symptoms that are causally linked to rape. Additionally, research has demonstrated that fewer than 5 percent of rapists were psychotic at the time of their rape (Abel *et al.,* 1980).

We view rape as behavior learned socially through interaction with others; convicted rapists have learned the attitudes and actions consistent with sexual aggression against women. Learning also includes the acquisi-

"Convicted Rapists' Vocabulary of Motives: Excuses and Justifications," by Diana Scully and Joseph Marolla, reprinted from *Social Problems,* vol. 31, no. 5, 1984, pp. 530–544.

tion of culturally derived vocabularies of motive, which can be used to diminish responsibility and to negotiate a non-deviant identity.

Sociologists have long noted that people can, and do, commit acts they define as wrong and, having done so, engage various techniques to disavow deviance and present themselves as normal. Through the concept of "vocabulary of motive," Mills (1940:904) was among the first to shed light on this seemingly perplexing contradiction. Wrong-doers attempt to reinterpret their actions through the use of a linguistic device by which norm-breaking conduct is socially interpreted. That is, anticipating the negative consequences of their behavior, wrong-doers attempt to present the act in terms that are both culturally appropriate and acceptable.

Following Mills, a number of sociologists have focused on the types of techniques employed by actors in problematic situations (Hall and Hewitt, 1970; Hewitt and Hall, 1973; Hewitt and Stokes, 1975; Sykes and Matza, 1957). Scott and Lyman (1968) describe excuses and justifications, linguistic "accounts" that explain and remove culpability for an untoward act after it has been committed. *Excuses* admit the act was bad or inappropriate but deny full responsibility, often through appeals to accident, or biological drive, or through scapegoating. In contrast, *justifications* accept responsibility for the act but deny that it was wrong—that is, they show in this situation the act was appropriate. *Accounts* are socially approved vocabularies that neutralize an act or it's consequences and are always a manifestation of an underlying negotiation of identity.

Stokes and Hewitt (1976:837) use the term "aligning actions" to refer to those tactics and techniques used by actors when some feature of a situation is problematic. Stated simply, the concept refers to an actor's attempt, through various means, to bring his or her conduct into alignment with culture. Culture in this sense is conceptualized as a "set of cognitive constraints—objects—to which people must relate as they form lines of conduct" (1976:837), and includes physical constraints, expectations and definitions of others, and personal biography. Carrying out aligning actions implies both awareness of those elements of normative culture that are applicable to the deviant act and, in addition, an actual effort to bring the act into line with this awareness. The result is that deviant behavior is legitimized.

This paper presents an analysis of interviews we conducted with a sample of 114 convicted, incarcerated rapists. We use the concept of accounts (Scott and Lyman, 1968) as a tool to organize and analyze the vocabularies of motive which this group of rapists used to explain themselves and their actions. An analysis of their accounts demonstrates how it was possible for 83 percent (n = 114)[1] of these convicted rapists to view themselves as non-rapists.

When rapists' accounts are examined, a typology emerges that consists of admitters and deniers. Admitters (n = 47) acknowledged that they had forced sexual acts on their victims and defined the behavior as rape. In contrast, deniers[2] either eschewed sexual contact or all association with the victim (n = 35),[3] or admitted to sexual acts but did not define their behavior as rape (n = 32).

The remainder of this paper is divided into two sections. In the first, we discuss the accounts which the rapists used to justify their behavior. In the second, we discuss those accounts which attempted to excuse the rape. By and large, the deniers used justifications while the admitters used excuses. In some cases, both groups relied on the same themes, stereotypes, and images: some admitters, like most deniers, claimed that women enjoyed being raped. Some deniers excused their behavior by referring to alcohol or drug use, although they did so quite differently than admitters. Through these narrative accounts, we explore convicted rapists' own perceptions of their crimes.

◉ Methods and Validity

From September, 1980, through September, 1981, we interviewed 114 male convicted rapists who were incarcerated in seven maximum or medium security prisons in the Commonwealth of Virginia. All of the rapists had been convicted of the rape or attempted rape (n = 8) of an adult woman, although a few had teenage victims as well. Men convicted of incest, statutory rape, or sodomy of a male were omitted from the sample.

Twelve percent of the rapists had been convicted of more than one rape or attempted rape, 39 percent also had convictions for burglary or robbery, 29 percent for abduction, 25 percent for sodomy, and 11 percent for first or second degree murder. Eighty-two percent had a previous criminal history but only 23 percent had records for previous sex offenses. Their sentences for rape and accompanying crimes ranged from 10 years to an accumulation by one man of seven life sentences plus 380 years; 43 percent of the rapists were serving from 10 to 30 years and 22 percent were serving at least one life term. Forty-six percent of the rapists were white and 54 percent were black. Their ranges ranged from 18 to 60 years; 88 percent were between 18 and 35 years. Forty-two percent were either married or cohabitating at the time of their offense. Only 20 percent had a high school education or better, and 85 percent came from working-class backgrounds. Despite the popular belief that rape is due to a personality disorder, only 26 percent of these rapists had any history of emotional problems. When the rapists in this study were compared to a statistical profile of felons in all Virginia prisons, prepared by the Virginia Department of Corrections, rapists who volunteered for this research were disproportionately white, somewhat better educated, and younger than the average inmate.

All participants in this study were volunteers. We sent a letter to every inmate (n = 3500) at each of the seven prisons. The letters introduced us as professors at a local university, described our research as a study of men's attitudes toward sexual behavior and women, outlined our procedures for ensuring confidentiality, and solicited volunteers from all criminal categories. Using one follow-up letter, approximately 25 percent of all inmates, including rapists, indicated their willingness to be interviewed by mailing an information sheet to us at the university. From this pool of volunteers, we constructed a sample of rapists based on age, education, race, severity of current offenses, and previous criminal records. Obviously, the sample was not random and thus may not be representative of all rapists.

Each of the authors—one woman and one man—interviewed half of the rapists. Both authors were able to establish rapport and obtain information. However, the rapists volunteered more about their feelings and emotions to the female author and her interviews lasted longer.

All rapists were given an 89-page interview, which included a general background, psychological, criminal, and sexual history, attitude scales, and 30 pages of open-ended questions intended to explore their perceptions of their crimes, their victims, and theirselves. Because a voice print is an absolute source of identification, we did not use tape recorders. All interviews were hand recorded. With some practice, we found it was possible to record much of the interview verbatim. While hand recording inevitably resulted in some lost data, it did have the advantage of eliciting more confidence and candor in the men.

Interviews with the rapists lasted from three hours to seven hours; the average was about four-and-one-half hours. Most of the rapists were reluctant to end the interview. Once rapport had been established, the men wanted to talk, even though it sometimes meant, for example, missing a meal.

Because of the reputation prison inmates have for 'conning,' validity was a special concern in our research. Although the purpose of the research was to obtain the men's own perceptions of their acts, it was also necessary to establish the extent to which these perceptions deviated from other descriptions of their crimes. To establish validity, we used the same technique others have used in prison research: comparing factual information, including details of the crime, obtained in the interview with pre-sentence reports on file at the prisons (Athens, 1977; Luckenbill, 1977; Queen's Bench Foundation, 1976). Pre-sentence reports, written by a court worker at the time of conviction, usually include general background information, a psychological evaluation, the offender's version of the details of the crime, and the victim's or police's version of the details of the crime. Using these records allowed us to clarify two important issues: first, the amount of change that had occurred in rapists' accounts from pre-sentencing to the time when we interviewed them; and, second, the amount of discrepancy between rapists' accounts, as told to us, and the victims' and/or police versions of the crime, contained in the pre-sentence reports.

The time between pre-sentence reports and our interviews (in effect, the amount of time rapists had spent in prison before we interviewed them) ranged from less than one year to 20 years; the average was three years. Yet despite this time lapse, there were no significant changes in the way rapists explained their crimes, with the exception of 18 men who had denied their crimes at their trials but admitted them to us. There were no cases of men who admitted their crime at their trial but denied them when talking to us.

However, there were major differences between the accounts we heard of the crimes from rapists and the police's and victim's versions. Admitters (including deniers turned admitters) told us essentially the same story as the police and victim versions. However, the admitters subtly understated the force they had used and, though they used words such as *violent* to describe their acts, they also omitted reference to the more brutal aspects of their crime.

In contrast, deniers' interview accounts differed significantly from victim and police versions. According to the pre-sentence reports, 11 of the 32 deniers had been acquainted with their victim. But an additional four deniers told us they had been acquainted with their victims. In the pre-sentence reports, police or victim versions of the crime described seven

TABLE 1 *Comparison of Admitters' and Deniers' Crimes Police/Victim Versions in Pre-Sentence Reports*

Characteristics	Percent Admitters n = 47	Percent Deniers n = 32
White Assailant	57	41
Black Assailant	43	59
Group Rape	23	13
Multiple Rapes	43	34
Assailant a Stranger	72	66
Controversial Situation	06	22
Weapon and/or Injury Present		
(includes victim murdered)	74	69

rapes in which the victim had been hitchhiking or was picked up in a bar; but deniers told us this was true of 20 victims. Weapons were present in 21 of the 32 rapes according to the pre-sentence reports, yet only nine men acknowledged the presence of a weapon and only two of the nine admitted they had used it to threaten or intimidate their victim. Finally, in at least seven of the rapes, the victim had been seriously injured,[4] but only three men admitted injury. In two of the three cases, the victim had been murdered; in these cases the men denied the rape but not the murder. Indeed, deniers constructed accounts for us which, by implicating the victim, made their own conduct appear to have been more appropriate. They never used words such as *violent,* choosing instead to emphasize the sexual component of their behavior.

It should be noted that we investigated the possibility that deniers claimed their behavior was not criminal because, in contrast to admitters, their crimes resembled what research has found the public define as a controversial rape, that is, victim an acquaintance, no injury or weapon, victim picked up hitchhiking or in a bar (Burt, 1980; Burt and Albin, 1981; Williams, 1979). However, as Table 1 indicates, the crimes committed by deniers were only slightly more likely to involve these elements.

This contrast between pre-sentence reports and interviews suggests several significant factors related to interview content validity. First, when asked to explain their behavior, our sample of convicted rapists (except deniers turned admitters) responded with accounts that had changed surprisingly little since their trials. Second, admitters' interview accounts were basically the same as others' versions of their crimes, while deniers systematically put more blame on the victims.

◉ Justifying Rape

Deniers attempted to justify their behavior by presenting the victim in a light that made her appear culpable, regardless of their own actions. Five themes run through attempts to justify their rapes: (1) women as seductresses; (2) women mean "yes" when they say "no"; (3) most women eventually relax and enjoy it; (4) nice girls don't get raped; and (5) guilty of a minor wrong-doing.

1) Women as Seductresses

Men who rape need not search far for cultural language which supports the premise that women provoke or are responsible for rape. In addition to common cultural stereotypes, the fields of psychiatry and criminology (particularly the subfield of victimology) have traditionally provided justifications for rape, often by portraying raped women as the victims of their own seduction (Albin, 1977; Marolla and Scully, 1979). For example, Hollander (1924:130) argues:

> Considering the amount of illicit intercourse, rape of women is very rare indeed. Flirtation and provocative conduct, i.e. tacit (if not actual) consent is generally the prelude to intercourse.

Since women are supposed to be coy about their sexual availability, refusal to comply with a man's sexual demands lacks meaning and rape appears normal. The fact that violence and, often, a weapon are used to accomplish the rape is not considered. As an example, Abrahamsen (1960:61) writes:

> The conscious or unconscious biological or psychological attraction between man and woman does not exist only on the part of the offender toward the woman but, also, on her part toward him, which in many instances may, to some extent, be the impetus for his sexual attack. Often

'a women [sic] unconsciously wishes to be taken by force—consider the theft of the bride in Peer Gynt.

Like Peer Gynt, the deniers we interviewed tried to demonstrate that their victims were willing and, in some cases, enthusiastic participants.. In these accounts, the rape became more dependent upon the victim's behavior than upon their own actions.

Thirty-one percent (n = 10) of the deniers presented an extreme view of the victim. Not only willing, she was the aggressor, a seductress who lured them, unsuspecting, into sexual action. Typical was a denier convicted of his first rape and accompanying crimes of burglary, sodomy, and abduction. According to the pre-sentence reports, he had broken into the victim's house and raped her at knife point. While he admitted to the breaking and entry, which he claimed was for altruistic purposes ("to pay for the prenatal care of a friend's girlfriend"), he also argued that when the victim discovered him, he had tried to leave but she had asked him to stay. Telling him that she cheated on her husband, she had voluntarily removed her clothes and seduced him. She was, according to him, an exemplary sex partner who "enjoyed it very much and asked for oral sex.[5] Can I have it now?" he reported her as saying. He claimed they had spent hours in bed, after which the victim had told him he was good looking and asked to see him again. "Who would believe I'd meet a fellow like this?" he reported her as saying.

In addition to this extreme group, 25 percent (n = 8) of the deniers said the victim was willing and had made some sexual advances. An additional 9 percent (n = 3) said the victim was willing to have sex for money or drugs. In two of these three cases, the victim had been either an acquaintance or picked up, which the rapists said led them to expect sex.

2) Women Mean "Yes" When They Say "No"
Thirty-four percent (n = 11) of the deniers described their victim as unwilling, at least initially, indicating either that she had resisted or that she had said no. Despite this, and even though (according to pre-sentence reports) a weapon had been present in 64 percent (n = 7) of these 11 cases, the rapists justified their behavior by arguing that either the victim had not resisted enough or that her "no" had really meant "yes." For example, one denier who was serving time for a previous rape was subsequently convicted of attempting to rape a prison hospital nurse. He insisted he had actually completed the second rape, and said of his victim: "She semi-struggled but

deep down inside I think she felt it was a fantasy come true." The nurse, according to him, had asked a question about his conviction for rape, which he interpreted as teasing. "It was like she was saying, `rape me'." Further, he stated that she had helped him along with oral sex and "from her actions, she was enjoying it." In another case, a 34-year-old man convicted of abducting and raping a 15-year old teenager at knife point as she walked on the beach, claimed it was a pickup. This rapist said women like to be over-powered before sex, but to dominate after it begins.

> A man's body is like a coke bottle, shake it up, put your thumb over the opening and feel the tension. When you take a woman out, woo her, then she says "no, I'm a nice girl," you have to use force. All men do this. She said "no" but it was a societal no, she wanted to be coaxed. All women say "no" when they mean "yes" but its a societal no, so they won't have to feel responsible later.

Claims that the victim didn't resist or, if she did, didn't resist enough, were also used by 24 percent (n = 11) of admitters to explain why, during the incident, they believed the victim was willing and that they were not raping. These rapists didn't redefine their acts until some time after the crime. For example, an admitter who used a bayonet to threaten his victim, an employee of the store he had been robbing, stated:

> At the time I didn't think it was rape. I just asked her nicely and she didn't resist. I never considered prison. I just felt like I had met a friend. It took about five years of reading and going to school to change my mind about whether it was rape. I became familiar with the subtlety of violence. But at the time, I believed that as long as I didn't hurt anyone it wasn't wrong. At the time, I didn't think I would go to prison, I thought I would beat it.

Another typical case involved a gang rape in which the victim was abducted at knife point as she walked home about midnight. According to two of the rapists, both of whom were interviewed, at the time they had thought the victim had willingly accepted a ride from the third rapist (who was not interviewed). They claimed the victim didn't resist and one reported her as saying she would do anything if they would take her home. In this rapist's view, "She acted like she enjoyed it, but maybe she was just acting. She wasn't crying, she was engaging in it." He reported that she had been friendly to the rapist who abducted her and, claiming not to have a home phone, she gave him her office number—a tactic eventually used to catch the three. In retrospect, this young man had decided, "She was scared and just relaxed and enjoyed it to avoid getting hurt." Note, however, that while he had redefined the act as rape, he continued to believe she enjoyed it.

Men who claimed to have been unaware that they were raping viewed sexual aggression as a man's prerogative at the time of the rape. Thus they regarded their act as little more than a minor wrongdoing even though most possessed or used a weapon. As long as the victim survived without major physical injury, from their perspective, a rape had not taken place. Indeed, even U.S. courts have often taken the position that physical injury is a necessary ingredient for a rape conviction.

3) Most Women Eventually Relax and Enjoy It

Many of the rapists expected us to accept the image, drawn from cultural stereotype, that once the rape began, the victim relaxed and enjoyed it.[6] Indeed, 69 percent (n = 22) of deniers justified their behavior by claiming not only that the victim was willing, but also that she enjoyed herself, in some cases to an immense degree. Several men suggested that they had fulfilled their victims' dreams. Additionally, while most admitters used adjectives such as "dirty," "humiliated," and "disgusted," to describe how they thought rape made women feel, 20 percent (n = 9) believed that their victim enjoyed herself. For example, one denier had posed as a salesman to gain entry to his victim's house. But he claimed he had had a previous sexual relationship with the victim, that she agreed to have sex for drugs, and that the opportunity to have sex with him produced "a glow, because she was really into oral stuff and fascinated by the idea of sex with a black man. She felt satisfied, fulfilled, wanted me to stay, but I didn't want her." In another case, a denier who had broken into his victim's house but who insisted the victim was his lover and let him in voluntarily, declared "She felt good, kept kissing me and wanted me to stay the night. She felt proud after sex with me." And another denier, who had hid in his victim's closet and later attacked her while she slept, argued that while she was scared at first, "once we got into it, she was ok." He continued to believe he hadn't committed rape because "she enjoyed it and it was like she consented."

4) Nice Girls Don't Get Raped

The belief that "nice girls don't get raped" affects perception of fault. The victim's reputation, as well as characteristics or behavior which violate normative sex role expectations, are perceived as contributing to the commission of the crime. For example, Nelson and Amir (1975) defined hitchhike rape as a victim-precipitated offense.

In our study, 69 percent (n = 22) of deniers and 22 percent (n = 10) of admitters referred to their victims' sexual reputation, thereby evoking the stereotype that "nice girls don't get raped." They claimed that the victim was known to have been a prostitute, or a "loose" woman, or to have had a lot of affairs, or to have given birth to a child out of wedlock. For example, a denier who claimed he had picked up his victim while she was hitchhiking stated, "To be honest, we [his family] knew she was a damn whore and whether she screwed one or 50 guys didn't matter." According to pre-sentence reports this victim didn't know her attacker and he abducted her at knife point from the street. In another case, a denier who claimed to have known his victim by reputation stated:

> If you wanted drugs or a quick piece of ass, she would do it. In court she said she was a virgin, but I could tell during sex [rape] that she was very experienced.

When other types of discrediting biographical information were added to these sexual slurs, a total of 78 percent (n = 25) of the deniers used the victim's reputation to substantiate their accounts. Most frequently, they referred to the victim's emotional state or drug use. For example, one denier claimed his victim had been known to be loose and, additionally, had turned state's evidence against her husband to put him in prison and save herself from a burglary conviction. Further, he asserted that she had met her current boyfriend, who was himself in and out of prison, in a drug rehabil-itation center where they were both clients.

Evoking the stereotype that women provoke rape by the way they dress, a description of the victim as seductively attired appeared in the accounts of 22 percent (n = 7) of deniers and 17 percent (n = 8) of admitters. Typically, these descriptions were used to substantiate their claims about the victim's reputation. Some men went to extremes to paint a tarnished picture of the victim, describing her as dressed in tight black clothes and without a bra; in one case, the victim was portrayed as sexually provocative in dress and carriage. Not only did she wear short skirts, but she was observed to "spread her legs while getting out of cars." Not all of the men attempted to assassi-nate their victim's reputation with equal vengeance. Numerous times they made subtle and offhand remarks like, "She was a waitress and you know how they are."

The intent of these discrediting statements is clear. Deniers argued that the woman was a "legitimate" victim who got what she deserved. For example, one denier stated that all of his victims had been prostitutes; pre-sentence reports indicated they were not. Several times during his interview, he referred to them as "dirty sluts," and argued "anything I did to them was justified." Deniers also claimed their victim had wrongly accused them and was the type of woman who would perjure herself in court.

5) Only a Minor Wrongdoing

The majority of deniers did not claim to be completely innocent and they also accepted some accountability for their actions. Only 16 percent (n = 5) of deniers argued that they were totally free of blame. Instead, the majority of deniers pleaded guilty to a lesser charge. That is, they obfuscated the rape by pleading guilty to a less serious, more acceptable charge. They accepted being over-sexed, accused of poor judgement or trickery, even some violence, or guilty of adultery or contributing to the delinquency of a minor, charges that are hardly the equivalent of rape.

Typical of this reasoning is a denier who met his victim in a bar when the bartender asked him if he would try to repair her stalled car. After attempting unsuccessfully, he claimed the victim drank with him and later accepted a ride. Out riding, he pulled into a deserted area "to see how my luck would go." When the victim resisted his advances, he beat her and he stated:

> I did something stupid. I pulled a knife on her and I hit her as hard as I would hit a man. But I shouldn't be in prison for what I did. I shouldn't have all this time [sentence] for going to bed with a broad.

This rapist continued to believe that while the knife was wrong, his sexual behavior was justified.

In another case, the denier claimed he picked up his under-age victim at a party and that she voluntarily went with him to a motel. According to pre-sentence reports, the victim had been abducted at knife point from a party. He explained:

> After I paid for a motel, she would have to have sex but I wouldn't use a weapon. I would have explained. I spent money and, if she still said no, I would have forced her. If it had happened that way, it would have been rape to some people but not to my way of thinking. I've done that kind of

thing before. I'm guilty of sex and contributing to the delinquency of a minor, but not rape.

In sum, deniers argued that, while their behavior may not have been completely proper, it should not have been considered rape. To accomplish this, they attempted to discredit and blame the victim while presenting their own actions as justified in the context. Not surprisingly, none of the deniers thought of himself as a rapist. A minority of the admitters attempted to lessen the impact of their crime by claiming the victim enjoyed being raped. But despite this similarity, the nature and tone of admitters' and deniers' accounts were essentially different.

❂ Excusing Rape

In stark contrast to deniers, admitters regarded their behavior as morally wrong and beyond justification. They blamed themselves rather than the victim, although some continued to cling to the belief that the victim had contributed to the crime somewhat, for example, by not resisting enough.

Several of the admitters expressed the view that rape was an act of such moral outrage that it was unforgivable. Several admitters broke into tears at intervals during their interviews. A typical sentiment was,

> I equate rape with someone throwing you up against a wall and tearing your liver and guts out of you. . . . Rape is worse than murder . . . and I'm disgusting.

Another young admitter frequently referred to himself as repulsive and confided:

> I'm in here for rape and in my own mind, its the most disgusting crime, sickening. When people see me and know, I get sick.

Admitters tried to explain their crime in a way that allowed them to retain a semblance of moral integrity. Thus, in contrast to deniers' justifications, admitters used excuses to explain how they were compelled to rape. These excuses appealed to the existence of forces outside of the rapists' control. Through the use of excuses, they attempted to demonstrate that either intent was absent or responsibility was diminished. This allowed them to admit rape while reducing the threat to their identity as a moral person. Excuses also permitted them to view their behavior as idiosyncratic rather than typical and, thus, to believe they were not "really" rapists. Three themes run through these accounts: (1) the use of alcohol and drugs; (2) emotional problems; and (3) nice guy image.

1) The Use of Alcohol and Drugs

A number of studies have noted a high incidence of alcohol and drug consumption by convicted rapists prior to their crime (Groth, 1979; Queen's Bench Foundation, 1976). However, more recent research has tentatively concluded that the connection between substance use and crime is not as direct as previously thought (Ladouceur, 1983). Another facet of alcohol and drug use mentioned in the literature is its utility in disavowing deviance. McCaghy (1968) found that child molesters used alcohol as a technique for neutralizing their deviant identity. Marolla and Scully (1979), in a review of psychiatric literature, demonstrated how alcohol consumption is applied differently as a vocabulary of motive. Rapists can use alcohol both as an excuse for their behavior and to discredit the victim and make her more responsible. We found the former common among admitters and the latter common among deniers.

Alcohol and/or drugs were mentioned in the accounts of 77 percent (n = 30) of admitters and 84 percent (n = 21) of deniers and both groups were equally likely to have acknowledged consuming a substance—admitters, 77 percent (n = 30); deniers, 72 percent (n = 18). However, admitters said they had been affected by the substance; if not the cause of their behavior, it was at least a contributing factor. For example, an admitter who estimated his consumption to have been eight beers and four "hits of acid" reported:

> Straight, I don't have the guts to rape. I could fight a man but not that. To say, "I'm going to do it to a woman," knowing it will scare and hurt her, takes guts or you have to be sick.

Another admitter believed that his alcohol and drug use,

> . . . brought out what was already there but in such intensity it was uncontrollable. Feelings of being dominant, powerful, using someone for my own gratification, all rose to the surface.

In contrast, deniers' justifications required that they not be substantially impaired. To say that they had been drunk or high would cast doubt on their ability to control themself or to remember events as they actually happened. Consistent with this, when we asked if the alcohol and/or drugs had had an effect on their behavior, 69 percent (n = 27) of admitters, but only 40 percent (n = 10) of deniers, said they had been affected.

TABLE 2 *Rapists' Accounts of Own and Victims' Alcohol and/or Drug (A/D) Use and Effect*

	Admitters n=39 %	Deniers n=25 %
Neither Self nor Victim Used A/D	23	16
Self Used A/D	77	72
Of Self Used, no Victim Use	51	12
Self Affected by A/D	69	40
Of Self Affected, no Victim Use or Affect	54	24
Self A/D Users who were Affected	90	56
Victim Used A/D	26	72
Of Victim Used, no Self Use	0	0
Victim Affected by A/D	15	56
Of Victim Affected, no Self Use or Affect	0	40
Victim A/D Users who were Affected	60	78
Both Self and Victim Used and Affected by A/D	15	16

Even more interesting were references to the victim's alcohol and/or drug use. Since admitters had already relieved themselves of responsibility through claims of being drunk or high, they had nothing to gain from the assertion that the victim had used or been affected by alcohol and/or drugs. On the other hand, it was very much in the interest of deniers to declare that their victim had been intoxicated or high: that fact lessened her credibility and made her more responsible for the act. Reflecting these observations, 72 percent (n = 18) of deniers and 26 percent (n = 10) of admitters maintained that alcohol or drugs had been consumed by the victim. Further, while 56 percent (n = 14) of deniers declared she had been affected by this use, only 15 percent (n = 6) of admitters made a similar claim. Typically, deniers argued that the alcohol and drugs had sexually aroused their victim or rendered her out of control. For example, one denier insisted that his victim had become hysterical from drugs, not from being raped, and it was because of the drugs that she had reported him to the police. In addition, 40 percent (n = 10) of deniers argued that while the victim had been drunk or high, they themselves either hadn't ingested or weren't affected by alcohol and/or drugs. None of the admitters made this claim. In fact, in all of the 15 percent (n = 6) of cases where an admitter said the victim was drunk or high, he also admitted to being similarly affected.

These data strongly suggest that whatever role alcohol and drugs play in sexual and other types of violent crime, rapists have learned the advantage to be gained from using alcohol and drugs as an account. Our sample were aware that their victim would be discredited and their own behavior excused or justified by referring to alcohol and/or drugs.

2) Emotional Problems

Admitters frequently attributed their acts to emotional problems. Forty percent (n = 19) of admitters said they believed an emotional problem had been at the root of their rape behavior, and 33 percent (n = 15) specifically related the problem to an unhappy, unstable childhood or a marital-domestic situation. Still others claimed to have been in a general state of unease. For example, one admitter said that at the time of the rape he had been depressed, feeling he couldn't do anything right, and that something had been missing from his life. But he also added, "being a rapist is not part of my personality." Even admitters who could locate no source for an emotional problem evoked the popular image of rapists as the product of disordered personalities to argue they also must have problems:

> The fact that I'm a rapist makes me different. Rapists aren't all there. They have problems. It was wrong so there must be a reason why I did it. I must have a problem.

Our data do indicate that a precipitating event, involving an upsetting problem of everyday living, appeared in the accounts of 80 percent (n = 38) of admitters and 25 percent (n = 8) of deniers. Of those experiencing a precipitating event, including deniers, 76 percent (n = 35) involved a wife or girlfriend. Over and over, these men described themselves as having been in a rage because of an incident involving a woman with whom they believed they were in love.

Frequently, the upsetting event was related to a rigid and unrealistic double standard for sexual conduct and virtue which they applied to "their" woman but which they didn't expect from men, didn't apply to themselves, and, obviously, didn't honor in other women. To discover that the "pedestal" didn't apply to their wife or girlfriend sent them into a fury. One especially articulate and typical admitter described his feeling as follows. After serving a short prison term for auto theft, he married his "childhood sweetheart" and secured a well-paying job. Between his job and the volunteer work he was doing with an ex-offender group, he was spending long hours away from home, a situation that had bothered his wife. In response to her request, he gave up his volunteer work, though it was clearly meaningful to him. Then, one day, he discovered his wife with her former boyfriend "and my life fell apart." During the next several days, he said his anger had made him withdraw into himself and, after three days of drinking in a motel room, he abducted and raped a stranger. He stated:

> My parents have been married for many years and I had high expectations about marriage. I put my wife on a pedestal. When I walked in on her, I felt like my life had been destroyed, it was such a shock. I was bitter and angry about the fact that I hadn't done anything to my wife for cheating. I didn't want to hurt her [victim], only to scare and degrade her.

It is clear that many admitters, and a minority of deniers, were under stress at the time of their rapes. However, their problems were ordinary—the types of upsetting events that everyone experiences at some point in life. The overwhelming majority of the men were not clinically defined as mentally ill in court-ordered psychiatric examinations prior to their trials. Indeed, our sample is consistent with Abel et al. (1980) who found fewer than 5 percent of rapists were psychotic at the time of their offense.

As with alcohol and drug intoxication, a claim of emotional problems works differently depending upon whether the behavior in question is being justified or excused. It would have been counter-productive for deniers to have claimed to have had emotional problems at the time of the rape. Admitters used psychological explanations to portray themselves as having been temporarily "sick" at the time of the rape. Sick people are usually blamed for neither the cause of their illness nor for acts committed while in that state of diminished capacity. Thus, adopting the sick role removed responsibility by excusing the behavior as having been beyond the ability of the individual to control. Since the rapists were not "themselves," the rape was idiosyncratic rather than typical behavior. Admitters asserted a non-deviant identity despite their self-proclaimed disgust with what they had done. Although admitters were willing to assume the sick role, they did not view their problem as a chronic condition, nor did they believe themselves to be insane or permanently impaired. Said one admitter, who believed that he needed psychological counseling: "I have a mental disorder, but I'm not crazy." Instead, admitters viewed their "problem" as mild, transient, and curable. Indeed, part of the appeal of this excuse was that not only did it relieve responsibility, but, as with alcohol and drug addiction, it allowed the rapist to "recover." Thus, at the time of their interviews, only 31 percent (n

= 14) of admitters indicated that "being a rapist" was part of their self-concept. Twenty-eight percent (n = 13) of admitters stated they had never thought of themselves as rapists, 8 percent (n = 4) said they were unsure, and 33 percent (n = 16) asserted they had been a rapist at one time but now were recovered. A multiple "exrapist," who believed his "problem" was due to "something buried in my subconscious" that was triggered when his girlfriend broke up with him, expressed a typical opinion:

> I was a rapist, but not now. I've grown up, had to live with it. I've hit the bottom of the well and it can't get worse. I feel born again to deal with my problems.

3) Nice Guy Image

Admitters attempted to further neutralize their crime and negotiate a non-rapist identity by painting an image of themselves as a "nice guy." Admitters projected the image of someone who had made a serious mistake but, in every other respect, was a decent person. Fifty-seven percent (n = 27) expressed regret and sorrow for their victim indicating that they wished there were a way to apologize for or amend their behavior. For example, a participant in a rape-murder, who insisted his partner did the murder, confided, "I wish there was something I could do besides saying 'I'm sorry, I'm sorry.' I live with it 24 hours a day and, sometimes, I wake up crying in the middle of the night because of it."

Schlenker and Darby (1981) explain the significance of apologies beyond the obvious expression of regret. An apology allows a person to admit guilt while at the same time seeking a pardon by signalling that the event should not be considered a fair representation of what the person is really like. An apology separates the bad self from the good self, and promises more acceptable behavior in the future. When apologizing, an individual is attempting to say: "I have repented and should be forgiven," thus making it appear that no further rehabilitation is required.

The "rice guy" statements of the admitters reflected an attempt to communicate a message consistent with Schlenker's and Darby's analysis of apologies. It was an attempt to convey that rape was not a representation of their "true" self. For example,

> It's different from anything else I've ever done. I feel more guilt about this. It's not consistent with me. When I talk about it, it's like being assaulted myself. I don't know why I did it, but once I started, I got into it. Armed

robbery was a way of life for me, but not rape. I feel like I wasn't being myself.

Admitters also used "nice guy" statements to register their moral opposition to violence and harming women, even though, in some cases, they had seriously injured their victims. Such was the case of an admitter convicted of a gang rape:

> I'm against hurting women. She should have resisted. None of us were the type of person that would use force on a woman. I never positioned myself on a woman unless she showed an interest in me. They would play to me, not me to them. My weakness is to follow. I never would have stopped, let along pick her up without the others. I never would have let anyone beat her. I never bothered women who didn't want sex; never had a problem with sex or getting it. I loved her—like all women.

Finally, a number of admitters attempted to improve their self-image by demonstrating that, while they had raped, it could have been worse if they had not been a "nice guy." For example, one admitter professed to being especially gentle with his victim after she told him she had just had a baby. Others claimed to have given the victim money to get home or make a phone call, or to have made sure the victim's children were not in the room. A multiple rapist, whose pattern was to break in and attack sleeping victims in their homes, stated:

> I never beat any of my victims and I told them I wouldn't hurt them if they cooperated. I'm a professional thief. But I never robbed the women I raped because I felt so bad about what I had already done to them.

Even a young man, who raped his five victims at gun point and then stabbed them to death, attempted to improve his image by stating:

> Physically they enjoyed the sex [rape]. Once they got involved, it would be difficult to resist. I was always gentle and kind until I started to kill them. And the killing was always sudden, so they wouldn't know it was coming.

❧ Summary and Conclusions

Convicted rapists' accounts of their crimes include both excuses and justifications. Those who deny what they did was rape justify their actions; those who admit it was rape attempt to excuse it or themselves. This study does not address why some men admit while others deny, but future research might address this question. This paper does provide insight on how men who are sexually aggressive or violent construct reality, describing the different strategies of admitters and deniers.

Admitters expressed the belief that rape was morally reprehensible. But they explained themselves and their acts by appealing to forces beyond their control, forces which reduced their capacity to act rationally and thus compelled them to rape. Two types of excuses predominated: alcohol/drug intoxication and emotional problems. Admitters used these excuses to negotiate a moral identity for themselves by viewing rape as idiosyncratic rather than typical behavior. This allowed them to reconceptualize themselves as recovered or "exrapists," someone who had made a serious mistake which did not represent their "true" self.

In contrast, deniers' accounts indicate that these men raped because their value system provided no compelling reason not to do so. When sex is viewed as a male entitlement, rape is no longer seen as criminal. However, the deniers had been convicted of rape, and like the admitters, they attempted to negotiate an identity. Through justifications, they constructed a "controversial" rape and attempted to demonstrate how their behavior, even if not quite right, was appropriate in the situation. Their denials, drawn from common cultural rape stereotypes, took two forms, both of which ultimately denied the existence of a victim.

The first form of denial was buttressed by the cultural view of men as sexually masterful and women as coy but seductive. Injury was denied by portraying the victim as willing, even enthusiastic, or as politely resistant at first but eventually yielding to "relax and enjoy it." In these accounts, force appeared merely as a seductive technique. Rape was disclaimed: rather than harm the woman, the rapist had fulfilled her dreams. In the second form of denial, the victim was portrayed as the type of woman who "got what she deserved." Through attacks on the victim's sexual reputation and, to a lesser degree, her emotional state, deniers attempted to demonstrate that since the victim wasn't a "nice girl," they were not rapists. Consistent with both forms of denial was the self-interested use of alcohol and drugs as a justification. Thus, in contrast to admitters, who accentuated their own use as an excuse, deniers emphasized the victim's consumption in an effort to both discredit her and make her appear more responsible for the rape. It is important to remember that deniers did not invent these justifications. Rather, they reflect a belief system which has historically victimized women by promulgating the myth that women both enjoy and are responsible for their own rape.

While admitters and deniers present an essentially contrasting view of men who rape, there were some shared characteristics. Justifications particularly, but also excuses, are buttressed by the cultural view of women as sexual commodities, dehumanized and devoid of autonomy and dignity. In this sense, the sexual objectification of women must be understood as an important factor contributing to an environment that trivializes, neutralizes, and, perhaps, facilitates rape.

Finally, we must comment on the consequences of allowing one perspective to dominate thought on a social problem. Rape, like any complex continuum of behavior, has multiple causes and is influenced by a number of social factors. Yet, dominated by psychiatry and the medical model, the underlying assumption that rapists are "sick" has pervaded research. Although methodologically unsound, conclusions have been based almost exclusively on small clinical populations of rapists—that extreme group of rapists who seek counseling in prison and are the most likely to exhibit psychopathology. From this small, atypical group of men, psychiatric findings have been generalized to all men who rape. Our research, however, based on volunteers from the entire prison population, indicates that some rapists, like deniers, viewed and understood their behavior from a popular cultural perspective. This strongly suggests that cultural perspectives, and not an idiosyncratic illness, motivated their behavior. Indeed, we can argue that the psychiatric perspective has contributed to the vocabulary of motive that rapists use to excuse and justify their behavior (Scully and Marolla, 1984).

Efforts to arrive at a general explanation for rape have been retarded by the narrow focus of the medical model and the preoccupation with clinical populations. The continued reduction of such complex behavior to a singular cause hinders, rather than enhances, our understanding of rape.

Endnotes

[1] These numbers include pretest interviews. When the analysis involves either questions that were not asked in the pretest or that were changed, they are excluded and thus the number changes.

[2] There is, of course, the possibility that some of these men really were innocent of rape. However, while the U.S. criminal justice system is not without flaw, we assume that it is highly unlikely that this many men could have been unjustly convicted of rape, especially since rape is a crime with traditionally low conviction rates. Instead, for purposes of this research, we assume that these men were

guilty as charged and that their attempt to maintain an image of non-rapist springs from some psychologically or sociologically interpretable mechanism.

[3]Because of their outright denial, interviews with this group of rapists did not contain the data being analyzed here and, consequently, they are not included in this paper.

[4]It was sometimes difficult to determine the full extent of victim injury from the pre-sentence reports. Consequently, it is doubtful that this number accurately reflects the degree of injuries sustained by victims.

[5]It is worth noting that a number of deniers specifically mentioned the victim's alleged interest in oral sex. Since our interview questions about sexual history indicated that the rapists themselves found oral sex marginally acceptable, the frequent mention is probably another attempt to discredit the victim. However, since a tape recorder could not be used for the interviews and the importance of these claims didn't emerge until the data was being coded and analyzed, it is possible that it was mentioned even more frequently but not recorded.

[6]Research shows clearly that women do not enjoy rape. Holmstrom and Burgess (1978) asked 93 adult rape victims, "How did it feel sexually?" Not one said they enjoyed it. Further, the trauma of rape is so great that it disrupts sexual functioning (both frequency and satisfaction) for the overwhelming majority of victims, at least during the period immediately following the rape and, in fewer cases, for an extended period of time (Burgess and Holmstrom, 1979; Feldman-Summers et al., 1979). In addition, a number of studies have shown that rape victims experience adverse consequences prompting some to move, change jobs, or drop out of school (Burgess and Holmstrom, 1974; Kilpatrick et al., 1979; Ruch et al., 1980; Shore, 1979).

References

Abel Gene, Judith Becker, and Linda Skinner. 1980. "Aggressive behavior and sex." Psychiatric Clinics of North America 3(2):133–151.

Abrahamsen, David. 1960. The Psychology of Crime. New York: John Wiley.

Albin, Rochelle. 1977. "Psychological studies of rape." Signs 3(2):423–435.

Athens, Lonnie. 1977. "Violent crimes: A symbolic interactionist study." Symbolic Interaction l(1):56–71.

Burgess, Ann Wolbert, and Lynda Lytle Holmstrom. 1974. Rape: Victims of Crisis. Bowie: Robert J. Brady.

———. 1979. "Rape: Sexual disruption and recovery." American Journal of Orthopsychiatry 49(4):648–657.

Burt, Martha. 1980. "Cultural myths and supports for rape." Journal of Personality and Social Psychology 38(2):217–230.

Burt, Martha, and Rochelle Albin. 1981. "Rape myths, rape definitions, and probability of conviction." Journal of Applied Psychology 11(3):212–230.

Feldman-Summers, Shirley, Patricia E. Gordon, and Jeanette R. Meagher. 1979. "The impact of rape on sexual satisfaction." Journal of Abnormal Psychology 88(1):101–105.

Glueck, Sheldon. 1925. Mental Disorders and the Criminal Law. New York: Little Brown.

Groth, Nicholas A. 1979. Men Who Rape. New York: Plenum Press.

Hall, Peter M., and John P. Hewitt. 1970. "The quasi-theory of communication and the management of dissent." Social Problems 18(1):17–27.

Hewitt, John P., and Peter M. Hall. 1973. "Social problems, problematic situations, and quasi-theories." American Journal of Sociology 38(3):367–374.

Hewitt, John P., and Randall Stokes. 1975. "Disclaimers." American Sociological Review 40(1):1–11.

Hollander, Bernard. 1924. The Psychology of Misconduct, Vice, and Crime. New York: Macmillan.

Holmstrom, Lynda Lytle, and Ann Wolbert Burgess. 1978. "Sexual behavior of assailant and victim during rape." Paper presented at the annual meetings of the American Sociological Association, San Francisco, September 2–8.

Kilpatrick, Dean G., Lois Veronen, and Patricia A. Resnick. 1979. "The aftermath of rape. Recent empirical findings." American Journal of Orthopsychiatry 49(4):658–669.

Ladouceur, Patricia. 1983. "The relative impact of drugs and alcohol on serious felons." Paper presented at the annual meetings of the American Society of Criminology, Denver, November 9–12.

Luckenbill, David. 1977. "Criminal homicide as a situated transaction." Social Problems 25(2):176–187.

McCaghy, Charles. 1968. "Drinking and deviance disavowal: The case of child molesters." Social Problems 16(1):43–49.

Marolla, Joseph, and Diana Scully. 1979. "Rape and psychiatric vocabularies of motive." Pp. 301–318 in Edith S. Gomberg and Violet Franks (eds.), Gender and Disordered Behavior: Sex Differences in Psychopathology. New York: Brunner/Mazel.

Mills, C. Wright. 1940. "Situated actions and vocabularies of motive." American Sociological Review 5(6):904–913.

Nelson, Steve, and Menachem Amir. 1975. "The hitchhike victim of rape: A research report." Pp. 47–65 in Israel Drapkin and Emilio Viano (eds.), Victimology: A New Focus. Lexington, KY: Lexington Books.

Queen's Bench Foundation. 1976. Rape: Prevention and Resistance. San Francisco: Queen's Bench Foundation.

Ruch, Libby O., Susan Meyers Chandler, and Richard A. Harter. 1980. "Life change and rape impact." Journal of Health and Social Behavior 21(3):248–260.

Scott, Marvin, and Stanford Lyman. 1968. "Accounts." American Sociological Review 33(1):46–62.

Schlenker, Barry R., and Bruce W. Darby. 1981. "The use of apologies in social predicaments." Social Psychology Quarterly 44(3):271-278.

Scully, Diana, and Joseph Marolla. 1984. "Rape and psychiatric vocabularies of motive: Alternative perspectives." In Ann Wolbert Burgess (ed.), Handbook on Rape and Sexual Assault. New York: Garland Publishing. Forthcoming.

Shore, Barbara K. 1979. An Examination of Critical Process and Outcome Factors in Rape." Rockville, MD: National Institute of Mental Health.

Stokes, Randall, and John P. Hewitt. 1976. "Aligning actions." American Sociological Review 41(5):837–849.

Sykes, Gresham M., and David Matza. 1957. "Techniques of neutralization." American Sociological Review 22(6):664–670.

Williams, Joyce. 1979. "Sex role stereotypes, women's liberation, and rape: A cross-cultural analysis of attitude." Sociological Symposium 25 (Winter):61–97.

☺ ☺ ☺

Questions

1. What are the distinguishing differences between "admitters" and "deniers"? Are there any similarities between these two groups? If so, what are they?

2. Define *justification*. Define *excuse*. How are the five justifications and three excuses discussed in this article similar? How are they dissimilar?

3. To what degree is there variation in the use of justifications and excuses by admitters and deniers? In other words, do admitters primarily use justifications or excuses for their behavior? What about deniers?

4. To what degree do you think rapists learn justifications through every-day socialization avenues (for example, family, peers, school, media, etc.)? To what degree might rapists learn justifications and excuses while in prison?

5. The authors conclude that their results somewhat refute the "medical explanation" of rape. They base this conclusion on rapists' ability to view and explain their behavior from a popular-culture perspective. Does this conclusion necessarily refute the "sick" or biological view of rape? Might rapists' *behavior* be psychopathological but the *explanations* for their behavior are framed in social terms? Explain your views on this possibility.

Rape by Acquiescence: The Ways in Which Women "Give in" to Unwanted Sex With Their Husbands

KATHLEEN C. BASILE

Sometimes rape is prominent with local and national media; at other times, it is not. When it is part of the "story of the day," very specific forms of rape are the focus, such as aggravated rape (e.g., physical force, use of weapons, assault). In the past decade or so, the focus has shifted from aggravated rape to date rape. There has also been a corresponding shift toward stranger rape: Stranger and aggravated rape tend to go hand-in-hand. But what about spousal rape? Can a man have sex with his wife without her consent (i.e., the "marriage contract" philosophy)? Can he forcibly make his wife have sex? Can he beat her psychologically into giving in and agreeing to have sex? If the man thinks that he has a "right" to have sex with his partner, how does he rationalize his actions? As you can see, there is an almost limitless supply of questions regarding spousal rape. In this selection, you will see how women are reluctant to call particular behavior "rape" and how their definition of the situation relies quite heavily on social context.

$\mathcal{T}$he commonly shared societal perception of rape is that it involves some kind of physical force. A woman walking through a deserted parking lot as a strange man grabs her by the throat, drags her down to the ground and rips her clothes off, or some variation of this, is the typical image that comes to mind (Hall, 1995). This image is what Estrich (1987) calls "aggravated rape." This type of rape has been defined as "one with extrinsic violence (guns, knives, or beatings) or multiple assailants or no prior relationship between the victim and the defendant" (Estrich, 1987, p. 4). The critical component of this societal image is the stranger status of the perpetrator.

Another context of rape that has dominated the rape literature in recent years is acquaintance or date rape. Research has raised awareness about the prevalence of rape by a nonstranger or someone known to the woman, and perhaps someone with whom she has previously been intimate (Koss & Cook, 1993; Warshaw, 1988).

Adding a new layer of ambiguity to the traditional idea of rape, this context, in a sense, bridges a conceptual gap between stranger rape and wife rape.

Perhaps the most intimate of contexts, rape by a husband against his wife, is even harder for many to comprehend. This is due in part to centuries-old legal ideas that excluded wives in definitions of rape. It is also due to cultural ideas about marriage that still prevail, such as the beliefs that a woman's consent to sex is assumed by virtue of a marriage license and that wives are obligated to sexually service their husbands. These societal beliefs make the idea of wife rape virtually inconceivable to many.

The recognition of wife rape as a social problem was a result of the women's movement of the 1970s (Brownmiller, 1975). At this time, feminist scholars were exploring the extent of the problem, rape crisis centers arose, and rape laws were beginning to be questioned (Brownmiller, 1975; Millett, 1970). The groundbreaking scholarship of Finkelhor and Yllo (1985) and Russell (1990) has shown that rape in marriage does in fact occur and is a critical problem in need of attention. Indeed, the important research about wife rape that continues to accumulate in the 1990s (See Bergen, 1996; Monson, Byrd, & Langhinrichsen-Rohling, 1996) illustrates that the problem of wife rape is still in need of attention. The continued push to spread awareness of the prevalence of wife rape and make legal strides against this crime, evidenced by the existence of organizations such as the National Clearinghouse on Marital and Date Rape, further confirms that wife rape is an important issue for legislators and others to work toward ending. It has been a long and tedious task to get to where we are today legally with regard to marital rape laws. Since the 1970s, all states in the United States have made changes in their laws in an effort to recognize wife rape by making it a crime in some or all sex crime statutes. However, the majority of states still have some exemptions for prosecuting husbands for rape. For example, some states have spousal exemptions in cases where the husband does not have to use force because his wife is vulnerable (i.e., physically or mentally impaired) and legally unable to give consent (Laura X, this issue).

Given the recent changes in the legal system with regard to this problem and the scholarly research that has accumulated since the 1970s, it seems safe to conclude that we as a society have taken steps to end unwanted sex that is physically forced on wives and girlfriends. The question that remains, though, is what are we doing to bring an end to coercive sex among intimates that is unwanted yet does not involve any physical force and sometimes does not involve threats or even discussion between partners? If this sex is identified by women as "unwanted," it should be of interest to scholars as well as those in the legal community to understand the contexts under which these experiences occur and how they relate to wife rape as it has been commonly defined. The issue is confounded, however, when examining unwanted sex among intimates when physical force is not involved, particularly when it occurs as a result of acquiescence on the part of the woman. These situations could occur because of the woman's perceived responsibilities as a spouse (i.e., the "wifely duty"), or could be due to threats of force and/or the woman's fear of force, among other things. How do we comprehend these more subtle forms of unwanted sex, particularly in the context of marriage, which is defined by ancient ideas of duty and obligation? More specifically, how does the idea of acquiescence fit into an understanding of sexual coercion in marriage? What are the different ways in which women "give in" to undesired sex with their partners? Furthermore, how do women make sense of their own reactions to the unwanted sex and other experiences within the relationships?

This article examines the ways in which women acquiesce to unwanted sex in marriage through in-depth analyses of 41 interviews with women who have experienced some form of unwanted sex in a marital or long-term intimate relationship. Various types of acquiescence are delineated and the contexts of these women's relationships within which these experiences occur are discussed. In addition, I examine the likelihood of women who use a given acquiescence type to believe that their experiences constitute rape.

❧ Review of the Literature

Despite popular myths about rape, namely, that the perpetrator is primarily unknown to the victim and that wife rape is essentially impossible, physically forced sex by an intimate partner is recognized by some as rape (Hall, 1995; Ward, 1995). For instance, 72% of Finkelhor and Yllo's (1985) sample of women who survived sexual assaults by their husbands agreed that their experiences qualified as rape. More recently, Bergen (1996) found that one third of the women in her sample initially defined their experiences with their partners as rape, and others redefined their experiences as rape as their relationships progressed. Even the average citizen now acknowledges that wife rape is prevalent and chronic. A recent national poll found that 76% of the general public believes husbands use force to make their wives have sex, and 80% believe it occurs often or somewhat often (Basile, 1998).

It is harder to assign a name to experiences of unwanted sex where there is no physical force and no lack of consent. Begging, bothering, pressuring, or manipulating in some way the actions of your partner all fall into the subtle realm of coercion without being clear-cut enough to qualify as rape. Reminiscent of Betty Freidan's (1963) "problem that has no name," which typified the frustration of housewives in the 1950s, married women have for centuries been subjected to coercive sexual activity but have been unable to name it. It is clearly not rape in the eyes of popular culture, the legal system, or most wives who experience it, for the two critical components of rape, force and consent, are not at issue. The unwanted sex that occurs in these relationships happens as a result of the wife's acquiescence, and it is often never known to anyone, even her husband, that the sex was undesired. These kinds of sexual relations sit in the gray area that most women define as the inconveniences of being married.

These kinds of coercive sexual acts are illuminated by the work of Finkelhor and Yllo (1985). They identified four types of coercion: (a) social, (b) interpersonal, (c) threatened physical, and (d) physical. Social coercion involves the social and cultural expectations that go along with being a wife. For instance, a woman might feel obliged to be dutiful and have sex with her husband. Social coercion must be viewed within the framework of the institutions that perpetuate it: the legal system, religion, and the institution of marriage itself. Rules about how to be a good wife are learned by women early on through socialization. Interpersonal coercion, according to these authors, is sex that results from threatening behavior on the part of the husband. Interpersonal coercion is not violent but instead entails threats of things such as cheating, withholding money or other resources, or general anger or unkindness if sex is not given by the wife.

Finkelhor and Yllo's (1985) third and fourth types of coercion are most closely linked to what is commonly recognized as rape. Threatened physical coercion is that which specifically implies the use of physical force if sex is not performed. Physical coercion, as its name suggests, is the use of physical force (punching, holding down) to have sex. Finkelhor and Yllo argued that all four types of coercion would constitute forced sex, but only the last two types (threatened physical and physical coercion) could be considered rape.

Finkelhor and Yllo's (1985) conceptualizations of sexual coercion, particularly social and interpersonal coercion, will be used in this article as a springboard from which to better understand the gray arena of coercion that leads many women to give in to sex without threats or force. For the purpose of this study, rape is defined as any sexual contact (vaginal, anal, or oral penetration) without consent through force or threat of force (Koss, Gidycz, & Wisniewski, 1987). As the issue of rape in marriage is primarily explained by men's control of power and resources (Finkelhor & Yllo, 1985), the focus here is exclusively on wife rape, or those incidents of rape perpetrated by men (husbands or intimate partners) on women (wives or girlfriends). Rape by acquiescence is defined as any unwanted sexual contact that a woman gives in to with a husband or partner. This definition is similar to Finkelhor and Yllo's (1985) social and interpersonal types of sexual coercion. It is distinct from rape in that it does not usually involve physical force on the husband's part, or lack of consent and/or struggle on the part of the wife. The types of acquiescence described in a later section of this article fit Finkelhor and Yllo's delineation of how women are "coerced, tricked, pressured, and bullied into having sex" (p. 86). Their ideas will be elaborated on in an effort to better understand these more subtle forms of forced sex in marriage.

❧ Theoretical Perspective

This research is guided by the feminist and social constructionist perspectives. A feminist theoretical perspective emphasizes power differentials between women and men that transcend all forms of social interaction between the sexes. As a woman-centered perspective, feminist theory conceptualizes society as patriarchal, wherein women are oppressed and subordinated socially, economically, and psychologically (Ward, 1995). Feminist scholars recognize the power and control of men over women that has allowed society to historically consider women as property and women's sexuality as a commodity for the use and enjoyment of men (Millett, 1970).

Feminists explain wife rape as stemming from an imbalance of power and resources between men and women in general, and husbands and wives specifically (Yllo, 1993). This is the result of a patriarchal society and is perpetuated in part by the gendered socialization of boys and girls (Millett, 1970). Applying a sex-role socialization perspective, boys learn early in their lives that they are valued if they are aggressive and dominant, whereas girls learn to be valued through passivity and submissiveness. Sexual attitudes, behavior, and expectations are also learned, and this dichotomy of male/female behavior is reproduced in the media, with books, movies, and television programs that romantically depict these scripted relationships between the sexes. This socialization crosscuts all forms of sexual aggression. This state of affairs has been described as the "rape culture" that Herman (1984) sees in this way: Our society "fosters and encourages rape by teaching males and females that it is natural and normal for sexual relations to involve aggressive behavior on the part of males" (p. 34).

The feminist perspective serves as backdrop in which we can understand the ways in which women "construct" their social worlds at a micro level. Using a social constructionist perspective, all reality is socially constructed, including our social roles and identities (Blumer, 1969). This perspective helps to identify the ways that women define, negotiate, and renegotiate their roles as wives within the larger patriarchal society. As elucidated in the work of Bergen (1996), the social constructionist approach in useful in understanding how wives make sense of their experiences with unwanted sex within the context of the marital identity.

◉ Method

Sample

This article is based on the results of semistructured, in-depth telephone interviews with 41 women previously involved in a national telephone poll of 1,108 randomly selected citizens. The national poll was conducted in the spring of 1997. The follow-up, in-depth interviews were conducted from June through October of 1997.

The women in this sample were fairly diverse with regard to social background in general. However, there was not as much racial diversity among these participants; the majority of the women were White. The participants were 71% White (n = 29), 20% multiracial (n = 8), 5% Hispanic (n = 2), 2% African American (n = 1), and 2% Native American (n = 1).[1] The ages of the women ranged from 21 to 74, and the average age was 43. There were 5 women in their 20s, 12 women in their 30s, 15 women in their 40s, 4 women in their 50s, 3 women in their 60s, and 2 women in their 70s at the time of the interviews. Of the women sampled, 9% had some graduate school or a graduate degree; 20% of the women were college graduates, but most of the women (39%) had some college credits. Twenty-two percent of the women had high school diplomas. The remainder of the sample (10%) had not graduated from high school. Using church attendance as an indicator of religiosity, 44% of the women said that they attend church less than a few times a year. However, 10 women (24%) said they attend church once a week.

Regarding residence, the largest number of women lived in the South (32% of the sample). Twenty-nine percent of the women lived in the Midwest, 27% resided in the West, and 12% lived in the Northeast. Although there are women in the sample representing all four regions of the country, this does not translate into a representative sample of the United States. Because more than half of the sample of women who had answered "yes" to unwanted sex and agreed to be called back were not interviewed, this sample is not generalizable. The benefit of this sample is that it can be used for exploratory and descriptive analyses of women's experiences as well as theory-building with regard to unwanted sex in marriage.

Procedure

Participants in this study were identified from a national telephone poll conducted in the spring of 1997. To qualify for an interview, women were asked whether they had experienced unwanted sex with a husband or intimate partner. Women who answered yes were asked if they could be called back for a longer telephone interview. Of the 602 women polled, 204 or 34% had experienced unwanted sex, and 96 of those women agreed to be called back for a longer interview. Forty-one interviews were successfully completed. The remaining 55 women did not complete interviews due to disconnected numbers, their inability to be reached after five or more attempts, and subsequent refusals to participate.

All interviews were conducted by the author, in line with a feminist technique of women-to-women talk (Spender, 1980), which has been found to be important in maintaining levels of comfort, trust, and a sense of shared experience. Interviews lasted from 20 minutes (only one interview) to 80 minutes. The average length of an interview was 45 minutes. All telephone interviews were transcribed verbatim into a computer with a word-processing program.

/𝘔easures

Women who answered affirmatively to having had unwanted sex were also questioned about different sexual coercion scenarios to determine if they had ever experienced unwanted sex under one or more of the seven circumstances. These scenarios were designed to be of increasing severity. The initial question ascertaining the occurrence of unwanted sex and the seven scenarios are listed in Appendix A. The first four scenarios are identified as less severe types of coercion, whereas the last three scenarios are considered to be severe forms of coercion.[2] Women were also asked about the frequency of unwanted sex. In addition, women who responded "no" to a scenario were asked if it had ever happened with a past partner.

Participants were asked to give detailed descriptions of the incident(s) of unwanted sex in their marriages or intimate relationships, including when, where, and the circumstances under which it happened. They were asked why they thought the incident(s) happened and how they felt while the unwanted sex was occurring (i.e., what emotions they were feeling at the time). They were asked the circumstances under which they chose to stay with or separate from their spouses or partners. Finally, similar to Finkelhor and Yllo's (1985) and Bergen's (1996) research, women were asked if they believe that they were raped. This was asked to see which of the women who have experienced unwanted sex at varying degrees of severity are willing to identify their experiences as rape. Given the harsh stigma associated with that word in our society, and the ambiguity related to marital relationships and rape, it is helpful to see which women use the term *rape* in describing their experiences.

/𝘈nalysis

A loosely defined grounded theory methodology with a feminist methodological approach was used to uncover the major themes in the interviews (Glaser & Strauss, 1967). A grounded theoretical approach is primarily inductive as it helps in discovering new theories "grounded" in the data through a method of line-by-line analysis. The feminist influence was introduced in the analyses through use of a "wide-angle lens" to understand the relationships discussed by the women (Yllo, 1993). In this way, I stayed mindful of the ways in which the gendered imbalance of power and resources in marriages and relationships could have affected women's choices and abilities to avoid unwanted sex, even if these gender differences were not explicitly considered by the women. In essence, use of a feminist perspective allowed me to highlight the interaction between gender and power while giving voice to the women who have survived the experiences. A feminist approach coupled with the use of the grounded theory method is commonly used with qualitative data analysis and, in this research, has proven useful in understanding these women's experiences with unwanted sex in their marriages (Reinharz, 1992).

◎ Findings and Discussion

There were 26 women (63%) who discussed unwanted sex with a past husband or partner and 13 women (32%) who described unwanted sex in their current relationships. The remaining 2 women had experiences with unwanted sex both in their current relationships as well as with previous partners. Most of the women (76%, or 31 women) were married at the time the unwanted sex occurred, and 7% (3 women) were cohabitating at the time the undesired sex took place. The remaining 7 women were involved in long-term relationships but did not live with their partners at the time that they had the unwanted sex. The length of the relationships ranged from several months to more than 50 years.

The women's experiences with unwanted sex were varied. Approximately half of the sample described severe experiences involving verbal bullying, physical force, and/or threats of force (21 women), and most of the rest of the women described less severe situations, where physical force and threats were not involved (17 women). The remaining 3 women could not be categorized as having suffered from either severe or minor coercion, as they experienced a combination of both or one type in the present and the other type in the past. Those women whose experiences were severe tended to have suffered the full gamut of minor as well as severe forms of sexual coercion. Of the 21 women who described severe coercion, 19 of them were describing past relationships.

Types of Acquiescence

By virtue of being in the sample, all of the women admitted to having unwanted sex. The issue at hand is the way in which women become involved in the undesired sex act. Although the contexts in which they faced the unwanted sex varied, results show that their reactions were often similar; more than half of the women (24 women, or 59%) admitted to having given in to sex with their partners once or more during their relationships. In other words, the women had sex with their husbands or partners often without any force by the partner and sometimes without any discussion of their disinterest. For a couple of the women (7%), all the acts of unwanted sex were experienced after they acquiesced, meaning that these women never initially wanted the sex, but instead, they always gave in to it. Findings reveal varying degrees of undesirability of the sex, making acquiescence to it easier to accept for those women who did not find it as extremely undesirable but rather as more of an inconvenience at the time it occurred. Through the course of the analyses, five types of acquiescence emerged. In this section, the types of acquiescence used by the women are described and examples of each are given in the words of the participants.

Unwanted Turns to Wanted

This type of acquiescence involves occasions when the women did not really feel up to sex initially but were able to enjoy it after a few minutes. It is perhaps the least severe way in which women gave in to undesired sex. These instances were usually the result of a romantic situation, where intimate kissing or a backrub preceded the sex act. Take, for example, the experience of Rita, a 27-Year-old who describes sex that was initially unwanted with her current husband:[3]

> Oh, let's see, just, you know, sometimes in the middle of the day or something and that's just not my time to have sex and they feel like it, and I guess kind of put you on a guilt trip if you don't want to, use things like, "you never want to when I do" or "you're always too tired," just stupid things, and so then you'll usually give in when initially you didn't feel like it and then afterwards, I was kind of glad that I did but initially I didn't feel like it.

Often the women ended up talking themselves into the sex, based on a feeling that they would be doing their partners a favor by making them feel good. The following quote is from Heidi, age 41, who spoke of her present husband:

> A lot of times if I don't really want to have sex and he does, sometimes after we start having sex it's like, it's okay, you know? It's like, well, yeah, you know. Okay, I can get into this too.

This type of acquiescence was used by 10% of the women. It occurred almost exclusively in relationships that were current and in relationships that were happy and healthy from the woman's perspective.

It's My Duty

This type of acquiescence is based on the idea of a wifely obligation inherent in the marital contract. This notion is bolstered by religious beliefs that women's role is to service their husbands. This was the most prevalent form of acquiescence among this sample. It occurred in current marriages and relationships that were defined as happy and healthy by the women, as well as in those past and present relationships that were filled with severe levels of physical abuse and/or physically forced sex. This method of acquiescence epitomized the "inconveniences of married life" for these women, but it was seen as an inherent responsibility of a wife and was virtually unchallenged. Denise, for example, was a 27-year-old who spoke about being pregnant a few months prior to the interview and having sex with her current husband because she thought it was her duty: "I felt like, you know, to be the dutiful wife, you know, you feel like you need to ... I don't know ... you just, kind of need to please him when he wants to, in order to keep everything happy."

As expressed in the above quote, the women saw their "wifely duty" as going hand-in-hand with "keeping peace" in the house-hold. In this sense, their role as wife included being peacemaker, and sex was often the best route to peace. In addition, being a "dutiful wife" also gave many women the assurance that their husbands would not stray, which is suggested by Hillary, age 51, who spoke of her current marriage: "I think that it's your responsibility to, you know, to keep them satisfied so they don't look other places."

The notion of a "wifely duty" was often connected to religious beliefs and upbringing, as this quote by Rhonda, a 37-year-old divorced woman, illustrates:

> Well, I guess, you know, I think of [wifely duty] in the biblical sense and whatever, the man takes a wife to bear him children and that type of thing. I guess that was always the way I was raised. The way life had portrayed it for me. When you're married, that's what you do.

Of the 41 women who were interviewed for this study, 31(76%) of them said that they sometimes had sex in their relationship because of a perceived wifely duty. Of the women sampled, 34% (or 14 women) saw a perceived wifely duty as the main reason they had unwanted sex. Of these 14 women, 9 were referring to current relationships.

Easier Not to Argue

This method of acquiescence occurred when verbal or nonverbal behavior from a woman's partner became too much for her to stand and giving in to sex was the easiest way out of the situation. It was often connected to various forms of emotional manipulation, pressure, and, in some instances, control. Manipulation surfaced in the form of guilt trips, verbal abuse, withholding of attention or a general level of unkindness and ill will toward her if she withheld sex. In this way, the consequence of not having sex became worse than just giving in, doing it, and getting it over with. If she gave in, she did not have to hear him complain, pout, or, in some cases, become angry or unpleasant for extended periods of time as a form of punishment for her. There were differing degrees of severity to this category of acquiescence. For example, Rebecca, age 36, described her experiences with a former live-in boyfriend:

> I was sort of nudged and then pestered and, never like pinned down and forced but it was easier to just give in than to have to deal with this guilt tripping and nudging and pestering and poking and you know, all this kind of thing that would just go on and on and on and I would just want to go to sleep, or get out of this situation or whatever.

To Rebecca and many of the women, having sex was the quickest escape, and often the fastest way to get some sleep. Ingrid, married and 26 years old, shared this sentiment: "If we just have sex then I can go to sleep faster than trying to have this discussion and whatever first and then getting to go to sleep."

For some women, acquiescence because it was easier not to argue occurred in a context of complete emotional control, as this quote by Terri, a 32-year-old divorced woman, exemplifies:

> It [sex] was something that I didn't want to do, and it was something that I didn't feel I could not do. Because I knew, it was just like, easier to do it, than to put up with the attitude I was gonna get, or, you know, the way he was gonna act afterwards.

Terri spoke of an alcoholic ex-husband who commonly threatened her and emotionally manipulated her. In this way, putting up with sex was easier than dealing with the verbal abuse that would result if she did not give in. Having sex because it was easier not to argue occurred among 27% of the sample (11 women).

Don't Know What Might Happen If I Don't

In this case, unwanted sex occurred due to fear of some negative reaction from the husband. In these cases, husbands commonly threatened their wives or acted in ways that were threatening and fearful to the wife, all in an effort to gain her complete acquiescence. These relationships were not usually characterized by physical force, just enough verbal threats to create an environment defined by fear and filled with the tension of wondering what might happen if she did not give in. Ellen, age 53, described why she always eventually acquiesced to her ex-husband:

> Oh, there was one point that he took out a gun, he had a little pistol, and uh, scared me half to death. I was shaking all over and he was looking for it and I had hidden it. He was looking through all my drawers and threw out everything from, you know, my bras and panties and things were all over the place, and he was looking for his gun. And so, after that episode, I just didn't dare, you know. I would just go through with it [sex], there was no way I was going to say no.

In another relationship, Nicole, age 31, suggests how she feared his potential reaction if she withheld sex: "The thing is, I didn't really fight it, but I think if I would have, that it probably would have gotten worse, not violent you know, but a little bit rougher for me so I would just give in." Although this type of acquiescence was less common than the others, it did occur among 7% of this sample. It was often a coping strategy employed after years of verbal threats and emotional control that culminated in the woman's complete acquiescence. As it involved more severe forms of emotional coercion, such as threats and bullying by the husband, it was most common among women who were no longer with the partner they discussed.

Know What Will Happen If I Don't

This form of acquiescence occurred in an effort to avoid any more of the prior experiences that they had with physical force and abuse from the partner. Similar to the previous type, women learned not to fight it and to essentially do whatever their husband or partner wanted because the women were totally controlled by them. However, unlike the previous type, the women in this category had firsthand experiences of physical abuse in their relationships and had frequently been physically forced to have sex with their partners. Agatha, age 74, described her acquiescence to her ex-husband in this way: "I guess you could say it was consensual when you feel like you are going to have your head beat so you feel like, why not?" Although not all women suffering from severe experiences fit into this category, 20% (or eight women) did acquiesce because they knew what would happen if they did not.

Most of these women (six women) experienced what Finkelhor and Yllo (1985) called battering rape, where physically forced sex occurred in the context of a battering relationship. Holly, a 33-year-old divorced woman, described unwanted sex with her ex-husband in this way:

> When you're intimidated by someone and they want to have sex no matter what the reason or what the situation, you do it, other-wise, you get the hell beat out of you to be quite honest ... you just let him do it. It's not him actually holding you down and forcing you but it is being forced because you can't say no.

Physical force was also used by Holly's alcoholic ex-husband to have sex, and in those cases she did define it as rape. Ronnie, age 46, was willing to liken her acquiescence to her alcoholic, abusive ex-husband to rape: "Sex-wise, he never physically abused me. I didn't want sex. ... I mean, you can call it rape, because I didn't want it. But I wouldn't say no because I knew what would happen if I said no." As seen in the above quotes, this type of acquiescence usually occurred along with the presence of alcohol, as 37% of the physically abusive husbands (15 in total) were described by the women as alcoholics. In addition, 5 women (12%) described drug-addicted husbands.

The environment created by the relationships described here, where the women acquiesced out of fear of violence, was an environment where the women were constantly monitoring their own behavior, teaching themselves to behave in ways that would not result in a negative reaction from their husbands. As Holly puts it, she "learned the things not to do" in order not to "push his buttons." In this manner, the women in this category often ended up (a) losing part of their identities as they molded themselves to react to the abuse and (b) blaming themselves for the predicament in which they found themselves, which served to perpetuate the abuse. Ronnie speaks of losing her identity: "I was no longer a person or an entity. I was a robot." Tammy, a 61-year-old woman who described her relationship with her emotionally manipulative ex-husband, talked about her self-blame: "I always felt that it was something in me that caused this sort of thing to happen." Roseanne, age 45 and divorced, said: "I still loved him ... and I would just blame myself for all the mistakes." Beatrice, age 44, who was formerly involved in a long-term relationship with an abusive boyfriend, saw herself to blame not only for the instances of abuse but also for the relationship as a whole: "I felt like I asked to be in the relationship so I, you know, held up my end to, you know, the relationship I guess." In this case, "holding up her end of the relationship" meant living for 12 years with frequent physical violence by her ex-boyfriend, coupled with his severe drug addiction.

Although most of the women (15%) who acquiesced as a result of physical force and violence described how they were completely controlled by their partners, some women fought back some of the time, and there were even women who only acquiesced when retaliation proved fruitless. For example, Kelly, age 47, when asked if she always fought with her ex-husband, replied,

> Until the point where he'd say if you keep on fighting, I'm going to keep on hurting you. He hurt my neck ... throat, choked [me] or uh ... so I just ... If I knew I couldn't fight anymore, I just laid there. In my mind I'm thinking, "when is this gonna end?"

Fighting back at one point or another in the relationship was described by 27% of the women.

Calling it Rape

Which women were likely to identify their experiences as rape? Results of this study make it clear that most women define their experiences as rape only when there is the clear use of physical force and when they did not give consent. In the sample as a whole, 15 of the women (37%) conceded that they had been raped, whereas 23 women (56%) did not see themselves as rape victims due to their failure to say no, and 3 women (7%) were not sure. Although some of the women who described previous relationships disclosed that they did not recognize their situations as rape at the time that it occurred, they were able to redefine their pasts and call it rape. Two common threads connecting most of the women who identified their experiences as rape were that they were subjected to severe levels of physical violence in their relationships, and their experiences of unwelcome sex were chronic. Of the 15 women who did think that they were raped, all of them had severe experiences where force and/or threats were used by their partner. Of these 15 women, 10 experienced unwanted sex with their husband once or twice a week or more, and for many of these 15 participants (6 women), every sex act was an unwanted one, especially near the end of the relationship.

Some women viewed acquiescence as something that they could not avoid, given the history of their relationship or the perceived consequences of denying sex. The majority of women who did call it rape (13 out of 15) were referring to relationships that have long since dissolved. Given the politicalization of wife rape that has occurred in recent years due to cases such as Lorena Bobbitt's, which have made the reality of wife rape a public issue, perhaps more women are now willing to identify their experiences as rape (Wiehe & Richards, 1995). Some of the women were even willing to identify their "acquiescence" as rape, even if the recognition remained solely in their minds. For example, take Robin, age 31, who described incidents of sex that she would consider rape:

> There were a lot of times, I did say no, and there was a few that I didn't say anything because he was gonna do whatever he wanted to anyway whether I said no or whether I didn't. There was a lot of times, instead of raising an issue, I wouldn't say anything.

Nina, a 35-year-old woman, described sex with her ex-husband that she thought would qualify as rape:

> Well, in the last six months that I was with him, I didn't want to have sex with him at all, it's more or less, I was there because I had no choice but to be there because I was terrified of him. So I don't know how many times we had sex in the last six months because I don't remember. I didn't even want to be there and I was terrified to leave, and the last six months any time we had sex that's exactly what it was [rape], because I wanted nothing to do with him.

Although the above example was considered rape to Nina, it also qualifies as acquiescence because she knew what would happen if she did not; she described an absolute fear with no conceivable way out. Nina's ex-husband had a history of being physically violent, and most of the violence culminated in unwanted sex. In this relationship, she felt totally controlled and trapped. When faced with the physical violence, she would negotiate with herself whether she would give in to sex or resist it and get beaten and eventually raped, which she said was as frequent as once a week in the last 6 months of the relationship.

As stated earlier, more than half of the women in this sample (23) did not characterize their experiences as rape. This supports other studies that have consistently found that many women do not consider themselves raped when they experience unwanted sex with an intimate (Bergen 1996; Finkelhor & Yllo, 1985; Koss, 1993; Warshaw, 1988). Most women in the sample (56%) were not willing to call their experiences rape, but rather they considered them inconveniences that they gave in to, particularly if physical force was not involved. However, there were 5 women in the sample who described severe experiences that they did not call rape. Nicole, age 31, in negotiating in her own mind whether her experience with her ex-boyfriend was rape, said: "I didn't necessarily consent, but ... I kind of gave in, I think if I wouldn't have given in and maybe fought it more ... that it possibly could have turned into something that I would have called rape." Ellen, age 53, did not see her experience as rape: "I would have had to tell him no, right off the bat, right?"

If they do not define their experiences as rape, women who give in to unwanted sex with their husbands have no shared language with which to describe the incidents. It is as if the only available cultural labels are "rape" or "not rape," and this dichotomy leaves no room to acknowledge or label undesired sex of a less violent and physically coerced nature.

❧ Conclusion

The central theme connecting the five types of acquiescence elaborated on here is the idea that they involved unwanted sex, therefore some level of coercion had to exist. These five types can be viewed as occurring in different marital contexts. Unwanted turns to wanted, the most seemingly innocuous of all the types of acquiescence, tended to occur in what the women defined as happy, noncoercive partnerships, and resulted in, as more than one woman put it, "the headache suddenly going away." Acquiescence as a result of a perceived marital duty, analogous to what Finkelhor and Yllo (1985) called social coercion, can be seen as a product of a history of societal tradition that dictates proper behavior for women and perceived expectations of wives. Whether this type of acquiescence occurred in relatively happy or in severely abusive and unhappy relationships, all women shared the idea that sex was a responsibility of a wife. Inherent in both of these types of acquiescence is the societal notion that women should sexually service their partners.

The last three types, on the other hand, can be viewed as coping strategies used by the women. "Easier not to argue" occurred in a context of guilt, insecurity, and hostility wherein the clearest path to peace perceived by the women was acquiescence. Types four and five were seen as ways to avoid potential and real physical danger, respectively, while managing to survive the situation.

When negotiating and enduring unwanted sex with an intimate, the definition of rape becomes ambiguous when women's consent is given under societal conditions of dominance and inequality. This is due, in part, to the ways in which men are socialized to believe "no" sometimes means "yes" or "maybe" or at least "keep trying" (Searles & Berger, 1995). As MacKinnon (1983) points out, the difference between acquiescence and consent becomes unclear. The marital context makes this already ambiguous situation even more confused, as is evidenced in the words of many women in the sample who had a hard time making sense of their experiences. Time was the one variable that seemed to help these women define their situations. Indeed, the overwhelming majority of severe experiences were described by women who were no longer with the abusive partner but had previously been subjected to physical force. These women were often redefining the experiences as abuse, which was now possible because they were not still involved with the abuser and they were in a safer (both physically and emotionally) place to reconstruct what had happened. This is evidenced by the fact that many women said that they would call the experience rape at the time of the interview but would not have at the time of the relationship. Two women even admitted that they would never have agreed to be interviewed at the time of the relationship, suggesting that they have come a long way in redefining their experiences as negative. These findings are similar to Bergen's (1996), who found that women did not immediately construct the unwanted sex as rape but only did so as the relationship progressed or after they had received outside help.

This article is an effort to recognize the varying degrees of force subsumed under the rubric of acquiescence. The processes and consequences of giving in to unwanted sex with an intimate have not been given as much attention as other forms of forced sex that have traditionally been identified as rape. Increased recognition of these more subtle forms of coercion is not suggested in an effort to dilute what is understood to be rape, a concern of Finkelhor and Yllo's (1985) that is well taken. The force or threat of force to gain sexual pleasures is a vicious and extremely damaging form of sexual assault that should not be compared or equated to the less severe forms of sexual coercion elaborated on in acquiescence types one, two, and three. However, types four and five, although they involved acquiescence on the part of the women, should be considered rape in the traditional sense, as they included threats and/or physical force. Indeed, each of the five types of acquiescence discussed in this article is a form of sexual coercion that has important implications. It is useful to consider different paths to unwanted sexual contact on a continuum of severity. This help us acknowledge the more subtle processes that result in women having undesired sex, while at the same time understanding the similarities of these subtle forms of coercion to the more severe forms that we recognize as rape. If we can make connections between subtle and severe experiences, we might make some headway in understanding the processes by which mildly coercive relationships become more coercive with time. We can also bring attention to and recognize the damage inherent in coercive experiences that have long been accepted by women as part of the marriage contract. All of this is done in an effort to come closer to the ultimate goal of feminist scholarship and all those working to end all forms of partner violence—to make intimate relationships equal for both partners.

⊛ Appendix

Sexual Coercion Items in the Spring 1997 National Telephone Poll

Initial question to qualify for study:
Some women have had sex with a husband or intimate partner when they really did not want to, and others have never had this experience. Have you ever had sex with a husband or intimate partner when you really did not want to?

Sexual coercion scenarios:
Now I am going to present several circumstances. Please think of your current or most recent relationship in answering the following questions. Thinking of your current or most recent partner, have you ever had sex with that person when you really did not want to?

"Less severe" coercion:
1. When you thought your husband or partner expected sex from you in return for certain actions, like spending money on you for a gift or taking you out for a nice dinner

2. because you thought it was your duty to have sex with your husband or partner when he wants to have sex

3. after a romantic situation, like after a back rub or after intimately kissing

4. after your husband or partner begged and pleaded with you to have sex

"Severe" coercion:

5. after your husband or partner said things to bully or humiliate you into having sex

6. after your husband or partner threatened to hurt you if you did not have sex

7. after your husband or partner used physical force on you in order to have sex

Endnotes

The sample used in this study was identified through a national poll conducted by the Applied Research Center at Georgia State University.

[1]The fact that this sample contains only one African American woman is disheartening. It should be noted, however, that among those who admitted to ever having unwanted sex, only 12% (24 women) were African American. Of that sample, there were only 9% (9 African American women) who agreed to be called back for an interview. Every effort was made to contact those nine women, but only one African American woman was reached and interviewed. The fact that 20% of the sample self-identified as "multiracial" could mean that there are actually more women of African American origin in the sample, although this cannot be determined.

[2]Eighteen experts in the field of social science were consulted about the ordering of the seven coercion items. A total of nine people responded, and the most common ordering was used. The dichotomizing of the items as "less severe" and "severe" was decided by the author, based on the ordering.

[3]All names of women quoted in this article were changed to protect the identities of the participants.

References

Basile, K. C. (1998). *Wife rape: Attitudes and experiences.* Unpublished manuscript.

Bergen, R. K. (1996). *Wife rape: Understanding the response of survivors and service providers.* Thousand Oaks, CA: Sage.

Blumer, H. (1969). *Symbolic interaction: Perspective and method.* Englewood Cliffs, NJ: Prentice Hall.

Brownmiller, S. (1975). *Against our will: Men, women, and rape.* New York: Fawcett Columbine.

Estrich, S. (1987). *Real rape.* Cambridge, MA: Harvard University Press.

Finkelhor, D., & Yllo, K. (1985). *License to rape: Sexual abuse of wives.* New York: Free Press.

Friedan, B. (1963). *The feminine mystique.* New York: Norton.

Glaser, B., & Strauss, A. (1967). *The discovery of grounded theory: Strategies for qualitative research.* Chicago: Aldine.

Hall, R. (1995). *Rape in America: A reference handbook.* Santa Barbara, CA: ABC-CLIO.

Herman, D. (1984). The rape culture. In J. Freeman (Ed.), *Women: A feminist perspective* (pp. 20–34). Palo Alto, CA: Mayfield.

Koss, M. P. (1993). Detecting the scope of rape: A review of prevalence research methods. *Journal of Interpersonal Violence, 8*(2), 198–222.

Koss, M. P., & Cook, S. L. (1993). Facing the facts: Date and acquaintance rape are significant problems for women. In R. J. Gelles & D. R. Loseke (Eds.), *Current controversies on family violence* (pp. 104–119). Newbury Park, CA: Sage.

Koss, M. P., Gidycz, C. A., & Wisniewski, N. (1987). The scope of rape: Incidence and prevalence of sexual aggression and victimization in a national sample of higher education students. *Journal of Consulting and Clinical Psychology, 55*(2), 162–170.

MacKinnon, C. (1983). Feminism, Marxism, method, and the state: Toward feminist juris-prudence. *Signs, 8*(4), 635–658.

Millett, K. (1970). *Sexual politics.* New York: Ballantine.

Monson, C. M., Byrd, G. R., & Langhinrichsen-Rohling, J. (1996). To have and to hold: Perceptions of marital rape. *Journal of Interpersonal Violence, 11*(3), 410–424.

Reinharz, S. (1992). *Feminist methods in social research.* New York: Oxford University Press.

Russell, D. E .H. (1990). *Rape in marriage.* Bloomington: Indiana University Press.

Searles, P., & Berger, R. J. (Eds.). (1995). *Rape and society: Readings on the problem of sexual assault.* Boulder, CO: Westview.

Spender, D. (1980). *Man made language.* London: Routledge Kegan Paul.

Ward, C. A. (1995). *Attitudes toward rape: Feminist and social psychological perspectives.* London: Sage Ltd.

Warshaw, R. (1988). *I never called it rape: The Ms. report on recognizing, fighting, and surviving date and acquaintance rape.* New York: Harper & Row.

Wiehe, V. R., & Richards, A. L. (1995). *Intimate betrayal: Understanding and responding to the trauma of acquaintance rape.* Thousand Oaks, CA: Sage.

X, Laura. (1999). Accomplishing the impossible: An advocate's notes from the successful campaign to make marital and date rape a crime in all 50 U.S. states and other countries. *Violence Against Women, 5*(9), 1064–1081.

Yllo, K. A. (1993). Through a feminist lens: Gender, power, and violence. In R. J. Gelles & D. R. Loseke (Eds.), *Current controversies on family violence* (pp. 47–62). Newbury Park, CA: Sage.

Kathleen C. Basile, Ph.D., is a research associate at the Applied Research Center and a periodic instructor for the Department of Sociology at Georgia State University. Her major research interest is violence against women.

◉ ◉ ◉

Questions

1. What do you think of the author's generally broad definition of rape?

2. How does the respondent's definition of "rape" (i.e., ay sexual contact without consent through force or threat of force) vary by social context?

3. Explain each form of acquiescence and provide an example from a source other than class material that corresponds to each form of acquiescence.

4. Explain how using psychological/emotional tactics affect spousal rape.

5. Although the author says the findings are not generalizable, how *might* these findings apply to other forms of rape?

6. There are some potential shortcomings methodologically in this article.

    a. "Because more than half of the sample of women who answered 'yes' to unwanted sex and agreed to be called back were not interviewed, the sample is not generalizable."

    b. "… however, there was not as much racial diversity among the participants."

    How might these methodological weaknesses affect the findings?

Through a Sociological Lens: Social Structure and Family Violence

RICHARD J. GELLES

Do you know who is most likely to engage in family violence? Why would someone use violence against an intimate associate or family member? In this article, Richard Gelles reveals how age, sex, position in the social structure, race and ethnicity, and contemporary family structure all affect our behavior. To show the explanatory power of a sociological perspective on family violence, he contrasts sociological theories with psychological and feminist theories.

The core of the sociological perspective is the assumption that social structures affect people and their behavior. The major social structural influences on social behavior in general, and family violence in particular, are age, sex, position in the socioeconomic structure, and race and ethnicity. In addition, (the structure of social institutions also influences social behavior. In the case of family violence, the structure of the modern family as a social institution has a strong overarching influence on the occurrence of family violence.

☺ *Social Facts and Social Influences*

Age

Violence in intimate relationships follows the same general patterns with regard to age as does violence between nonintimates. The rates of violence

---

(both victimization and offending) are highest for those between the ages of 18 and 30 years (Gelles & Straus, 1988; Straus, Gelles, & Steinmetz, 1980; U.S. Department of Justice, 1991; Wolfner & Gelles, 1993). Family violence, with the exception of the victimization of the elderly, is a phenomenon of youth, thus explanations for family violence need to consider issues such as life-span development, stage in the family life cycle, and human development if explanatory models are to reflect accurately the relationship between age and violence.

Sex

Interpersonal violence outside of intimate relationships takes place primarily between male offenders and male victims. The data on sex and family violence are somewhat different and often controversial. Much of the research on child maltreatment indicates that mothers are as, or more, likely to maltreat their children as are fathers (Burgdorf, 1980; National Center on Child Abuse and Neglect, 1988; Straus et al., 1980; Wolfner & Gelles, 1993). The sex difference, however, is not as clear as it might appear. First, the social construction of child maltreatment, especially the process of designating a perpetrator in official reports of child maltreatment, leaves females and mothers vulnerable to being identified as abusers and neglecters even if they are not directly responsible for the harm their children experience. Mothers are nearly always cited as offenders in cases of child neglect, not because they are the ones who directly caused harm to their children, but because cultural and societal views hold mothers responsible for the welfare of their children. Similarly, mothers are sometimes cited as maltreaters in official reports of child sexual abuse even when the perpetrator was the male partner or some other male, because child protective workers often assume that mothers have the responsibility for protecting their children from sexual abuse.

The data on physical abuse also indicate that females are nearly as, or more, likely than males to assault and abuse their children physically. However, as Margolin (1992) explains, these data fail to consider the different levels of responsibility males and females have for child care. When the level of responsibility for child care is controlled—for instance, comparing abuse committed by male and female baby-sitters (Margolin, 1991) or comparing abuse by single parents (Gelles, 1989)—males are actually more likely to be physical abusers than are females.

344

The data on physical violence and abuse between spouses are even more controversial than the data on child abuse. . . . Some students of family violence, especially those who use a feminist perspective, . . . argue that females are vastly disproportional victims of adult intimate violence. Their point of view is supported by data on wife abuse derived from shelters and other helping agencies (see, for example, Dobash, Dobash, Wilson, & Daly, 1992). On the other hand, Murray Straus, among others, argues that there are far more women using violence toward men than the shelter data indicate. Although I cannot resolve this issue, . . . the data do suggest that males are the more likely offenders and females the more likely victims of family violence, consistent with a gender pattern of interpersonal violence found in other settings and groups.

Sex is also a factor in abuse of the elderly. Data indicate that women are the most likely victims of elder abuse. Data on offenders are somewhat more controversial. . . . Skinmetz's conceptualization of elder abuse supports the claim that middle-aged females who are under stress from their caretaking obligations are the most likely abusers of the elderly. Pillemer's . . . conceptualization that abuse is a result of the dependency of the offender is more neutral on which sex would be the most likely offender.

Position in the Social Structure

Wife abuse, child abuse, elder abuse, and other forms of family violence tend to occur in all social and economic groups. Violence and abuse can be found among truck drivers and physicians, laborers and lawyers, the employed and the unemployed, the rich and the poor. The fact that violence can be found in all types of homes leads some people to conclude that social factors, especially income and employment, are not relevant in explaining family violence. But although family violence does indeed cut across social and economic groups, it does not do so evenly. The risk of child abuse, wife abuse, and elder abuse is greater among those who are poor, who are unemployed, and who hold low-prestige jobs (Gelles & Straus, 1988; Pelton, 1978; Straus et al., 1980; Wolfner & Gelles, 1993). One of the mechanisms that explains why family violence is more likely to be found among those who are poor and unemployed or holding low-prestige jobs is social stress. The more stressful experiences individuals and families have to deal with, the greater the likelihood of the occurrence of some form of family violence

(Milner & Chilamkurti, 1991; Starr, 1988; Straus, 1980a, 1990; Straus et al., 1980).

Race and Ethnicity

The data on family violence and race and ethnicity are somewhat contradictory. If one looks at official report data on child abuse, blacks and other minority racial groups are vastly overrepresented among those reported for child maltreatment (see, for example, American Association for Protecting Children, 1988; Gil, 1970). On the other hand, two national surveys of recognized and reported child maltreatment found that blacks were not overrepresented among those recognized for child maltreatment (Burgdorf, 1980; National Center on Child Abuse and Neglect, 1988). Other studies have found that blacks have lower rates of child maltreatment than do whites (Billingsley, 1969). Survey data indicate that blacks are more likely to use violence and abusive violence toward their children (Hampton & Gelles, 1991; Straus et al., 1980). This higher rate is the result of blacks having lower incomes and higher rates of unemployment than whites (Cazenave & Straus, 1979).

Official report data and survey data both agree that the rate of violence toward women is higher among blacks than among whites (Goetting, 1989; Hampton, Gelles, & Harrop, 1989).

The Second National Family Violence Survey, conducted in 1985, included an oversample of Hispanic families. The rates of husband-to-wife violence and parent-to-child violence among Hispanic respondents were significantly higher than those among non-Hispanic whites (Straus & Smith, 1990). As with blacks, the higher rate of violence in Hispanic homes is largely a function of the strong links among family violence, low income, urbanization, and youthfulness. Hispanic families are likely to have lower incomes than are white non-Hispanic families, are more likely to live in urban areas, and are younger than non-Hispanic whites.

I should point out that some official records, particularly official reports of child abuse and data from criminal justice agencies on wife abuse, reflect both the reality of the greater risk of abuse and violence in these groups *and* the fact that abuse and violence in these groups are overreported to official agencies. Newberger, Reed, Daniel, Hyde, and Kotelchuck (1977) and Hampton and Newberger (1985) found that poor and minority children are more likely to be correctly *and incorrectly* reported for child abuse, whereas white and middle- and upper-class families are much less likely to be correctly and incorrectly reported for abuse. Similarly, wife abuse and elder abuse in lower-income and minority families is much more likely to come to the attention of the police and courts than is violence in more affluent homes.

❧ Structure of the Family as a Social Institution

The psychological perspective, because it looks for the causes of violence within the individual perpetrator, ignores the special and unique structure of the family as a social institution. The feminist perspective focuses only on the influence of gender and gender-structured relations on the institution of the family and the violence and abuse therein. The family, with the exception of the military in times of war and the police, is society's most violent social institution (Straus et al., 1980). The likelihood of being a victim of violence at the hands of a stranger or on the streets is measured in terms of risk per 100,000 people, but the risk of family violence is measured in terms of a rate per 100 individuals (Gelles & Straus, 1988). Thus a comprehensive perspective that explains family violence must consider the attributes of the family as a social institution that create such a high risk for violence.

In work published in 1979, Murray Straus and I identified the unique characteristics of the family as a social group that contribute to making the family a violence-prone institution (Gelles & Straus, 1979). Later, Straus, with his colleague Gerald Hotaling, noted the irony that these same characteristics we saw as making the family violence-prone also serve to make the family a warm, supportive, and intimate environment (Straus & Hotaling, 1980). Briefly, these factors are as follows:

1. *Time of risk:* The ratio of time spent interacting with family members far exceeds the ratio of time spent interacting with others, although the ratio varies depending on the stage in the family life cycle.

2. *Range of activities and interests:* Not only do family members spend a great deal of time with one another, the interaction ranges over a much wider spectrum of activities than does nonfamilial interaction.

3. *Intensity of involvement:* The quality of family interaction is also unique. The degree of commitment to family interaction is greater. A cutting remark made by a family member is likely to have a much larger impact than the same remark in another setting.

4. *Impinging activities:* Many interactions in the family are inherently conflict structured and have a "zero-sum" aspect. Whether a disagreement involves a decision about what television show to watch or what car to buy, there will be both winners and losers in family relations.

5. *Right to influence:* Belonging to a family carries with it the implicit right to influence the values, attitudes, and behaviors of other family members.

6. *Age and sex differences:* The family is unique in that it is made up of different ages and sexes. Thus there is the potential for battles between generations *and* between sexes.

7. *Ascribed roles:* In addition to the problem of age and sex differences is the fact that the family is perhaps the only social institution that assigns roles and responsibilities based on age and sex rather than interest or competence.

8. *Privacy:* The modern family is a private institution, insulated from the eyes, ears, and often rules of the wider society. Where privacy is high, the degree of social control will be low.

9. *Involuntary membership:* Families are exclusive organizations. Birth relationships are involuntary and cannot be terminated. There can be ex-wives and ex-husbands, but there are no ex-children or ex-parents. Being in a family involves personal, social, material, and legal commitment and entrapment. When conflict arises it is not easy to break off the conflict by fleeing the scene or resigning from the group.

10. *Stress:* Families are prone to stress. This is due in part to the theoretical notion that dyadic relationships are unstable (Simmel, 1950). Moreover, families are constantly undergoing changes and transitions. The birth of children, maturation of children, aging, retirement, and death are all changes recognized by family scholars. Moreover, stress felt

by one family member (such as unemployment, illness, bad grades at school) is transmitted to other family members.

11. *Extensive knowledge of social biographies:* The intimacy and emotional involvement of family relations reveals a full range of identities to members of a family. Strengths and vulnerabilities, likes and dislikes, loves and fears are all known to family members. Although this knowledge can help support a relationship, the information can also be used to attack intimates and can lead to conflict.

❧ Sociological Theories of Family Violence

Position in the social structure is clearly and strongly related to family violence. In order to illustrate how the sociological perspective applies and uses the empirical data on proximate correlates of family violence and the unique features of the family as a social institution, this section presents summaries of four primarily sociological theories of family violence: general systems theory, resource theory, exchange/social control theory, and subculture of violence theory.[1]

General Systems Theory

Murray Straus (1973) and Jean Giles-Sims (1983) developed and applied a social system approach to explain family violence. Here, violence is viewed as a system product rather than as the result of individual pathology. The family system operations can maintain, escalate, or reduce levels of violence in families. General systems theory describes the processes that characterize the use of violence in family interactions and explains how violence is managed and stabilized. Straus (1973) presents eight propositions to illustrate how general systems theory relates to family violence:

1. Violence between family members has many causes and roots. Normative structures, personality traits, frustrations, and conflicts are only some.

2. More family violence occurs than is reported.

3. Most family violence is either denied or ignored.

4. Stereotyped family violence imagery is learned in early childhood from parents, siblings, and other children.

5. The family violence stereotypes are continually reaffirmed for adults and children through ordinary social interactions and the mass media.

6. Violent acts by violent persons may generate positive feedback; that is, these acts may produce desired results.

7. Use of violence, when contrary to family norms, creates additional conflicts over ordinary violence.

8. Persons who are labeled violent may be encouraged to play out a violent role, either to live up to the expectations of others or to fulfill their own self-concepts of being violent or dangerous.

Giles-Sims (1983) elaborates Straus's basic model and identifies six temporal stages that lead to wife battering:

1. establishing the family system

2. the first incident of violence

3. stabilization of violence

4. the choice point

5. leaving the system

6. resolution or more of the same

Resource Theory

The resource theory of family violence assumes that all social systems (including the family) rest to some degree on force or the threat of force. The more resources—social, personal, and economic—a person can command, the more force he or she can muster. However, according to William Goode (1971), the more resources a person actually has, the less he or she will actually use force in an open manner. Thus a husband who wants to be the dominant person in the family but has little education, has a job low in prestige and income, and lacks interpersonal skills may choose to use violence to maintain the dominant position. In addition, family members (including children) may use violence to redress grievances when they have few alternative resources available.

Exchange/Social Control Theory

In earlier work I have elaborated on the basic propositions of an exchange theory of aggression and developed an exchange/social control model of family violence that proposes that wife abuse and child abuse are governed by the principle of costs and rewards (Gelles, 1983). Drawing from exchange theory, I have noted that violence and abuse are used when the rewards are higher than the costs. Drawing from social control theories of delinquency, I have proposed that the private nature of the family, the reluctance of social institutions and agencies to intervene—in spite of mandatory child abuse reporting laws—and the low risk of other interventions reduce the costs of abuse and violence. The cultural approval of violence as both expressive and, in the case of disciplining children, instrumental behavior raises the potential rewards for violence.

Subculture of Violence Theory

The subculture of violence theory is perhaps tile most fully developed and widely applied sociocultural explanation of violence (see Wolfgang & Ferracuti, 1967, 1982). This theory asserts that social values and norms provide meaning and direction to violent acts, and thus facilitate or bring about violence in situations specified by these norms and values. Subculture of violence theory explains why some sectors, or subcultures, of society or different societies are more violent than others, especially when they have cultural rules that legitimate or require violence.

◉ The Attractiveness of Psychological Explanations

The initial discussions of child abuse and wife abuse tended to overlook or downplay the relevance of social factors in explaining or helping to understand family violence. By and large, this was a consequence of the medical, or psychiatric, model that was applied by those who first discussed child abuse in the professional literature (see, for example, Kempe, Silverman, Steele, Droegemueller, & Silver, 1962; Steele & Pollack, 1968). As Barbara Nelson (1984) points out, the first people to identify a problem often shape how others will perceive it (p. 13).

The early writings on family violence discounted social factors as playing *any* causal role in the etiology of abuse. As Steele and Pollock (1968) put it "If all the people we studied were gathered together, they would not seem much different than a group of people picked by stopping the first several dozen people one would meet on a downtown street" (p. 92). They went on:

> Social, economic, and demographic factors . . . are somewhat irrelevant to the actual act of child abuse. Unquestionably, social and economic difficulties and disasters put added stress in people's lives and contribute to behavior which might otherwise remain dormant. But such factors must be considered incidental enhancers rather than necessary and sufficient causes. (p. 94)

For Steele and Pollock and other early students of child abuse, the explanation for abuse was that abusers suffered from significant psychopathology.

Leroy Schultz's (1960) examination of 4 cases of wife assault from a caseload of 14 spouse assaulters focused on mother-child dynamics as a means of explaining wife assault. Schultz noted that each assaulter was characterized by a domineering-rejecting mother relationship in which the child experienced primary rejection. The result was a passive-submissive individual who avoided conflict at all costs. Schultz noted that a uniformly poor mother-child relationship makes for a frustrated dependency in which the child's emotional needs are never met. He went on to explain that children who cannot permit aggressive impulses to break through during youth have difficulty as adults in entering into interpersonal relationships that do not duplicate their original dependency as children. These individuals seek to recreate dependent relationships with their spouses, but when their dependency needs are frustrated, the men tend to attack the objects of their frustration—their wives.

Current psychological explanations of child abuse, wife abuse, and family violence are considerably more sophisticated than the earlier notions of psychopathology or frustration-aggression arising out of disturbed patterns of mother-child relationships. Psychological theories of family violence also draw heavily on social learning as an explanation for child abuse, spouse abuse, elder abuse, and other forms of family violence (see

O'Leary, 1988 . . .). However, psychological explanations of violence continue to overlook and minimize the contributions of social and structural factors to the occurrence and persistence of violence and abuse in intimate relationships.

The notion that social factors are not relevant, or not as relevant as psychological factors, in explaining family violence is often manifested in assertions and statements such as "Family violence can be found in all social groups and in all income levels." Anecdotal examples of violence and abuse in wealthy families, or among physicians or lawyers, are also offered as proof that social factors play only a minimal causal role in family violence.

There continues to be a heavy psychological bias in most theoretical conceptualizations about the causes and explanations of child abuse, wife abuse, elder abuse, and other forms of family violence. The enduring stereotype of family violence is that the abuser is mentally disturbed or truly psychotic and that the victim is a defenseless innocent. The typical reaction to a description of a case of domestic violence or a photo of an abused woman or child is that "only a sick person" would do such a thing. The stereotype is so strong that unless the offender fits the profile of the mentally disturbed, psychotic alien and the victim is portrayed as innocent and defenseless, there is a tendency not to view the event as "abuse." The stereotype is so strong that some women who have been abused fail to define their experiences as abuse because the violence was not as severe as that depicted in such popular media accounts as the television movies *The Burning Bed* and *A Cry for Help: The Tracey Thurman Story*. Thus considerable public attention is focused on the most sensational cases of intimate violence. Horrible torture of women and children, sexual abuse in day-care centers, and the killing of babies and the elderly make news, not only because such cases are somewhat unusual (although less unusual than the public thinks), but because they fit the stereotype of what really is "family abuse."

We want to believe that the family is a safe, nurturant environment. We also do not want to see our own behavior and the behavior of our friends, neighbors, and relatives as improper. Thus most people want to envision "family violence" as terrible acts committed by horrible or bizarre people against innocents. This allows us to construct a problem that is perpetrated by "people other than us."

The theory that abusers are sick is often supported by a circular argument. Those who use the psychological level of analysis sometimes note that one of the character disorders that distinguishes child abusers is an "inability to control aggression." This seems a simple enough diagnosis. However, it is circular. How do we know that these people cannot control their aggression? Because they have abused their children. The abuse is thus the behavior to be explained *and* the means of explaining the behavior. When clinicians try to assess individuals without knowing whether or not they have abused their offspring or spouses, they find that they cannot accurately determine whether someone abused a family member based only on a psychological profile. In fact, only about 10% of abusive incidents are caused by mental illness. The remaining 90% are not amenable to purely psychological explanations (Steele, 1978; Straus, 1980b).

◉ The Attractiveness of Feminist Theory

Feminist theory is becoming the dominant model for explaining violence toward women. There are significant strengths in the feminist explanation of wife abuse, as well as some important weaknesses. One major strength of the feminist approach is its "praxis" or "advocacy" approach. Feminist theory is about women's victimization as a social problem and the need to do something about the patterned, continuing, and harmful use of psychological and physical coercion to control and dominate women. . . . Feminist theory provides the explanation *and* the formulation to both explain and end violence toward women.

A second strength of feminist theory is the diverse, yet consistent, empirical support for the proposition that gender inequality explains violence toward women. A number of recent studies by different researchers who used different methodological approaches on different populations have all found that gender inequality explains variations in the incidence and rates of violence toward women. Rebecca Morley (in press) used both in-person interviews and mailed questionnaires to study wife abuse in Papua New Guinea. Her findings cast significant doubt on the traditional hypothesis that modernization and the resulting social disorganization of modernization produce increased risk of wife beating. Although modernization does produce new pressures, expectations, and changes in women's support systems, the underlying explanation for the abuse of women is the husband's perceived right to control his wife and a social structure that "allows" husbands to assert this right. Murray Straus (in press) analyzed data from the Second National Violence Survey as well as aggregate-level data to examine patterns of wife assault in the 50 U.S. states. Straus's findings parallel Morley's New Guinea data. Social disorganization does not entirely explain variations in the rates of violence toward women in the United States. The greater the inequality between men and women and the greater the degree of social disorganization, the higher the rate of assault on wives.

Two additional researchers have employed data from newspapers to examine the abuse of women. Devi Prasad (in press) conducted a formal content analysis of newspaper articles on dowry-related violence in India, and Ko-Lin Chin (in press) used a less formal analysis of newspaper reports on violence toward "out-of-town brides" in the Chinese American community. The anecdotal data presented by Prasad and Chin add further weight to a gender inequality model of wife assault. The structurally inequitable positions of out-of-town Chinese brides and Indian women increase their risk of victimization.

The recent studies cited above support the earlier work of feminist scholars and sociologists who found that structured gender inequality is strongly associated with violence toward women. In addition, Straus and Morley both compare the explanatory power of competing theoretical models (social disorganization versus gender inequality) and find stronger support for the gender inequality model. Finally, the results come from a range of scholars who examined wife abuse using different methodologies and different theoretical approaches.

A final strength of the feminist perspective is that many feminist scholars, such as Yllö, Kurz, Dobash and Dobash, and Pagelow, are sociologists. They apply the sociological imagination, social facts, and sociological frames of reference to explaining violence toward women. Thus their approach is not entirely different from the theoretical approach used by sociologists, or those Yllö has labeled "family violence researchers."

The limitation of feminist theory is the other side of the coin of the theory's strength. Although the "gendered lens" provides a clear focus on violence toward women, the lens is a telephoto lens, not a wide-angle lens. The telephoto focus on violence toward women examines factors such as patriarchy, dominance, and control, and excludes from the vision other salient and important aspects of social structures and social institutions. The main problem with the feminist perspective is that it uses a single variable, patriarchy, to explain the existence of wife abuse. Moreover, the theory fails to account for the lack of variance of this single variable across time and cultures. Although the feminist perspective provides a politically attractive theory that is amenable to broad social action, it does not provide a useful theory to explain the complex nature of family violence. Feminist theory offers a single-variable analysis, albeit a powerful one, in a multivariable world. Moreover, feminist theory is an analysis of only one type of violence or victimization. The gendered lens does not, and apparently cannot, account for a wide range of objective phenomena that fall under the general label of "family violence." Neither Yllö . . . nor other feminist scholars and theorists have been able to apply the feminist perspective to child abuse, sibling abuse, violence by women, or abuse of the elderly.

◉ Summary

The sociological perspective provides the widest and most inclusive perspective from which to understand and explain family violence. A sociological perspective neither excludes nor diminishes the contributions of psychological or social psychological variables; rather, it places these variables within a wider explanatory framework that considers the impact of social institutions and social structures on social behavior. Similarly, sociological theory offers a more complex formulation for the varied phenomena of violence and abuse between intimates and is applicable to a wider range of victimization than is feminist theory.

Yet the sociological perspective has a major drawback. Because the sociological perspective *does not* focus on a single characteristic of social life (e.g., personality or gender inequality), sociological theories are by definition complex. The sociological theories reviewed in this chapter are complicated, and such theories do not lead to simple solutions, either in clinical or practice settings or in terms of social policy. One cannot easily use a sociological theory to inform clinical practice. Nor can one use it to develop a simple legislative package for a state or federal legislative body. Those who seek simple answers and simple solutions will find little of value in the sociological perspective.

References

American Association for Protecting Children. (1988). *Highlights of official child neglect and abuse reporting, 1986.* Denver: American Humane Association.

Billingsley, A. (1969). Family functioning in the low-income black community. *Casework, 50*, 563–572.

Burgdorf, K. (1980). *Recognition and reporting of child maltreatment.* Rockville, MD: Westat.

Cazenave, N., & Straus, M. A. (1979). Race, class, network embeddedness, and family violence: A search for potent support systems. *Journal of Comparative Family Studies, 10*, 280–299.

Chin, K.-L. (in press). Out-of-town brides: International marriage and wife abuse among Chinese immigrants. In R. J. Gelles (Ed.), Family violence [Special issue]. *Journal of Comparative Family Studies.*

Dobash; R. P, Dobash, R E., Wilson, M., & Daly, M. (1992). The myth of sexual symmetry in marital violence. *Social Problems, 39*, 71–91.

Gelles, R. J. (1983). An exchange/social control theory. In D. Finkelhor, R. J. Gelles, G. T. Hotaling, & M. A. Straus (Eds.), *The dark side of families: Current family violence research* (pp. 151–165). Beverly Hills, CA: Sage.

Gelles, R. J. (1989). Child abuse and violence in single parent families: Parent absence and economic deprivation. *American Journal of Orthopsychiatry, 59*, 492–501.

Gelles, R. J., & Straus, M. A. (1979). Determinants of violence in the family: Toward a theoretical integration. In W. R. Burr, R. Hill, F. I. Nye, & I. L. Reiss (Eds.), *Contemporary theories about the family* (Vol. 1, pp. 549–581). New York: Free Press.

Gelles, R. J., & Straus, M. A. (1988). *Intimate violence: The causes and consequences of abuse in the American family.* New York: Simon & Schuster.

Gil, D. (1970). *Violence against children: Physical child abuse in the United States.* Cambridge, MA: Harvard University Press.

Giles-Sims, J. (1983). *Wife-beating: A systems theory approach.* New York: Guilford.

Goetting, A. (1989). Patterns of marital homicide: A comparison of husbands and wives. *Journal of Comparative Family Studies, 20*, 341–354.

Goode, W. (1971). Force and violence in the family. *Journal of Marriage and the Family, 33*, 624–636.

Hampton, R. L., & Gelles, R. J. (1991). A profile of violence toward black children. In R. L. Hampton (Ed.), *Black family violence: Current research and theory* (pp. 21–34). Lexington, MA: Lexington.

Hampton, R. L., Gelles, R. J., & Harrop, J. (1989). Is violence in black families increasing? A comparison of 1975 and 1985 national survey rates. *Journal of Marriage and the Family, 51*, 969–980.

Hampton, R. L., & Newberger, E. H. (1985). Child abuse incidence and reporting by hospitals: The significance of severity, class, and race. *American Journal of Public Health, 75,* 56–60.

Kempe, C. H., Silverman, F. N., Steele, B. F., Droegemueller, W., & Silver, H. K. (1962). The battered-child syndrome. *Journal of the American Medical Association, 181,* 17–24.

Margolin, L. (1991). Abuse and neglect in nonparental child care: A risk assessment. *Journal of Marriage and the Family, 53,* 694–704.

Margolin, L. (1992). Beyond maternal blame: Physical child abuse as a phenomenon of gender. *Journal of Family Issues, 13,* 410–423.

Milner, J. S., & Chilamkurti, C. (1991). Physical child abuse perpetrator characteristics: A review of the literature. *Journal of Interpersonal Violence, 6,* 345–366.

Morley, R. (in press). Wife-beating and modernization: The case of Papua New Guinea. In R. J. Gelles (Ed.), Family violence [Special issue]. *Journal of Comparative Family Studies.*

National Center on Child Abuse and Neglect. (1988). *Study findings: Study of national incidence and prevalence of child abuse and neglect: 1988.* Washington, DC: U.S. Department of Health and Human Services.

Nelson, B. J. (1984). *Making an issue of child abuse: Political agenda setting for social problems.* Chicago: University of Chicago Press.

Newberger, E. H., Reed, R. B., Daniel, J. H., Hyde, J. N., Jr., & Kotelchuck, M. (1977). Pediatric social illness: Toward an etiologic classification. *Pediatrics, 60,* 178–185.

O'Leary, K. D. (1988). Physical aggression between spouses: A social learning perspective. In V B. Van Hasselt, R. L. Morrison, A. S. Bellack, & M. Hersen (Eds.), *Handbook of family violence* (pp. 31–56). New York: Plenum.

Pelton, L. (1978). Child abuse and neglect: The myth of classlessness. *American Journal of Orthopsychiatry, 48,* 608–617.

Prasad, D. (in press). Dowry-related violence: A content analysis of news in selected newspapers. In R. J. Gelles (Ed.), Family violence [Special issue]. *Journal of Comparative Family Studies.*

Schultz, L. G. (1960). The wife assaulter. *Journal of Social Therapy, 6,* 103–111.

Simmel, G. (1950). *The sociology of Georg Simmel* (K. Wolf, Ed.). New York: Free Press.

Starr, R. H., Jr. (1988). Physical abuse of children. In V. B. Van Hasselt, R. L. Morrison, A. S. Bellack, & M. Hersen (Eds.), *Handbook of family violence* (pp. 119–156). New York: Plenum.

Steele, B. (1978). The child abuser. In I. Kutash, S. B. Kutash, L. B. Schlesinger, and Associates (Eds.), *Violence: Perspectives on murder and aggression* (pp. 285–300). San Francisco: Jossey-Bass.

Steele, B., & Pollock, C. (1968). A psychiatric study of parents who abuse infants and small children. In R. E. Helfer & C. H. Kempe (Eds.), *The buttered child* (pp. 103–147). Chicago: University of Chicago Press.

Straus, M. A. (1973). A general systems theory approach to a theory of violence between family members. *Social Science Information, 12,* 105-125.

Straus, M. A. (1980a). Social stress and child abuse. In C. H. Kempe & R. E. Helfer (Eds.), *The battered child* (3rd ed., pp. 86–102). Chicago: University of Chicago Press.

Straus, M. A. (1980b). A sociological perspective on the causes of family violence. In M. R. Green (Ed.), *Violence and the family* (pp. 7–31). Boulder, CO: Westview.

Straus, M. A. (1990). Social stress and marital violence in a national sample of American families. In M. A. Straus & R. J. Gelles (Eds.), *Physical violence in American families: Risk factors and adaptations to violence in 8,145 families* (pp. 181–201). New Brunswick, NJ: Transaction.

Straus, M. A. (in press). State-to-state differences in social inequality and social bonds in relation to assaults on wives in the United States. In R. J. Gelles (Ed.), Family violence [Special issue]. *Journal of Comparative Family Studies.*

Straus, M. A., Gelles, R. J., & Steinmetz, S. K. (1980). *Behind closed doors: Violence in the American family.* Garden City, NY: Anchor/Doubleday.

Straus, M. A., & Hotaling, G. T. (Eds.). (1980). *The social causes of husband-wife violence.* Minneapolis: University of Minnesota Press.

Straus, M. A., & Smith, C. (1990). Violence in Hispanic families in the United States: Incidence rates and structural interpretations. In M. A. Straus & R. J. Gelles (Eds.), *Physical violence in American families: Risk factors and adaptations to violence in 8,145 families* (pp. 341–367). New Brunswick, NJ: Transaction.

U.S. Department of Justice. (1991). *Criminal victimization in the United States.* Washington, DC: Government Printing Office.

Wolfgang, M., & Ferracuti, F. (1967). *The subculture of violence.* London: Tavistock.

Wolfgang, M., & Ferracuti, F. (1982). *The subculture of violence* (2nd ed.). London: Tavistock.

Wolfner, G., & Gelles, R. J. (1993). A profile of violence toward children. *Child Abuse and Neglect, 17,* 197–212.

❂ ❂ ❂

Questions

1. Suppose your friend believes that family violence is almost always committed by men who suffer from mental disorders. How would you explain to your friend why this common-sense understanding of family violence is inaccurate?

2. What unique features of the family make it a violent-prone institution?

3. Which theoretical perspective described in this article seems to offer the most useful explanation for family violence? Which seems least useful? Explain your responses.

4. What is the fundamental premise of the "exchange-control theory"? How relevant is this theory for understanding other forms of deviant or violent behavior?

5. Given the various sociostructural factors that contribute to family violence, how would *effective* programs to reduce family violence work?